THE BEST INTENTIONS

THE BEST INTENTIONS

Kofi Annan and the UN
in the Era of American World Power

JAMES TRAUB

BLOOMSBURY

Bloomsbury Publishing Plc
36 Soho Square
London W1D 3QY

A CIP catalogue record for this book is
available from the British Library

ISBN 978 0 7475 8728 6

10 9 8 7 6 5 4 3 2 1

Printed in Great Britain by Clays Ltd, St Ives plc

The paper this book is printed on is 100% post-consumer waste recycled

www.bloomsbury.com

To my coalition of the willing—E.W.E. and A.E.T.

Contents

Preface

THE UNITED NATIONS. IN CONVERSATION, AT LEAST IN THE United States, and after 9/11, those words carry a whiff of the not-altogether-serious, of the ever-so-slightly-embarrassing. The giant sculpture on the lawn in front of the General Assembly Building, of a gun with the barrel twisted into a knot—that says it all. The UN means standing by amid the butchery of Somalia, Bosnia, Rwanda, palavering with Saddam Hussein rather than taking him on. That tall glass building towering above the East River in Manhattan is the beautiful and illusory empire of good intentions. In short, the world is hard, and the UN is soft. And of course Kofi Annan, head of peacekeeping and then secretary-general, the gentle, kindly African with the silver goatee and the rueful, yellowing eyes—Kofi Annan is the very image of all this high-minded, ruinous blundering.

So why the UN, and why its incarnational figure? Well, first of all, I just like the place. No doubt I would feel different if I had first encountered the UN when the Security Council was twiddling its thumbs while Hutus were slaughtering Tutsis in Rwanda in the spring of 1994. But I didn't. I first wrote about the UN and about Kofi Annan when Annan made his thrilling dash to Baghdad in February 1998, a plucky little Daniel in the lion's den of Saddam's murder factory, and emerged with a pact that prevented—well, forestalled—war. Here was not only cliff-hanging drama but drama in the most satisfyingly allegorical form. And I liked the people around Annan, the political advisers and speechwriters and peacekeepers. Far from being mere bureaucrats, they were, by and large, highly intelligent people who had seen a great many things and spoke a great many languages, people who believed deeply in the UN's mission, no matter how acutely aware they were of its failures.

And I was fascinated by the UN's works—not the sculptures on the lawn or the tedious orations inside the buildings, but the actual work in the world, and above all the work of peacekeeping and nation-building, impossible but indispensable in the post–Cold War world of warlords and collapsing states. Over the years I spent time in many of the UN's great laboratories and cockpits, including East Timor, Sierra Leone, Haiti, and Kosovo. FDR and his aides had imagined the UN as a global police force, squashing conflict before it blazed into war. That dream flickered out in the first days of the Cold War, and yet here, instead, was a sort of global emergency medical force, performing desperate interventions and devising long-term cures for profoundly sick nations. And yes, these places were both laboratories and cockpits, where UN officials labored to hatch police forces and civil services and legal systems while peacekeeping troops tried to keep yesterday's combatants from each other's throats. The very idea of building, from the outside and in a matter of a few years, institutions that in successful countries accrete slowly over generations seemed faintly absurd. And yet was there any more important work in the world? And any more intriguing?

The UN had grown enormously over the years, in part because it shared the general tendency of bureaucracies to expand into all available space, but also because it did things no one else did. More than sixty thousand UN peacekeepers operated in Congo and Sierra Leone and Ethiopia and Cyprus and Lebanon and East Timor and elsewhere. UN administrators organized "post-conflict reconstruction" in Afghanistan and served as the sovereign authority in Kosovo. The UN High Commissioner for Refugees superintended the care of twenty million people who had been uprooted by conflict in Africa, Asia, and South America. The UN Development Programme and the UN Children's Fund, or UNICEF, as well as semiautonomous bodies within the UN family like the World Health Organization and the World Food Programme, operated in virtually every poor country. The International Atomic Energy Agency sent nuclear inspectors into dozens of countries, including Iran, and tracked the global black market in nuclear material. Nine thousand members of the UN Secretariat, the body of international civil servants who reported to the secretary-general, were scattered around the world, with the largest number by far working in UN headquarters along the East River in New York.

It was Kofi Annan's good fortune to become secretary-general in 1997, when the world was largely at peace. During his first term, Annan had been perhaps the most popular figure ever to occupy the office. He had restored the prestige of an institution that had fallen into disrepute, at least in the United States. His combination of modest charm and moral gravity had established him as a world leader and afforded him a freedom of action that few of his predecessors had known. He had lectured Third World nations on human rights and the imperative of "humanitarian intervention"; he had reproached industrialized nations for their niggardliness on development assistance and the response to AIDS. And of course he had made that melodramatic dash to Baghdad. The agreement he had gained had lasted for only ten months, but it had imparted a heroic glow to this gentle soul. In 2001, Annan had won the Nobel Peace Prize. He was lionized around the world and much cherished in the most rarefied social circles in New York, where he and his wife, Nane—tall, blond, reserved, the niece of Raoul Wallenberg, the Swedish hero of the Holocaust—constituted the ultimate catch.

And then the long run of good luck came to an end. In September 2002, President George W. Bush challenged the UN to confront Saddam Hussein—or to concede its irrelevance. When I spent time with Secretariat officials and Security Council diplomats that fall, I found the atmosphere charged with fear—not so much about Saddam Hussein's intentions as about President Bush's, and about the very future of the institution. The Brazilian ambassador, Gelson Fonseca, talked about "dual containment"—of Iraq and of the United States. The UN and the United States had been at loggerheads for years, above all over the American failure to pay hundreds of millions of dollars in arrears. But this was different, for now America's unrivaled power, its aggressive assertion of national interest, its unwillingness to be bound by the mechanism of multilateral decision-making all posed an existential threat to the UN. Kofi Annan, who until now had painstakingly threaded his way through every maze, found himself blocked at every turn. Here was a problem without a solution. In the end, when the diplomats fell back exhausted and resentful, and Washington and its allies went to war without Security Council approval, it really did feel as if this sixty-year-old experiment in global governance had hiccuped, coughed, and died.

The UN failed, and with the whole world watching. And from this failure came the whiff of fecklessness. One heard a kind of easy contempt for the institution even from people uncomfortable with the war, as if the Security Council's refusal to bless the American war effort proved that the UN would rather frustrate the United States than confront violent threats (a charge that in fact would stick against a number of its members). And it wasn't only a matter of trying to contain Gulliver. The UN seemed to be teetering on the brink of archaism. It was a parliament of states, designed to prevent or punish conflict between them. But countries didn't fight each other anymore; states waged war on their own citizens, or warlords fought over the carcass of defunct states. Kofi Annan had said a great deal, and much to the point, about the obligation to protect citizens from their own states, but when, while the world was watching the bloodshed in Iraq, the government of Sudan had confronted a rebellion in the Darfur region by organizing a campaign of ethnic cleansing, what had the Security Council done? Nothing, despite all the dire recollections of Rwanda. And this time you couldn't blame Washington; it was China and Russia, and their allies in Africa and Asia, who had refused to intervene in Sudan's internal affairs. The UN had no private stock of political will, any more than it had a private stock of soldiers; it could not act where its members did not wish to act.

And yet for all that, for all the blockage and the failure, the UN was not, in fact, irrelevant. The Bush administration, which had been quite content to let the UN put together a government in Afghanistan the year before, found that after it had declared victory in Iraq it needed the UN for the same purpose once again, for Iraqi leaders who would not so much as meet with coalition officials were willing to trust a UN envoy. And the administration discovered as well that while it could fight a war without Security Council approval, it could not restore sovereignty to a new Iraqi state without Security Council approval. That "legitimacy" which Washington unilateralists had viewed as a collective fiction turned out to have a power beyond the reach of the greatest military machine the world had ever known. And in the very different setting of Darfur, where the problem was not action but inaction, the UN retained ownership; for a long, agonizing period, no one else, no other neighbor or regional body, wanted any part of the disaster. The UN's inevitability, or indispensability, seemed to be a thing quite apart from its effectiveness. Even in this weirdly asymmetrical era—not so much the post–Cold War world as the post-9/11 world—with disintegrating states and stateless terrorists on the one side, and a grimly determined "hyper-power," as the French called the United States, on the other, the UN had or did or was something quite precious. It was supremely *relevant.*

At the end of 2003, I asked Kofi Annan if he would agree to cooperate for a book about the institution and about his own place in it. I explained that I did not want to write a biography of him, but rather a book about the era that began after the Gulf War put a decisive end to the UN's long post–Cold War paralysis, a period during which, first as head of peacekeeping and then as secretary-general, he had played a central role, and in fact had come to incarnate the institution for better and for worse. (I don't think I wrote that last part.) But I also wanted to sit in the background and watch over the next year or so as he and his aides and the institution itself struggled to operate, and to remain central, in the post-9/11 world—which is why I needed his cooperation. Annan finally agreed. I could sit in on meetings, subject to his approval, with his staff and with outsiders (though I would be permitted to quote the others only with express approval); I would travel with him, and he would speak to me regularly and candidly.

In June 2004, just weeks after Annan acquiesced, I joined him in Sudan, where he hoped to persuade the government to call off the camel-borne Cossacks, known as Janjaweed, whom it had unleashed on the villagers of the vast desert region of Darfur. Annan visited the refugee camps into which the terrified and starving citizens of Darfur had been herded; one camp had vanished by the time he arrived, the thousand or so inhabitants having been trucked away in the dead of night, apparently to prevent the UN secretary-general from witnessing the squalor in which they lived. Several months later Annan returned to Africa on a kind of diplomatic barnstorming tour designed to address the conflicts in Sudan, Congo, and Iraq. And in the beginning of January 2005, I joined him as he toured the region devastated by the tsunami—first Indonesia, then Sri Lanka, and finally the tropical outback of the Maldive Islands.

Annan had one of the world's most frantic schedules, and at times as many as two months would go by between our conversations. But he proved to be a conscientious subject, and between the summer of 2004 and the fall of 2005 we spoke, by my count, eighteen separate times, sometimes for as little as thirty minutes, at others for as long as two hours. I spent large chunks of this period haunting the thirty-eighth floor of the Secretariat Building, where the secretary-general and his staff are quartered, and it was there that Annan and I usually talked. I found it a serene and muted place—none of that antic wisecracking or shouting into telephones familiar from *The West Wing*—and my visits there had a pleasingly ritualistic quality. When I arrived, the guard at the reception desk would call Annan's office, and then one of his assistants, Laura Donini, would catch my eye from the end of the hall and indicate with a tiny gesture that I was to approach. I would then be ushered into a waiting room furnished with leather chairs and in-house literature, including *A World of Art: The United Nations Collection*. After a few minutes, Laura would peek in and say, "The secretary-general will see you," and then deliver me to his wood-paneled office, where we would sit together on a black leather couch under a serene and muted landscape showing a stream curving off into a dark stand of trees and a little fisherman sitting patiently at the bend.

Annan is the most gracious of men, and he would usually greet me with a big smile and a roundhouse handshake, a kind of domesticated soul gesture. He rarely failed to ask after my wife, my son, and my parents, and while I spoke, he would listen intently, nodding his head ever so slightly and sometimes even repeating back to me tiny fragments of my own narrative—an unconscious display of regard that, coming from a man who occupied so majestic a position, was both disarming and ever so slightly odd. He was an easy man to talk to, rarely calculating or cagey; he never asked to go off the record, never bridled at even the most impertinent question, never pleaded ignorance. He would, it's true, sometimes sheer off into platitudes when I probed into a particularly painful area—when I asked, for example, about his virtual incapacitation in the aftermath of the Iraq debate—but I always felt that he had roped off such areas from his own scrutiny, and thus had no light to shed on them for others. Like so many successful men, he had very little to say about himself, because it was a subject that he almost never dwelled on.

Annan is a career civil servant; he has the habits and the outlook of what the French call an *haut fonctionnaire*. And so have the men and women closest to him. His chief of staff, Iqbal Riza; his counselor, Lamin Sise; his spokesman, Fred Eckhard; his longtime assistant, Elisabeth Lindenmayer; and the head of public information, Shashi Tharoor, had spent virtually their entire careers in the UN and in diplomacy. What's more, they had worked by his side for years. They were not sycophants; Annan had neither the need nor the wish to dominate those around him. But they had been molded by the same kinds of experiences he had had, and they looked at the world very much as he did—which sometimes produced the same effects as sycophancy. Indeed, the air of dignity, of deference, of solemn reserve that suffused the thirty-eighth floor came not only from Annan himself but from his chief courtiers, who regarded him with a respect that often bordered on awe.

Annan's closest aides understood his views, of course; more important, they understood *him*. The secretary-general said a very great deal less than he thought, and left much to be inferred; the true adepts knew what he thought without asking. "He's very controlled," Kieran Prendergast, the head of the Department of Political Affairs, once said to me, "but I find his tiny facial movements quite expressive. I can tell when he feels under pressure he doesn't want to be under. Madeleine Albright"—the former U.S. ambassador and secretary of state in the administration of President Bill Clinton—"would try to push him into something when he wasn't ready to make a decision, and you could see the muscles in his jaw tense just fractionally." Prendergast also understood that Annan himself was reading people in this intuitive way. "He's extremely aware of body language and mood," he said. "He can tell who's in a good mood, who's in a bad mood, who's not feeling well. If you're in a crowd, he'll always know that you're there, or that you're not there." I, too, learned to interpret his silences and his bland utterances.

The year or so I passed in the company of this benevolent and somewhat cryptic sovereign, and of his genteel courtiers, could well have been stultifying, but it wasn't, for during this time the court was rocked, and almost shattered, by catastrophe, and also galvanized by great ambitions. The catastrophe was, of course, the scandal over the Oil-for-Food Programme, which had been developed a decade earlier to mitigate the effect of sanctions the UN had imposed on Iraq. American conservatives, still furious over the failure of both Annan and the Security Council to support the Iraq war, wielded the evidence of misdeeds in the program as a battering ram to smash both the secretary-general and the institution. By the fall of 2004, the conservative media were afire with accusations against the UN, Annan, and his son, Kojo, who had an extremely tenuous connection to Oil-for-Food.

And the secretary-general, who had remained above personal reproach even as he had been pummeled on Iraq, or earlier on Bosnia and Rwanda, who had not long before been the darling of public opinion, was bewildered and devastated by the onslaught. Annan's friends in the global elite, always so eager to see him at Davos, had gone deathly quiet. And the brow-heralds of the upper floors saw that his skin had gone matte and his voice had gone ghostly. The place was seized by a sense of collective panic. No secretary-general since the very first, the ineffectual Trygve Lie, had stepped down in the middle of a term. Would the SG—one referred to him only as "the SG"—make it past the end of the year? Was he strong enough to do a 60 Minutes interview, to face the UN press, to stare down his persecutors? It was—or at least felt like—an apocalyptic moment. The moment passed, but the terror returned, like an inexpungible cancer, each time the committee investigating the scandal issued a new report.

And then there was a countervailing movement—a movement toward rebirth. Annan had responded to the challenge flung at the UN by President Bush with a burst of reform activity. The UN, Annan had said in the fall of 2003, had reached a "fork in the road." Either it would remake itself to adapt to the new world in which it lived or it would accept a slow subsidence toward irrelevance. He had appointed a High-Level Panel on Threats, Challenges, and Change to reexamine the whole range of issues touching on peace and security, including the UN Charter's ban on preemptive war, which Washington had allegedly violated. A separate report on economic development would issue a call to arms on global poverty and disease. The panel was to publish its conclusions a year hence, states were to consider and debate them, and the reforms would be adopted in September 2005, when the world's heads of state would gather in New York for the General Assembly session celebrating the UN's sixtieth anniversary.

The year running up to the GA session was thus also a time of intellectual debate and policy formulation, of public marketing and private diplomacy, of encouraging the recalcitrant and cooling off the single-minded. All this was tonic for the beleaguered Annan. He could barely stir himself to fight for his own survival, but he was happy to exhaust himself fighting for the survival of the institution. In the spring of 2005 he issued his own version of the high-level panel report, grandly titled "In Larger Freedom." It was, by general agreement, a remarkably ambitious, coherent, honest, and forceful blueprint for reform. But in the bitterly contentious atmosphere of the UN in the summer of 2005, forging consensus behind ambitious change was well-nigh impossible. Annan, his chief aides, and a team of diplomats threw themselves into a campaign to promote the package, while the member states, few of whom had clamored for reform in the first place, threatened to reduce the document to a pulp.

It is too simple to say that the UN's crisis—its convergence of crises—was wholly brought on by the United States, but this isn't far off. The debate over the Iraq war had brought the UN to the "fork in the road." Oil-for-Food, for all the legitimate issues it raised, was Annan's punishment for having taken "the wrong side" in that debate. The UN's relation to the United States had come to feel like an insoluble equation. Did it have to be so? The end of the Cold War, which had divided the world into implacable camps and thus paralyzed the UN, had seemed to be the most precious of gifts for the world body. And the U.S.-led and UN-sanctioned Persian Gulf War in 1991 had appeared to usher in a splendid new era of comity and concerted action. That burst of euphoria had expired in the dust of Mogadishu, but Annan had done much to repair relations with Washington in his first term. Then the American people had elected a Republican president with deep reservations about multilateral institutions, jeopardizing even this more modest and pragmatic relationship. And 9/11, which for all the talk of "global threats" had targeted the United States and the United States alone, had launched Washington on a path that had little, if any, place for the United Nations. Yes, the Bush administration had returned to the Security Council on Iraq and on a range of other issues, but it practiced "multilateralism à la carte." And why shouldn't it? Other countries would pursue their national interests just as single-mindedly if they had the power to do so.

Now, incredibly, you could almost be nostalgic for the Cold War. It was easier to maneuver between two more or less equal blocs than between a demanding superpower and everyone else—especially when the relentless demands only hardened the resistance of many of the UN's members. Kofi Annan, peacemaker and consensus seeker, exhausted himself trying to accommodate an administration that seemed quite content to see him forced from office; this, in turn, earned him the contempt of many of his own employees. But he couldn't fight back, for that would be fatal to the UN, and perhaps also for him. The UN couldn't survive without the United States, but the opposite was scarcely true. It was grotesquely unfair, but it was, for the UN, a fact of life. It was this fact, this all-but-insoluble equation, that had defined Kofi Annan's second term in office, and it will continue to shape the UN long after he has stepped down.

PART I

CHAPTER ONE

A Greater Magna Carta . . .

INSTITUTIONS OF GLOBAL ORDER ARE AN AMERICAN INVENtion. A nation that occupied and swiftly conquered a continent of its own had little need of the intricate and perpetually shifting web of alliances that had bound European sovereigns since the Peace of Westphalia in 1648; a nation that understood itself as having been formed and guided by Providence naturally viewed its national interests in universalistic terms—even as it asserted its dominion, brutally at times, over that continent. American leaders scorned the calculations of a Metternich or a Palmerston—the philosophy known as *raison d'état*—as cynical and corrupt. And when that old order came to an abrupt and shocking end with World War I, a hideous and thoroughly avoidable conflict that made the old treaty system look like a death pact, the United States, which had emerged from the war as the world's supreme power, was prepared to impose its idealistic vision on the exhausted combatants. A war that had begun on European terms would thus end on American ones. President Woodrow Wilson, the scholar and Christian moralist who had led a reluctant America into war to save Europe from itself, sought a peace in which the victors would not carve up the spoils and territories of the vanquished but rather would band together in a League of Nations designed to end war itself.

The League failed, of course, but not only because the U.S. Congress refused to ratify it. The body had been designed as a kind of circuit-breaking institution to prevent nations from marching blindly into a war none of them really wanted. But that nineteenth-century diplomatic minuet had disappeared forever in Flanders field. The authoritarian and militaristic states that arose in the ensuing vacuum were bent on crushing weaker neighbors or picking off helpless colonies. Only the threat of a greater force could stop these aggressors, and the League, which had no such mechanism, proved helpless in the face of Japanese, Italian, and German expansionism.

Planning for a new organization began inside President Franklin Roosevelt's State Department in 1939, more than two years before the United States was drawn into World War II. To FDR, an earthier and more tough-minded figure than Wilson, the League demonstrated the absurdity of trying to counter aggression by summoning men to their better angels. Wilson had rightly recognized that only America could, or would, subordinate its own supremacy and limit its own freedom of action in order to ensure world peace. But FDR's vision was to place might at the disposal of right. The president was open to all sorts of variations in design, but he "adhered unswervingly," as the historian Stephen C. Schlesinger writes, "to one central realpolitik tenet derived from his disillusion with the League's enforcement operations, that the four powers—China, the Soviet Union, Great Britain, and the United States—should act as policemen and provide security for any world organization."

FDR became the driving force behind the establishment of the United Nations, a name he had dreamed up soon after Pearl Harbor, when he had gathered twenty-six nations in Washington to sign a United Nations Declaration vowing to defeat the Axis powers. By the end of 1943, he had persuaded Stalin and Churchill to accept a world body with the "Four Policemen," as they were known, at its heart. In August 1944, American, Russian, British, and Chinese diplomats met at Dumbarton Oaks in Washington to flesh out the proposal. Working from a State Department draft, they agreed on an organization that would have an eleven-member Security Council with five permanent members. (France, second only to Germany among the Continental powers, had by now been added to the original four.) The Big Five would have a right of veto over all substantive matters—a critical distinction from the League, which depended on consensus and thus effectively awarded the veto to all. A General Assembly consisting of all members would discuss non-security questions, and the whole would be guided by a professional secretariat.

As the war drew to a close, Roosevelt became consumed with establishing the world body. In February 1945, he put his increasingly frail health at risk by traveling to Yalta, on the Black Sea, to meet with Churchill and Stalin and overcome Stalin's remaining objections to the UN. Several weeks later, in one of the last interviews he gave before his death, Roosevelt told a *New York Times* reporter that "all his hopes of success in life and immortality in history were set on getting an international organization in motion." It's just as well for Roosevelt that his place in history does not depend on the UN, but he is, without question, the institution's progenitor.

The signatories of the United Nations Declaration, in the global equivalent of a constitutional convention, gathered in San Francisco on April 25, 1945, to write the UN Charter. The world press descended on this charming seaside city and relayed breathlessly to readers the portentous debates over the hatching of this great instrument of peace. The issues that most agitated the delegates mattered less than the very public narrating of the debate, for during those weeks, and in the ensuing months, a world public exhausted with fighting came to believe, or at least to hope, that mankind really had begun to put the savage madness of war behind it.

At its core, the UN was, as FDR had always wished, an institutionalized form of the wartime alliance. It was understood that the Big Five would provide the bulk of the troops available to the UN; Article 47 of the Charter established a Military Staff Committee, consisting only of delegates of the five, which was responsible for the "strategic direction of any armed forces placed at the disposal of the Security Council." Attempts by smaller countries to limit the veto largely failed, which both ensured the supremacy of the Big Five and allowed each of them to block any use of the council's enforcement powers that they opposed. The council and the General Assembly would be served by a professional secretariat, with a secretary-general functioning as the UN's "chief administrative officer." But unlike the League of Nations's chief executive, who had been expected to tend strictly to internal affairs, the UN secretary-general, according to Article 99 of the Charter, was empowered to "bring to the attention of the Security Council any matter which in his opinion may threaten the maintenance of international peace and security." Precisely what this vague assertion meant was in no way clear.

The United Nations was much more than an instrument for global policing; the new body also aspired to affirmatively shape a new and more just world order. An Economic and Social Council would seek to alleviate the poverty and injustice that often lay at the root of conflict; a Trusteeship Council would promote self-government in colonized states, with an ultimate eye to sovereignty; and a World Court would adjudicate international disputes.

The UN Charter was bequeathed to, and greeted by, the world public as if it were the Decalogue brought straight from Mount Sinai. The most sober figures described it in the most intoxicated language. John Foster Dulles, an adviser to the U.S. delegation and future secretary of state, called the Charter "a greater Magna Carta." Senator Arthur Vandenberg, a Republican and former isolationist whom President Truman had shrewdly included in the team sent to San Francisco, presented the document to the Senate as "a new emancipation proclamation for the world." The Senate, which a generation earlier had rejected the League of Nations and which continued to harbor a good many men deeply suspicious of the world beyond America's borders, ratified the Charter by the astonishingly lopsided total of 89 to 2. Men, including hardheaded men, so ardently wished to put an end to conflict between nations that they allowed themselves to believe that this mechanism they had built might actually make war, at least catastrophic war, obsolete.

The General Assembly held its opening session on January 17, 1946. The meeting was held amid the rubble of war-torn London, but two months later the UN moved to New York, where it occupied the Bronx campus of Hunter College, a municipal college for women. Workmen hurriedly redecorated the college gym to make room for the deliberations of the Security Council. The UN's first important order of business was choosing a secretary-general. The Americans wanted Lester Pearson, the Canadian ambassador to Washington and future prime minister and Nobel Peace Prize recipient, but the Soviets would not accept a figure close to the United States. They wanted someone from a country not aligned with the United States, and so settled on Norway's thoroughly undistinguished foreign minister, Trygve Lie, who was then swiftly approved. "There was no consideration of who might be best for the job," writes Brian Urquhart, one of the UN's most illustrious civil servants as well as one of its leading historians. Urquhart served as one of Lie's personal assistants and describes him as a simple and simpleminded man "out of his depth" as head of the new world body, "jealous of his position and at the same time nervous of it." Ralph Bunche, the American diplomat and high UN official, records his first impression of the new SG: "a huge, flabby-looking man" said by British colleagues to be "a politician first, last and all the time." In its initial act the UN thus established an implicit rule of the lowest common denominator, an early sign that this new organization might not live up to the noble ideals with which it was forged.

The Soviets were under no illusions about the supposed commonality of interests between themselves and their former allies; they *wanted* a weak Secretariat, because they feared that a more activist one would abet the Western cause. In fact, the spirit of comity to which so many hosannas had been dedicated began to dissipate almost as soon as the UN, and especially the Security Council, opened its doors. In mid-February, the Soviet ambassador, Andrey Vyshinsky, cast a veto, a weapon the framers had expected to be used only in hopelessly intractable situations, on an American resolution calling for the withdrawal of British and French troops from Syria because he found the language too weak—an act of almost calculated insouciance. Soon thereafter, his successor, Andrei Gromyko, stormed out of the council when he failed to block a discussion of the Soviet troop presence in Iran.

The hardheaded FDR had, it turned out, misjudged the future almost as thoroughly as Wilson had, believing that the antifascist coalition which had fought World War II would continue to make common cause after the fascists were gone (though FDR's insistence on the veto had much to do with his fears of Soviet intentions). In fact, the world was as implacably divided over Communism as it had been over fascism. In the Security Council, the Soviets opposed the other four permanent members on almost every question of importance and made liberal use of the veto to block action. They also reneged on the promise to make troops available to the council, thus reducing the Military Staff Committee to a meaningless appendage, as it would remain forever after. The euphoric expectations of 1945 did not even survive 1946. By 1950, a Gallup poll found that only 27 percent of Americans thought that the UN was doing a good job; 36 percent judged its performance "poor."

And yet during those rare crises when the Soviets did not cast or threaten their veto, the UN showed that it had potential far beyond that of the League. Both the United States and the Soviet Union supported the creation of the Jewish state, and in November 1947 the General Assembly voted to accept a British plan to divide its mandate territories into a Jewish and an Arab state—a soul-stirring triumph for the cause of Zionism. The following year, after war had broken out between the new nation of Israel and Egypt, Ralph Bunche, an indefatigable and endlessly resourceful figure, negotiated an armistice between them. Bunche then spent months hammering out agreements between Israel and deeply reluctant representatives of Jordan, Syria, and Lebanon, an achievement for which he was ultimately awarded the Nobel Peace Prize.

The Security Council took one momentous decision in these early years. On June 24, 1950, North Korean troops crossed the 38th parallel into South Korean territory. That line of demarcation was monitored by UN observers, who had been dispatched several years earlier to supervise elections meant to reunify the country. The invasion was thus not only a violation of the Security Council resolution establishing the mission; it was precisely the kind of naked act of aggression the UN had been created to prevent or to reverse. Trygve Lie reacted to news of the invasion by blurting out, "That's war against the United Nations." It was also war against an important American ally, which is to say that the core principles of the UN coincided with the strategic interests of its most powerful member. The State Department asked Lie to call an emergency session of the council on the following day, a Sunday; the secretary-general eagerly complied.

By this time, the forces of the Chinese Communist Party under Mao Tse-tung had overthrown the Chiang Kai-shek government. But the UN continued to recognize the so-called Nationalist regime, which had close ties to Washington, as China's rightful representative. For the previous six months the Soviets had been boycotting council sessions to protest the refusal to seat the Communist Chinese. The Soviets continued to absent themselves during the discussion over North Korea, thus sparing the council an almost certain veto. And so the Security Council swiftly adopted an American resolution condemning the attack. Two days later the council adopted another American resolution, calling on all members to help South Korea repel the invasion. The American-led force that would fight the Korean War would thus be acting under UN authorization. President Truman made it clear that he would have gone to war with or without the imprimatur of the Security Council. But the imprimatur was no mere afterthought. Another UN historian, Stanley Meisler, quotes Truman as telling a diplomat, "In the final analysis I did this for the United Nations. I believed in the League of Nations. It failed. Lots of people thought it failed because we weren't in it to back it up. Okay, now we started the United Nations. It was our idea, and in this first big test we just couldn't let them down." Even if Truman was only half sincere, it's startling to hear an American president worrying about letting the UN down, rather than the other way around.

The Soviets were furious over Lie's collaboration with the United States, and in mid-1950, as his five-year term was drawing to a close, they announced that they would oppose a second term. In fact, Lie's ties with Washington went far deeper than the merely diplomatic. For the last year, he had been secretly cooperating with the FBI in order to ensure that the Secretariat hired no Americans with alleged Communist sympathies; it was he, in fact, who had approached the Truman administration about the idea. The Americans would not have anyone but Lie. He may have been a mediocrity, but he was *their* mediocrity. Ultimately, the General Assembly awarded him only an additional three years. (The Charter had not fixed a secretary-general's term of office.) The Soviets refused to recognize him, torturing Lie's vanity by refusing to invite him and his wife to Eastern bloc receptions and declining to present to him their diplomats' credentials. In November 1952, not quite two years into his second term, Lie abruptly tendered his resignation.

No consensus candidate had emerged by the following March,

when the Security Council convened to nominate a successor. (The General Assembly formally elects the candidate.) The Soviets were not prepared to accept anyone acceptable to the United States (and vice versa). In order to break the deadlock, the French ambassador submitted a list of names to his Soviet counterpart. The only one the Soviets did not reject out of hand was Dag Hammarskjöld, a Swedish diplomat known to almost no one. Hammarskjöld must have seemed like the very definition of harmless neutrality; and so, in the single greatest misapprehension in the history of this selection process, a brilliant, fearless, and deeply self-willed man became the UN's second secretary-general.

Dag Hammarskjöld is the standard against which all successive secretaries-general have been measured, and found wanting, for the very simple reason that the Security Council did not make the same mistake twice. Hammarskjöld was a man of high intelligence as well as deep convictions. It is true that he lacked many of the conventional attributes of leadership: he was solitary, melancholy, introspective, sensitively attuned to the eddies of his own consciousness. And yet there was nothing in him of the indecisive Hamlet; he was always prepared to thrust himself into situations where he believed he could make a difference. And his formidable intellect allowed him to pick his way nimbly through situations that would have frustrated a lesser man.

Hammarskjöld first demonstrated both his gifts and his understanding of the job in late 1954, when the Chinese shot down an American B-29 bomber and a C-47 transport plane and captured eleven Air Force crewmen and two civilians, whom they accused, probably rightly, of being CIA agents. American public opinion was outraged, and the General Assembly, at that time still highly pro-American, condemned the decision of the Chinese to try the crew members as spies rather than release them as prisoners of war. What made the issue yet more inflammatory was that the Nationalists continued to occupy China's seat in the UN and on the Security Council, thus effectively barring the Communist regime from the debate. Hammarskjöld, however, had gotten the delegates to insert in the resolution a request for him to "act in the name of the United Nations" to free the airmen. Lie had never sought such an opportunity, but Hammarskjöld sensed that his unique status as impartial representative of the world body might allow him to act in a situation where neither adversary could make concessions to the other but both feared escalation. Hammarskjöld wrote to Chinese prime minister Chou En-lai for permission to come to Peking, not as an emissary from the Security Council—and thus from the chief belligerent—but in his own right as secretary-general. Chou agreed, and the airmen were ultimately released.

By his dramatic and highly personalized intervention, Hammarskjöld loosened the stays that had bound his own office, and indeed the entire Secretariat. His so-called Peking Formula stipulated that the secretary-general had an affirmative obligation to act when peace and security were threatened. The authority for such acts lay not in the actual words of the Charter but in its penumbra—or rather in Hammarskjöld's own quasi-mystical sense of calling. FDR's vision of an organization that would coordinate the use of force to deter or defeat acts of aggression had already receded into history. Hammarskjöld offered an alternative understanding of the UN as the institutional embodiment of the idea of the neutral or disinterested position. The UN's strength, in effect, arose from its weakness: what it had lost in coercive power it had regained through its unique, supra-partisan status.

Hammarskjöld never lost sight of either the delicacy or the power of the UN's mediatory role. He was outraged when, in 1956, the French and the British secretly conspired with Israel to drive Egypt from territory it had occupied along the Suez Canal and to smash its military capacity. In the course of a Security Council meeting over the so-called Suez Crisis, he loosed one of his most majestic rhetorical blasts. "The principles of the Charter," he said, "are, by far, greater than the organization in which they are embodied, and the aims which they are to safeguard are holier than the policies of any single nation or people." As a servant of the organization, he went on, the secretary-general has a duty to maintain neutrality in disputes between states, but that obligation "may not degenerate into a policy of expediency," above all when members violate the terms of the Charter. The secretary-general was the defender of the Charter, much as the pope was the defender of the Church.

It was in response to Suez that Hammarskjöld invented UN peacekeeping. The General Assembly had passed a resolution demanding that foreign forces withdraw from the area and instructing the secretary-general to draw up a plan to establish "an emergency international United Nations force to secure and supervise the cessation of hostilities." Nobody really knew what such a force would look like. Finding soldiers was not the problem, for many countries were eager to staff this novel UN force for peace. But what were they to do? Hammarskjöld stipulated that the troops would supervise the withdrawal of all combatants and then patrol the disputed area, but they would not seek to settle, or in any way prejudice, the underlying political question, which would have to be settled among the parties. This allowed the British and the French to withdraw without formally admitting defeat. The UN Emergency Force, or UNEF, as it was called, would report not to the various national authorities but to a UN "force commander"; they could be identified by the blue helmets and blue berets they wore. And though the soldiers would be armed, they would use their weapons only in self-defense.

This strange doctrine flew in the face of military tradition and training. Brian Urquhart, who had more to do with the theory, practice, and culture of UN peacekeeping than any other individual, described it as "the projection of the principle of non-violence onto the military plane." The premise was not that violence was wrong, but rather, as Urquhart writes, that "the moment a peacekeeping force starts killing people it becomes part of the conflict it is supposed to be controlling, and therefore a part of the problem." The peacekeeping force, like the UN itself, would have to hold itself rigorously above the combatants in order to preserve the impartiality that was the source of its unique standing.

Stanley Meisler describes Suez as "one of the most spectacular single achievements of the UN during its first fifty years." Though American support was critical, he notes, it was the UN's own moral prestige, especially in Britain and France, that forced the European powers to accept defeat, and it was Hammarskjöld's artfulness that buffered the humiliation of that defeat. The six-thousand-man peacekeeping force, made up of troops from the Scandinavian countries as well as India, Indonesia, Colombia, and others, deployed rapidly, secured the withdrawal of occupying forces, and suffered no serious challenge for many years. But Meisler also notes that when, during the same period, the Soviet Union crushed the Hungarian uprising and executed its leader,

Imre Nagy, the General Assembly issued a futile bleat of protest, and the Soviets went about their grim business unimpeded. The UN could act forcefully only when circumstances brought the American and Soviet views into alignment.

Almost four years passed before Hammarskjöld was able to once again insert himself into a situation of the first importance. In early July 1960, only five days after Belgium had granted independence to the long-suffering and hopelessly unprepared Congolese people, army troops in the Kinshasa barracks (then Léopoldville) rebelled against their Belgian officers; the riot quickly became general, endangering the country's large European population. Belgium rushed in additional troops. Congo's prime minister, Patrice Lumumba, asked President Eisenhower to intervene. Ike instead brought the issue to the UN. The United States and the Soviet Union had begun vying for influence among the emerging nations of Africa; both wanted to see the Belgians removed. An emergency session of the Security Council accepted Hammarskjöld's plea to establish a peacekeeping force to replace the Belgians and restore order.

Peacekeeping was still an immensely popular endeavor, and Hammarskjöld was able to deploy a force with astonishing speed: by July 23, the blue helmets had replaced Belgians at most of Congo's key installations. But Congo was disintegrating faster than the UN could hold it together. Moise Tshombe, a strongman in the mineral-rich eastern province of Katanga, announced in the first days of the chaos that the province had seceded. In mid-September, the army chief of staff, Joseph Mobutu, had Lumumba imprisoned. Four months later Lumumba was put on a plane to Katanga, allegedly with CIA connivance. Tshombe's men beat him savagely during the flight; barely alive, the prime minister was then taken out and shot. UN troops made no attempt to intervene—it was not within their mandate.

Hammarskjöld was fiercely criticized for the passivity of his forces. The doctrine of noninterventionist peacekeeping looked laughable in the face of the Congolese chaos—just as it would thirty years later amid the brutality of Somalia, Rwanda, and Bosnia. But the UN was not yet habituated to a fatalistic acceptance of institutional limits. In February 1961, a month after Lumumba was murdered, Hammarskjöld sought and received from the Security Council a new mandate to use force to keep the nascent state intact—the first time that UN peace-keepers had been so authorized. And when the Katangese insurgency continued to boil, the peacekeepers, incredibly, went to war. The first battle, in September 1961, ended in a cease-fire. By early December, the UN force had been augmented to included jet fighters and heavy artillery; President Kennedy had essentially lent the UN America's military airlift capacity to ensure the swift delivery of the new armaments. But commanders on the ground made a hash of the campaign, while pilots mistakenly bombed civilian targets in Katanga's capital, Elisabethville (now Lubumbashi). The battle lasted two weeks, resulted in more than two hundred deaths, and left the UN looking like an inept bully.

Tshombe built up his forces again and began testing the UN troops. This time, however, he had made a mistake. In December 1962, Major General Dewan Prem Chand of India launched the rakishly titled Operation Grand Slam. Commanding troops from India, Sweden, Ireland, and Ghana, backed by Swedish air support, General Prem Chand swept through Elisabethville, mowed down the Katangese gendarmerie, choked off Tshombe's supply route, and captured key cities. Tshombe surrendered the following month. In the first test of the impromptu doctrine of peacekeeping-as-enforcement, the UN had won a stunning, if very messy, victory. But it was a Pyrrhic victory, for many of the UN's supporters stood aghast at this triumph of might. FDR's muscular vision was a distant memory; the UN was supposed to be above violence, not a party to it. Never again would UN peacekeepers bomb targets or take cities; almost forty years would pass before a UN force would even openly take sides in a civil conflict.

What's more, by 1960 Hammarskjöld's unflinching independence had at one time or another infuriated all the major powers, and above all the Soviets. In the General Assembly session of September 1960, Nikita Khrushchev scornfully called on Hammarskjöld to "muster the courage to resign." (It was during this session, several weeks later, that Khrushchev famously banged his shoe against the table.) The secretary-general defended himself in the majestically impersonal terms he had long mastered, but it was clear that he had reached, and exceeded, the limits of his office. We'll never know how this conflict would have been resolved. On September 17, 1961, Hammarskjöld climbed into a DC-6B for a seven-hour flight from Léopoldville to Ndola, in Northern Rhodesia, where he planned to meet with Tshombe in hopes of ending the first battle of Katanga. The plane approached the Ndola airport and then abruptly disappeared; the smoking wreckage was found the next day a few miles north of the airport. All thirteen passengers were dead.

"Hammarskjöld's death left an aching void at the United Nations," Brian Urquhart later wrote. "He had been the life and soul of the institution even in the last year of criticism and violence, and without him there was a terrible feeling of emptiness." What Hammarskjöld had achieved he had done wholly by dint of his own extraordinary gifts; he had expanded the powers and the prestige of his office far beyond what the authors of the Charter had envisioned. A heroic figure appears to change the rules, but the rules reestablish themselves when the hero leaves.

For the tens of millions of men and women living not in independent states but in colonies, the UN looked less like an organ of collective security than like a promise of self-determination. The UN Trusteeship Council, headed by the estimable Ralph Bunche, had shepherded a number of so-called Trust Territories to independence during the 1950s; it had, more important, helped make decolonization a burning moral issue. In 1960, the General Assembly passed a "Declaration on the Granting of Independence to Colonial Countries and Peoples," calling for an unconditional grant of sovereignty to remaining colonies. These were deeply stirring words for people struggling to gain independence. Joaquim Chissano, later to serve as the president of Mozambique, a territory then in thrall to Portugal, says, "We felt that we had a right which is recognized by the world, so that our wishes are also becoming the wishes of the entire world." Over the next few years, the steady pace of decolonization became an avalanche. And the effect on the UN was overwhelming: by 1963, the membership of the organization had swelled from the original 51 to 114, with the majority of new members in Africa and Asia.

By the time Hammarskjöld died, the moment had plainly come for a non-Western secretary-general. The Soviets, having learned the danger of trusting neutral nations, were open to such a candidate, as were the Americans. Once the patently unsuitable ones, and those who leaned too far to one side or the other, were weeded out, the remaining figure was the ambassador from Burma, U Thant, whom Hammarskjöld had thought of as a potential successor. Thant was a small, unassuming man, a Buddhist with the virtues of the Buddha himself— gentleness, serenity, wry humor, self-restraint. These were the kinds of virtues that recommended themselves to members tired of being dominated by a forceful secretary-general.

The air of turbulence and high drama that had roiled the UN during Hammarskjöld's tenure receded after his death. Thant wasn't timid: it was he who authorized the final assault on Katanga in late 1962. Nor was he altogether unwilling to take on the great powers, for he criticized the Vietnam War privately and, much less often, publicly. But this modest man had little of Hammarskjöld's grandiose conception of his calling, or of his ability to marshal political support for personal diplomacy. At a White House visit in 1964 he proposed that he initiate back-channel discussions with Ho Chi Minh; the secretary-general never understood that neither President Lyndon Johnson nor the president's aides took him seriously, and he was crestfallen when the United States backed out of a planned meeting with him in early 1965. Thant then had the temerity to tell reporters, "As you know, in times of war and of hostilities, truth is the first casualty." Secretary of State Dean Rusk put the secretary-general in his place by shouting over the telephone, "Who do you think you are, a country?"

For all that, one of the most dramatic moments in the history of the Cold War was played out in the Security Council during this period. On October 22, 1962, President Kennedy, in a solemn television address, announced that the United States had "unmistakable evidence" that the Soviets had placed nuclear missiles in Cuba. The following day the Security Council met in an emergency session, where U.S. ambassador Adlai Stevenson and Soviet ambassador Valerian Zorin exchanged provocations. Stevenson demanded that Zorin confirm or deny the American allegation, and then added, "Yes or no—don't wait for the translation—yes or no." When Zorin frostily asserted that he would supply an answer "in due course," the famously genial Stevenson rejoined, "I am prepared to wait for your answer until hell freezes over, if that's your decision." And then, in a coup de théâtre, aides wheeled out easels on which U-2 photographs of the missiles were fastened, leaving Zorin speechless.

Neither Thant nor the Security Council could play an important role in so grave a crisis; the same was true of the other great Cold War confrontations of the time, including the Vietnam War and the Soviet invasion of Czechoslovakia in 1968. The Americans and the Soviets were equally unwilling to permit the Security Council or the secretary-general to mediate disputes within their spheres of influence. Both entities fell into a kind of half-conscious state, destined to come fully awake only when the Cold War stalemate came to an end. The council and the secretary-general subsisted on second- or third-order conflicts. When Greece and Turkey threatened to go to war over control of the island of Cyprus in early 1964, both sides agreed to accept a UN peacekeeping force. As with UNEF in Egypt, the Cyprus mission had no political component; it was designed to give the combatants breathing space to work out the problem. And as with UNEF, it became a semipermanent feature of the landscape as the political situation remained in deadlock. When war broke out between India and Pakistan in August 1965, on the other hand, U Thant flew to the region amid great fanfare, but neither side would budge, and the war continued until India won a decisive victory.

The one really discreditable episode in U Thant's tenure came two years later, in May 1967, when Egyptian forces declared that they would cross the line in the Suez manned by UN peacekeepers and asked the UNEF mission to voluntarily withdraw. This had been the UN's first peacekeeping mission, and a very visible symbol of its commitment to preventing conflict. But Thant, insisting that peacekeepers served only so long as both parties to a dispute wished them to, caved in to Nasser's demand without even putting up an argument. The secretary-general had thus dismantled one of the UN's enduring legacies in the name of niggling legalism and impartiality at all costs. The Israelis neither forgot nor forgave the abrupt abandonment. "What is the use of a fire brigade which vanishes from the scene as soon as the first smoke and flames appear?" Israel's foreign minister, Abba Eban, said in the General Assembly. In early June, the Israelis launched the devastating preemptive strike on their Arab neighbors that provoked the Six Days' War, permanently altering the map of the Middle East.

By this time, the Security Council had faded as the locus of activity in the UN—not only because it had been paralyzed by the Cold War but also because it was remote from the concerns of the overwhelming majority of members. The UN in the 1960s changed into a forum for issues of development. UN economists churned out studies on poverty. The World Health Organization vowed in 1966 to wipe out smallpox in a decade. (It missed the mark by only one year.) The UN sponsored world conferences on hunger, the environment, population growth, and women's rights. New bodies were established, including regional economic commissions, the UN Conference on Trade and Development, the UN Development Fund for Women. This vast swarm of activity had, with a few exceptions (such as the eradication of smallpox), a very indirect effect on the real world, or no effect at all. But it constituted a new UN that aspired to mediate not between combatants but between the wealthy countries of "the North" and the dozens of new members from the generally impoverished "South."

In 1971, the Security Council selected as U Thant's successor Kurt Waldheim, an Austrian diplomat who had openly campaigned for the job after losing in a run for his country's presidency. The fact that Waldheim had served as a Wehrmacht officer in the early years of World War II was not held against him, while the Soviets vetoed the American candidate, Max Jakobson, on the grounds that the Arab world would never accept a Jew. This led Daniel Patrick Moynihan, later to serve as U.S. ambassador to the UN, to quip, "Our candidate had been a Jewish socialist, but we settled for a German infantry officer." Much later, in fact, it emerged that Waldheim had joined Nazi youth groups, that he had remained in the German army far longer than he had admitted, and that he had served as an officer in a unit that had rounded up Greek Jews for transport to the death camps and murdered thousands of villagers in reprisal killings. "In retrospect," Stanley Meisler remarks, "it seems like a fortuitous metaphor for the United Nations to be led during the 1970s by a Nazi and a liar."

Waldheim accomplished very little of note, and said very little of note, during his ten years as secretary-general. Even a sympathetic biographer delicately observes that Waldheim "slowly recognized that he was safest articulating positions supported by UN consensus." But his poor reputation chiefly rests (in addition to his status as Nazi and liar) on the polarizing, fruitless, and in some cases barbarous debates that consumed the UN during his time in office. By 1971, the UN's membership rolls had reached 134; the Third World was now firmly in the saddle, while the prestige of the United States continued to decline, thanks both to the Vietnam War and to the increasing radicalization of opinion in much of the developing world. The East-West axis of the Cold War gave way, at least ideologically, to a North-South divide, in which the free markets and resource consumption of the North were understood to be responsible for the poverty of the South.

Developing nations united around the demand for a New International Economic Order, including a large-scale transfer of resources from the rich to the poor and the dismantling of multinational corporations and global controls on commodity prices to rectify trade imbalances. In the United Nations Educational, Scientific, and Cultural Organization, or UNESCO, an original UN body chartered to promote mutual understanding among peoples, developing nations pressed for something called the New World Information and Communication Order, which would redress inequalities in information, in part by requiring media outlets to focus on wrongs perpetrated against the Third World. Few, if any, of the advocates of this doctrine permitted the press freedoms taken for granted in the West, as critics were quick to note. Both of these proposals stimulated serious debate, and serious proposals for change. But ultimately very little came of either, and perhaps little was expected to. The UN was increasingly becoming a rhetorical institution, where nations who felt ill-treated could even the score, if only in words, against their powerful foes.

Western nations, including the United States, had generally taken the view that these Marxist rodomontades were best treated like so many firecrackers, irritating but not harmful. In Daniel Patrick Moynihan, however, President Richard Nixon had appointed a UN ambassador who believed deeply that words and ideas mattered, and that the United States could not afford to let the anti-Western polemic, of which the Soviet Union had made itself chief sponsor, harden into conventional wisdom. In a famous article in *Commentary* titled "The

United States in Opposition," Moynihan had written: "To have halted the great totalitarian advance only to be undone by the politics of resentment and the economics of envy would be a poor outcome to the promise for a world society." Moynihan was passionate and expostulatory, an Irish stem-winder, showboat, and polymath. Nobody relished the prospect of gladiatorial combat more than he.

Moynihan chose to make a stand on the issue of Israel, a subject that consumed an astonishing amount of energy at the UN considering how very little the organization could do to affect the political and military situation in the Middle East. In 1974, the General Assembly devoted eight days to debating "the question of Palestine." Yasser Arafat, head of the Palestine Liberation Organization, was not only treated as a head of state but permitted to wear a holster (apparently empty) as he spoke in the chamber. By the time of Moynihan's appointment, no UN conference, no matter its subject, was complete without a ritual denunciation of Israel. In the fall of 1975, the Group of 77, as the Third World bloc styled itself, decided to bring a resolution condemning Israel to the General Assembly itself. When the United States and several of its allies strongly objected, the resolution was withdrawn and replaced with another stating simply that "Zionism is a form of racism and racial discrimination."

Adroit diplomacy at this point might have made the whole issue go away. But Moynihan believed that diplomacy had allowed the more virulent Third World nations to hijack the UN as a global forum for their annihilationist ideology; both the anti-Israel faction and the UN itself needed to be called to account. In mid-October, the UN conducted a bitter and vituperative and very public debate on the "Zionism equals racism" resolution. Before the calling of the vote, whose outcome was never in doubt, Leonard Garment, the U.S. representative to the UN Human Rights Commission, a man of great eloquence and, not irrelevantly, a Jew, rose to state the American position. "This committee," he said, "is preparing itself, with deliberation and foreknowledge, to perform a supreme act of deceit, to make a massive attack on the moral realities of the world . . . I choose my words carefully when I say that this is an obscene act." The resolution passed, 70 to 29, with 27 abstentions. Four months later Ambassador Moynihan, having made enemies enough for a lifetime, resigned. Waldheim, on the other hand, remained so circumspect throughout this tumultuous drama that he emerged unscathed. The "Zionism equals racism" resolution became, in the eyes of the West, and above all of Jews, an ineradicable stain on the UN.

By the early 1980s, the United Nations had become a matter of such indifference in Washington that the highly conservative administration of President Ronald Reagan supported Waldheim's request for a third term. When this was blocked, no consensus candidate emerged. Javier Pérez de Cuéllar, a Peruvian diplomat who had retired only a few months earlier after serving as under-secretary-general at the UN, emerged as "everyone's last choice," in the words of an African diplomat. As a young man, Pérez de Cuéllar had served on the Peruvian delegation to the first General Assembly session in London; later he had been Peru's ambassador to the UN, and Waldheim's special representative to Cyprus. He was the first secretary-general to have grown up with the UN, and he was, like the UN itself, elegant, gracious, highly professional, elaborately noncommittal. It was famously said of him that he couldn't cause a splash by falling out of a boat.

The UN in the early 1980s was still careening down the ruinous path it had been charting for the previous decade. Now, however, it was confronting an American administration that was every bit as ideological as the world body, save in the opposite direction. The Reagan administration, committed to the proposition that the Soviet Union needed to be confronted rather than simply contained, spared no pieties for the global forum of diplomacy. American conservatives found an inviting target in UNESCO, whose single-minded focus on controlling media for the benefit of the developing world they considered especially noxious. UNESCO's secretary-general, Amadou-Mahtar M'Bow, was an imperious figure who brooked no dissent from the developing world line on information and cultural issues. M'Bow made himself vulnerable to criticism by building himself a lavish penthouse atop UNESCO's Paris office, and by presiding over a nest of mismanagement and nepotism. In late 1983, the Reagan administration announced, to a good deal of domestic applause, that it would withdraw from the organization absent reform. Though this threatened not only political but economic catastrophe for UNESCO, which depended on the United States for a quarter of its budget, M'Bow would not stoop to mollify his critics. The United States withdrew, followed shortly by Great Britain and Singapore. The UN appeared to be drifting onto the shoals of irrelevance.

And then, quite abruptly, it wasn't. In September 1987, Mikhail Gorbachev, the reform-minded Soviet president, wrote a celebrated article in *Pravda* and *Izvestia* proposing "a wider use of . . . the institution of UN military observers and UN peace-keeping forces" and calling for the five permanent members to serve as "guarantors" of international security. Gorbachev wanted to move the Soviets out of their sterile position of permanent opposition; the UN was the perfect forum in which to do so. And so geopolitics, which had shackled the institution for forty years, now made it new. Pérez de Cuéllar had urged the five to meet among themselves to thrash out solutions to the senseless slaughter then pitting Iran against Iraq; they began discussing other issues as well, including Cambodia, a brutalized pawn in the old Cold War game.

As the Cold War at last began to thaw, entire regions of the world became accessible to diplomacy and mediation, and thus to the tools with which both the Security Council and the secretary-general were equipped. In the twelve years following the establishment of an observer force along the India-Pakistan border in 1966, the Security Council had authorized all of three peacekeeping or observer missions, each in the Middle East; in 1988 and 1989 alone, it established five such missions—on the Iran-Iraq border and in Afghanistan, Angola, Namibia, and Central America.

In some instances, the Security Council was able to open up its own dead-case files. In 1978 the council had passed a resolution establishing an interim UN authority in Namibia, a colony of South Africa which had brutally suppressed a local insurgency, known as SWAPO. It was a classic Cold War standoff, for both the Soviets and the Cubans supported rebel movements in the region; the United States, fearful of falling African dominoes, backed South Africa despite the outcast status of the apartheid regime. But the Soviets were quickly shedding an ideological empire they could no longer afford, while the South Africans had tired of fending off well-trained Cuban soldiers. In late 1988 and early 1989, the Cubans agreed to leave neighboring Angola, while South Africa agreed to surrender Namibia, which was formally under the protection of the UN Trusteeship Council. A UN peace-keeping mission, known as UNTAG, undertook to do something no peacekeeping mission had done before: to act as the sovereign author-ity until elections could establish a legitimate government. An astonish-ing 97 percent of Namibians turned out for the UN-run election, held in early November. The ballot was conducted, by a beautifully fitting coincidence, at just the moment when the Berlin Wall was coming down. It was an enthralling token of what the UN might accomplish in the post–Cold War era. Pik Botha, the foreign minister of South Africa, later called the Namibia operation "probably the most important event in southern Africa in the last forty years."

In the midst of this period, Saddam Hussein did the Security Council a favor of incalculable value by invading Kuwait, which he did in the predawn hours of August 2, 1990. Not since the North Koreans crossed the 38th parallel almost exactly forty years earlier had the council been confronted with such a brazen attempt to annex the terri-tory of a sovereign state. Washington had backed Saddam in the war with Iran. But this time the Iraqis, like the North Koreans, had made the mistake of attacking a key American ally, which is to say that once again the imperative to respond to a gross violation of the Charter coin-cided with American self-interest. Better still, from the point of view of council unity, no oil-consuming state could afford to be indifferent to Saddam's naked attempt to add Kuwait's oil reserves, and perhaps even Saudi Arabia's, to his own. Finally, the Soviets, who had been conve-niently AWOL in 1950, were eager to demonstrate their return to membership in the family of nations. The planets in the UN system were perfectly aligned. Within hours of the invasion, the Security Council had adopted a resolution condemning the violation of Kuwaiti sovereignty and demanding immediate withdrawal. The council acted under Chapter VII of the Charter, which authorized the use of sanc-tions as well as military force. The measure carried with fourteen votes, including that of Cuba. (Yemen abstained.) Over the next two months the council passed one punitive resolution after another.

President George H.W. Bush, a former UN ambassador himself, was every bit as eager to work through the Security Council as Harry Truman had been in 1950. But his reasoning was more pragmatic. In his memoirs, written with the former national security adviser Brent

Scowcroft, Bush wrote that while he had preferred to act multilaterally, "This was, in part, a practical matter. Mounting an effective military counter to Iraq's invasion required the backing and bases of Saudi Arabia and other Arab states. Building an international response led us immediately to the United Nations, which could provide a cloak of acceptability to our efforts and mobilize world opinion behind the principles we wished to project." Even Bush, perhaps the most pro-UN American president since Kennedy, did not feel that he *needed* the council imprimatur to legitimize a war to roll back Iraqi aggression. Had he failed to gain that support, the president wrote, "we would back away from a UN mandate and cobble together an independent multinational effort built on friendly Arab and allied participation"—what later became known as "a coalition of the willing."

But of course this never proved necessary. At a climactic meeting on November 29, presided over by Secretary of State James Baker and attended by a dozen other foreign ministers, the council passed resolution 678 authorizing "all necessary means" to enforce the earlier resolution requiring Iraqi withdrawal. The vote was 12 to 2, with Cuba and Yemen in opposition and China abstaining. All understood the significance of the vote: 200,000 troops, principally American, had already gathered in the Gulf. It was a solemn moment, but also an enthralling one, full of promise that the UN's future would look very different from its past. Secretary Baker hit just that transcendent note. "With the Cold War behind us," he told the council, "we now have a chance to build the world which was envisioned . . . by the founders of the United Nations. We have the chance to make the Security Council and this United Nations true instruments for peace and justice across the globe."

President Bush had no interest, either ideological or tactical, in removing the "cloak of acceptability" from the naked fact of U.S. power and engagement. He agreed to allow an additional seven weeks for diplomacy. He sent Secretary Baker to negotiate with the Iraqis, and he did not stop Pérez de Cuéllar from embarking on a futile mission of his own to Baghdad. He put together a military coalition that included France, Great Britain, and several major Arab countries—none of whom, of course, he actually needed to do the job. And when coalition ground forces smashed Iraqi resistance in a matter of days, he called a halt to the war rather than move on to Baghdad, in part out of fear of violating the terms of his UN mandate and thus eroding his international support. Bush had played his hand with consummate skill.

In the euphoria of the moment, it was easy to overlook two central facts. First, the United States had attained such global dominance with the collapse of the Soviet empire that it could afford to act on its own, even if it preferred not to. Second, Saddam's attempt to forcibly annex his neighbor was an archaism: The UN, like the League before it, had been established to cure a disease from which the world no longer suffered. In the post–Cold War era, states would collapse from within rather than being toppled from without. Henry Kissinger wrote that "historians in all likelihood will treat the Gulf crisis as a special case rather than a watershed." The Gulf War certainly *felt* like a watershed for the UN, for it showed how very powerful the organization's consensus-building and legitimating functions could be once the paralysis of the Cold War had lifted. But that paralysis had also concealed the fundamental defects in the UN's machinery. The euphoria of 1991 would prove as transitory as the euphoria of 1945.

CHAPTER TWO

A Gold Coast Man

THE GOLD COAST OF AFRICA, WHERE KOFI ANNAN WAS born in 1938, was one of the more benevolent corners of empire. Independence was a distant dream, and the British colonial government provided opportunities for young men of talent. Annan was born into the uppermost reaches of the tribal order; both of his parents were of noble lineage, his mother from the Fante tribe, his father both Fante and Ashanti. Both were Westernized and Christianized, his father going by the name of Henry Reginald, his mother, Rose. Their son was baptized Anthony, but by this time the fashion had shifted toward the African name, and he was always known as Kofi, save by the occasional elderly aunt. "Kofi" means "born on Friday"; his twin sister was named Efua, the female equivalent. Annan also had a brother and two older sisters.

Henry Annan was a chief, with a chiefly temperament, "a strong person in a quiet way," as Annan recalls. He was part of the first generation of modern men in Africa, an educated man who wore a suit to his work with the United Africa Company, a subsidiary of Unilever, a Dutch multinational. Henry Annan retired as a director of the company and as commissioner of the Ashanti region, an administrative position that the independent government of Ghana gave to tribal leaders. Kofi revered his father, whom he thought of less as a chief than as a man of importance, a man to whom other men listened. Local notables were forever dropping in to the Annan household to ask advice or, increasingly, to talk politics. Kofi sat in the background, neither speaking nor expected to speak.

Local politics had been dominated for years by the United Gold Coast Convention, which represented the sober and solid professional class, among whom it was understood that independence was best sought incrementally and without conflict. But in 1949, Kwame Nkrumah, a firebrand who had spent many years in England and the United States, broke away to form the Convention People's Party, which would use the Indian tactic of nonviolent resistance to demand immediate independence. Henry Annan had never been a party man, but his sympathies naturally lay with the United Gold Coast Convention. And it was in Kofi's nature to accept the views of his father and his father's friends. He had been sent off at age eleven to Mfantsipim, the country's oldest and most prestigious boarding school. Even in this redoubt of privilege, Kofi was known as a Gold Coast man. He was a respectful lad, but he was not altogether compliant. The boys talked constantly about the independence struggle, and perhaps a grain of the spirit of Nkrumah seeped into him. He led a boycott of the cafeteria food—the boys took the precaution of eating before they arrived for dinner—and the authorities were forced to make changes. It was to be one of the few overtly confrontational acts of his career.

Ghana, as the new country was called, gained its independence, without bloodshed, in March 1957. Kofi Annan was eighteen; he had seen his world transformed, and with remarkably little friction. His father's circle never got the ministerial jobs, but Annan saw people emerge from jail to take up important posts in the new government. Nkrumah was a revered leader. Annan absorbed from this national triumph a faith that things work out, that events are malleable, that one can, in fact, play a role and be an agent of history. It was, he has said, "an exciting and electrifying time" when bright young men like him felt beckoned to join the great enterprise of nation-building. He enrolled in college, and he assumed that after graduation he would join the government.

Henry Annan wanted Kofi to take a good job with a company like United Africa and accept his place within the tribal hierarchy. But independent Ghana had much more to offer an ambitious young man. Annan enrolled at the University of Science and Technology and became vice president of the Ghana Student Union. At a meeting of student leaders in Freetown, Sierra Leone, he learned of a Ford Foundation grant to study in the United States. Annan applied and won. In 1959, he was sent to Macalester, a liberal arts college in St. Paul, Minnesota, which was so internationally minded that it flew the UN flag. One might imagine that this West African princeling would have reeled before lily-white, ice-bound Minnesota, but it wasn't so; Annan had the gift of making himself comfortable anywhere and of inducing others to be comfortable with him. He was a much-liked and much-admired figure on campus. He was given a scholarship for a second year so that he could graduate. He majored in economics and set the school record in the sixty-yard dash.

Annan says that he closely followed the civil rights movement then unfolding, yet race was essentially a matter of indifference to him. Once he was out walking along the Minnehaha Creek with a German girl he knew, and a group of drunken louts in a boat began shouting racist abuse. The two barely escaped what could have been a serious beating. But what Annan remembers most about the incident is the fury of his white friends on hearing of it, and the fact that he later received a personal apology from the mayor of Minneapolis on mayoral stationery. "I'm considerate of my color and of my deep African roots," he says. "But from my student days I've always remembered the wonderful comment 'No one can make you feel inferior without your consent.'" What is perhaps more to the point is that in his own mind he was not "black"; he was African. And in the African hierarchy he occupied a far more exalted social position than those who tried to insult him or condescend to him.

Annan was the kind of exemplary newcomer upon whom Americans enjoyed shedding their bounty. After graduating from Macalester, he received a Carnegie grant to continue his studies in economics in Geneva. Annan had little academic interest in the subject—he was a good student without being a person of intellectual passion—but he felt that he would need French to return to West Africa. And Annan thrived in Geneva as he had at Macalester. According to Toni Goodale, a well-heeled New Yorker then doing her junior year abroad at the University of Geneva, "This was a very sophisticated crowd, a lot of rich kids, and you wouldn't think they would take easily to this Ghanaian.

But he was the star of our group. Women adored him; he had a different girl every day."

Opportunities came to Annan without his particularly seeking them, and at the time his own plans—learn French, return to Ghana—were sufficiently tentative that he was happy to lay them aside for something better. In 1962, when he was offered a job as an administrative and budget officer at the World Health Organization, he left his graduate studies to become a P1—the lowest civil-service grade—at WHO's Geneva headquarters. The UN's lofty ideals, its impeccable anticolonial credentials, and its emerging focus on social and economic development all appealed to a young West African with high expectations for himself. Annan wanted to put his talents at the service of Africa. After a few years in his post he went to the director of personnel and asked to be sent to openings in Congo-Brazzaville or Alexandria. The official was stupefied, since almost all of Annan's colleagues had been scheming to stay in cushy posts in Europe. He offered this eager beaver a posting in Copenhagen. Annan politely resigned, and instead took a job in Addis Ababa with the Economic Commission for Africa, a UN planning body and think tank for macroeconomic and structural issues. He was only an administrator, but he still felt that he was playing a modest role in the rise of a new Africa. Because the Organization of African Unity also met in Addis, Annan had the opportunity to watch and listen to the great independence leaders—Nyerere and Nkrumah, Kenyatta and Senghor.

In Geneva, Annan had been introduced by his uncle to Titi Alakija, a Nigerian woman from a family of more or less equal standing to the Annans. They married in 1965 and had their first child, a girl named Ama, in Addis, in 1969. The second, Kojo, came four years later. By the late 1960s, Annan was growing restless once more. He wasn't sure he wanted to stay with the UN; he still felt he had a role to play in Ghana. In 1971, he took a sabbatical to study at the Sloan School of Management at MIT. It was, he says, "a period of reflection. I was trying to figure out what to do next, where I can make the best contribution." Annan always felt comfortable in the genteel and collegial setting of a university. Nevertheless, he found the work at Sloan extremely hard, and he succeeded only by dint of great discipline.

Annan then returned to Geneva to work for the UN High Commissioner for Refugees, and then once again left headquarters to serve as an administrator with the UN Emergency Force, the peacekeeping force along the Suez that Hammarskjöld had deployed in 1956. He still felt a sense of unsatisfied obligation to his home country; in 1974 he returned to Ghana to take a job with the state tourist board. By this time, however, the Ghana that Annan and his friends had dreamed of had already slipped into memory. The autocratic Nkrumah had been ousted in a military coup in 1966. And the economy was failing. Like Nehru, Nyerere, and other champions of the anticolonial movement, Nkrumah had seen socialism as the path to mass prosperity, and so had nationalized much of Ghana's assets. While capitalist Ivory Coast thrived next door, socialist Ghana spiraled downward. Annan himself had become persuaded of the merits of capitalism, and of the American way generally, during his time at Macalester. Now he spent two frustrating years inside a Soviet-style economy; what's more, he found his proposals blocked at every turn by the generals who had infiltrated the state.

Annan had spent years waiting to return home to make his contribution; now he understood that there was no place for him there. His idealism and optimism, his patience and quietude, ill suited him for the increasingly harsh and brutal world of Ghanaian politics. These very attributes, on the other hand, made him the UN official nonpareil. Annan accepted the inevitable, returning to the organization in 1976. By this time, he had been pegged as a manager, a behind-the-scenes figure who knew how to keep the mechanism working. He was sent to New York to work in the Department of Human Resources. This work put the thirty-eight-year-old Annan about as far as it was possible to get from the UN's moral core, for in matters of personnel the organization surrendered to politics and cronyism with barely a fight.

Indeed, the UN as insiders knew it bore almost no resemblance to the noble, if beleaguered, institution visible to the outside world. With so little actually to do, and thus to be held accountable for, the UN had become a giant paper-processing factory, a stultifying bureaucracy where, save in its uppermost reaches, sensible people kept their heads down. Its culture was overwhelmingly risk-averse, careerist, and politically hypersensitive. In *Defeat of an Ideal*, her devastating, if highly tendentious, account of a decade of service at the UN, the novelist Shirley

Hazzard acidly noted that "more goodwill has perhaps been brought to the United Nations Secretariat than to any other modern organization, and more wasted." Merit was no match for politics.

The Charter stipulated that the "paramount consideration" in the hiring of staff should be ensuring "the highest standards of efficiency, competence, and integrity," but added that "due regard" should be paid to the widest possible geographical distribution of posts. The main point tended to get lost as members used geographical distribution as a pretext to treat the UN as a giant jobs bank, turning the organization into a cushy redoubt for time-servers. And they met with little resistance. On the occasion of U Thant's retirement, *The New York Times* noted that "as far as is known he never challenged a member government when it nominated an ill-equipped man to a position on the staff." Waldheim, too, silently acquiesced in this system.

It was a low era at the UN, with the General Assembly convulsed by fruitless and ugly debates and the Security Council helpless to break the Cold War deadlock. It's not easy to imagine what would keep an intelligent and ambitious—and still young—person coming to work at Turtle Bay. Annan acknowledges that the institution did itself "lots of damage" by its fights with Israel, with capitalism, with the Western media. But, he says, "I really had come to believe in the ideals of the UN. And for those of us who believe in the ideals, you keep trying to improve it, you keep hoping it will get better, you keep saying, 'It's the only organization we have where you can do something, because you can talk to the member states so they will understand it's in their interest to put their bitter differences aside and work on issues of common concern.'"

By 1979, Annan had separated from his wife. He was taking care of Kojo, and Ama was to go to boarding school in England. Annan was no longer agitating for a position in Africa; now it made sense to go back to Geneva. In the spring of 1980 he accepted a position as deputy director for management and administration at the Office of the High Commissioner for Refugees. The job brought him closer to the substantive work of the UN, and to the ideals he cherished. In 1981 the Nobel Peace Prize went to the commission for its work in the giant refugee camps in Thailand, Pakistan, and elsewhere. Annan took frequent trips to the camps, though he was plainly a "headquarters" man rather than a "field" man.

In 1981, Annan met Nane Lagergren, a tall, blond Swedish lawyer then also working at UNHCR. She was, like him, quiet, composed, profoundly gracious, and perhaps a bit unworldly. She had about her the same aura of simple goodness that people felt in Annan. Lagergren had a young daughter, and she was divorced. In retrospect, an air of predestination hung over the union; at the time, it was love at first sight. The two were married in 1984, not long after Annan's divorce was finalized. That same year Annan returned to New York as head of the budget department, another assignment that would keep him chained to a desk, far from the UN's good works. But it was another rung up the ladder, and Annan accepted the job without hesitation.

Annan spent the 1980s climbing to the uppermost rungs of the UN bureaucracy. In 1987 he became assistant secretary-general for human resources; in 1990 he became the head of budget and planning. These are not terribly glamorous jobs anywhere, but they were particularly unappealing at the UN, where the General Assembly maintained a death grip on administrative decisions, down to the last line of the budget and the lowliest post in the hierarchy. Annan says vaguely that he had spoken to some "senior people" about moving into a different kind of job, but apparently nothing came of it. He had been typecast as an administrator, and it was understood that administrators did not move to peacekeeping or political affairs. He was widely respected inside the UN as a gentleman, a quietly competent professional, and a warm colleague—but no more than that. Brian Urquhart, who had stared down many a rifle barrel in an illustrious career as a UN peacekeeper, thought of Annan as a bit of a hothouse plant. "He was always considered a cordial chap who liked to go to cocktail parties," Urquhart recalls. "Nobody ever thought that he would develop in this way."

But there was a part of Annan that wasn't satisfied going to cocktail parties, even if he kept it quite successfully under wraps. And his chance came in 1990, when Iraq's lightning invasion of Kuwait suddenly stranded nine hundred UN international staff members in the two countries. Javier Pérez de Cuéllar turned to Annan to personally negotiate their release with the Iraqis. Annan had never before faced so

fraught a situation, yet he confronted it with a surprising show of resolution. When Elisabeth Lindenmayer, a longtime aide, asked if he was
worried that the mission might miscarry, he said, "Don't ever speak to
me negatively when I'm about to negotiate. We'll make it—and I don't
want to hear that we may not make it."

When Annan arrived in Baghdad, he found that the UN personnel
constituted a small fraction of the foreigners trapped by the war. There
were Westerners whom Saddam Hussein was holding hostage, and
thousands of Filipinos, Sri Lankans, Bangladeshis, and others who
worked in Kuwait, and were free to leave but unable to do so, since
flights had been grounded and banks closed. Annan persuaded the
Iraqis to release the UN officials. They would not allow the Asians to
leave directly from Kuwait, so Annan was able to bring them to Baghdad, and then organized a caravan across the desert to Amman. From
there he kept a fleet of planes shuttling back and forth between Jordan
and various Asian capitals until the trapped workers had reached home.

Annan had labored anonymously throughout the UN's anonymous
years. Now, by a happy coincidence, he had distinguished himself from
his fellow bureaucrats at precisely the moment when the organization
had begun to matter as its founders had envisioned. His true history,
and the organization's, would begin at virtually the same moment. On
February 1, 1992, the new secretary-general, Boutros Boutros-Ghali,
appointed Annan to a new job, as deputy chief of the Department of
Peacekeeping Operations, or DPKO.

The machinery of peacekeeping had rusted over in the long years of the
Cold War impasse. In the late 1980s, peacekeeping missions were operated by six officials sitting around a table in what was known as the
Office of Special Political Affairs. The group was dominated by its
head, Marrack Goulding, a punctilious Englishman who inspected
every word that went out under his name, and rewrote many of them.
Goulding had inherited the job from Brian Urquhart, for peacekeeping
was a British domain, with a specifically British culture of fair play,
self-discipline, and doctrinal clarity. It was a practice very much defined by what it wasn't: peacekeepers did not take sides or discharge
firearms, save in self-defense, or meddle in politics. The doctrine had

proved serviceable in the few instances in which it had been applied in recent years. Whatever questions arose as to the applicability of the model in particular cases were settled by Goulding.

But by the beginning of 1992, when Javier Pérez de Cuéllar was succeeded by Boutros Boutros-Ghali, an Egyptian diplomat, this small and tidy world had already become an anachronism. The Security Council was sending peacekeepers all over the world. States held together by one of the twin hegemons of the Cold War were coming apart at the seams; there was talk of sending blue helmets into the whirlpool of the Balkans. One of Boutros-Ghali's first decisions was to create the Department of Peacekeeping Operations, and to make Goulding under-secretary-general for peacekeeping. As a matter of bureaucratic standing, Goulding wanted a deputy who was an assistant secretary-general. He thought well of Kofi Annan, who had distinguished himself in Iraq. Goulding also felt that it would be a good idea to have an African, since many of the new operations were occurring in Africa. "I thought we could unload Africa and the Middle East on him," Goulding says. It was true that Annan had only the briefest experience of peacekeeping, but the rapid increase in missions had created an administrative tangle that he was well suited to sort out.

Annan had arrived at the UN's second great moment of euphoria. The end of the Cold War had made possible what had once been unthinkable. UN political officials and peacekeepers had run a country of their own in Namibia; in El Salvador, they ended a civil war, instituted meaningful human rights standards, and helped establish a legitimate political process. In late January 1992, the Security Council instructed the secretary-general to submit a plan to strengthen the UN's capacity for preventive diplomacy and peacekeeping. In June, Boutros-Ghali issued the grandiloquently titled "Agenda for Peace." Capturing the spirit of hope and possibility, the authors observed that "in the past few months a conviction has grown, among nations large and small, that an opportunity has been regained to achieve the great objectives of the Charter . . . This opportunity must not be squandered. The Organization must never again be crippled as it was in the era that has now passed."

The time had come, Boutros-Ghali maintained, to revitalize Article 42 of the Charter, which authorized the Security Council to take military action in the face of threats to peace. The moribund Military Staff Committee should be revived and should become the operational arm of a military force raised from among members, and available for enforcement actions against recalcitrant foes. The council should also have access to "peace-enforcement units," essentially peacekeeping troops with an offensive capacity who would be deployed when, for example, one side refused to honor a cease-fire, thus compelling the UN to take sides in order to enforce the agreement. This muscular doctrine constituted a radical departure from peacekeeping as Brian Urquhart and Marrack Goulding had known it. Washington was scarcely less giddy than Turtle Bay. Colin Powell, then chairman of the Joint Chiefs of Staff, spoke movingly of peacekeepers as "warriors of freedom." President George H.W. Bush offered to let the UN train its soldiers at Fort Dix, in New Jersey.

In the initial months of 1992, UN peacekeeping missions were sent to Cambodia, to monitor elections, protect human rights, oversee the return of refugees, and rebuild the war-shattered infrastructure; to Croatia, to separate warring Serbs and Croats; and to Somalia, to protect the supply of humanitarian goods in the midst of a famine. Peacekeeping seemed to have no limits. The underlying mentality, says Shashi Tharoor, a career UN official who had begun working with Goulding in 1989, was, "Now that we are no longer divided on ideological grounds, every problem can come to us and we will prescribe a resolution. Boutros-Ghali spoke rashly of 'a problem of too much credibility.'"

This problem did not last long, for the Security Council made no serious effort to match the size and capacity of the peacekeeping force to the setting in which it was being deployed. In April, the council declared that the immense scale of suffering in Somalia constituted a threat to international peace and security. The suffering, in fact, threatened no one but the Somalis, but widely broadcast scenes of mass starvation impelled the council to act, and peacekeepers had become the UN's all-purpose weapon against evil. So the council acted: the members authorized a force of five hundred troops to secure humanitarian supplies in the midst of a madhouse run by rival warlords. As if this weren't feckless enough, the Pakistani contingent that agreed to serve took five months to arrive.

Annan had sent Elisabeth Lindenmayer to Mogadishu to organize the peacekeeping presence; she was horrified to discover that the Pakistanis had come with virtually no equipment and no preparation. Pinned down by the forces of the chief warlord, Mohammed Aideed, the peacekeepers could barely move beyond the confines of the airport, much less protect the distribution of food. People all over the world saw televised images of starving Somalis juxtaposed with helpless UN troops. The warlords were stealing the aid and using the proceeds to buy guns. Under pressure from Boutros-Ghali, the Bush administration agreed in December to send in a large force to protect the relief supplies. Having already lost his reelection bid to Bill Clinton, President Bush may have wished to leave the stage with an act of unprecedented magnanimity. An astonishing thirty-seven thousand troops, twenty-eight thousand of them American, took over the job from the five hundred Pakistanis. While Americans had on several occasions fought in UN-sanctioned wars—most recently, of course, in the Persian Gulf—never before had American troops served in a UN peacekeeping operation designed to achieve classic peacekeeping goals rather than to advance strategic national interests.

Restore Hope, as the operation was called, succeeded in keeping the warlords at bay and thus saving massive numbers of Somalis from starvation. But it was always understood as a stopgap: the Americans would not disarm the factions or attempt to fill the vacuum of state power. And the commitment was unsustainable. The new Clinton administration could not continue to underwrite a massive deployment that had no obvious end in sight. "From the moment I got to the UN," says Madeleine Albright, then the U.S. ambassador, "my instructions were to get the U.S. out of Somalia and get it transferred to the UN." At the end of March, the Security Council established a new peacekeeping mission and tasked it not only with humanitarian protection but with everything the vastly better-trained and better-armed Americans would not do: disarming the factions and systematically rebuilding the wrecked country. Annan was scrambling to find replacement troops, and they were coming from Third World countries, not Europe. No one on the council seemed to have given any thought to how the new force would achieve the objectives it had been handed.

And then the situation got worse. On May 1, 1993, Annan told Lindenmayer, by then back in New York, to come to his office right away. General Çevik Bir, the force commander in Mogadishu, was screaming over the telephone: "They've left! You've got to get command and control!"

"Who's left?"

"The Marines! They left during the night. They're gone."

It was true—ten thousand Marines had suddenly pulled up stakes. The patchwork force left behind felt terribly exposed in a lunatic environment where teenagers careered around on pickup trucks firing machine guns. It was an absurd situation. "What kind of signal do we send to potential spoilers when the big boys walk away?" asked Hedi Annabi, then head of DPKO's Africa division. "Of course it didn't take long for Aideed to get the message." One month later, on June 5, Aideed's troops ambushed two Pakistani units, killing twenty-six soldiers. This shocking act felt like an attack not only on the soldiers but on the UN itself. Boutros-Ghali, who from the outset had championed a full-bore response in the UN's one major African mission, was outraged; both the secretary-general and the Pakistanis demanded that Aideed be punished. Only one day after the attack, the Security Council passed a resolution authorizing "all necessary precautions against all those responsible for armed attacks." The posse would hunt down the warlord.

The campaign had elements of grotesque travesty, with American forces killing innocent civilians and launching surprise attacks on what turned out to be UN officials. And of course it ended in catastrophe on October 3, when Aideed's men shot down a U.S. Black Hawk helicopter and killed eighteen Army Rangers. President Clinton publicly blamed Boutros-Ghali for the fiasco, but by this time American soldiers in Somalia were operating through an American chain of command, and the decision to send the Ranger mission was taken by the Special Operations command in Florida. "It definitely was not the UN's fault," says Madeleine Albright. "I think the U.S. let down the UN on that." Clinton, to his credit, kept American troops in Somalia until the following March.

In Somalia the UN—and the Clinton administration as well—discovered how utterly unprepared it was for the new world into which it had so boldly and blithely plunged. Every decision was precipitate, every commitment either grossly inadequate or unsustainable. The UN did not know how to operate in a country with no functioning state, nor how to foster the institutions that might ultimately coalesce into a state. (Neither, of course, did anyone else.) Somalia was a profound shock to the system; the giddy sense of possibility that began with the Gulf War ended with sickening images of the corpses of American soldiers dragged through the dusty streets of Mogadishu. Diplomats and UN officials invoked "the Mogadishu line" whenever a new mission or operation loomed in which peacekeepers might have to take sides and thus become combatants. In January 1995, when Boutros-Ghali issued the "Supplement to an Agenda for Peace," he conceded the futility of his visionary hopes of 1992: "Neither the Security Council nor the Secretary General at present has the capacity to deploy, direct, command or control [enforcement] operations except perhaps on a very limited scale."

CHAPTER THREE

Peace, Not Justice

I N FEBRUARY 1993, SECRETARY-GENERAL BOUTROS BOUTROS-Ghali abruptly informed Marrack Goulding that he was being transferred to the Department of Political Affairs, or DPA, then a gloomy backwater heavily populated by Russian timeservers. Goulding was devastated, and his colleagues, who had functioned as subalterns under Goulding's obsessively controlling command, were scarcely reassured to learn that Kofi Annan was to become under-secretary-general for peacekeeping. Goulding was the very embodiment of peacekeeping and its arcane tradecraft, while Annan was an amiable technocrat with one year of experience under his belt. Peacekeeping itself was undergoing a revolutionary transformation. And yet for this very reason, Annan, an outsider, an African, may have been better suited to the job than Goulding, immersed as he was in a tradition dating to Suez. And it turned out that Annan had been hiding his light under a clerical bushel.

Iqbal Riza, a career official who had known Annan since the mid-1970s and predated him in DPKO, became Annan's deputy in 1993. "It was only when we started working in peacekeeping," says Riza, "that I, who had worked on the political and peacekeeping side, realized his very exceptional abilities and qualities. He had political insights, he had perspectives, he saw options. When he took over, we were in the middle of Bosnia, Cambodia, Somalia, Rwanda, El Salvador, Mozambique, Angola; we had fifteen or sixteen operations. We had a meeting

with the perm reps"—the permanent representatives, or ambassadors—"in the midst of these crises, and I could sense a certain skepticism. 'Is he able to manage?' I'd say that lasted about five to six weeks."
Annan encountered at least as much skepticism from his own colleagues, but won them over with a combination of professionalism,
courtesy, and deference. Goulding had rewritten every cable; Annan
sized up his colleagues and offered almost complete autonomy to those
whose abilities he trusted.

Annan quickly displayed his diplomatic gifts, playing a key role in
coaxing the government of Angola and the rebel force known as
UNITA to sign a peace agreement and similarly prodding the military
junta in Haiti to agree to the return of President Jean-Bertrand Aristide, whom they had deposed. He had somehow put together a force to
replace the Americans in Somalia. The enormous and impossibly ambitious mission in Cambodia had organized and protected a reasonably
fair election that had led to the first peaceful transfer of power in that
country's history. These were not trivial achievements, but they would
be remembered by only a few.

DPKO's very real successes were soon to be blotted out by the endlessly protracted agony of Bosnia, which demolished every bright hope
of the post–Cold War moment and came very close to demolishing
peacekeeping itself. The war in the Balkans had begun in the summer
of 1991, when Croatia had declared independence from Yugoslavia and
the Yugoslav president, Slobodan Milošević, had responded with a military campaign designed to subjugate the province. In November, army
troops had massacred civilians in the Croatian town of Vukovar,
prompting calls for a UN peacekeeping presence. Boutros-Ghali, the
incoming secretary-general, wanted to focus the organization on Africa,
not Europe. When he met with Pérez de Cuéllar just before taking office, he said, "Yugoslavia is a European problem; let the Europeans deal
with it." Indeed, Lord Carrington, the chief negotiator on the Balkans
for the European Union, had famously intoned, "The hour of Europe
has come." But now, confronted with the greatest horror on the Continent since World War II, the Europeans, and above all the French and
the British, who were driving policy in the region, insisted on sending
UN forces, rather than their own, into the area.

The Secretariat could not and did not resist the Security Council, and the following month UN military observers were sent to monitor a cease-fire line drawn after Serbian conquests in Croatia. But as un-armed observers, they could do nothing about repeated Serbian viola-tions of the line. Milošević now understood that the blue helmets had their uses: he could seize territory, and then, in effect, use the UN to consolidate his gains. In April 1992, Serbian paramilitaries and government forces began a siege of Sarajevo, Bosnia's capital, prompt-ing calls for a proper peacekeeping force. Boutros-Ghali dispatched Goulding, who was every bit as opposed as he was to such a deploy-ment. Upon Goulding's return, Boutros-Ghali informed the council that "in its present phase the conflict is [not] susceptible to the UN peacekeeping treatment." But the Europeans once again would not take no for an answer. In June, the council expanded the mission, known as UNPROFOR, to include infantry. Three months later the council tasked the mission with protecting an emergency airlift that had been organized to bring supplies to the people of Sarajevo.

By the time Kofi Annan became head of DPKO, the Balkan slaugh-ter was in full spate. Serbian militias had embarked on their systematic campaign of ethnic cleansing in Bosnia, driving women and children into the countryside and interning men in concentration camps. On April 12, a Serb shell killed fifty-six people at a market in Srebrenica, and graphic scenes of carnage flashed around the world. Days later, council members passed a resolution establishing a "safe haven" around Srebrenica, to be enforced by UNPROFOR; a month later the safe havens concept was extended to four other beleaguered Bosnian towns. Over the course of eighteen months, a mission established to separate enemy combatants, in classic UN fashion, had been changed and expanded five times to encompass tasks the UN had never before attempted. Here was mission creep with a vengeance.

Boutros-Ghali continued to make no secret of his distaste for the entire enterprise. On New Year's Eve 1992, he had blithely told the people of Sarajevo, "You have a situation that is better than ten other places in the world . . . I can give you a list"—this at a moment when Serb shells were raining down from the hills on helpless civilians. Boutros-Ghali resented the expenditure of men and money on what he called "a white man's war" while the Security Council took a pass on yet more brutal conflicts in Africa—the ones on the "list." Goulding urged Bhoutros-Ghali to confront the Security Council over the safe havens issue. But Kofi Annan felt otherwise; he was not committed to a canonical view of peacekeeping, nor was he one to keep ethnic or geographical lists. "I had the view that it was going to be extremely difficult for the UN to say we were walking away from this," he says. "How can you go and tell the world, and the Bosnians, that you're going to walk away, that this is not for us?"

UNPROFOR officials considered the policy unenforceable, and feared that it would compel them to side openly with the Bosnians against Serb attackers in violation of the sacrosanct peacekeeping principle of impartiality. The force commander sent a long cable to New York arguing that the havens would have to be large enough to allow Bosnia's citizens to move freely beyond the range of Serbian guns; seventy thousand troops would be required to police such tracts. Boutros-Ghali presented this absurdly high figure to the Security Council; he seemed to be registering his opposition to the enterprise rather than helping to implement it. In mid-June, after another resolution, he proposed either a "heavy option," involving thirty-four thousand troops, or a "light option," involving fewer troops along with a threat of the use of airpower. The Security Council, which effectively meant Britain and France, chose the light option and reduced the proposed troop strength to seventy-six hundred.

This was a decisive, and genuinely catastrophic, moment in the history of peacekeeping, and indeed of the UN itself. The Serbs had made no secret of their ambition to annex Bosnia through a combination of terror and forced evacuation. The Americans and the Europeans, unwilling to fight a war to save Bosnia, had instead mounted a vast humanitarian effort to counter the consequences of Serb aggression, and then, as they had in Somalia, instructed the UN to protect that effort. But this time there would be no crack American divisions. Instead, seventy-six hundred lightly armed peacekeepers were to prevent the Serbs from terrorizing Bosnian civilians. Even at the time, the decision seemed either grossly cynical or profoundly deluded. It was, Annan says, "almost as if they were persuaded that the presence of the blue helmets in the zone itself would dissuade attacks, thinking these guys were so civilized that they wouldn't attack the UN."

David Hannay, the British ambassador, insists that he suffered from no such fantasy. "Nobody liked the idea of the safe areas," he says. They were meant to function as a stopgap measure until the Serbs accepted the so-called Vance-Owen peace plan, then under serious discussion. And when the peace plan in fact collapsed, the safe areas remained as a Band-Aid. Hannay also argues that the heavy option was unworkable, because the Serbs would never allow such a vast assemblage of troops in key areas without a fight, which in turn would provoke a war. "The solution lay in airpower," he says, "not ground troops." But peacekeeping officials as well as troop contributors blocked almost every proposed air strike in the ensuing year, and Milošević soon discovered that the threat was, in fact, a bluff. While the safe havens held throughout 1993—which is to say that they might have been remembered as a brilliant expedient had the peace plan succeeded—the towns, above all Srebrenica, Goražde, and Bihać, became killing zones starting in early 1994.

` All of this could have been foreseen, and indeed was foreseen by critics of the safe havens policy. Why, then, did the UN adopt a policy that led to humiliation and, ultimately, death? The obvious answer is that the major powers simply would not bring sufficient force to bear to stop the Serbs. The Americans wanted to bomb but were unwilling to put troops on the ground; those NATO countries that had provided troops were not about to expose them to the inevitable wrath of the Serbs after a bombing campaign. And there was very little public pressure at the time to do otherwise: the Americans were unwilling to die, and the Europeans to kill, in order to stop Milošević. Had Boutros-Ghali proposed, for example, that the peacekeepers be withdrawn in order to let NATO bomb the Bosnian Serbs, the Americans would have supported him, but the other NATO countries would not. The Secretariat could not compel the Security Council to enforce its own mandates. As Shashi Tharoor says, "You cannot expect the implementation of a policy to substitute for the will on which the policy was granted."

This is the story line endlessly repeated inside the UN. It is true, but insufficient. "The Secretariat was the dog that didn't bark," says David Harland, who served as the chief political officer to the UNPROFOR force commander from 1993 to 1995 and later co-authored the Srebrenica report, the UN's own study of what went wrong in the Balkans. "They were hearing about the atrocities, they knew how bad it was, they knew there were alternatives, but they didn't bark." Thant Myint-U, a young UN official who was sent to Sara-jevo in 1994 as assistant spokesman for UNPROFOR, found himself fighting constantly with Yasushi Akashi, the head of the UN mission, and General Sir Michael Rose, the force commander in Bosnia, both of whom insisted on a rigid impartiality between the two sides even when the brutal facts cried out otherwise.

"Akashi could have said something, but he chose not to," says Thant. "We used the authority of the UN to characterize the situation in such a way as to preserve an environment in which we could carry out the humanitarian mission." The Serbs created a humanitarian ca-tastrophe, and then permitted the UN to minister to the victims so long as the organization did not blame the Serbs. The effect of this moral myopia, so far as Thant and other, generally younger, offi-cials were concerned, was to blunt the argument for a more forceful in-tervention and thus to postpone an inevitable day of reckoning. "I couldn't accept a policy of lying to preserve a position of neutrality," says Thant. He tried to resign, but his resignation was not accepted; then he was fired for, as he sees it, speaking honestly to the press.

After forty-five years of ardent conflict prevention, the muscular body fashioned by FDR and Churchill seemed to have degenerated into a fearful pacifism. "The UN was interested in peace, not justice," as the journalist David Rieff writes in *Slaughterhouse*, his mordant ac-count of the early years of the war. And this peace-at-any-price men-tality had the effect of aligning the UN with the Serb cause. "UNPROFOR's job was to facilitate . . . humanitarian assistance," Rieff writes. "What was getting in the way? The fighting. And who was keep-ing the fighting going? The Bosnian government side, which was not prepared to accept the dismemberment of the country. To many in the UN, the Bosnians became the ones 'getting in the way' of the aid effort by continuing their resistance."

General Rose and Akashi and the other chief figures in Bosnia were in daily contact with DPKO. Rose has written that when he first took up his command, he visited Annan and explained that he would adhere strictly to the mandate of humanitarian protection. He was, he writes, gratified to find that DPKO officials entirely shared his views. Shashi Tharoor was every bit as skeptical of the value of air strikes as General

Rose was, and just as committed to the traditional tenets of peacekeeping. Across the hall, though, sat Iqbal Riza, a Pakistani Muslim who felt deep sympathy for the Bosnians. Riza was not a UN careerist and thus had not so deeply absorbed the UN's institutional norms; his prior career, as a diplomat, had come to an abrupt end in 1977, when he quit in protest after Pakistan's civilian president, Zulfikar Ali Bhutto, ordered troops to fire on unarmed civilians.

The Balkans were in Tharoor's portfolio, not Riza's, and he was far too restrained and courtly a figure to overstep his authority. But in meetings and in conversations with Annan he took the position that UNPROFOR's commitment to neutrality had made it effectively an instrument of Serb war aims. He could not abide the self-righteous General Rose, who had, he thought, "no sense of compassion for what was happening to the Bosnians." And he felt "a tremendous amount of impatience and frustration" that both DPKO and Boutros-Ghali were blocking forceful action at every turn. On two occasions, in late 1993 and early 1994, when he was serving as head of the office in Annan's absence, Riza sent sharp notes to the secretary-general asking him to push the Security Council to take stronger action on the basis of international law. After the second note, Boutros-Ghali curtly instructed him to cease communicating with him directly.

And where, in all this, was Kofi Annan? Which side was he on? The loyal Riza exempts Annan from this division of opinion, though he says that Tharoor's views "had a great deal of influence on Kofi." Critics like David Rieff, on the other hand, see Annan as the fountainhead of peace at any price. Annan himself does not speak of views at all, but rather of trying to manage his way through an impossible situation. He recalls struggling desperately to find the seventy-six hundred troops who were to police the safe areas. "I had discussions with NATO officials," he recalls. "I had discussions with European and American officials. We not only didn't have enough troops; we didn't have the quality of troops we wanted." Moreover, this was a period of almost nonstop crisis in peacekeeping. The immense operation in Somalia was winding down under the most chaotic conditions. Annan was personally negotiating the end of the Haitian junta. The unspeakable catastrophe of Rwanda began in April and continued to consume Annan and his aides over the ensuing months.

Annan saw himself as an administrator, not a theoretician or even a tactician. His "views" were essentially what he understood the institution's views to be. His sense of what ought to be done was profoundly shaped by his understanding of what could or, rather, couldn't be done. At a decisive meeting with the British foreign secretary, Douglas Hurd, in mid-1994, Rose writes that Annan seconded his argument against a more aggressive military posture, saying that this had been the lesson of Somalia. Like Tharoor, equally deep-dyed in UN culture, Annan was acutely sensitive to the limits of political will. After the Security Council resolution authorizing the "light option" in the safe havens, and the prerogative of air strikes, Tharoor wrote a memo to UNPROFOR, which Annan signed, emphasizing that air strikes were to be used only in the event of a grave threat to the mission (rather than to Bosnian civilians). The effect, according to David Harland, was to remove the only threat that might have made the policy enforceable.

Indeed, the unwillingness to jeopardize the humanitarian operation or the peacekeeping troops became the central predicament of the UN presence in the Balkans and led ultimately to the most terrible event of the war, the massacre in Srebrenica in July 1995. Whenever the Serbs had shelled one of the safe havens—Srebrenica, Goražde, Bihać—the UN or NATO had threatened air attacks and then pulled back. And when NATO finally launched a "pinprick" attack, in late May 1995, the Serbs had responded by taking 350 UN peacekeepers hostage. Immediately afterward, Bernard Janvier, the deeply cautious force commander, widely considered pro-Serb, held a secret meeting with Serbian commanders, after which the UN announced that it would adhere henceforward to "strictly peacekeeping principles"—that is, no more bombing. The hostages were duly released.

The Serb assault on Srebrenica began July 6. The six hundred lightly armed Dutch soldiers protecting the town issued desperate requests for air support, but to no avail. On July 11, Srebrenica fell. By the fourteenth, it was clear that something terrible was happening to the town's Muslim population: the Serbs had deported women, children, and the elderly, but, Akashi reported to Annan, "4000 draft-age males" could not be accounted for. He suggested that this information be kept confidential in order not to jeopardize UN forces. Akashi himself revealed so little of what he had heard that on the eighteenth

DPKO sent him a cable asking, "What about the reports of mass murder coming from refugees?" In the end, the Bosnian Serbs killed about seventy-four hundred men and boys—by far the greatest atrocity in Europe since World War II.

Srebrenica shattered any remaining illusions about the aims of the Bosnian Serbs. And yet weeks more would pass before the allies would act. On July 21, the allied leaders held an emergency meeting in London, agreeing that NATO, which itself had been fearful of provoking the Serbs, would no longer give the UN a veto over bombing decisions. In early August, after the Serbs had laid siege to the other safe havens, President Clinton sent his national security adviser, Tony Lake, to inform the allies that the United States was prepared to attack the militias, with or without allied support. On August 28, a Bosnian Serb mortar shell landed in a marketplace in Sarajevo, killing thirty-seven people. This was the trigger: the NATO bombing campaign, Operation Deliberate Force, began on the thirtieth and continued until the Bosnian Serb leadership, already reeling from a renewed Croatian onslaught, signed a draft of a peace agreement two weeks later.

The safe havens policy had been predicated upon a view of Serb war aims that was barely supportable at the time, and had been exposed as naive, or disingenuous, long before Srebrenica. In the words of the Srebrenica report, "The civilian inhabitants of the enclave were not the incidental victims of the attacks; their death or removal was the very purpose of the attacks upon them." And while the report, which was issued under Annan's name, is unsparing on the member states who shaped the policy, it is no less harsh on the UN professionals who carried it out, concluding that "the management of UNPROFOR" failed to "adapt mandates to the reality on the ground." And this lapse was a matter less of shortsightedness than of institutional culture and entrenched principles. Though the Serbs were ultimately checkmated not through diplomacy but force, the authors observe, "the Secretariat had convinced itself early on that the broader use of force by the international community was beyond our mandate and anyway undesirable."

I read a portion of this lacerating self-criticism to Annan while we were having one of our periodic lunches in the dining room of his office suite—white-gloved steward, choice of red wine or white, splendid view westward through a wall of glass. I asked if he felt, in retrospect, that he and his colleagues had refused, as the report alleged, to look the truth in the eye. The question plainly made him uncomfortable, and he said, "We had to rely on our commanders on the ground. They made judgments. In hindsight it became clear, but in the heat of the moment we had lots of questions, but we didn't learn the truth from headquarters."

This was a surprisingly impersonal, and even guilt-free, answer; the report he had commissioned and issued was far harsher on the peace-keeping office than Annan himself was. It wasn't clear whether he felt personally implicated in the catastrophe. Riza, who had shepherded the report through the bureaucracy and warded off all efforts at dilution, had no doubt that UNPROFOR had allowed the Serbs to savagely exploit the UN's commitment to neutrality and humanitarian protection. Immediately after Srebrenica, he had walked across the conference room that separated his office from Annan's and said, "Kofi, if we don't act in Bosnia, I will have to tender my resignation. And you know that I've done it before." The NATO bombing had saved Riza from having to perform his second act of career suicide (though it's true that he had delivered this ultimatum only after having been a party to this failed policy for several years).

I asked Annan what, if anything, he felt that he had done wrong or had failed to do. "I relied too much on the commanders from the ground," he repeated. "We should not have relied so much on their judgment, and should have probed a bit more. But we have to be careful not just to blame the commanders, because the troop contributors imposed their own limitations on the commanders, which of course played into the hands of the Serbs." Perhaps, he conceded, it was true that the Serbs could be stopped only by force, but since there was no willingness to use force until the very end, no purpose could have been served by calling for a drastic change in tactics.

Of all the failures in the history of the United Nations, and in the career of Kofi Annan, none had such swift and shattering consequences as the failure to act in the face of genocide in Rwanda. Bosnia was an endless agon; Rwanda was a sudden cataclysm in which 800,000 people were slaughtered in one hundred days. In the Balkans, the UN intervened timidly and clumsily; in Rwanda, it did not intervene at all.

Rwanda was the classic post–Cold War mess: a little country of no strategic importance located in a region where rival ethnic groups routinely vied for power by slaughtering each other. In Central Africa, the UN and other peacemaking groups tried to persuade the factions to stop fighting and accept systems of power sharing. In August 1993, the Rwandan state, controlled by the Hutu majority, signed such an agreement, known as the Arusha Accords, with a rebel group made up of the minority Tutsis. The agreement was to be policed by a UN peacekeeping force. The peacekeeping department asked for twelve hundred troops, with more to come later; the Security Council authorized a force of eight hundred.

Belgium, Rwanda's former colonial master, agreed to supply troops for the mission, known as UNAMIR, but rather than furnish the motorized infantry battalion or the armored personnel carriers that the council had requested, they offered four hundred and fifty lightly armed soldiers with little transport. The battalion was rounded out by Bangladeshi soldiers, who arrived with nothing save their personal arms. And troops that arrived later from Ghana and elsewhere generally showed up without transport or spare parts, short of ammunition and small arms, with no more than two days' worth of rations, drinking water, or fuel. And they dribbled in over time, thus presenting an even less formidable spectacle.

This patched-together force might have been able to implement the peace agreement, but the truth was that neither party to the accord had reconciled itself to peace. More important, the real danger in Rwanda came not from the Tutsi rebels but from a "third force" of Hutu militias known as the Interahamwe, but since the militias hadn't been a party to Arusha, UNAMIR's mandate took no account of them. By late 1993, Rwanda's capital, Kigali, was rife with violence and with portents of renewed killing. But the peacekeeping department, acutely aware that the council's commitment to Rwanda was marginal, especially after the catastrophe in Somalia, soft-pedaled the bad news.

On January 11, 1994, the force commander, Roméo Dallaire, a Canadian general, sent the most notorious cable in UN history to General Maurice Baril, Boutros-Ghali's military adviser. Dallaire wrote that a high-level government official had put him in contact with an official in the Interahamwe who said that he had been ordered to register all Tutsis in Kigali, he assumed for execution. His men, he said, could kill up to a thousand Tutsis in twenty minutes. Moreover, he said, a plot had been hatched to murder the Belgian peacekeepers, thus provoking them to leave the country and give the militias free rein. He had also told Dallaire of an arms cache that was to be used on the Belgians. Dallaire wanted to protect the informant and seize the weapons. But he was so concerned that the UN mission's civilian head, Jacques-Roger Booh-Booh, a Cameroonian considered sympathetic to the Hutus, would countermand or dilute his request that he had violated UN procedure by sending the message directly to New York rather than through the office of the SRSG (special representative of the secretary-general). Dallaire was giving advance notice, not seeking permission. *"Peux ce que veux,"* he wrote in conclusion—"Where there's a will, there's a way."

This appalling news provoked a swift response—but scarcely the one Dallaire had in mind. After Baril showed the cable to peacekeeping officials, Iqbal Riza wrote, and Annan signed, a note to Booh-Booh—not Dallaire—saying that nothing should be done "until clear guidance is received from Headquarters." Booh-Booh responded that he had received confirmation of Dallaire's intelligence from the highest levels and that the plan was to go forward in twenty-four to forty-eight hours. But Riza wrote back that UNAMIR must not seize the weapons, for doing so would violate the Security Council mandate on Rwanda, which did not include protecting civilians or seizing illegal arms. He instructed the two officials instead to pass on the intelligence to diplomats from the United States, France, and Belgium and to Rwandan president Juvenal Habyarimana. The cable ended by admonishing that "the overriding consideration is the need to avoid entering into a course of action that might lead to the use of force and unanticipated repercussions."

How could the avoidance of the use of force have come to be seen as "the overriding consideration"? Avoiding the use of force was, of course, almost *always* an overriding consideration in peacekeeping missions; it had been so in Bosnia. Only six months earlier the Security

Council had blithely departed from this policy by authorizing the use of
force to track down Mohammed Aideed, and that mission had ended in
a fiasco that threatened to discredit the doctrine of aggressive peace
enforcement foreseen in "An Agenda for Peace." When I asked Annan
why he hadn't acquiesced in Dallaire's impassioned plea, he said, "You
can't look at Rwanda without thinking of what happened in Somalia; in
fact, they were happening almost simultaneously." The U.S. Rangers
had been killed in the course of enforcing a Security Council resolution. What would happen if another contingent took casualties in *violation* of their mandate? Dallaire was thinking about Rwanda, but Annan
had to think about the whole enterprise of peacekeeping. "We were
concerned," Annan said, "given the limited number of men Dallaire
had at his disposal, if he initiated an engagement and some were killed,
we would lose the troops."

But why didn't he at least bring the issue to the Security Council?
"Obviously we don't take pieces of cables to the Security Council," Annan said. In any case, he added, "I think we conveyed the urgency and
the danger of the situation." Several of the council members, he says,
had better information than the Secretariat did; the issue, as ever, was
will, not knowledge. He concedes, however, that the shadow of Mogadishu may have made him too skittish. "It was probably not a good
call," he says.

But other peacekeeping officials are less willing to concede even
this measure of wrongdoing. Shashi Tharoor, who was not involved in
the decision making, points out that Rwanda happened to be sitting
on the Security Council at the time. "Would it have made any sense,"
he asks, "for Kofi Annan to do the responsible thing, go to the Security
Council, say, 'We have these warnings, we take them seriously, we seek
your mandate to intervene'? It would have blown the whole thing sky-
high." Tharoor believes that the peacekeeping department has nothing
to apologize for.

Finally, the peacekeepers felt that it wasn't their decision to make.
Iqbal Riza points out that every cable sent to DPKO was copied to
Boutros-Ghali, where it was read by Chinmaya Gharekhan, one of the
secretary-general's chief advisers. "He doesn't have to wait for us to say,
'Please bring this to Mr. Boutros-Ghali,'" Riza says. What's more,
Boutros-Ghali had instituted a policy, infuriating to his department

heads, that only Gharekhan could brief the council. And so bureaucratic pettiness, on both sides, entered into the decision. "We all said,
'He's got the cable; let *him* decide what to do with it,' " Riza recalls. It
wasn't their responsibility; it was the secretary-general's. Boutros-Ghali,
who has never expressed remorse over any of the catastrophes that took
place on his watch, blames the member states (and notes in his memoirs that throughout January he was "away from New York and not in
close touch with the Rwanda situation"). And the chief member states
blame the Secretariat for failing to keep them informed. Where did the
buck stop? Nowhere.

An independent inquiry into the UN's role in Rwanda later concluded that the peacekeeping department erred in not bringing the cable to the Security Council's attention; worse, though, was the failure
to subsequently press President Habyarimana to take action against the
militias. Indeed, while Dallaire grew more and more agitated, the advice from New York remained emollient and passive. After the force
commander prepared a security analysis at the end of January fleshing
out his plan to seize illegal weapons, he received another cable under
Annan's signature advising that UNAMIR could "respond positively, on
a case-by-case basis, to requests by the government and the RFP"—the
Tutsi rebels—"for assistance in illegal arms recovery operations. It
should be clearly understood, however, that while UNAMIR may provide advice/guidance for the planning of such operations, it cannot, repeat, cannot take an active role in their execution." Dallaire would later
describe this missive as "yet another body blow."

As the situation in Rwanda deteriorated, council members grew increasingly impatient with both parties. On April 5, 1994, the council
passed a resolution extending the mission for only another five weeks.
This was intended to pressure the antagonists into beginning the
power-sharing process, but since the antagonists had no intention
of doing so, the actual message it sent—and above all, to the Hutu
militias—was that the international community was looking for a way
out. And this was true: with large-scale operations mounted in Bosnia,
Somalia, Cambodia, and Mozambique, among other sites, the cost of
peacekeeping had zoomed to $3 billion a year. Colin Keating, then the
ambassador from New Zealand, which held the presidency of the
council, has written that the UN was under pressure, particularly from

the United States, the largest donor, to prove that it could shut down a mission; UNAMIR was considered the likeliest candidate. Earlier in the year, in fact, when Belgium had pressed the council to reinforce the mission and strengthen its mandate, the United States and the U.K. had blocked the proposal.

Whether by coincidence or by design, on the very next day President Habyarimana's plane was blown out of the sky by a missile. The systematic killing began within hours. At midnight on April 7, Dallaire spoke to Annan and Riza and proposed siding with Hutu moderates in the hope of empowering them against the killers—probably a futile gesture by that time. "The answer came back loud and clear," he writes: "I was not to take sides, and it was up to the Rwandans to sort things out for themselves." Two days later, with Security Council members increasingly ready to withdraw from this Central African nightmare, Annan sent a cable to Kigali stating that UNAMIR could no longer carry out its mandate and might have no choice save to withdraw. The Secretariat had so deeply internalized the "Mogadishu line" that one could no longer say whether it was anticipating Security Council timidity or helping to rationalize it.

The Interahamwe had taken the measure of the international community. On April 10, ten members of the Belgian contingent were murdered, just as Dallaire's informant had predicted. Four days later the Belgians announced that they were immediately withdrawing their forces from their former colony. Seeking cover for this abject flight, Foreign Minister Willy Claes called the U.S. secretary of state, Warren Christopher, to gain support for a complete withdrawal of UNAMIR. And Christopher, incredibly, complied: the following day he informed Madeleine Albright that "the international community must give highest priority to full, orderly withdrawal of all UNAMIR personnel as soon as possible." Though infuriated by Christopher's humiliating instructions, the ambassador proceeded to do just that.

Albright now says that "information about what was going on inside Rwanda never rose to such a level that we fully understood what was going on." But in fact the administration ignored warnings from some of its own officials and discounted Dallaire's reports as overheated alarmism. And while it is true that at first the violence appeared to be yet another episode of the endless Central African bloodletting, it had already become clear by the time of Christopher's cable that the killing was systematic and widespread. No matter: intervention in Rwanda was simply unthinkable. Mogadishu had traumatized the administration, very much including President Clinton. UN peacekeeping suddenly felt like just the kind of idealistic folly from which a hardheaded Democratic administration had to distance itself. Congressional Republicans were loudly crying that the administration had "subcontracted" its foreign policy to the much-mocked Boutros Boutros-Ghali. National security officials had just finished drafting a presidential finding, known as PDD-25, that would prohibit the United States from participating in or even supporting peacekeeping missions that did not have an explicit goal and exit strategy, did not entail U.S. interests, lacked clear support among the public and allies, and so on. No emergency response to atrocities would ever meet this standard.

The Clinton administration's refusal to act in the face of growing evidence of genocide was, if anything, overdetermined. Indeed, to this day many former administration officials do not believe that they could have or should have acted otherwise. Madeleine Albright blames the failure to act on a lack of information and the "volcanic" nature of the genocide. Michael Sheehan, a Special Operations officer with long experience in peacekeeping settings and then a senior official at the U.S. Mission to the UN, is much more blunt about the dominant thinking at the time: "The U.S. pulls its last forces out of Mogadishu March 31, our soldiers were going back humiliated, PDD-25 was being passed, saying never again will we without the proper resources get involved in empty resolutions. So what happens? Six days later the plane is shot down. The U.S. wasn't about to turn around those ships in the port of Mogadishu. It was not clear there was going to be a genocide yet, no one knew who was a Hutu or a Tutsi, no one knew where Rwanda was, there was no strategic interest—it just wasn't happening. There was no advocate for it anywhere in the U.S. government or the Congress." The media, preoccupied with the Balkans, did not apply the kind of pressure that might have forced the administration's hand.

Nor, it is important to note, was there an advocate for intervention elsewhere in the world. On April 19, Boutros-Ghali sent Security Council members a letter imploring them to intercede, if necessary by "forceful means." But the Rwandan delegate had persuaded several

Third World nations that the Tutsi rebels were at fault, and in any case that there were no grounds for intervention. Other members felt that they had to make good on their threat to close down the mission if the parties refused to cooperate—even though it was plain that the killing was the work of *génocidaires* who had not been party to the Arusha Accords. Troop-contributing countries feared for the safety of their soldiers. And Boutros-Ghali was scarcely an effective advocate of his own position. He sent the council a proposal with three options: massive reinforcement, reduction to a token force, or total withdrawal. The safe havens experience presumably had taught him the consequence of giving the council a choice between an enormous commitment and a scanty one. The wisdom of providing three options, rather than two, was that members, including the United States, could take comfort in choosing something rather than nothing. After much debate, Albright agreed to accept what she herself called a "skeletal" force of two hundred and seventy.

By the end of April, estimates of deaths had reached as high as half a million, and the newspapers and airwaves were filled with accounts of unspeakable savagery, and yet the UN continued to behave as if Rwanda presented a conventional problem of political reconciliation. The independent inquiry concluded that it was "disturbing that records of meetings between members of the Secretariat, including the Secretary-General, with officials of the so-called Interim Government show a continued emphasis on a cease-fire, more than the moral outrage against the massacres, which was growing in the international community." Boutros-Ghali did not use the word "genocide" until early May. Still, this was considered an act of boldness and even tactlessness, for the Clinton administration was by then twisting itself into rhetorical knots to avoid using the word at all for fear of triggering the provisions of the UN Convention on the Prevention and Punishment of the Crime of Genocide, which requires signatories to "prevent and punish" such crimes.

In early May, the council finally agreed to ask the Secretariat to draw up a plan to reinforce UNAMIR. The council stipulated that the report be drafted not as an official document but as a "non-paper," which would not carry the force of Boutros-Ghali's endorsement, and thus could be all the more safely ignored. Dallaire put together a proposal for fifty-five hundred additional troops, to be deployed wherever large concentrations of Tutsis had sought shelter. The plan was perfectly straightforward. "Go where there are concentrations of people at risk," as Hedi Annabi puts it, "and say, 'If you try to kill them, you're going to have to kill me first. And if you try, I'm going to kill you.' This wasn't Somalia, with guys in technicals [jeeps with machine guns on the hood]. It was a bunch of thugs armed with machetes."

Since over the past month even tiny, ill-equipped squads of peacekeepers had been able to scare off the mobs, there was good reason to believe the Dallaire plan would end the killing. Nevertheless, the Clinton administration didn't like it. Vice President Al Gore had earlier promised Boutros-Ghali that the United States would help with logistics, though not with troops. But Pentagon officials feared that any soldiers sent to Rwanda to help with the airlift would be forced to act against the killing—an unacceptable entanglement. The administration devised an alternative to the Dallaire plan, in which the UN, with American logistical aid, would establish safe havens outside of Rwanda.

In mid-May, with Hutus dying by the thousands every day, a group of American diplomats and military planners came to DPKO to explain the concept. As one peacekeeping official recalls, "They pulled out this secret map—they wouldn't let us have a copy of it—which showed that the people had already left and were concentrated in big pockets outside of Rwanda. And we said, 'But we have people on the ground, and they tell us they're being killed *inside* Rwanda.' We checked with Dallaire, and he said, 'This makes no sense.' " But the United States would not approve a mission inside Rwanda. Albright, again acting on instructions, had the vote postponed. Finally, on May 17, the United States accepted the resolution—after rendering it meaningless by insisting that only eight hundred soldiers could be deployed in an initial stage.

Perhaps it wouldn't have mattered, since neither Rwanda's neighbors nor any of the usual peacekeeping sources were willing to send soldiers into the Central African cauldron. Annan later estimated that he canvassed a hundred countries over the ensuing months. According to Annabi, "Kofi Annan would call for a meeting of troop-contributing countries. Nobody would ask for the floor, so finally Annan would give the floor to somebody who didn't ask for it. And they would be terribly embarrassed, and say nothing." Paul Kagame and the Rwandese Patriotic Front took Kigali, declared a cease-fire, and then formed a new government on July 19. Only a week or so afterward did DPKO receive the first pledge of troops. As Annabi recalls, "Kagame is telling us, 'What are you coming to do? When I needed you, you ran away. Now I don't really need you.'"

The Rwandans suffered from catastrophically bad timing. In the aftermath of Mogadishu, there was simply no willingness to put troops in harm's way. But that trauma also offered a convenient excuse. Nancy Soderberg, then a high-ranking official in Clinton's National Security Council, has written that "even if the tragedy in Somalia had never occurred, it is unlikely President Clinton would have ordered U.S. troops to deploy to Rwanda or supported a United Nations–authorized force to enter the country to try to stop the killing once it occurred . . . The ugly truth is that at the root of the failure to act is a belief . . . that the United States has little responsibility to protect the lives of the victims of an ongoing genocide." And in this the United States was little different from its fellow members of the so-called international community.

But as with Bosnia, the failure of political will was not the whole story. The independent inquiry observed that while UNAMIR was established to monitor a peace agreement, "the onslaught of the genocide should have led decision-makers in the United Nations . . . to realize that the original mandate, and indeed the neutral mediating role of the United Nations, was no longer adequate and required a different, more assertive response, combined with the means necessary to take such action." Annan bridled at the criticism, feeling that the report placed far too much blame on the UN and too little on the members, above all the United States. Riza felt similarly ill-treated, though more because he felt that Boutros-Ghali and his staff and Jacques-Roger Booh-Booh had received nothing like their appropriate share of blame. Both were initially inclined to respond to the report, but other aides persuaded them to take their lumps and move on. And in fact in his letter accepting the report, Annan expressed his own "deep remorse," writing, "All of us must bitterly regret that we did not do more to prevent it."

All these years later, Iqbal Riza has not shaken his sense of personal responsibility for Rwanda. "I live with it," he says—by "it" he means his failure to push Gharekhan to go to the Security Council and sound the alarm. Does Annan, too, live with it? When I asked him, as I had about Bosnia, whether and in what way he felt personally culpable for the failure in Rwanda, he paused and thought, and paused a bit more. "In retrospect," he finally said, "and this is also the culture of the house, we should have used the media more aggressively, and exposed the situation for them to see. Of course, at that time this organization was media-shy." And that was it.

Somalia, Bosnia, Rwanda—each of these ventures was so vast and terrible that one can't help thinking of them as separate, freestanding narratives. And yet they occurred at almost the same moment. UN officials had no prior experience with the boiling madness of civil war, but whatever they might have learned from the one disaster they had no time to apply to the next. The only thing they could bring to bear was the flinch mechanism that comes with pain. The Secretariat learned that it could not afford to bring bad news to the Security Council. The members of the council learned that the instrument developed for Sinai and Cyprus could not operate in the midst of civil war—that one could not, in an expression that became all too popular, engage in peacekeeping where there was no peace to keep. The lessons were almost wholly negative. More encouraging and practicable lessons would come over time. The feeling at the moment, however, was that an era that began with such brilliant hopes had ended in despair.

CHAPTER FOUR

The American Candidate

BOUTROS BOUTROS-GHALI WAS ONE OF THE MOST QUALI-fied and talented men to be appointed secretary-general. His diplomatic lineage was impeccable: his grandfather had been prime minister of Egypt, and he himself had served as both deputy foreign minister and deputy prime minister. Boutros-Ghali was quick-witted, erudite, analytical—the most intelligent man, perhaps with the exception of Hammarskjöld, to occupy the post. But "talent," for a diplomat, is at least as much a matter of character as of intellect. And Boutros-Ghali did not have the temperament for self-effacing adjudication or for the patient searching out of common ground. He was condescending, arrogant, secretive, status-conscious. He was prone to interrupt an ambassador in the midst of a presentation with an airy "Yes, I know, I just discussed this yesterday with your foreign minister." He dwelled like Zeus within the cloud-capped majesty of the thirty-eighth floor, confiding in only a few trusted advisers, often leaving even his own department heads in the dark about policy. He could not, quite understandably, tolerate the endless tedium of Security Council meetings, but neither would he send whichever official could bring his expertise to bear on the discussion—thus the arrangement with Chinmaya Gharekhan that so vexed officials in DPKO and elsewhere.

Boutros-Ghali had an understanding of his job commensurate with his sense of his own worth. The Holy Writ he was wont to cite was not Article 99 of the Charter, which permitted the secretary-general to raise with the Security Council matters touching on international peace and security, but Article 100, which admonished members to "respect the exclusively international character of the responsibilities of the Secretary-General and the staff and not to seek to influence them in the discharge of their responsibilities." The watchword of the secretary-general, Boutros-Ghali said, must be "independence." This was a principled and defensible interpretation of the Charter; it was also extremely naive, or perhaps disingenuous. Though he had opposed the peacekeeping mission in Bosnia, Boutros-Ghali insisted on his own primacy in running it. He instituted a "dual-key" policy that gave him veto power over NATO bombing decisions; even when NATO asked him, in the fall of 1994, to relinquish control over target selection, though not over the actual decision to bomb, he refused.

The secretary-general's unwillingness to approve air strikes infuriated American policy makers, who came to view the secretary-general, in the words of James Steinberg, then deputy national security adviser, as "an implacable obstacle to solving the Bosnia problem." But it wasn't only with Clinton administration officials that the secretary-general's stock began to plummet. "Boutros-Ghali blocked the liberal intellectual support of the UN," says Jamie Rubin, then Madeleine Albright's press secretary, "because by saying he was going to hold the key and having the wrong view on Bosnia, he lost guys like me who supported the UN for the moral side. Boutros took an amoral position on Bosnia."

Boutros-Ghali also suffered from extremely bad luck, for the American internationalism that was at high tide when he took office crested and broke halfway through his term. Somalia, Bosnia, and Rwanda soured American public opinion, and especially American elites, on the UN. At the same time, the congressional election of 1994 placed conservative Republicans in power in the House and Senate. This was a toxic combination. At a time when the UN seemed like a handmaiden to catastrophe, President Clinton found himself answering to the likes of North Carolina senator Jesse Helms, who viewed the institution as a colossal waste of money and a threat to American sovereignty. Isolationists like Pat Buchanan, the polemicist and television personality, and conspiracy theorists like the televangelist Pat Robertson became prominent voices in the public debate over foreign policy. Conservatives wanted to withhold dues payments to the UN until the organization accepted a long list of "reforms." Others were happy simply to bid the organization goodbye.

A more emollient figure might have found a way of drawing the poison from these serpents, but Boutros-Ghali was not such a man. He had to refute every absurdity and hypocrisy, even if doing so would cost him, and his institution, dearly. The secretary-general rarely passed up an opportunity to needle the United States for failing to pay its dues, failing to provide troops, failing to stay the course. Every time he opened his mouth he gave more ammunition to the administration's conservative foes. And yet the secretary-general, serenely sure of the rightness of his case, was always eager to venture into the lion's den. According to Madeleine Albright, "He made a terrible impression in a place where I needed a good impression—Congress. There was a sense of arrogance about him that they did not like. But he was so convinced of his own infallibility and that he was selling the UN story so well that he didn't understand that having him come to Washington a lot didn't help." Enemies of the UN could scarcely have invented a better caricature of the institution than Boutros-Ghali, with his hauteur, his Francophilia, his diplomatic punctilio, and even his absurd-sounding name. In the 1996 presidential campaign, Bob Dole, the Republican nominee and until this point a dependable internationalist, never failed to draw a laugh when he stretched out the secretary-general's name to "Booo-tros."

By the fall of 1995, leading White House and State Department officials were convinced that Boutros-Ghali could not be permitted to serve a second term. A small group began working on a plan, dubbed Operation Orient Express, to oust him; in order to keep the plot secret, nothing was committed to paper for months. In January, Albright won President Clinton's approval for the plan; in March, the team produced a memo, under Albright's signature, laying out their reasoning. The memo, according to Albright's memoirs, read in part, "[Boutros-Ghali] is not committed to, or capable of achieving, our urgent reform goals. Blocking his second term will significantly improve our chances to obtain funds from Congress, to pay our arrearages and sustain our obligations in the future. Finally the chances of ensuring a domestic consensus that supports UN actions in the future will be greatly improved if he departs from the scene."

Though Albright and others were open to a number of alternate candidates, the memo mentioned only one: Kofi Annan. To those administration officials who worked with him, Annan felt like the anti-Boutros. He was pragmatic, straightforward, unmarred by either ego or ideology. "On former Yugoslavia and a whole host of other issues," says a former official with the U.S. Mission to the UN, "we felt that Kofi Annan was an extremely nuanced, extremely serious man with whom we agreed most of the time. The discussions were just more sensible when he was involved than with some others." And if the Clinton officials blamed anyone for the UN's failures in Bosnia and Rwanda, it was Boutros-Ghali, not Annan.

From official Washington's point of view, in fact, Bosnia had been Annan's proving ground, as it had been Boutros-Ghali's Waterloo. When the administration had committed itself to a massive bombing campaign in late August 1995, NATO could not continue to abide by the "dual-key" arrangement. On August 29, with Boutros-Ghali on a flight and allegedly unreachable, Annan instructed UN officials to temporarily surrender their veto over air strikes. "Kofi made a historic decision," says Richard Holbrooke, then assistant secretary of state and the administration's chief negotiator on Bosnia. "Without that decision, we might never have gotten to the table. As long as the Serbs believed we were never going to hit them hard, they would never have been incentivized to act."

Annan was also admired for the role he had played in Haiti, where the United States was determined to restore Jean-Bertrand Aristide, the elected president, who had been ousted in a coup. After a humiliating episode in the fall of 1993, when an American ship carrying U.S. soldiers and Canadian police officers turned around in Port-au-Prince harbor rather than face a jeering, stone-throwing rabble, the Security Council imposed sanctions on the Haitian government, and then gave its blessing to a U.S.-led multinational force to drive the junta from power. This time around the soldiers deployed, the generals fled, Aristide returned, and at the end of March 1995 the multinational force handed off to UN peacekeepers. Annan was widely credited with managing this smooth transition, and with assembling a highly effective UN mission that, at least for the next several years, kept the peace in Haiti and laid the foundations for development.

Among administration policy makers, Haiti was taken as the proof of something important. Few foreign-policy issues seemed more urgent in the otherwise peaceful mid-1990s than getting peacekeeping right. PDD-25, the new national security directive, was meant not to put an end to peacekeeping but to prevent the United States from backing into starry-eyed or ill-prepared ventures, and, not incidentally, to forestall congressional criticism. Haiti offered proof that this new, hard-headed relationship with the UN could bring results. But the relationship would work only if the UN changed as well. According to Robert Orr, then a junior officer at the National Security Council working on the team to oust Boutros-Ghali, "People personalized it, that we hated Boutros-Ghali and we liked Kofi Annan. In fact, it was all about the policy. Kofi could do it. Very few secretaries-general had worked with the U.S. military. Here we were in an era where the U.S. military was going to be a big part of the equation. You needed a secretary-general who understands that the U.S. military is not the enemy."

Annan was certainly aware of Boutros-Ghali's sinking fortunes and his own rising star. Shashi Tharoor says that when he and Annan had gone out for a drink in 1994, he had spoken to his boss of the growing dissatisfaction of Clinton officials. "Look around you," he had said. "You are the best-qualified person. And on top of that, you can work with these people." Annan, as was his wont, listened and said nothing. In late 1995, Boutros-Ghali made the extremely odd decision to send Annan to Zagreb as his special representative in the Balkans, a move that was widely interpreted as an attempt to exile a potential rival to Siberia. When Annan returned the following spring, having further enhanced his reputation in this thankless job, Michael Sheehan, a member of the secret White House team, says that he began keeping Annan informed of the plans. "I didn't say, 'You're our guy,'" Sheehan says, "because he wasn't. But he generally knew what was happening, and we kept him informed."

Annan insists that until mid-1996 he considered the whole issue moot, because Boutros-Ghali seemed undislodgeable. Even then he did nothing to put himself forward. It is generally considered unseemly to campaign to be secretary-general, just as it is unseemly to campaign for the papacy. But it would have been certain death to Annan's ambitions to be seen as an American alternative to a sitting officeholder.

Some of the people closest to Annan organized a stealth campaign, speaking regularly to officials in the U.S. Mission, sounding out key diplomats, casually dropping Annan's name to leading members of the UN press, who then began talking him up.

The American campaign went public in June, when Secretary of State Warren Christopher leaked the news that the United States would oppose a second term. Boutros-Ghali immediately rallied his forces. President Jacques Chirac of France called to say that he and President Hosni Mubarak of Egypt had agreed to stand up to the Americans. A French cabinet official pointedly threatened, "The right of veto does not belong only to the Americans. France also has the right." The French had none of the problems with the gratifyingly Francophile Boutros-Ghali that Washington did. And nothing grated on the French more than being railroaded by the Americans. The dominant attitude, as a leading French diplomat puts it, was "Why should we on this issue accept the diktat of one country against the strong view affirmed and reaffirmed by the other fourteen?"

No secretary-general had ever seen his bid for a second term vetoed; indeed, all of Boutros-Ghali's predecessors had been reelected. And despite intensive diplomacy by Albright and others, and despite a broad dissatisfaction with Boutros-Ghali, no other nation signed on to the administration's cause. Who wanted to get on the wrong side of a secretary-general who might well continue to serve? The Organization of African Unity endorsed the reelection bid; Nelson Mandela spoke of Boutros-Ghali as "my brother." President Clinton was getting besieged by calls from Chirac, Mubarak, and others. Clinton hated being the bad guy. He browbeat Tony Lake, the national security adviser, who then suggested to Albright that they call off the dogs. Albright berated Lake for going soft. Suddenly she was alone in an administration that was itself isolated.

But what Albright had on her side was that the administration had come a long way, for better or ill, since 1993. Clinton had come into office vowing to work closely with the UN; his chief aides were committed multilateralists. They still were, but they now saw themselves as unillusioned multilateralists. They had slowly come to terms with the fact of American primacy, above all in Bosnia, where the world had waited for the United States to act. Moreover, they were under relentless pressure from Republicans, who accused them of "subcontracting foreign policy to the UN." For all its misgivings and hesitations, the Clinton administration was far more willing to aggressively defend its interests, even with little or no support, than it had been before; the battle over the renomination was, in fact, an early episode of the willingness to act alone that was to become the defining element of American foreign policy in years to come. Albright and her allies eventually succeeded in stiffening the president's spine.

On November 17, Albright went to the secretary-general's residence in a final bid for compromise. Would he be willing to accept the chairmanship of some high-level foundation, along with the title "Secretary-General of the United Nations Emeritus"? Boutros-Ghali brushed aside this rather ludicrous blandishment, as he had others. The Americans, he later wrote in *Unvanquished*, a memoir whose very title conveys the air of self-glorification that pervades the text, "can not grasp that I have to defend a principle: the integrity of the United Nations and the independence of the secretary-general." Two days later the United States made good its vow to veto Boutros-Ghali's bid for renomination; the vote was 14 to 1. But Boutros-Ghali's solid front of African support began to dissolve once the United States made it clear that they would support another African for the office. Now the question became: Which African?

And this provoked a new round of infighting. There were four, or possibly five, plausible African candidates, and their fortunes shifted throughout early December as the Security Council took straw polls almost every day. The permanent and non-permanent members used different-colored slips for the straw polls, so it was always possible to know who would face a veto in an actual vote. Annan always had one veto, from the French, who were incensed by the White House campaign against Boutros-Ghali and who rightly viewed Annan as Washington's man. Amara Essy, the foreign minister of the Ivory Coast and by now France's alternative African candidate, always faced two vetoes, presumably from the United States and Britain. Annan's chances brightened considerably when President Clinton announced in early December that Madeleine Albright would be the new secretary of state. There was no percentage in blocking the will of such a powerful figure. Annan's numbers rose with each straw poll.

Boutros-Ghali still hoped that the French would remain intransigent, forcing the Americans to back down. An article had appeared in *Le Monde* reporting concerns that Kofi Annan did not, as the French say, speak the language of Molière. Perhaps this would be the pretext for rejecting his candidacy. An alarmed Jamie Rubin maneuvered himself next to Nane Annan at a dinner party to ask whether her husband spoke French. In fact, he did, though more like a high-school teacher than the seventeenth-century playwright. Annan himself says that no one forced him to take a *dictée*. "The only thing they were interested in was that I not dismiss multilingualism," he says. "I would respect the use of the two languages in making appointments and that sort of thing. Pierre-Louis LeBlanc, who had been de Gaulle's spokesman, tried to impress on me what bilingualism means. He said there are two legal systems, and two systems of government, the French and the Anglo-Saxon." Annan, who can fool the unwary into thinking he agrees with practically anything, nodded gravely.

By December 12, the vote was 14 to 1 for Annan, with the French still holding out. But the French could not afford to be as willful as the Americans. Annan's aides had begun receiving inquiries from French diplomats on the order of "Can we get DPKO?" Iqbal Riza was hoping to take over his boss's old job, but Annan agreed to toss the French this bone (and in fact did so once he became secretary-general). On December 13, President Chirac instructed his ambassador to vote for Annan. Four days later the vote was confirmed by the General Assembly. Boutros-Ghali, barbed to the last, used his valedictory speech before the assembly to cast his successor as an American puppet, observing, "The holder of this office must never be seen as acting out of fear of, or in an attempt to curry favor with, one state or group of states."

Annan immediately moved from the very modest apartment he and Nane rented on Roosevelt Island, an unfashionable spot in the middle of the East River, to a suite at the Waldorf hotel. He appointed Riza and Lamin Sise, longtime friends and colleagues, to head his transition team. Theodore Sorensen, another friend who had been President Kennedy's speechwriter, began drafting an acceptance speech full of soaring, Kennedyesque phrases—most of which were scrubbed by UN bureaucrats trained to avoid controversy at all cost.

Kofi Annan did not arrive on the thirty-eighth floor with anything so formal as an agenda; he was a lifelong civil servant who thought in terms of problems and solutions rather than sweeping formulations or ideological positions. Unlike his predecessors, however, he knew very well what a disorganized mess lay behind the gorgeous curtain of rhetoric. And with his MIT management degree, he had a fairly good idea, at least in the abstract, of what effective organizations looked like. Part of his appeal to Washington, in fact, was that he might push the kinds of reforms that would mollify the fire-eaters in Congress.

The least self-aggrandizing of men, Annan immediately signaled that Boutros-Ghali's imperial reign was a thing of the past. Relevant officials, rather than the SG's designated emissary, would brief the Security Council. Boutros-Ghali had permitted only his own note taker to record meetings with departments, thus centralizing information in his own office; Annan instructed department heads to bring their own note takers. The departments themselves—political affairs, humanitarian affairs, peacekeeping, and so on—were notorious for operating as moated castles, and Annan sought to bring them together by dividing the work of the UN into such broad categories as "peace and security" and "economic and social affairs," with each overseen by an executive committee. And every Wednesday morning, Annan convened a meeting of the heads of the committees as well as the directors of the major funds and programs, many of them piped in from remote locations by videoconference. The idea that the many branches of the UN should view themselves as a single entity and act in concert seems too obvious to state, but since they had never acted this way before, the senior management group was, according to Kieran Prendergast, the new chief of the political affairs department, "a revolutionary thought."

In the popular imagination, the UN was something like a large, diversified corporation, with a CEO—the secretary-general—occupying the commanding heights. This was an almost completely misleading analogy. First of all, the secretary-general was merely "the chief administrative officer" of the Secretariat, according to the Charter, and thus the servant, not the master, of the members themselves. And second, he had direct authority over only the various departments of the Secretariat, including peacekeeping, political affairs, and so on. The heads of UN "funds and programs," including such bodies as UNICEF, the UN Development Programme, and the Office of the High Commissioner for Refugees, reported to their own boards, though they were appointed by the secretary-general and in various ways accountable to him. The "specialized agencies," including UNESCO, the World Health Organization, the International Monetary Fund, and the World Bank, were wholly autonomous. Any secretary-general who imagined himself a CEO would quickly learn otherwise. Annan was, of course, highly sensitive to the limits of his own power.

In July, Annan delivered to the General Assembly a ninety-five-page document proposing wholesale institutional reform. The report, written by Maurice Strong, a friend of Annan's and a fellow veteran of the institution, was plainly written with one eye on the U.S. Congress, for it noted that Annan had already instituted 550 "efficiency projects" designed to enhance "cost-effectiveness" and to permit a 10 percent reduction in head count, to nine thousand. But most of the proposals in the report required the cooperation of the UN's member states, who had thwarted virtually every serious effort at reform in the past. He suggested that the General Assembly, which every year passed a great stack of resolutions to which scarcely anyone paid attention, focus its work on a few major issues every session; review old mandates in order to phase out the irrelevant or defunct; and apply a "sunset provision" to future initiatives. He proposed, in the most delicate language possible, that the assembly stop micromanaging the budget and dictating high-level appointments to the Secretariat. The assembly, unmoved both by the analysis and by the diplomacy, refused to adopt any of these proposals.

The "Quiet Revolution," as Annan tellingly called his agenda, was arguably more quiet than revolutionary. One of the crucial concerns of the aides and outside experts who helped craft the document was to force the humanitarian agencies—UNICEF, the World Food Programme, and so on—to coordinate their response to emergencies with one another and with aid organizations, something they had conspicuously failed to do in years past. An earlier draft had proposed that the UN High Commissioner for Refugees serve as the "lead agency" in emergencies. But both UNICEF and WFP publicly objected to any eclipse of their authority or autonomy. And in a raw demonstration of independence, the leaders of the two bodies—both American— enlisted sympathetic congressmen and several major nonprofit organizations, who also foresaw a loss of status, in a campaign to quash the decision. The proposal was first relegated to an annex, and then eliminated altogether. Thomas Weiss, an academic and former UN official who had helped devise the proposal, later observed that the secretary-general could hardly expect to overcome resistance from the member states if he could not even bring his own agencies to heel.

Though no one was more familiar with the UN's careerist and risk-averse culture than the new secretary-general, the passage in the reform document on "the human resources dimension" gave little hint of the urgency of reform. Rather, Annan listed the sensible but modest initiatives he had been able to undertake on his own, and concluded by fully committing himself to "the Organization's goals of geographical representation and gender balance." The whole exercise persuaded Weiss that Annan's long career at the UN had so habituated him to the institution's pathologies that he would never confront them head-on. He would push for change, but he was so sensitive to what the market would bear that he would push only so hard.

Annan understood that his most urgent task lay in the realm of external diplomacy rather than internal reorganization. He had to demonstrate to the United States that the UN was no longer hostile territory. He decided that for his first official trip as secretary-general he would go to Washington. Riza and others warned him that he would be demeaning himself by going to kiss the White House ring. What of Boutros-Ghali's sacred Article 100, which also warned the secretary-general to do nothing to compromise his exclusively international status? Annan was not an Article 100 absolutist: he took the position, as he said, that if someone owes you a billion dollars, you can't worry about appearances. In an Oval Office meeting, President Clinton, a shrewd judge of political horseflesh, sized up the secretary-general and said, "You could be a star in this country. You're the face of the UN. You've got to get out and talk to the American people." Annan met with both Democratic and Republican legislators and was amazed to find them lining up to have their picture taken with him, like kids with the star center fielder. His charm offensive lifted the cloud of ill feeling without, however, having any noticeable impact on the willingness of Congress to pay American arrears or finance peacekeeping missions.

In those first months Annan also had to confront the lethal post–Cold War cocktail of ethnic violence, civil war, and collapsing states. In the aftermath of the Rwandan genocide and the victory of the Tutsi rebel force, over a million Hutus had crossed the border into eastern Zaire in a refugee flight of epic, hopelessly unmanageable proportions. Worse still, thousands of members of the Interahamwe had escaped in the flight and reestablished themselves in the vast, squalid camps set up by UNHCR. In November 1996, Rwandan president Paul Kagame, fearing a renewed attack, sent his army across the border to smash the camps, sending terrified refugees either back to Rwanda or deeper into the Zairean forest. By the time Annan became secretary-general, a monstrous, almost formless civil war had broken out in eastern Zaire, with Rwanda, Uganda, and a band of Zairean insurrectionaries on one side and Zairean President Joseph Mobutu, Interahamwe fighters, and local tribal allies on the other. Tens of thousands of Hutu refugees—no one knows exactly how many—starved or were slaughtered in the jungle in a kind of Rwandan counter-genocide. In May, Mobutu fled, and was replaced by the guerrilla leader Laurent Kabila.

The UN had been helpless to restrain, much less stop, the anarchic violence. And the brutal control that the *génocidaires* had asserted over the camps had presented UNHCR with the agonizing choice of feeding and sustaining mass murderers or cutting off support and allowing hapless, desperate refugees to starve. (The agency chose the former.) Now, with Kabila at least nominally in control of Zaire, which he renamed, with grim irony, the Democratic Republic of the Congo, the UN demanded that he reckon with the atrocities committed by his forces and their allies. Kabila agreed, but refused to cooperate with a UN investigation. Annan met with him in early June and implored him to permit a UN team to travel to the affected areas and conduct interviews. Kabila agreed once more, but then he stalled and stonewalled and introduced new conditions, and eventually Annan was compelled to withdraw the investigative team with several hundred thousand Rwandan refugees still unaccounted for. The full measure of the horror was never plumbed.

By the end of his first year in office, Annan was a very different figure from the one he had been before. He was well on his way to becoming the star that Bill Clinton thought he was meant to be. He barnstormed the country as a kind of traveling incarnation of the UN, drawing large and enthusiastic crowds almost everywhere he went. And he was becoming a very different kind of global figure from what Boutros-Ghali had been. Annan's predecessor had spoken for the developing world to the rich world. He had, for example, deprecated the importance of human rights as "an instrument of intervention to serve the political objectives of the developed world." Annan, by contrast, was a universalist; he took it as a given that Africans had exactly the same rights as Westerners. And he was determined to say so.

In June 1997, in his maiden speech before the Organization of African Unity—the regional UN of his home continent—Annan spoke of "respect for fundamental human rights," and then added, "I am aware of the fact that some view this concern as a luxury of the rich countries for which Africa is not ready. I know that others treat it as an imposition, if not a plot, by the industrialized West. I find these thoughts truly demeaning, demeaning of the yearning for human dignity that resides in every African heart." When Annan finished speaking, the hall was eerily silent. And then the audience, perhaps with the hypocritical tribute that vice pays to virtue, rose in a standing ovation. Salim Salim, then secretary-general of the OAU, came over to the podium and said, "Kofi, you are probably the only one who could say that and get out of this room without being lynched." And that was precisely why Annan felt it was so important for him to say it.

Like any UN bureaucrat, Annan had been a thoroughly anonymous figure beyond the confines of Turtle Bay, but now he embraced his celebrity. His old friend James Goodale says, "Kofi and I spent a lot of time talking about the role of the UN in the new media world. Under Boutros-Ghali, the place had just disappeared off the map. He understood that the only way to get your story out was to personalize it." The

Goodales threw him a "coming-out party" at the Four Seasons and organized dinner parties at their home, where Annan and Nane could meet the New York elite, especially the media elite. "All we had to do was introduce him to people," says Toni Goodale, "and they immediately took to him." Brooke Astor, the socialite nonpareil, took him up and incorporated him into the social whirl. Annan had been an utterly indifferent dresser, but after Iqbal Riza had advised him to start dressing like a secretary-general, Annan began to sport beautifully cut dark gray suits from Brioni. Indeed, he took the advice so well that he was soon appearing on best-dressed lists.

Kofi and Nane, both enormously attractive and disarmingly modest, the one short and black and the other tall and blond, made for a dazzling couple; they projected a kind of moral glamour. This did not necessarily sit well back at the office. "All those pictures of him in *The New York Times* dancing with the jet set—I was never in favor of it," says Elisabeth Lindenmayer. "We are the organization of the poor and the humble." And yet Annan never seemed compromised by the social whirl; his growing reputation as a source of moral authority, even "a secular pope," immunized him against charges of elitism or certainly frivolity. He was something quite new in the history of the UN: a spokesman for mankind who looked wonderful in a tuxedo.

CHAPTER FIVE

Kofi in the Lion's Den

I FIRST MET KOFI ANNAN LATE IN THE MORNING OF FRIDAY, February 13, 1998. One week earlier he had told the Security Council that he was prepared to travel to Baghdad and meet with Saddam Hussein in order to resolve a deadlock over council-mandated weapons inspections that was threatening to lead to war. Since that time, the five permanent members of the council had debated furiously, and almost ceaselessly, over the wisdom of this melodramatic proposal. The French and the Russians had been pressing Annan to go for weeks, while the Americans and the British, whose warships were now gathering in the Persian Gulf, were deeply worried that Hussein would bully or dupe the gentle secretary-general into relaxing the inspection regime. Earlier that morning, in fact, U.S. secretary of state Madeleine Albright had called to warn Annan against going without the approval of all five. It was, by an order of magnitude, the most grave and pressurized moment of Annan's tenure as secretary-general.

Annan came around from behind his desk to greet me and invited me to sit next to him on his black leather couch rather than, as I would have imagined, on the far side of the desk. It was a trusting, almost an intimate, gesture. I put my tape recorder between us on the couch. When Annan began speaking, I quickly discovered that he was scarcely audible, and certainly not tape-recordable, from more than a few feet away. Was that all the volume he could muster? Perhaps Annan understood that his breathy wisp of a voice disarmed the visitor, just as his cozy seating plan did—by bringing him so close, and thus dismissing the exalted status that came with his title. It was, in its way, a terribly seductive manner, if not necessarily a reassuring one. The secretary-general did not inspire faith in his capacity to slay monsters so much as a wish to protect him from those monsters.

I asked about the call from Albright, but Annan was not interested in reflecting on the poor odds of success. "I think what is important is that the permanent five is talking among themselves," he said. "The British and the Americans were on one side, and the French and the Russians were engaging the Iraqis, and the Chinese were in the middle. And I brought them together and said, 'If we're going to have a diplomatic solution, we're going to have to try to break the difference between the permanent five and come up with an approach or an arrangement that will allow us to get the inspections, even if we have to give the Iraqis some way out.'" Rather than wait for the council to reach consensus, he was pointing them toward common ground and then pushing them to seek it. And he would embark on his self-appointed mission the moment the five permanent members had found a mutually acceptable formulation. It was a bold stroke in a career that until then had been marked by caution and circumspection. Annan and I spoke for about half an hour, and then an aide tiptoed in with a note: Sergei Lavrov, the Russian ambassador, was on the phone. The endless round of consultations resumed.

The crisis had begun three months earlier, though it had been building up for years. In the aftermath of the Gulf War, the Security Council had imposed crippling economic sanctions on the Saddam Hussein regime, with the chief goals of preventing Saddam from re-building his war machine and of accounting for and eliminating suspected stocks of weapons of mass destruction. It was this latter job with which the weapons inspectors had been entrusted. Saddam had consistently denied seeking a nuclear weapons capacity, but the nuclear inspectors of the International Atomic Energy Agency had almost immediately discovered massive installations designed to produce nuclear fuel. The team from the United Nations Special Commission, or UNSCOM, which was responsible for finding biological and chemical weapons material, had unearthed a trove of documents demonstrating the progress the Iraqis had made by the time of the Gulf War but no signs of an ongoing program. But because the Iraqis had so blatantly lied about the past, the inspectors no longer trusted their assertions about the present. The Iraqis, in turn, came to feel that they would never get out from under the sanctions or the inspections. And so the inspectors became more aggressive, and the Iraqis more intransigent.

In July 1997, Annan appointed Richard Butler, a blunt Australian diplomat, as the new head of UNSCOM. Butler's confrontational style only increased the tensions. The Iraqis began to complain bitterly of the "indignities" they had suffered, and some of the people closest to Annan sympathized with their plight. Iqbal Riza, a fellow Muslim, believed that the Iraqis had good reason to take umbrage. "You can't insult them and expect them to behave themselves," he says today. "And the behavior was insulting, in a culture where insults are unacceptable and are not forgotten." Many top UN officials did not consider Iraq a danger to anyone, and certainly not to the United States; their chief concern was ending a sanctions regime that had brought such suffering to ordinary Iraqis. "Saddam was weakened to a degree that being kept in the box didn't require starving the Iraqi people," says Lakhdar Brahimi, the former foreign minister of Algeria and one of Annan's trusted advisers. "He was not a menace to anyone." Annan himself believed that it was worth accommodating Iraqi sensitivities in order to keep the inspectors at work.

In the first days of November, Annan asked a three-man team, headed by Brahimi, to go to Baghdad in order to break the impasse. Butler felt that the visit would undermine his authority unless the deputation simply reiterated Iraq's obligations under various council resolutions. Annan agreed, and Gustavo Zlauvinen, Butler's political adviser, wrote up what he said were narrow and explicit instructions. Brahimi proceeded to ignore them. "The only thing we did in Baghdad is allow the Iraqis to speak," Brahimi says, "and to treat them with great respect." On their first day in Baghdad, the team listened to a litany of complaints from Tariq Aziz. On the second day, they watched a video showing American inspectors breaking in windows and smashing locks. Zlauvinen was forced to sit outside, so that he could not explain that the Iraqis often showed up to installations without a key. Butler writes that the Iraqis took the visit "as a further confirmation that Annan was committed to a diplomatic solution to Iraq's recalcitrance, without

obliging it to be disarmed." The Iraqis do appear to have been emboldened by the visit. On November 13, they demanded that all American
inspectors leave the country at once. Butler responded by evacuating
the entire team.

This new crisis precipitated an extraordinary, and increasingly hec-
tic, round of global diplomacy. The Russians and the French, both of
whom had generally supported Iraq in the Security Council, sought a
diplomatic solution. UNSCOM returned to Iraq, but the atmosphere
grew only more embittered; the Iraqis blocked site visits and directed
fierce invective against the mission in the state-controlled media.
Emissaries from the Arab League and the Organization of the Islamic
Conference, as well as the foreign minister of Turkey, tried and failed
to mediate the situation. The Security Council was hopelessly dead-
locked. Annan came to feel that Butler was playing to the British and
the Americans and making no attempt to work with the others; Butler
felt that the others were moved by cynical or greedy calculations. And
the warships gathered in the Gulf.

The crisis played out as one of appeasement versus containment,
or, from the opposite point of view, of bellicosity versus compassion.
But underneath the melodrama was a problem of policy to which no
one had a good answer. The UN Security Council imposes sanctions
not as a punishment but as an inducement to change behavior, in effect by raising the cost of that behavior; the classic, if rather solitary,
example of success was the sanctions imposed on South Africa until it
ended the apartheid regime. Sanctions have a chance of working only if
the target regime can make the calculation that changing its ways will
bring relief. Saddam was perfectly content to permit the sanctions to
reduce his once middle-class nation to utter penury; he had, in fact,
brilliantly exploited his people's suffering, for which he was chiefly responsible, in order to discredit the entire sanctions regime. And it had
worked; in 1995 British and American diplomats, worried that the
sanctions were becoming unsustainable, had devised the so-called Oil-
for-Food Programme, which allowed the Iraqis to sell limited amounts
of oil and use the proceeds to buy humanitarian goods. Saddam had accepted the program only because he knew that he could manipulate it
for his own purposes. His ultimate goal was always to ride out the sanctions until the weapons inspectors had given him a clean bill of health.

Free from inspections and sanctions, he could then rebuild his military and industrial plant.

In October, the nuclear inspectors submitted a report concluding that nothing remained of Iraq's nuclear program. The Iraqis, with French and Russian support, pushed to have the "nuclear file" closed; Washington refused. The Americans, as well as the British, had concluded that Saddam was simply too dangerous to be let out of his cage, whether he complied or not. In November, President Clinton said that "sanctions will be there until the end of time, or as long as [Saddam] lasts." But of course if sanctions would never be lifted, then Saddam had no further incentive to accommodate the inspectors. The status quo, which had lasted a remarkable seven years, was now disintegrating. The Security Council was poised between two unpalatable options: inspectors without sanctions, or sanctions without inspectors. The French and the Russians were willing to accept the first; the Americans, and to a lesser extent the British, were willing to risk the latter, with the stick of a threatened invasion, rather than the carrot of lifted sanctions, ensuring Saddam's docility.

The thread was bound to be snapped; the precipitating incident was access to what the Iraqis called "presidential sites." These were vast but ill-defined areas that Tariq Aziz had declared off-limits to inspectors. The Iraqis insisted it was another matter of dignity; Butler believed that the prohibition was just another phase in the endless game of cat and mouse. Iraq's allies on the Security Council, as well as officials in the Secretariat, scrambled to devise a formulation that would give inspectors access to the sites consistent with Iraq's dignity. By the time I arrived on the scene, the state of play had grown incredibly complicated. Annan was being deluged with demands from world leaders and religious authorities that he go to Baghdad to prevent war. He was meeting with the permanent five and, separately, with the other ten members of the council; the P5, as the permanent members of the security council are known, were meeting among themselves. He was trying to get Butler to tone down his language while warding off demands for Butler's head from Arab countries. By this time, Annan was almost desperate to go to Iraq to prevent the impending war. "The pressure on him to go is so enormous," his aide Shashi Tharoor told me the day before I first met Annan, "that not going would be seen by many countries as a betrayal of his responsibilities." The Americans were willing to let him go only to deliver an ultimatum. Javier Pérez de Cuéllar had done just that on the eve of the Gulf War and come home empty-handed. Annan felt that he needed more space than that.

The Americans still didn't want him to go and negotiate, and both Albright and the deputy U.S. ambassador Peter Burleigh told him so directly. But neither were they comfortable about bombing Iraq, a decision that might prove politically unpopular, especially among Democrats; Annan's trip would at least permit them to say that they had exhausted every alternative. On Sunday, Albright came to Annan's home on Sutton Place for lunch and read him a list of "red lines" he must not cross—all sites must be accessible, and for multiple visits, and without time limits, among other things. Annan agreed. The trip began to take on an air of inevitability. The Americans wanted Annan to go with written instructions formalizing his understanding with Albright, but Annan did not want to be seen as a "messenger boy." Finally, on Monday night, the British ambassador, John Weston, suggested to his colleagues that he read "speaking notes" to Annan that incorporated the British-American red lines. Annan would have no written instructions, but neither would he be free to improvise. This piece of diplomatic legerdemain proved acceptable to all, including Annan himself.

It was a dramatic moment, not only for Annan, but for the office he occupied. A few days earlier, Iqbal Riza had asked to see a copy of Brian Urquhart's biography of Dag Hammarskjöld: he wanted to reread the passage about the "Peking Formula," lest Annan need to furnish some justification for this exercise in personal diplomacy. Annan himself was no such legal stickler, but his view of the office assumed just such a right and an obligation. When I spoke to him on Tuesday, while his aides were consumed with a frenzy of preparation, he used language worthy of his great predecessor: "There may be times when the secretary-general has to stand alone and use the moral authority of the office, and one should not shy away from that and I do not intend to shy away from that."

Annan's plane, lent by President Jacques Chirac, arrived at Saddam Hussein International Airport outside of Baghdad at 6:30 on the evening of February 20. The Iraqis, who felt that a great propaganda victory was in the offing, had decided to admit the international press, and two hundred or so reporters were crowded into a roped-off space near the terminal. We stared across a vast empty stretch of tarmac crumbling after years of disuse; weeds sprouted through long cracks. A violent orange sun was setting as Annan's Falcon 900 rolled to a stop. Tariq Aziz, in military uniform—not a good sign—strode to the base of the plane's gangway. CBS's Mike Wallace emerged—that's how big a story this was!—and then Annan himself. The secretary-general and the Iraqi diplomat made brief remarks, Annan inaudible as always, and then sped off in Annan's motorcade.

Annan was driven to the big whitewashed villa where he was to spend the next several days. In a country where even doctors could barely afford to buy a few eggs or tomatoes, and practically everyone depended on the rations provided by Oil-for-Food, the villa was a miniature version of the famously opulent presidential palaces. The place was a monument to Baathist kitsch, with a birdbath filled with sculpted figurines, a giant crystal chandelier, and a three-paneled painted mirror featuring a Regency dandy in curled wig holding a glass of punch. Iraqi protocol officers spent hours crowded together on a white couch, sipping sweet tea and chatting. They had all been to New York, and they fondly remembered the Upper East Side neighborhood where the Iraqi consulate was located.

Annan and his team spent the next day, a Saturday, closeted with Aziz and other Iraqi officials. During a break in the action, I went up to the villa and talked to Shashi Tharoor. "From 10:00 to 11:20 they really talked turkey," he said. "Then from 11:25 to 1:25, they delivered a lecture." They complained bitterly about the "cowboys" in UNSCOM and about the strictures of Oil-for-Food. Still, it seemed the Iraqis wanted to find a solution. Annan was to speak to Saddam Hussein the following day. "Where is not known, when is not known, in whose company is not known," Tharoor said. Officials could not even say whom Annan could bring with him; that would depend on how many of his private drivers Saddam would send, for only they knew of his whereabouts. Tharoor believed that a historic breakthrough might be at hand, one that would testify to his boss's combination of painstaking preparation and supreme commitment. But did this supposed space really exist?

Some of the stories out of Washington quoted senior administration officials predicting that the mission would fail. Maybe they wanted a failure that would justify hostilities.

Later that afternoon I spoke with Annan in the large, scruffy garden behind the villa. The secretary-general slowly picked his way along the border paths to a corner where a little rusty swing and two garden chairs had been placed. He turned the chair to face straight into the sun—an African heliotropism. Annan was perfectly composed and, under the circumstances, astonishingly gracious. "How has Baghdad been treating you?" he asked. How were the other journalists doing? Annan's sympathies plainly extended to the Iraqis as well, which was just what the Iraqis and their allies had hoped, and what the Americans and the British had feared. "Talk to some of your Arab friends," he said, "or talk to Brahimi; ask them to talk about dignity. It's like the Chinese losing face—it's that important. It's not a joke. The sense of humiliation or losing your dignity or losing face—they would die or go to war over that."

Butler had feared that Annan would come to accept the view of some in the Secretariat, and on the council, that the problem lay with the inspectors, not the Iraqis. This he would never do altogether, for to do so he would have to forsake the tiny patch of middle ground he had staked out. But the Iraqis had plainly won his sympathies that morning. "They say, 'We have cooperated and worked with the inspectors for seven years.' It's not the Security Council resolutions or UNSCOM per se. It's certain individuals and their behavior, and the sense that they have a national agenda." They had accused Butler, Annan said, "of playing an American game." Annan had warned them that the Americans were serious about bombing if they did not cooperate. On the other hand, he had promised that if "they would accelerate their cooperation," the UN "would accelerate the process and lift the sanctions." The Americans and the British had said otherwise, but this did not yet seem irremediable.

Annan was trying to thread a needle—but it was the Iraqis who were holding the needle. The Iraqis would not accept the idea of repeat, open-ended inspections of the presidential palaces. When the negotiations finally ended at 2:00 that morning, the odds of success looked about fifty-fifty. Annan, who does not have a particularly hardy constitution, went to sleep at 3:30 and woke up at 6:00. Unexpectedly, another meeting was suddenly called Sunday morning at the Foreign Ministry. Annan's team raced off, and then returned to the villa and waited. Finally, at a few minutes before noon, three black Mercedes sedans pulled into the U-shaped driveway. Annan was told that he could take three aides and a bodyguard. Ahmad Fawzi, the spokesman for Annan's delegation, asked one of the Iraqis where Annan was being taken. "He looked at me like I was a cockroach," Fawzi said later. "I think he wanted to take me out back and have me shot."

In fact, Annan was driven a few miles down a broad boulevard, through a vast gate, and then down another boulevard to a much bigger villa, a palace that had been bombed during the Gulf War and then rebuilt—the finest architecture in the world, the security officers assured Fawzi. The marble floors were covered with fine carpets, but the rooms themselves were utterly empty—a precaution, it was explained, for the coming war. Saddam, in a navy double-breasted suit rather than his military uniform, greeted the secretary-general. Annan was struck that the same officials who had been lecturing him with blustering bravado became as meek as church mice when they were before Saddam; only then did he fully understand what fear the tyrant engendered.

Annan sat down with Saddam, Tariq Aziz, and several other aides. Saddam ran down the usual litany of supposed outrages, insults to Iraqi pride, and so on. As the conversation meandered along, Annan began to worry that he would be dismissed without an agreement. Finally, after an hour, Saddam stood up. Everyone else stood up. Annan feared that his moment had already passed until his interpreter whispered that he was to remain behind. The sycophants departed, leaving only the secretary-general, the dictator, and their translators. The two men spoke for three hours.

Before leaving, Annan had sought advice from Pérez de Cuéllar, who had, after all, embarked on a very similar mission. Pérez de Cuéllar had said that Saddam often paused for so long that he would appear to have finished his thought; one must wait, however, and under no circumstances interrupt. This was almost superfluous advice for Annan, who was loath to interrupt schoolchildren, much less homicidal tyrants, but he reminded himself to grant Saddam all the time he wished. Saddam's manner, Annan said later, was "very correct, very calm, almost serene." At times he took notes on a yellow pad. He offered Annan a Cuban cigar, which he accepted; both men smoked.

Annan was not a man who had to be told to watch his words, but now he had to inspect every single syllable he uttered. He could not offer anything that transgressed the British-American red lines. At the same time, he knew that he could not threaten or even criticize Saddam. Instead, he would appeal to Saddam's delusional sense of himself as a latter-day Saladin—his sense of glory and magnanimity. He was, Annan said, a "builder" who had built modern Iraq, a statesman, a man of vision and courage. It was in his hands to avert war, to preserve his people from suffering, and so on. But Annan also bluntly told the dictator that none of Iraq's allies would be able to prevent America from bombing the country should he remain intransigent. He produced the memorandum of understanding that his legal adviser had worked out with Iraqi officials; the problem areas were marked with brackets. He and Saddam began to go over the text. Saddam complained about the word "inspections," as applied to his palaces; they agreed on "entries." He demanded a few other changes in language. And in the end, he accepted what Tariq Aziz did not have the authority to accept: openended inspections of the palaces. The aides were summoned, and Annan announced that they had reached an agreement.

The following morning I showed up at the villa at 8:00, and Annan agreed to see me. I was ushered into an elegant parlor, where I found him sitting bolt upright on the edge of an Empire couch, his hands in his lap, as if in rigid defiance of his obvious exhaustion. The previous afternoon he had returned to the villa, asked for a room to lie down in, rose after half an hour, and then began making phone calls: Clinton, Tony Blair, Chirac, Mubarak, Yevgeny Primakov, the Russian foreign minister. He told each that he had "a good text" but refused to provide details, lest any of them try to unravel what he had so laboriously tied up. He had fallen asleep, and then at 2:30 a.m. Madeleine Albright had called, demanding to have the text read to her. Albright was very fond of Annan, but she tended to browbeat him, especially when she feared he was going soft. Annan's circle had adopted an increasingly dim view of her, seeing her as the chief impediment to a peaceful resolution of the Iraq crisis. Elisabeth Lindenmayer, who accompanied Annan on all trips, begged Albright to call the next morning, but she refused. Albright cross-examined the groggy secretary-general, who put her off with uncharacteristic asperity. "She was," Annan said, "quite nervous and agitated."

Annan himself was exhilarated, and he came as close as he ever did to reflecting on his own achievement. "It's really quite something," he said, with as much bewilderment as delight. "The concentration and attention, the creativity you need to move people along and to convince them." Annan was probably thinking of the Americans as much as the Iraqis. He had persuaded Saddam to accept something he had not been prepared to accept, and perhaps would not have accepted from anyone else. Now, he understood, he would have to persuade the Clinton administration, which would be just as hard. "We say Iraq is isolated from the international community," he said, "but the international community is also isolated. We want them to comply, but I'm not sure we make the effort to understand what is going on." He was picking his words with exquisite care; this, too, was a minefield. "I believe we have demonized Iraq. I have to be careful; I was going to say something I shouldn't have. I was going to say we have demonized him, and maybe with some justification. But to not go beyond that . . ." He, certainly, had gone beyond that.

Annan returned to, quite literally, a hero's welcome: hundreds of staff members had gathered in the foyer of UN headquarters and greeted him with an ovation. The Security Council, despite some reservations from the Americans, the British, and the Japanese, approved the memorandum of understanding unanimously. Richard Butler, who had the power to pop the swelling balloon of adulation with one well-aimed barb, was uncharacteristically gracious, praising the agreement on the Sunday-morning talk shows. Annan himself was deluged with media requests. He did, it's true, make one all-too-characteristic mistake: At his first press conference, he described Saddam Hussein as "a man I can do business with." Of course, Annan had just *done* business with Saddam, and he believed that it was his obligation to do business with anyone in the interests of peace and security. But the comment made him sound like a dupe, and led Trent Lott, then the majority leader of the U.S. Senate, to denounce both Annan and President Clinton.

Annan was never going to satisfy the Republican conservatives. But both Clinton and Albright felt that he had avoided war without giving away the store. When I spoke with Jamie Rubin, Albright's spokesman and confidant, a few weeks after Annan returned, he said, "Other than a few ill-chosen words"—the I-can-do-business-with business—"it was a brilliant diplomatic exercise." Rubin said that Annan "could be one of the great secretary-generals of our time," so long as he wasn't taken captive by the anti-American crowd around him. Richard Butler was equally enthusiastic: "He brought home the bacon," he told me. "He brought home an agreement that, if implemented faithfully by Iraq, will solve the problem without any diminution of our professional role or ability."

Butler has since written in his memoirs that he was always more skeptical than he let on; when Albright asked him what he thought of the agreement, he says, he told her that he was deeply troubled by the final paragraph, in which Annan promised to bring Iraq's wish to see the sanctions lifted "to the full attention of the members of the Security Council." Albright herself says that the reaction to the agreement in the White House was "This is the guy you thought was going to be so good?" Albright said that she had to explain that Annan's job was to "try to find consensus and develop peace," which was not an endorsement but an explanation. James Steinberg, at the time the deputy national security adviser, says that he and others considered the mission a "disaster." "It was," he says, "part of Saddam's game, which was to undermine the whole thing, and thus to undermine the inspection regime. Everything was going to be negotiable, and so it encouraged Saddam to continue to whittle away at the sanctions. In the end, it deepened the crisis rather than defusing the crisis."

A good deal of this has the ring of wisdom after the fact. Since Annan's mission to Iraq did not ultimately succeed in averting war, there may well have been some retrospective rearranging of opinion. It's true that in the long run, the Iraq trip lowered rather than raised Annan's stock among many American policy makers, who concluded that his penchant for the peaceful resolution of disputes, his faith in the powers of negotiation, and his trust in the goodwill of others could make him an obstacle when force, or the threat of force, was required. But the immediate and overwhelming effect of Annan's dramatic mission was to raise him to heights of public esteem that no secretary-general since Dag Hammarskjöld had attained. He was a gentle, forceful peacemaker—a Gandhi, a Mandela. I myself played a role in this mythmaking. In my cover story on Annan in the March 29, 1998, issue of *The New York Times Magazine*, I portrayed him, only half ironically, as a Daniel in the lion's den and a Zen master of diplomacy.

The Iraqis, however, began backing away from the agreement before Annan reached New York. On February 23, the same day he signed the memorandum, Tariq Aziz sent Annan a letter claiming, absurdly, that it had been understood that Iraq would control the transport and accommodation of the teams visiting the presidential sites and that any analysis of material taken from the sites would be conducted in Baghdad, with the material itself shared with the Iraqis. Annan wrote back, curtly observing that his team had specifically rejected these proposals. It was a taste of things to come: relations between Aziz and Richard Butler began to degenerate almost from the moment Butler and his team returned to Baghdad, and hopes for cooperation disappeared down a whirlpool of recrimination. In August, Aziz belligerently informed Butler that Iraq was now fully disarmed. If UNSCOM wasn't prepared to certify this status, it should leave right away. Once again, the inspections came to a thudding halt.

Annan's aides were more convinced than ever that UNSCOM had become the problem rather than the solution. Scott Ritter, the most notorious of the "cowboy" inspectors, had just resigned from the body while unleashing a torrent of stupendous allegations—Butler was a tool of the U.S. government, UNSCOM itself had become a front for CIA intelligence gathering. The fact that Ritter had gone overnight from UNSCOM's biggest hawk to its harshest detractor cast some doubt on his claims; nevertheless, the CIA does seem to have used monitoring equipment it supplied to UNSCOM for freelance intelligence gathering. Whatever the case, the allegations had the effect of vindicating the darkest suspicions. In early October, Annan proposed that the Security Council bypass UNSCOM and make its own determination of Iraq's compliance with a view to ultimately relaxing or eliminating the sanctions.

The United Kingdom was then presiding over the Security Council, and Sir Jeremy Greenstock, the new ambassador, was not about to let Annan once again insert himself into the process in order to forestall military action. Instead, the council produced its own version of "comprehensive review," which contained no promise of the much-discussed light at the end of the tunnel. Iraq repudiated it and reiterated its refusal to deal further with UNSCOM. From that time on, Greenstock says, "Kofi realized he couldn't do the Security Council's business, and he left the council to handle its own problems on this." This marked the end of the great experiment in expanding the authority of the office that had begun nine months earlier.

On November 11, Butler, having been warned of impending air strikes, withdrew his personnel from Iraq. U.S. and British warplanes prepared to strike Iraqi targets. At the last minute, Tariq Aziz sent a letter to Annan reversing the Iraqi position, and President Clinton rescinded the attack order an hour before it was to become effective. The inspectors returned to their work, receiving the usual mixture of cooperation and confrontation. The "comprehensive review" process was still open; Butler was to tell the Security Council whether, in language carefully crafted by the Americans, Iraq had "returned" to "full cooperation." It hadn't, of course; but the inspectors saw signs of modest progress. On the morning of December 16, Butler handed the final draft of the report to his political aide, Gustavo Zlauvinen. "The first four pages, which described the situation, was what he had agreed on," Zlauvinen recalls. "The fifth page was completely new, on a different computer. It was totally different, and totally harsh." Zlauvinen accused Butler of taking dictation from the Clinton White House, which Butler angrily denied. Zlauvinen said, "The Iraqis are doing their best, within the limits we've set. If you present this, the Americans are going to bomb. That means innocent people are going to die, and inspections are going to come to an end." Zlauvinen refused to present the document to the council.

Zlauvinen was right. On December 16, while the Security Council debated the report, word arrived that Operation Desert Fox had begun. The inspectors would not return to Iraq for four years.

———

What are we to make of this thrilling but ultimately futile exercise in brinkmanship? At the time, Kofi Annan's genuine heroism, and the almost absurd melodrama of the moment, tended to blind onlookers (like me) to the inherent limitations of the mission. Annan was an entrepreneur of diplomatic space, and yet the tiny slice of space that he wedged himself into turned out to be illusory. There was, in fact, no common ground. As Jeremy Greenstock says, "It was a classic Kofi Annan compromise, and a very clever one, but it contained the seeds of the trouble all the way through. In his brilliant compromise to get around the problem that they wouldn't deal with the inspectors, he did enough for the Americans not to rupture the whole business but not quite enough to make it clear that the inspectors were in charge of the inspections."

Does this mean Annan shouldn't have gone at all? When I asked him this question, he said, "Let's assume I hadn't gone, and we had gone to war at the beginning of 1998, because the palaces are closed, and we didn't go the last mile. Don't forget that we are also an organization of peace, though we are not pacifists. The inspectors would have been thrown out much earlier, and inspections would have come to a halt. Being constantly in their hair was quite effective." All that is true. And though James Steinberg may have been right in feeling that the very act of propitiating Saddam Hussein, and of acknowledging the legitimacy of his concerns, emboldened him to push for more, that peril should scarcely have been sufficient to make Annan ignore the pleas to intervene that he had been receiving from every corner of the globe.

Yes, he should have gone; but should he have so readily credited Saddam's commitment to the "dignity" of his people? Annan came away from the experience feeling that Iraq and Saddam had been unfairly demonized. But in fact they had been *fairly* demonized. Madeleine Albright had called Saddam the most evil man since Hitler. Annan blanched when I recalled his Baghdad comment, but the moral judgment seems about right. Saddam was in fact contemptuous of his people's dignity and welfare; he had intentionally starved them while assaulting the world's ears with the cruelty of the sanctions. Saddam and Tariq Aziz had both told Annan that they had reached agreement only because they trusted him, and then Aziz had tried to rewrite the pact as soon as the secretary-general's back was turned. Hadn't they played him for a fool? Annan thinks otherwise. "This is a region where honor and pride is so high," he says, "that they had to sell it to the people as if they had not in fact made any concessions." Perhaps. But it is also true that Annan was too willing to believe the best of both men. He felt that if he treated people with respect, they would behave as if they were worthy of that respect. It's a fine belief, but it doesn't apply to people like Saddam Hussein. And it was precisely this credulity that made the "I can do business with" Saddam comment stick to Annan. Here, as in Bosnia, Annan's genuine horror of violence was prone to make him find interlocutors where there were none.

But no secretary-general, Annan included, has the final say in such momentous affairs. It is the calculus of the great powers that define these dramas, and that delineate the space within which a secretary-general can operate. And the Americans and the British, who were driving the debate, had no good answer to the problem of Iraq. With President Clinton consumed by the Monica Lewinsky scandal, the administration was in no condition for bold strokes or far-reaching strategy. Annan constantly asked, "After the bombing, what?" But there was no answer. The bombing campaign, known as Operation Desert Fox, lasted four days and produced precisely the effect that Annan and others had predicted: Saddam's hold on power was, if anything, strengthened, and with the inspectors banished, it was no longer possible to know what he was up to. Iraq moved to the back burner, since no one knew what to do about it. And there it remained until the terrorist attacks of 9/11 made Saddam's intentions, whatever they were, seem far more menacing than they had before.

CHAPTER SIX

Bosnia Never Again

IN APRIL 1998, ANNAN HIRED EDWARD MORTIMER, A COL-umnist for the *Financial Times*, as his chief speechwriter. Mortimer was exceedingly tall, exceedingly thin, exceedingly intelligent, an immoderate person of moderate views, with the stammer and the nervous tics and the palpable air of discomfort that seem, among the English, to be highly correlated with I.Q. It was Mortimer's voice, and that of his principal aide, Nader Mousavizadeh, that Annan would be channeling in years to come. And it was thanks to them and to others in the speech-writing department that in his prepared remarks Annan sounded so much more reflective, and even witty, than he did in interviews or off-the-cuff remarks.

Mortimer was to begin work in July, but he volunteered to write the speech Annan was to deliver in late June at Ditchley, the annual retreat for elite figures in British diplomacy and international relations. When Mortimer learned that the secretary-general wished to speak on "the challenge of governance," his heart sank. But then Shashi Tharoor called to say that Annan wanted to talk instead about "intervention," a subject about which Mortimer had thought, written, and spoken a great deal. When Annan came through London, Mortimer went to see him at the Dorchester hotel to ask what, exactly, he wanted to say on the subject. Annan was hopelessly vague. He didn't know what he thought, but he knew what he felt. He said, "Look at my speech when I left Sarajevo in December of 1995." What he had said at the time was that in the face of terrible crimes, each of us has an obligation to search our conscience and ask, "Could I have done more?"

It wasn't in Annan's nature to dwell on his or his institution's failures; rather, he would externalize them as "issues" and seek to resolve them in the form of changes in policy. The great, besetting failures were, of course, Bosnia and Rwanda. The UN had to act, and act robustly, in the face of atrocities. But what kind of action was acceptable, and under what circumstances? Annan felt that finding the answer to this problem would be central to his tenure as secretary-general. In the spring of 1997, at one of the first dinner parties at which he hosted his carefully balanced selection of media stars, statesmen, heroes of conscience, and socialites, he asked Elie Wiesel, the author and Holocaust survivor, to talk about "intervention." He then asked each table to discuss the issue, and appoint a speaker to get up during the dessert course to recount their thoughts. No conclusion was reached, and Annan himself said little. That was his way: He marinated himself in the thoughts of people more verbal and philosophical than he. This helped him get a feel for the shape of a subject, and for where he himself might fit in.

By the spring of 1998, grave crimes were incubating once again in Slobodan Milošević's dreadful laboratory. The Balkan strongman kept a choke hold on the southern province of Kosovo, which was ethnically Albanian rather than Serbian, and Muslim rather than Christian. But as Yugoslavia had begun to dissolve into its constituent parts, the Kosovars had moved from peaceful resistance to low-level guerrilla war. In early 1998, as weapons began to flow across the border from Albania, the Kosovo Liberation Army, as the insurgent force styled itself, began attacking Serbian police and paramilitary officers. The Serbs, as ever, responded with yet greater ferocity: in early March, police units equipped with artillery wiped out fifty-eight members of one of the leading families of the resistance. The tit-for-tat violence spiraled upward throughout the spring, with Serbian forces burning villages and attacking civilians and guerrillas alike with helicopters. These gathering horrors convinced Annan that the time had come to talk about the subject that had been ripening in his mind since his time in Sarajevo.

It was an extraordinary speech—densely reasoned, unflinching, and passionate (and written entirely by Mortimer and other aides). Annan began by saying that his listeners were probably assuming that as an African, and as the leader of an organization dedicated to the principle of sovereignty, he would "preach a sermon against intervention." Not at all, he said. "The Charter protects the sovereignty of peoples. It was never meant as a license for governments to trample on human rights and dignity. Sovereignty implies responsibility, not just power." Wasn't that, after all, the principle that lay behind such lesser interventions as the condemnation of apartheid in South Africa? And if sovereignty did not, in fact, convey responsibility, then what could possibly be the meaning of the Convention on the Prevention and Punishment of the Crime of Genocide? "State frontiers," Annan said, "should no longer be seen as a watertight protection for war criminals or mass murderers. The fact that a conflict is 'internal' does not give the parties any right to disregard the most basic rules of human conduct." This was a doctrine known in the realm of political thought as "conditional sovereignty."

And while in 1997 Annan might have understood "intervention" chiefly in economic or diplomatic terms—as sanctions or political isolation—now he did not shy away from the orthodox meaning of the word. While these lesser forms of intervention, with the consent of all parties, he went on, are vastly to be preferred to military operations without such consent, could anyone doubt that, say, the Vietnamese intervention to end the genocide in Cambodia was justified? The real problem was that it had been mounted unilaterally, for if every state is to be the judge of its own right of intervention, then "will we not be forced to legitimize Hitler's championship of the Sudeten Germans?" Only the Security Council had the global legitimacy to govern the exercise of this duty.

Annan closed by reminding his audience of the failure to act effectively in Bosnia and Rwanda. "Each of us as an individual has to take his or her share of responsibility," he said, reprising his words in Sarajevo. This time, he went on, if the simmering violence in Kosovo explodes into another campaign of ethnic cleansing, "no one will be able to say that they were taken by surprise . . . All our professions of regret; all our expressions of determination to never again permit another Bosnia; all our hopes for a peaceful future for the Balkans will be cruelly mocked if we allow Kosovo to become another killing field."

Annan had laid down for the first time the core principles that would distinguish his first term in office and make him the kind of moral actor that the UN had lacked since the time of Hammarskjöld. At the time, however, scarcely anyone beyond his immediate audience took any notice of the speech. Kosovo was not a UN issue. Russia, the historic ally of the Serbs, opposed any consideration of the subject in the council. And President Clinton, every bit as determined as Annan was not to endure once again the shameful paralysis of Bosnia, was not about to let the UN serve as the arbiter of this grave moral responsibility. Indeed, Madeleine Albright writes that when British Foreign Secretary Robin Cook explained to her in the summer of 1998 that "his lawyers told him a [Security] council mandate would be needed if NATO were to act," she told him to "get himself new lawyers." Such a precedent, she pointed out, would give Russia and China an effective veto over NATO action. In September, the council did pass a resolution declaring the ethnic violence a threat to international peace and security, demanding that Serb forces in Kosovo be confined to their garrison, and seeking a negotiated solution to Kosovo's bid for secession. The Russian ambassador promptly insisted that the resolution did not authorize force should the Serbs fail to comply.

Starting in March, Annan and his aides had managed to sneak Kosovo onto the council's agenda through the procedural back door of "other business." Throughout the remainder of the year, Secretariat officials periodically briefed the council on the rising tide of violence in Kosovo and on the swelling ranks of internally displaced people, who by the summer had reached 200,000, or about 10 percent of the province's population. Annan was striving to keep the UN at the center of decision making over Kosovo, not only because this was his reflexive response to almost everything, but because his new doctrine of humanitarian intervention depended on the council for its legitimacy. But whenever he tried to assert himself, he was blocked. On several occasions in late 1998 and early 1999, Annan raised Kosovo in meetings with the council, and "he was told more or less to mind his own business," according to Kieran Prendergast. When European diplomatic efforts stalled, Annan decided to appoint Pauline Neville-Jones, a retired British diplomat with long experience in the Balkans, to engage in a quiet round of visits to the major capitals on his behalf. But when Prendergast approached U.K. ambassador Jeremy Greenstock on the subject, he was told that "the British would take it very badly, at the level of No. 10 [Downing Street]." Albright felt the same way.

Washington and London may have feared that Annan would try a repeat performance of his eleventh-hour intervention in Baghdad. Annan's willingness to accept almost any sign of good intentions from the Iraqis, even while they were obstructing the weapons inspectors, and his open opposition to the Desert Fox bombing raid had done real harm to his reputation in Anglo-American circles. In a profile of Annan that appeared in *The New Republic* in early February, David Rieff, who had never forgiven the UN for its role in Bosnia, described his subject as "a decent man who has presided over shocking indecency" and argued that Annan was "committed to the peaceful resolution of conflicts at almost any price." This was an unusually harsh view, but Annan was, in fact, gaining a reputation as a peacenik. The Ditchley speech would argue otherwise, but no one knew about that.

In late October, with NATO threatening imminent air strikes, Milošević agreed to implement the terms of the September council resolution, and to admit unarmed international monitors to verify compliance. But the Serbs were not about to be deterred by unarmed monitors. The violence, the bouts of ethnic cleansing, grew more brutal. On January 15, in a reprisal for a KLA attack, Serbian police entered the town of Racak and systematically murdered forty-five Kosovar civilians. This was a provocation the West could not ignore. NATO began to prepare its war machinery, while the Bosnia Contact Group, which consisted of the United States, the U.K., Germany, France, Italy, and Russia, and which had been coordinating diplomatic efforts, called for a last-ditch attempt at negotiations in the French resort of Rambouillet.

The UN had no real role at Rambouillet, just as it had had no role at the Dayton talks that brought the Bosnian war to an end. Europeans did not need a UN interlocutor in order to talk to other Europeans. But the parties had not yet exhausted themselves with fighting, and so Rambouillet, unlike Dayton, failed. Milošević did not even attend, and while the KLA ultimately signed a peace agreement, former Yugoslavia, as the rump state was known, did not. The failure of the political route gave the UN a second chance, and the Canadians, who held the presidency of the Security Council in February, lobbied members to unite behind a resolution authorizing the use of force. But it was fruitless: even though most members of the council were prepared to vote for such a resolution, the Russians stated flatly that they would veto it. Paul Heinbecker, the Canadian ambassador, says that his country even contemplated forcing the Russians to veto and then bringing the issue to the General Assembly under a seldom-used procedure known as Uniting for Peace. But he worried that the Yugoslavs could keep the question bottled up for weeks. What's more, several NATO members adhered, he said, to "a connect-the-dots legal position" that would have prohibited hostilities once a council resolution had been defeated.

On March 24, NATO initiated a bombing campaign that was to last seventy-seven days. Here was the response to atrocities that Annan had foreseen in Ditchley, and all but invited in Brussels, but without the legitimation that he considered the only bulwark against self-righteous militarism. Was he to deplore the violation of the Charter, or accept that a higher form of legitimation might lie in the imperative to stop atrocities? A debate raged around the thirty-eighth floor, but Annan would not wrap himself in the Charter. "When you look at the Declaration of Human Rights," he says, "the principle behind the intervention in Kosovo was quite legitimate. The fact that the council couldn't come together doesn't make it not legitimate." Annan issued a statement in which he blamed the Yugoslavs for rejecting a political settlement, and then stated, "It is indeed tragic that diplomacy had failed, but there are times when the use of force may be legitimate in the pursuit of peace." Self-evident though this sounded, the use of the word "legitimate" to describe hostilities undertaken in the absence of a Security Council mandate was close to heresy in the world of the UN. For this reason, Paul Heinbecker says, "Kofi showed a lot of courage on Kosovo, though only in the UN could you say that not resisting the right thing takes courage."

That the bombing campaign was in fact the right thing is not altogether self-evident. The Serbs, who could not strike back at NATO bombers, struck back instead at Kosovar civilians. Before March 24, about twenty-five hundred Kosovars had been killed and close to half a million made homeless; during the course of the air war, about ten thousand people died, chiefly at the hands of the Serbs, while a stepped-up campaign of ethnic cleansing forced another million or so to flee, displacing virtually the entire country. Had NATO been willing to target Serbia's infrastructure or to introduce ground troops, the war might have ended much faster, and with far less suffering to the victim population. But political constraints made European leaders withhold permission for more aggressive bombing, and made President Clinton flatly rule out the use of infantry.

Of course, the resistance Annan faced was not from those who wanted to prosecute the war more aggressively but from those who opposed it altogether. Third World nations generally viewed the bombing not as a humanitarian action but as a colonial one, a blatant violation of Serbian sovereignty. But many of Annan's own aides were equally upset about the violation of the Charter, which was as sacrosanct for them as the principle of nonintervention was for others. In fact, the debate over Kosovo split Annan's team down the middle. On one side was John Ruggie, his American adviser; Iqbal Riza, the chief of staff; and the speechwriters, Edward Mortimer and Nader Mousavizadeh. Mortimer was the intellectual author of Annan's ringing declaration of "Never again." Mousavizadeh had spent several years at *The New Republic* and had absorbed the magazine's "liberal interventionist" position, and had then worked with Riza in the Balkans. Though of Danish and Iranian background, Mousavizadeh was essentially American and, like Ruggie, could not view international law as the *summum bonum*.

But this was precisely the view taken in the departments of political affairs and legal affairs. When General Klaus Naumann, the military head of NATO, came to see Kieran Prendergast, the DPA head got out his much-thumbed copy of the UN Charter to prove that force would be illegitimate absent Security Council approval. "For those of us who care about multilateralism and collective action," Prendergast says, "this action by NATO was a crossing of the Rubicon, because for the first time countries like Norway and Denmark and the Netherlands, that had always given primacy to the international rule of law, were willing to go along with the action." Prendergast took the distinctly minority view that more sensitive diplomacy could have brought the Russians around and thus rendered the whole issue moot. But he also considered the war a stupid blunder that caused unnecessary suffering.

The two sides fought over the language of the reports that would lay out the secretary-general's view of the conflict. DPA would prepare a draft and send it to Riza; the *chef de cabinet* would forward the document to Mousavizadeh, who would flag the more egregious phrases and then draft a memo to DPA under Riza's name. In the last of these memos, written March 16 and sent to Álvaro de Soto, a high-ranking DPA official, Riza writes, "In answer to your statement that you have 'no evidence' that the Serbian authorities' use of force against the civilian Kosovar population . . . . is continuing . . . I refer you, *inter alia*, to page A1 of today's *New York Times*." Riza also harshly takes de Soto to task for describing the crisis as "an ongoing dispute in whose resolution we have no involvement"—a breathtaking repudiation of Annan's evolving doctrine of humanitarian intervention. He concludes by noting, "I cannot agree with your explicit and implicit suggestion that the KLA are largely to blame for the calamity that has befallen the people of Kosovo. Regrettably, I must add that it reminds me of a most disagreeable argument made about the last victims of Mr. Milosevic's brutal policies, namely the people of Bosnia."

The internecine struggle came to a head in the drafting of Annan's response to the bombing. In the initial draft of the proposed statement, Annan merely expressed his "regret" for the failure of diplomacy. Mousavizadeh wrote a heated note to his mentor predicting that such a statement would be read as a defense of "the right of the Yugoslav authorities to do as they wish with the people of Kosovo." Would this general expression of regret, he asked, "reflect adequately the lessons about the use of force which we claim to have learned from our experience in Bosnia"? Riza needed no persuasion; Mousavizadeh and Mortimer drafted a new statement, with its prominent and startling use of "legitimate." Mortimer says that when he delivered the new version, Annan gazed at it fixedly and finally said, "This is the most difficult statement I have had to make as secretary-general." And then he agreed to issue the statement.

The argument continued to rage throughout the spring. For most liberal internationalists, the question of humanitarian intervention was simple enough: What level of atrocities justified a resort to force? But for Annan and others at the UN, the issue was much more complicated: Did this moral imperative, whatever its standards, fall within the compass of international law? How could one ensure that such decisions bore the legitimating stamp of the Security Council? (No one questioned, as Madeleine Albright and a great many others did, that it was the council that provided such legitimation.) In June, at Kieran Prendergast's suggestion, Annan impaneled the Working Group on the Post-war Security Framework. ("Post-war" here meant Kosovo, not the Cold War.) The group included officials on both sides of the Kosovo debate, as well as a number of prominent outsiders. Its deliberations, according to minutes of the sessions, offer a capsule version of the state of opinion on this consuming question inside the UN, and in the surrounding policy and intellectual community.

The first meeting was held June 10, the very day when the Security Council ratified the peace agreement that NATO bombing had forced Milošević to sign. And yet many of those present believed that it was the war, not the failure to act, that called the UN's very purpose into question: "The question for the UN is whether it owes its existence to fundamental principles in common to all"—that is, the Charter—"or was just tolerated while there was a division in power during the Cold War." The question, which sounds very much like Prendergast's, was whether those with power, and above all the United States, now felt free to act as they wished. The United States didn't need a mandate; NATO didn't need a mandate. "A central question to be asked is: what is the Secretary-General for? The Charter is his Bible. If an action takes place that violates the Charter, how can he now stand up for it? If he starts accepting the idea that the Charter does not matter, he is undermining his own foundation."

Over time, the group seemed to become ever more skittish about the doctrine that Annan himself had enunciated; or rather, the uncomfortables increasingly carried the day. Lakhdar Brahimi, who had served as a crucial adviser to Annan during the Iraq crisis, argued that "the more distance the Secretary-General kept from this issue, the better, at least for the moment." Both he and Ibrahim Gambari, a DPA official, worried that merely by identifying itself with this alleged right or obligation, "the UN risked being used to legitimise intervention by a powerful country." What about "the consent of the host state?" Gambari asked. "What should happen if this consent were not given?" Edward Mortimer, one of the few voices on the other side, pointed out that "one of the reasons the UN had a bad public image was precisely because it was seen as an association of states that compromised on values and principles." But Mortimer agreed that the secretary-general should find ways of talking about intervention that involved "relieving human suffering" rather than military action.

In Annan's own world, in short, the "lesson of Kosovo" was not "The UN must never again be a mute witness to atrocities," but "Intervention without UN approval must not be condoned." The imperative to protect international law, and the UN itself, trumped the imperative to protect civilians. But dry legalism was contrary to Annan's nature, and so was the premise that two supreme goods could be irreconcilably opposed to each other. He devoutly believed both sides of this equation: only by accepting the moral imperative of humanitarian intervention could the UN retain its own legitimacy, and only by conferring UN approval could such an action retain *its* legitimacy. Annan knew very well that many members, especially the ex-colonies in the Third World, repudiated the doctrine of conditional sovereignty and viewed their "internal affairs" as inviolable. Nevertheless, he decided to make humanitarian intervention the theme of his speech opening the upcoming session of the General Assembly in September, the secretary-general's equivalent of the State of the Union address. "We had made it too comfortable for the member states," he says. "I thought it would be good if we had a real debate and put things on the table."

Annan began his speech by restating the conditional sovereignty principle: "The state is now widely understood to be the servant of its people, and not vice versa." The sovereignty of the individual had, at the same time, been "enhanced" by a growing respect for human rights. It was this fundamental change in relations between the individual and the state that underpinned the doctrine of humanitarian intervention. This doctrine, Annan went on, was wholly consistent with the language and spirit of the Charter, which permitted the use of armed force in the common interest. "But what is the common interest?" he asked. "Who shall define it? Who will defend it—under whose authority and under what means of intervention? These are the monumental questions facing us as we enter the new century."

He went on to offer preliminary answers to these questions. Intervention, he said, must be "fairly and consistently applied"—an axiom designed to forestall claims that the doctrine would serve as a tool of the powerful. Member states must embrace a "more broadly defined, more widely conceived definition of national interest," a conception that would include the systematic extermination of the citizens of a strategically insignificant state. The Security Council must "rise to the challenge," as it conspicuously had failed to do both in Rwanda and in Kosovo. And the commitment to intervene must extend beyond hostilities to post-conflict reconstruction. Implicit in each of these propositions was Annan's central premise: that the UN, and only the UN, could authorize and adjudicate such interventions. Only the UN had the global legitimacy to underwrite the moral claims of the intervenors, whoever they should be. And for this very reason, Annan warned his audience in closing, they must not, indeed could not, shrug off so monumental a burden: "If the collective conscience of humanity . . . cannot find in the United Nations its greatest tribune, there is a grave danger it will look elsewhere for peace and for justice." And of course this collective conscience, if that's what it was, had done just that in the case of Kosovo.

Annan did not have to wait long for an answer from the member states. The third speaker, President Abdelaziz Bouteflika of Algeria, a country deeply shaped by its violent struggle against French colonialism, said that while he would not deny that the UN "has the right and the duty to help suffering humanity," Algeria was "extremely sensitive to any undermining of our sovereignty, not only because sovereignty is our final defence against the rules of an unjust world, but because we have no active part in the decision-making process in the Security Council nor in monitoring the implementation of decisions." This last proviso may have been disingenuous, for Bouteflika seemed far more worried about the threat that Annan's doctrine posed to states than about the threat that murderous states posed to their citizens. "We firmly believe," he declared, "that interference in internal affairs may take place only with the consent of the State in question."

This turned out, not surprisingly, to be the overwhelming sentiment of the membership. At a diplomatic reception soon after the speech, Dr. Theo-Ben Gurirab, the ambassador of Namibia and the president of the General Assembly, used his toast to assail Annan's remarks—an astonishing breach of etiquette. The G77, as the bloc of developing countries is known, formally repudiated the doctrine of humanitarian intervention as an unacceptable violation of state sovereignty. But this was not Annan's principal audience; he was speaking, as the pope does, *urbi et orbi*—to the city and the world. And to the larger world, or at least to the world of public opinion, Annan had identified himself, and the United Nations, with the great moral imperative of the day. In certain circles Annan would never be able to shed his reputation as a confirmed peacenik, and yet he had courted the wrath of the developing world by rejecting anticolonialism in favor of moral principles cherished in the West.

And then, strikingly, he clammed up. In the ensuing months, according to John Ruggie, Annan declined invitations to revisit the subject. He recognized that he could advance the argument no further by throwing down the gauntlet once again. He would instead let the debate he had provoked swirl on without him. Ruggie came to think of the secretary-general as a "norm entrepreneur" who understood precisely when and how far he could press a large and controversial principle, whether the universality of human rights or the doctrine of intervention. Perhaps there was a strong element of timidity in Annan's sagacity; if so, it was a caution born of long experience.

At the 2000 convening of the General Assembly, Canadian Prime Minister Jean Chrétien announced that he would impanel a commission to study the issues Annan had raised. The commission's highly regarded report, "The Responsibility to Protect," greatly advanced Annan's argument and gave it the imprimatur of an important member state. Year by year, the responsibility to protect gained standing in world opinion until finally, in 2005, it would be embraced by the UN itself (rhetorically, if scarcely in practice). It may not only be pride of authorship that leads Edward Mortimer to say, "I firmly believe that if Kofi Annan had achieved nothing beyond gaining broad acceptance for the responsibility to protect, that by itself would constitute a major achievement."

Just as Annan was pressing his muscular new doctrine, another humanitarian catastrophe forced itself on the world's attention, as if to make the argument for intervention inescapable. This was the nightmare of East Timor. There were few more persistent and shameful examples of the UN's willingness to abide even the most brutal assertions of sovereign power than this tiny island province. The Portuguese had colonized this lush and mountainous region, ringed with lovely, if crocodile-infested, beaches, in the sixteenth century. (The Dutch, who owned the western half, surrendered it to Indonesia in 1949.) When the Portuguese up and left, in 1975, Indonesia filled the vacuum and acted as the worst kind of colonist, not only sucking out resources but filling every desirable job and reducing the native population to a kind of servitude. The Indonesian military brutally suppressed a local insurgency, and then initiated a reign of terror that led to more than 180,000 deaths—out of a population of fewer than 1 million. East Timor was one of the notorious human rights nightmares of the 1980s, but the Security Council refused to address the situation on the grounds that it was a purely internal Indonesian matter.

By the 1990s, Indonesia was no longer a crucial piece of the Cold War chessboard; the era of impunity was drawing to a close. In 1998, the longtime president, Suharto, was forced from office and replaced by B. J. Habibie, a pious and eccentric gentleman deemed acceptable by the all-powerful military. The following January, President Habibie startled the world by announcing that the Timorese would be permitted to choose between autonomy within Indonesia or independence. The president appears to have blithely assumed they would choose the former. UN officials, on the other hand, understood both the Timorese passion for independence and the backlash it would produce. The UN had gained a great deal of experience organizing elections in dangerous and chaotic settings since doing so in Cambodia in 1993, and Habibie agreed to let them run the popular consultation in East Timor. Annan pressed Habibie to accept an armed force to protect UN civilians during what was bound to be a very turbulent period, but the Indonesians insisted that the army and police would provide security. These were the same forces that had kept the island under their thumb for decades; they would not be pleased at the prospect of losing control. "We were like the dog lying on its back with its throat exposed," as Kieran Prendergast says. But there was no choice. On May 5, Indonesia, Portugal, and the UN agreed to hold a popular consultation in mid-June.

By all accounts, the UN mission, known as UNAMET, did an extraordinary job of organizing a ballot in a desperately impoverished country with no tradition of elections. Militia forces in league with the Indonesian army terrorized the Timorese and did their best to intimidate the unarmed civilians. Annan was forced to delay the election twice and might well have put it off altogether had not the Timorese people so passionately embraced the opportunity to determine their fate. On August 30, an astonishing 98 percent of eligible voters went to the polls. On the morning of September 4, it was announced that almost 80 percent of Timorese had voted for independence. This was the signal for organized militia violence to begin. Gangs of young men moved from village to village, killing with machetes and burning with jerricans of gasoline. Political figures were hunted down and murdered; virtually the entire population was forced to flee into the hills. And the Indonesian army, plainly in league with the militias, was abetting the violence rather than trying to control it.

Kofi Annan almost always responded to crisis in the same way: he would get on the phone and talk to the heads of state and foreign ministers of the protagonists and their allies, or anyone else who might have influence on the parties. Often, as with Kosovo or, ultimately, with Iraq—anyplace where the United States had a deep interest—the action moved beyond him, and he was helpless. But Portugal and Australia, the chief supporters of the Timorese, had no wish to act unilaterally. And Annan seemed to be the one person Habibie would trust, and even listen to. So from the outset, Annan played a central role in a dedicate, complex, and frighteningly fast-moving situation. The killings had unavoidable echoes of Rwanda and, more immediately, of Kosovo. The UN had failed in Kosovo. Another such failure would render Annan's doctrine of humanitarian intervention—and indeed the UN itself—a grotesque irrelevance.

But the geopolitics of the situation was not promising. East Timor was a remote place of absolutely no importance; Indonesia was one of the colossi of the developing world and an important ally of China. What's more, both China and Russia had stated that they would veto any force to which the Indonesians did not consent, just as they were prepared to do in Kosovo. Neither state, for obvious reasons, put much stock in "the sovereignty of peoples." And Malaysia and several other developing countries on the council were equally adamant about Indonesia's sovereign rights. Annan's only hope was to somehow persuade the Indonesians—not only Habibie, but the military—to swallow their pride and request an international force. And at the same time he would have to persuade nations in the region—and thus acceptable to Indonesia—to join that force, and to be prepared to deploy within days.

By the end of August, Annan had begun speaking daily with Habibie, urging him to instruct military officials to enforce order. These conversations had an unnerving air of unreality. The exchanges, Annan recalls, typically ran as follows:

"Mr. President, the situation is desperate, they're burning the places down."

"No, the report I'm getting is that these are Indonesians who after all these years are disappointed to leave, and they're burning their own homes and cars rather than leaving it behind for others."

"No, that's not the case."

"But I have the military report right *here*."

Annan assumed that the military was feeding Habibie misinformation, but he could never be sure who, if anyone, was calling the shots. Certainly neither the president nor his military chiefs wanted to acknowledge the truth. Movements for independence or autonomy were sprouting from end to end of the vast archipelago; giving the Timorese their independence would embolden the freedom movements elsewhere.

On September 5, the day after the worst of the violence began, Prime Minister John Howard told Annan that Australia would lead the multinational force. This was a critical breakthrough, since Australia had close ties with Indonesia and also possessed a highly professional army not to be trifled with. Annan called Habibie that night and urged him to accept the deployment of a "security component." Habibie demurred, but said he was thinking of declaring martial law in the territory.

With the violence reaching apocalyptic levels, Annan kept turning the wheel inch by painstaking inch. By the sixth, he had won the president's agreement that if the Indonesian military could not restore peace within twenty-four to forty-eight hours, an outside force would do so. He then explained the terms of the understanding in phone calls to Xanana Gusmão, the jailed leader of the Timorese rebel army, for Gusmão would have to instruct his lieutenants to accept such a force.

He also briefed Clinton, Howard, and Prime Minister António Guterres of Portugal. For the previous week, Kieran Prendergast had been trying to persuade the Security Council to send a mission to Indonesia and East Timor to demonstrate their seriousness; finally they had agreed. Annan briefed the ambassadors who would be going, urging them to drive home the twenty-four- to forty-eight-hour deadline. He then issued a public statement declaring that if the violence were not brought quickly under control, "the international community will have to consider what other measures it can take to assist the Indonesian government." He spoke again with President Clinton, asking for American help with the rapid-deployment force. But Clinton, despite brave words on East Timor, made no offer.

At 2:00 on the morning of the eighth, Prendergast was awoken by a call from Ian Martin, the head of UNAMET, saying that militia forces were besieging the compound. He would have to withdraw, for the lives of hundreds of unarmed UN officials were at risk. Prendergast called Annan, who immediately called Habibie. It was now 3:25 a.m. The president woolgathered for an hour, claiming that all was well. The secretary-general, a listener of epic patience, absorbed it all, then politely but firmly insisted that this was not so, and reminded the president of his pledge. Annan conferred once again with the heads of state of countries he was hoping would join the rapid-deployment force, including President Clinton, as well as of nations on the Security Council. At 11:30 that night he spent another half hour trying fruitlessly to get Habibie to request a foreign force. "You could see he was in a very difficult situation," says the ever-sympathetic Annan. "His country was falling apart, there was lots of international pressure on him to act, and internally he wasn't a Sukarno or a Suharto," whose unchallenged authority would have seen him through any such crisis.

By the following day, the security situation around the UNAMET compound had grown desperate. Annan worried that the twelve hundred refugees who had taken shelter in the compound would be helpless if the mission departed; instead, he ordered a partial withdrawal. Eighty staff members had volunteered to stay behind while the others were evacuated. Militia members fired weapons and entered the school in the compound where many of the refugees had gathered. One militia member played with a grenade at the entrance. Indonesian soldiers watched or pitched in. "We passed a terrible night—for some of us, the worst night of our lives," says Nicholas Birnback, a former Air Force officer and veteran of some of the hairiest of peacekeeping missions. If he and others left, Birnback assumed, the militias would wreak vengeance on the local UN staff members they left behind. So they stayed.

By this time, President Clinton had finally found a way of applying American power by threatening to block loans from the World Bank and the IMF if the violence continued. Annan himself ratcheted up the pressure, publicly declaring on September 10 that "the time has clearly come for Indonesia to seek help from the international community." He had now assembled a truly multinational force, and he listed the nations that had agreed to join. And he raised the prospect of war-crimes tribunals for those responsible for the orchestrated violence. On the eleventh, the Security Council mission, which had been stalled in Jakarta, was finally permitted to fly to East Timor's capital, Dili, where they were able to witness for themselves a scene of incomprehensible destruction, all wrought within the space of a single week. General Wiranto, Indonesia's top military officer, had also come to Dili. He was plainly shocked by what he saw, though some UN officials believe that Wiranto had already decided to accept the international force and was now engaged in something of a pantomime. Wiranto's arrival also put a swift end to the threats at the UN compound. In New York, the Security Council held an open meeting at which fifty delegations spoke about East Timor; even Russia, China, and India urged the Indonesians to accept an outside force. This was not, after all, an "intervention" but a mission in support of the government of Indonesia—at least officially.

On Sunday the twelfth, the council mission returned to Jakarta and went to the presidential palace to demand that Habibie relent. But Habibie would make this concession only to Annan. Keeping the diplomats waiting, he called the secretary-general and issued a formal request for a UN-mandated force "as soon as possible." He was sending his foreign minister to New York right away to work out the details. "From my side," the president said, "there are no conditions." Annan thanked him for his courageous decision and immediately called Gusmão, Prime Minister Howard, and Prime Minister Guterres. On September 15, the Security Council unanimously passed a resolution authorizing a multinational force, to be known as INTERFET. And five days later, an Australian-led force of twenty-five hundred waded ashore. It was the fastest emergency deployment since the UN first sent a force into Congo in 1960.

Was this the realization of the doctrine Annan had promulgated in Ditchley? Not quite. For years, the Security Council had looked on with placid unconcern while Indonesia squeezed the life from its helpless territory. The response to the crisis had been swift, but not swift enough: by the time the multinational force arrived, after all, there was virtually nothing left of East Timor to preserve. A united Security Council could have forced the Indonesians to accept the multinational force earlier, or could have voted to go in anyway—the essence of the doctrine of humanitarian intervention. Richard Holbrooke, the U.S. ambassador, who played an important role both in pressuring the Clinton administration and in rallying council members, got it about right when he said that the intervention was just what Roosevelt and Churchill had dreamed of when they founded the UN; "it only took twenty years, a staggering number of wasted lives, and pillaging and rampaging by the Indonesian military."

But whatever good had been accomplished would have been unimaginable absent Annan's own tireless engagement. Operating under the same limits that he had faced in Kosovo—more severe, in some ways—he had been able to shape the situation so that this time it was the UN that brought an end to hostilities. In talking with Habibie, he had combined flattery, persuasion, and threat with the mastery of a great chef. He so thoroughly made himself the president's lifeline that Danilo Türk, a UN political affairs official deeply involved with the discussions, says, "Whenever we raised anything, Habibie would say, 'I've already talked to the SG about that,' or, 'I will talk to the SG about that.'" But Annan also marshaled world opinion, leaving the Indonesians to feel that they had no choice but to capitulate, even though they could have blocked council action by withholding consent.

With each new crisis, Annan was exploring the ambit of his authority, and that of his institution. In matters of the highest importance to the great powers, and above all to the United States, such as the standoff with Iraq, he could squeeze out a role for himself only with great persistence and circumspection, and even then he, and the UN, could be brushed aside at any moment. But on any issue that did not implicate the vital interests of the five veto-bearing members of the Security Council, Annan at least had room to maneuver, both through quiet diplomacy and through public rhetoric. The great limiting factor, in all such cases, was the political will of the member states.

CHAPTER SEVEN

The Exquisite Ironies
of Benevolent Colonialism

U N PEACEKEEPING HAD SUFFERED THE INSTITUTIONAL equivalent of post-traumatic stress syndrome in the aftermath of Somalia, Bosnia, and Rwanda. Between 1996 and 1998, the Security Council authorized only one sizable new mission, in eastern Slavonia, a province of Croatia. This owed something to coincidence, since in the years after 1995 very few conflicts had been settled in a way amenable to UN engagement. But it was also true that the fiascoes of the mid-1990s had discredited peacekeeping, and indeed the UN itself, for it was above all through the deployment of blue helmets that the UN realized its founding ideals. Boutros Boutros-Ghali had shown no interest in examining failures in which he himself might have had a part. In late 1996, when Prince Zeid Ra'ad Zeid al-Hussein arrived in New York as Jordan's UN ambassador, he was shocked to discover that Srebrenica had disappeared down a memory hole. Zeid had just completed a two-year stint as political affairs officer for UNPROFOR, and his disgust at the mission's cult of neutrality was still fresh. He teamed up with the ambassadors from Bosnia and Croatia to push for a thoroughgoing investigation of the UN's role. The following year, the three men met with Shashi Tharoor and Hedi Annabi to explore the idea. "Their attitude," says Zeid, "was that they would just put together the reports the UN had been writing during that time. We said, 'No, it's going to have to be a serious document. And if you try to down-scale it, the story is going to get out anyway.'"

The secretariat had no wish to expose its dirty laundry. Zeid and his confederates, having begun aboveboard, decided to operate below-decks. First they persuaded a producer at *Sixty Minutes* to demand access to secret cables, and then they got Bianca Jagger, at the time a high-profile activist, to call for an investigation. Though Annan's repu-tation rests in no small part on his resolute insistence on anatomizing past UN failure, the truth is that he capitulated to, rather than de-manded, a report exposing the failures of the office which he had run. "We had to drag him through the mud to get to this position," says Zeid, who was confounded by the resistance of a figure with whom he had worked closely in the Balkans and whom he deeply respected. In November 1998, the General Assembly passed a resolution calling for a report assessing the UN's role in the rape of Srebrenica.

Responsibility for the report fell to Iqbal Riza. The *chef de cabinet* had no wish to "down-scale" the study, for he believed that much of the UN, including some of his own colleagues in the peacekeeping depart-ment, had been far too willing to accept the bona fides of the Serbs. And so the report was assigned to David Harland and Salman Ahmed, two of the most brilliant young officials at UN headquarters. Both had served with UNPROFOR during this crucial period, and neither had any illusions about the UN's performance.

Harland and Ahmed spent six months interviewing officials, includ-ing leading political and military figures in Bosnia, Croatia, and Serbia; European and American diplomatic and political figures; journalists and scholars; and virtually every UN official who played an important role in this endless drama, up to and including then-Secretary-General Boutros Boutros-Ghali. The report, a book-length 100,000 or so words, offered an exhaustive account of the decisions made by all the major players, and the consequences of those decisions, from the establish-ment of the safe havens policy to the cataclysm at Srebrenica, and was scathingly critical both of the member states and of the Secretariat.

Riza assigned the all-important "Assessment" section of the report to his former aide in the Balkans, Nader Mousavizadeh, whose views were at least as hawkish as Harland's or Ahmed's. Mousavizadeh's con-clusions were extremely harsh. The summary section, written as if in Annan's own voice, declares that Boutros-Ghali, his senior advisers—including Annan and Shashi Tharoor—and his chief representatives in the Balkans failed to use airpower even when it was clear that nothing else could have deterred the Serbs. They had failed at times to give the Security Council an honest accounting of Serb atrocities, in part owing to "a general tendency to assume that the parties were equally responsible for the transgressions that had occurred." Officials in the field had engaged in negotiations with war criminals like General Ratko Mladić that at times "amounted to appeasement." And the report suggested that these failures had their origin in the culture and collective psychology of the Secretariat, which had so come to see itself as a bulwark against "the culture of death"—a phrase used by Boutros-Ghali—that it could not accept the imperative to use force.

The report was every bit as uncompromising on "the community of nations" represented in the Security Council, declaring that neither an arms embargo nor a peacekeeping force nor humanitarian aid constituted an adequate response to a "problem which cried out for a political/military solution." The council had, in effect, insisted on a fantasy—that the Serbs would abide by the rules—which the Secretariat had proved all too willing to execute. In Srebrenica, as again later in Kosovo, the report concluded, "the international community tried to reach a negotiated settlement with an unscrupulous and murderous regime. In both instances it required the use of force to bring a halt to the planned and systematic killing and expulsion of civilians."

The Srebrenica report had to navigate a gauntlet of internal criticism. Many current and former officials in the departments of political affairs and peacekeeping objected, sometimes furiously, both to assertions about specific actions and to the report's broader moral claims about the failed doctrine of neutrality. Mousavizadeh recalls fierce line-by-line arguments with Tharoor, who had served as the DPKO desk officer on the Balkans. John Ruggie says that his chief responsibility was to "offer a shield" to the three authors "and to make sure that what they wanted to say got as far as Kofi." Riza, too, protected these young officials from the wrath of their seniors. And in fact the report that Annan saw was the report that the three had written. And despite his own role, Annan, according to all three authors, changed nothing, though he did insist on removing the names of UN officials when specific actions were cited.

Annan was less inclined to shine a light on the UN's other shameful failure. In June 1998 he had traveled to Rwanda in order to deliver an extremely belated apology. But he had given the distinct impression that he was apologizing on behalf of someone or something else. At a press conference in Nairobi, his last stop before Rwanda, he had characterized criticism of the peacekeeping department's role as "an old story which is being rehashed" and had added, categorically, "I have no regrets." In Kigali, he was preceded to the podium by Rwanda's foreign minister, who delivered a scathing attack on the UN's failure to protect the Rwandan people, first during the genocide and then in the refugee camps. Annan was startled and offended. And though aides had suggested that in Kigali he speak informally and from the heart, he delivered his speech in his usual wooden and impersonal style. And though he said that "the world must deeply repent this failure," he said nothing of his own sense of repentance. Worse still, he made a point of reminding his listeners that the genocidal violence "came from within," a hard truth which, as victims of that violence, they were in no mood to hear. The visit was a disaster.

Annan really didn't feel personally culpable (as he was to make clear to me in our later conversations). "He's a bureaucrat by temperament and training," as Edward Mortimer says. "His way of thinking is 'I was doing the job assigned to me; I was not really the main person responsible.' " But, says Mortimer, Annan "came to understand that, politically, Rwanda was a millstone around his neck." The UN had to face Rwanda, as it had to face Srebrenica. In March 1999, Annan agreed to establish an independent inquiry into the genocide; the panel published its report in mid-December, one month after the Srebrenica report appeared.

The Rwanda report proved every bit as devastating as the Bosnia one had. The panel concluded that even the modest force of twenty-five hundred peacekeepers present when the violence broke out should have been able to "stop or at least limit" the massacres. It had not, because virtually every aspect of the peacekeeping process had failed: UN officials had missed the warning signs of impending disaster and then soft-pedaled the truth to the Security Council, while the council itself had provided the force with an impossibly weak mandate. And then, once the killing began, "the instinctive reaction within the Secretariat seems to have been to question the feasibility of an active United

Nations response, rather than actively investigating the possibility strengthening the operation to deal with new challenges on the ground." But the panel concluded that the troop-contributing countries that had withdrawn their soldiers or ordered them to keep out of harm's way, and the Security Council members who had pressed for a total withdrawal of the force, had shown the same ignominious instincts. Ultimately, the Rwanda report described the same collective cognitive failure, or act of willful blindness, that the Srebrenica report had found: the insistence on characterizing a situation as amenable to traditional UN instruments despite the increasingly transparent reality that it could be resolved only by force.

Annan was initially inclined to dispute aspects of the report. He thought that the UN had come in for too large a share of blame because the Secretariat had opened its files to the panel, while the important member states had made far less available. "We felt that they pulled their punches," he says. But his advisers persuaded the secretary-general that this was a fight he could not win and should not wage. Annan accepted the report as it was written. And in his letter transmitting it to the council, he adopted a very different tone from the one he had used the year before. "All of us must bitterly regret that we did not do more to prevent [the genocide]," he wrote. "On behalf of the United Nations, I acknowledge this failure and express my deep remorse."

Even the harshest critic of the institution would have been hard put to dispute Annan's assertion that the report, as well as the earlier one on the Balkans, "reflects a determination to present the truth about these calamities." The UN had never subjected itself to such painful self-scrutiny. Nor, of course, had most of its member states, including the democratic ones. Whether or not Annan actually experienced the sense of remorse he expressed, his willingness to accept institutional blame, as Boutros-Ghali never would, demonstrated that it really was a new day at the UN, that the institution, or at least the secretary-general, understood how very deep and urgent was the need for change. Though both reports reflected badly on Annan's role in an earlier day, this act of humility and transparency had the effect of enhancing his standing as a moral actor.

If the period from 1995 to 1998 had offered little business for UN peacekeepers, 1999 and 2000 provided a bumper crop of cease-fires, peace agreements, and half-open windows of opportunity—not only in Kosovo and East Timor, but in Sierra Leone and the Democratic Republic of the Congo as well. And by this time not only the UN Secretariat but the chief troop-contributing countries and the major powers had gained a much clearer idea of what UN peacekeeping could and could not do. This was especially true of the Clinton administration, whose grandiose ambitions for the UN had splintered on the rocks of Bosnia.

The transformation of American foreign policy played a crucial role in the revival of the UN. Somalia, Bosnia, Rwanda, and Haiti had put an end to all the bright talk of "assertive multilateralism," a phrase Madeleine Albright had coined, and lived to regret. But these post–Cold War battlefields, localized but savage, also demonstrated that America could not withdraw into a peaceable and mercantile relationship with the world. The world needed American power, which had turned the tide in the Balkans and in Haiti. And stability in both places clearly served important American interests. America would act where it needed to, and where it could; that was the essence of the national security document PDD-25. And the UN had a crucial, if sharply circumscribed, role in this new dispensation. As Nancy Soderberg, a former Clinton administration national security official, writes in *The Superpower Myth*, "The UN would be left to political negotiations where there is a peace to make and to peacekeeping where there is a peace to keep. The UN and regional organizations other than NATO would focus on institution and capacity building, and NATO and coalitions of capable forces, led by the United States, would take on the wars, or so-called enforcement operations."

This was, in fact, precisely the formula that the United States and its NATO allies, the UN, and various European bodies worked out in Kosovo. NATO fought the war, but returned to the Security Council for a resolution retrospectively blessing the war effort and mapping out the postwar terrain—unlike in Bosnia, where the terms of settlement were determined by a conference among the combatants. There could be no question of sending UN peacekeeping troops into a place as volatile as Kosovo, any more than there had been in Bosnia; forty thousand NATO troops fanned out across this tiny province. But while the

Dayton Accords had divided authority for the civil administration of
Bosnia among the UN, the European Union, and the Organization for
Security and Co-operation in Europe, the Security Council vested civil
control in the UN, with the two European regional bodies, among
others, reporting to an SRSG. Here was a straightforward statement,
in institutional terms, of what the UN could and couldn't do. The
subsequent nation-building effort in Kosovo proved far slower and
more frustrating than anyone had imagined at the time, but that says
more about the inherent limitations of the undertaking than about the
assignment of powers.

In the first days of 1999, unfamiliar men began to appear in the streets
of eastern Freetown, the capital of Sierra Leone. The men said they
were fleeing from the marauding rebel force that had been laying waste
to much of the country's interior. In fact, they were the rebels' advance
guard. On January 6, they commenced what the rebels called, with characteristically grisly humor, Operation No Living Thing. The name
was all too accurate. Edmond Jah, a hotel clerk who lived in the neighborhood, said that he was awoken around midnight by shots and ran
outside into a nightmare: "The rebels were shooting at anyone, killing
babies, women, old men." Jah fled, and in the ensuing days he saw
stacks of bodies piled up outside the municipal hospital, rebels advanc-
ing using women as human shields, and Nigerian soldiers, making a
desperate stand at the road that led up to the president's house, shooting the women and then killing the insurgents. By the time the rebels
had been repulsed, after two weeks, as many as six thousand civilians
lay dead. Thousands of women had been raped, and thousands of men,
women, and children had had their hands chopped off—the rebels' dis-
tinctive signature in human flesh.

Sierra Leone's president, Ahmad Tejan Kabbah, a former UN official, appealed to Kofi Annan, his old colleague and fellow West African,
for UN peacekeeping assistance. At this very moment, NATO was
threatening to bomb Slobodan Milošević into submission unless he
withdrew his forces from Kosovo. But there was no appetite for intervention in this remote and strategically insignificant corner of Africa,
and the UN was not about to send a peacekeeping mission into the

midst of a maelstrom once again. Madeleine Albright visited Freetown and saw for herself the horrors that the rebels had perpetrated. But, as she writes in her memoirs, "the lesson of Somalia was that [the UN] invited disaster when it took sides in a conflict. The lesson of Rwanda was that the UN invited disaster when it heeded the lesson of Somalia . . . The solution to these conflicts had therefore to be found through diplomacy, with outside force introduced rarely and selectively." And so Sierra Leone got diplomacy. Annan sent a special representative to seek a settlement between President Kabbah and Foday Sankoh, a cashiered junior officer who since 1991 had led the rebel force, known as the RUF, on its maniacal sprees through the countryside.

By 1999, President Kabbah had run through all his sources of protection. The Sierra Leone army, whose conscripts earned two dollars a day, had long since melted into the opposition forces; citizens had coined the term "sobel" to describe soldiers who wore the national uniform by day and joined the rebels at night. Kabbah's predecessor, in desperation, had turned to a South African mercenary firm, Executive Outcomes, which had almost single-handedly beaten back a rebel attack in 1995; but Kabbah had been forced to dispense with the firm when he signed a peace agreement in November 1996. The pact crumbled almost immediately, and Kabbah had to flee to neighboring Guinea along with 200,000 civilians. In March 1998, Nigerian soldiers, acting on behalf of a regional organization called the Economic Community of West African States, or ECOWAS, retook Freetown and restored Kabbah to power. But after this latest assault, the Nigerians had tired of fighting Foday Sankoh's drug-crazed teenagers, and Kabbah was forced once again to sue for peace. In July 1999, the president agreed to accept the rebels into the government, while the RUF agreed to lay down its arms and reconstitute itself as a political party, as if the group had ever stood for some principle greater than self-enrichment through violence. Kabbah was even forced to give the repellent Sankoh the Ministry of Mines, thus formalizing the RUF's control over the diamond mines that had long been Sierra Leone's treasure, and its curse.

Now, at last, the Security Council could answer Sierra Leone's entreaty. In October, the council authorized a peacekeeping force of six thousand to monitor the terms of the agreement and to carry out such key tasks as the "disarmament, demobilization and reintegration" of the country's forty-five thousand or so soldiers. The peacekeeping department then began to canvass traditional troop-contributing countries, but no Western country would send its soldiers into this hellhole. Only India, among countries with highly professional armies, agreed to send troops. The rest of the contingent would be made up of soldiers from the ECOWAS countries—Nigeria, Guinea, Ghana—as well as from Zambia and Kenya.

Sierra Leone was probably the most dangerous environment into which UN peacekeepers had been introduced since Bosnia. The government's writ barely extended beyond President Kabbah's mansion at the brow of one of Freetown's highest hills; in fact, the president rarely left the mansion save to speed to the airport. Sierra Leone had no army and no police. And despite the documents Foday Sankoh had signed, he and his ragtag followers had obviously not given up their hopes of taking the country by force. The rebels began testing these new recruits the moment they arrived, and they quickly discovered just how flimsy they were. The Guinean contingent had orders not to engage until they joined the main force, so they meekly surrendered their weapons when RUF soldiers accosted them after they crossed the border. The Zambian contingent, too, was disarmed. Annan feared that a fiasco was brewing. UNAMSIL, as the mission was called, was the first peacekeeping mission in a really dangerous place in three years; if it failed, the UN might not be asked again. In January 2000, after the soldiers had been humiliated, he asked the Security Council to increase the troop ceiling to eleven thousand and to strengthen the mandate, and the council agreed.

I arrived in Freetown in April, during an interval of relative tranquillity, and flew to the Indian encampment at Daru, in the east. Over the previous two months, the Indians had pushed farther eastward over the shattered, swaybacked roads that sliced through the jungle. They had established a beachhead in Kailahun, seventy miles to the east, an RUF bastion where the rebellion had begun almost a decade earlier. There they'd found a town where trees were growing through the middle of houses, and no one but soldiers remained. And they had begun a campaign to win over the locals. The peacekeepers had brought in a doctor who treated the rebels, no question asked, and even requisitioned a helicopter to bring the more severely wounded to Freetown. They dug a well and brought in water-purification equipment. People began trickling back into town; in Daru, the Indian base, the population rose from three thousand to thirty thousand. And the Indians had found their own firm but nonlethal way of dealing with intransigence. Lieutenant Colonel Amit Sharma, who acted as my guide, told me that in mid-February a large Indian convoy had been stopped by a roadblock in a place called Bendu Junction. By this time he had gotten to know the local RUF leaders, and he had been called in to mediate. "Look, guys, you know we can't let this stand," he said.

"We've got orders not to let UNAMSIL pass," the soldier in charge replied. The convoy stayed; more rebels arrived. After thirty-six hours, four hundred or so rebels, clutching AK-47s, were gathered on the other side of the roadblock. Finally Sharma said, "We're leaving, but you're going to see us again." UNAMSIL got word through to Foday Sankoh, and several days later the regional RUF commander personally escorted them through Bendu Junction.

The Indians struck me as highly professional peacekeepers, but the truth was that their professionalism, and their campaign to win hearts and minds, were completely wasted on the RUF. The rebels feared the Nigerians, who could be almost as ruthless as they were; they had learned that they did not have to fear the peacekeepers, who talked but did not shoot. On May 1, only weeks after I left, the rebels seized five hundred peacekeepers, chiefly Kenyan and Zambian, but some Indians as well. Back in New York I wondered if some of my exquisitely polite and gently chaffing Indian pals were sitting with guns pointed at their heads. Unlike the earlier incidents, the kidnapping was widely reported. The UN, it seemed, had learned nothing from its failures. The Security Council had dispatched troops at the invitation of a coalition government, but the coalition, and thus the invitation, was only a legal formality. The peacekeepers had proved unwilling or unable to speak the only language the rebels understood: the language of force. The most ambitious mission since Bosnia was looking like Bosnia redux.

And yet it turned out that the rebels had overplayed their hand. The British, despite their usual engagement with former colonies, had remained passive while Sierra Leone descended into madness. But now, amid fears of a fresh attack on Freetown, Prime Minister Tony

Blair evacuated British and other nationals, and then sent a force of seven hundred paratroopers to Freetown. Seven Royal Navy warships arrived offshore with a fleet of jet aircraft and attack helicopters. It was the largest British mobilization since the Falklands, in 1982. And the British, operating wholly outside the UN chain of command or mandate, accomplished almost effortlessly what their predecessors had achieved only by wading through blood: they confronted and disarmed a particularly vicious gang known as the West Side Boys, established roadblocks and fortified positions, trained and patrolled with UNAMSIL troops, secured the airport, and pushed the rebels to release the hostages. And they were able to begin drawing down their forces within weeks. It was a dramatic demonstration of what could have been accomplished at almost any time in the past—before so much devastation and agony—with a sufficient show of force.

The British intervention was a shock to the RUF, which until then had operated with virtual impunity. Emboldened by the sudden swing of fortune, the outraged citizens of Freetown marched on Foday Sankoh's home. Sankoh fled in women's clothing, and then was captured, stripped naked, and paraded through the streets before being handed over to government officials to be tried for war crimes. And the UN was emboldened as well. The Nigerians agreed to send three thousand more soldiers to reinforce UNAMSIL. The United States would not send troops, but it would use Sierra Leone as a test case for its somewhat erratic commitment to peacekeeping. Over the summer, the Security Council passed a series of resolutions increasing UNAMSIL's size and requiring peacekeepers to go after the RUF more aggressively, calling for the creation of a war-crimes tribunal, and passing an embargo on the "conflict diamonds" that were the rebels' chief source of wealth. The Indian force commander was stripped of his post. Both the Indian contingent and another from Jordan refused to serve in the redefined mission; UNAMSIL lost five thousand soldiers almost overnight. But Pakistan, eager to demonstrate its military prowess and to show up its regional rival, agreed to send a large and heavily armed contingent.

In May 2001, Hedi Annabi, deputy head of peacekeeping, traveled to RUF headquarters in the north to deliver a message: "We're increasing to 17,500 troops, and we're going to deploy 4,000 Pakistanis in your heartland, and they mean business." After that, Annabi says, "things started to turn around as the RUF began to understand that pursuing a military option was no longer viable." By January 2002, 45,000 soldiers had been disarmed. In May 2002, President Kabbah was reelected in a ballot beset, but at least not wholly undermined, by fraud. UNAMSIL began to shift from peacekeeping to "peace-building." The British trained a new national army, while Commonwealth countries worked to rebuild the police force. Sierra Leone remained one of the most profoundly impoverished countries in the world, but the consuming air of menace had dissipated. By 2005, only 3,200 of the 17,500 UN troops remained; many of the others were moved to the crisis next door, in Liberia. The people of Sierra Leone had had to endure unspeakable suffering, and then prostrate themselves at the feet of their tormentors, before UN peacekeepers would arrive on the scene. But once the UN had stopped trying to adapt Sierra Leone's reality to its own limits, and instead changed the limits in order to deal with the reality, it had risen to the challenge and learned how to operate in a dangerous place. Sierra Leone demonstrated that it was very hard, but not impossible, to adapt peacekeeping to the post–Cold War world of warlords and failed states.

When I arrived at the airport in Dili in March 2000, a Timorese employee of the UN took my passport and stamped it with the insignia of UNTAET—United Nations Transitional Administration in East Timor. East Timor was not a country, like Sierra Leone; it was a province of a larger state, but one that had been granted the opportunity to choose independence. The only thing standing in the way of East Timor's actually becoming a country was the fact that it had nothing—no army or police, no doctors, teachers, nurses, accountants, lawyers, and no buildings to put them in. The revered resistance leader, Xanana Gusmão, emerging from years in an Indonesian prison, freely acknowledged that East Timor wasn't ready to fly its own flag. And so sovereignty had been temporarily vested in the UN.

The militias had largely fled before the Australian force, and the Timorese themselves, from Gusmão down to the ordinary citizen, seemed remarkably free from the wish to avenge themselves on their former oppressors. Crime operated on a small scale, perhaps because there was almost nothing to steal. And the chief border problem was coaxing citizens who had fled to West Timor back home, despite threats from militia groups in the west. On the other hand, the country was a blank. Hansjoerg Strohmeyer, the mission's counsel and a veteran of the rebuilding effort in the Balkans, said, "In Kosovo we had judges, lawyers, prosecutors; the problem was finding one who didn't have a Yugoslav past or a Serbian collaborator past. Here, you don't have a single lawyer." Strohmeyer had tracked down all seventy law-school graduates remaining in East Timor; thanks to the logic of Indonesian domination, none had been permitted to practice law. The militias had also burned or stolen every law book in East Timor and wrecked all the courthouses. Andrew Whitley, the head of the Civil Service, had had so much trouble finding Timorese with the credentials for even middle-rank jobs that he had been forced to advertise in Indonesia. He would, he said, consider anyone who hadn't been "formally accused of a major crime," like burning down a neighbor's house.

There was something almost comical about the UN's role as East Timor's last colonial master. UNTAET operated from the Governor's House, a lovely, colonnaded structure facing the ocean that had served as the headquarters for both the Portuguese and the Indonesian administrations. Sergio Vieira de Mello, the "transitional administrator," worked from the same spacious second-floor office that had housed his Indonesian predecessor. The East Timor Authority, as the new state apparatus was called, was quartered in an auditorium behind the Governor's House. The international civil servants who had been charged with inventing this new state sat on a raised gallery around the rim of the building; you could tell which ministry you had reached by the name tacked on the back of their computers—Civil Service, Water Supply, Agriculture, Judicial Affairs, and so on.

UNTAET was engaged in nation-building in the most literal sense, operating from cleared ground not only physically but conceptually. The effort at times seemed to be taking place in a laboratory, as if the political philosophers' notional "state of nature" had been realized for the purpose of a real-life experiment. The Security Council had vested the transitional administrator with virtually dictatorial powers, but stipulated that he was to work "in close consultation and cooperation with the Timorese people," in whose name, after all, the UN was ruling. Thus the first statute Vieira de Mello passed, or rather decreed, delineated UNTAET's own authority and stipulated that Indonesian law would remain in force save where it conflicted with UN human rights standards or the UN mandate. Everything had to be developed *ab ovo*. UNTAET could not pay its employees until it had promulgated a banking law and settled on a currency, nor punish lawbreakers without a body of criminal law.

But of course East Timor wasn't a Rousseauean pastoral; it was a prostrate and desperate place. The UN, working with aid organizations, had to feed people whose livelihoods had been destroyed and house people whose homes had been torched; driving through the countryside, you could see Timorese unloading galvanized zinc sheets for roofing from UN trucks and then trudging through the woods to their homes like long lines of snails, their houses carried on their backs. The UN coordinated the vast program of resettlement for the 70 percent of the population that had fled. The UN flew currency into the island and distributed it by helicopter to government employees.

It was an astonishing exercise even when it failed, as it often did, but at the heart of the whole affair was the paradox of benevolent colonialism. The UN was busily hammering the square pegs of Western norms, Western institutions, Western jurisprudence into the round holes of Timor's traditional culture. Is this what the Timorese wanted? How could one know? What's more, the UN had given the hammers to Western experts. What had happened to the imperative of building the Timorese capacity for self-government? And if you did everything for the Timorese, what would happen when you left? In one of his first acts, Vieira de Mello had set up a National Consultative Council of leading Timorese figures, and he had a close and trusting relationship with Gusmão, but it was the UN official who held all the power. In July, he would replace the consultative council with another body consisting wholly of Timorese and establish a new cabinet whose posts were shared equally between Timorese and internationals. The auditorium of technocrats would give way to the East Timor Transitional Administration. Nevertheless, real power still flowed from the Security Council mandate to the UN mission, and the previously patient Gusmão complained that he was sick of receiving regulations from the

Governor's House and watching as international largesse was dispensed from the hundreds of white four-wheel-drive UN vehicles that dominated Dili's streets. Many of the private humanitarian workers who had flocked to Dili treated the spectacle, of which they themselves were a part, with equal contempt.

But the administrators themselves could not afford to be doctrinaire about the methods and mores of neocolonial rule. As David Harland, who was sent to East Timor to run the governance program soon after finishing the Srebrenica report, recalls, "You have these people who say, 'You fool, you've ignored local capacity.' But you have to take a real decision which affects real people about what you're going to do tomorrow. The Australians said, 'Okay, we're leaving, and we're turning the airport over to you.' I thought, 'Fine, I'll hire the downtrodden and culturally oppressed Timorese air controllers, and then I'll sit on the veranda and drink gin and tonics.' And then it turned out that the only Timorese air controller was in Indonesia. There was not a soul in East Timor who could run an airport." The same was true with finding a harbormaster for the port, and telephone technicians, and of course judges. And so Harland found internationals to do the job while Timorese were trained to take over. "Is there an inherent arrogance to that?" he asks. "Yes. But I'm not sure there was an alternative."

In *You, the People*, a study of UN transitional administrations, Simon Chesterman, a scholar of international law, describes the UNTAET mandate as "the most expansive assertion of sovereignty by the United Nations in its history." Yet the Timorese, despite complaints, submitted to UNTAET's yoke. At one point, in fact, Gusmão wanted to slow the drive to statehood lest East Timor be left on its own before its political institutions were ready. What made this peaceful transition possible was not only Gusmão's extraordinary patience and restraint but the fact that the Timorese knew that they would soon reach independence. They had no reason to suspect the UN of hidden imperialist designs. Indeed, East Timor's first elections, two years to the day from the referendum that sent the province reeling into the arms of the UN, "were so calm as to be almost boring," Chesterman writes—this despite a competition among sixteen parties. Gusmão was elected president in April 2002, and East Timor gained its sovereignty in May. Timor-Leste, as the new nation was known, reached independence as the poorest nation in the region. It remained, however, largely at peace.

For all its dire poverty, East Timor was less a test case than an ideal case of the state-building process. The obvious contrast was with Kosovo, another neglected and impoverished region that had been rescued by the international community and was now being administered by the UN in collaboration with the local government. But Kosovo, which I visited in early 2003, four and a half years after the Serb paramilitaries had fled, was a sullen, suspicious, profoundly gloomy place. Economic activity was nil, save for a thriving racket in guns, drugs, girls, and anything else that could be moved clandestinely across borders. The effort to integrate the remaining Serbs with the Albanian population had failed almost completely. The Serbs I met feared the Albanians they had once despised; the Albanians, with some very important exceptions, despised those they had previously feared. Serbs were increasingly gathering in homogeneous enclaves; the northern city of Mitrovica, near the border with Serbia, had become wholly Albanian south of the Ibar River, which bisected it, and wholly Serbian to the north. Kosovar leaders had grown thoroughly sick of UNMIK, the UN mission. "In five years, we have seen not a single act which shows Kosovo what is democracy, what is rule of law, what is justice," Ilir Deda, the prime minister's political adviser, bitterly told me.

It was true that Kosovo had no Xanana Gusmão—few places do. And it is also true that UNTAET had learned from some of UNMIK's mistakes. Officials in Kosovo had entrusted the criminal justice system to local lawyers and judges, who promptly reduced it to an instrument of punishment for the Serbs and impunity for Albanians. The East Timor mission had a heavier "footprint," in UN parlance, than the Kosovo one had. But the critical difference between the two missions lay in the prospects they held out to subject peoples. The Kosovars, like the Timorese, had suffered and fought in the name of independence. But this was precisely what the UN could not guarantee. Serbia still viewed the province as integral to its sovereignty, and both Russia and China supported its claims. The UN could not simply declare Kosovo an independent state; Serbia would have to agree. Even if the proto-government met the "standards" that UNMIK had set for it, Kosovo would qualify for only a *discussion* of its final status. And by the time I arrived in Priština, the Kosovar leadership class had lost whatever sense of incentive it once had to jump through the UN's hoops. NATO still had thirty-eight thousand soldiers in this tiny province. And they were needed: a few months after I left, the country erupted in riots between Albanians and Serbs.

By the middle of 2000, UN peacekeepers seemed to be committed everywhere; their numbers had grown from fifteen thousand a year earlier to forty-five thousand. And yet the institution had no such thing as a "peacekeeping doctrine." DPKO barely had the resources to manage its burgeoning portfolio, much less to codify a set of principles and procedures. Missions were cobbled together on the fly and thrust into utterly unfamiliar and often terrifying settings. The mission was often hopelessly overmatched by the setting, but the UN would blunder in nevertheless, like a novice surgeon learning on his hapless patients. Annan worried that this mismatch was bound to produce another catastrophe. Peacekeeping needed a doctrine not only to guide future missions but to limit future demands. In March, he convened a high-level panel on peace operations and asked Lakhdar Brahimi, his adviser and special envoy to Afghanistan, to chair the group. The panel delivered its report in August.

The Brahimi report was every bit as blunt, and as crisp, as the Srebrenica report (in part because much of the prose was crafted by Salman Ahmed, the co-author of the earlier study). Its central proposition was as follows: "There are many tasks which the United Nations peacekeeping forces should not be asked to undertake, and many places they should not go. But when the United Nations does send its forces to uphold the peace, they must be prepared to confront the lingering forces of war and violence with the ability and determination to defeat them." The idea that the UN should learn to say no was itself novel. Peacekeepers, Brahimi wrote, need "clear, credible and achievable mandates"; without them, or without "solid commitments from Member States" for the needed forces, the Security Council should refrain from action.

The panel argued that the UN had to adapt itself to a far messier world than the one for which it was created: "United Nations operations . . . do not deploy into post-conflict situations so much as they deploy to create such situations." Rather, peacekeepers seek to "divert the unfinished conflict . . . from the military to the political arena, and to make that diversion permanent." The old Marquis of Queensberry rules would no longer apply if UN troops were to confront the lingering forces of war and violence. Rules of engagement "should allow ripostes sufficient to silence a source of deadly fire," and at times should permit troops to take the battle to the adversary. Impartiality must not be mistaken for neutrality, "which can amount to a policy of appeasement"— a reference, of course, to the Balkans. And the Secretariat must demand all the force it needs, rather than "apply best-case planning assumptions to situations where the local actors have historically exhibited worst-case behavior." Brahimi also called for a rapid-deployment capability, to be filled either by standing reserves of military, police, and civilian officials or by "extremely reliable standby capacities."

The report placed peacekeeping at the center of a continuum of interventions, beginning with prevention and ending with peace-building. Only an environment with stable and self-sustaining institutions, Brahimi wrote, provides an exit strategy for peacekeeping. How to get there? The report reflected the painful lessons the UN had learned on securing the rule of law: "Where peace-building missions require it, international judicial experts, penal experts and human rights specialists, as well as civilian police, must be available in sufficient numbers to strengthen rule of law institutions." The report offered specific advice on strategies for disarmament, demobilization, and reintegration, on the centrality of human rights, on coordination among UN agencies. Brahimi also called for the development of a kind of National Security Council of peacekeeping, a body that would gather information about conflict situations, disseminate knowledge, and formulate policy analysis and long-term strategy.

The Brahimi report offered an eloquent argument for a far more systematic approach to peace operations. Brahimi noted that thirty-two officials at DPKO headquarters in New York were expected to supervise 27,365 peacekeepers, a "headquarters/field ratio" of 0.1 percent. No professional military would dream of operating this way. But of course UN peacekeeping had been a largely mechanical exercise for decades; only in the last year or so had it become plain that "transitional administrations" and deployment in chaos would be its lot. The Brahimi report offered a new doctrine for a new age, the first attempt to rethink peacekeeping since Boutros-Ghali's "Agenda for Peace" in 1992. That document took wing on what turned out to be a very brief gust of optimism. This one was many shades darker—an unillusioned policy for a chastened age.

The Brahimi report had a profound impact on the culture of peacekeeping. It gave Secretariat officials the courage and the cover to offer blunt assessments to the Security Council. The report, as well as the humiliating failures it described, forced the council to be more realistic about the mandates it drafted; "robust peacekeeping" became more than a contradiction in terms. But the institutional changes Brahimi championed never happened—no intelligence-gathering unit, no standby force of troops, no civil administrators or police held in reserve. The members did not, at bottom, want peacekeeping to be much more forceful, or perhaps much more effective, than it already was.

CHAPTER EIGHT

Romancing Cousin Jesse

THE UNITED STATES IS ONE OF THE VERY FEW COUNTRIES in the world whose foreign policy can be significantly shaped by its legislative as well as by its executive branch. Congress will normally defer to the president on international affairs so long as they are of the same party, or if the president is exceptionally popular. But after 1994, when the Republicans swept to power in both houses of Congress, a legislature dominated by conservatives faced a Democratic president who had been elected with 42 percent of the vote; they were determined to replace Clinton's agenda, as far as possible, with their own. And the UN was a rich target, both substantively and symbolically. To this new generation of conservatives, many of whom had never even traveled abroad, the UN, with its suave diplomats and its ideology of collective action, offered almost a perfect summation of the cosmopolitan, statist liberalism they had sworn to dismantle. And the seigneurial Boutros Boutros-Ghali, lecturing Americans on their global obligations, made the perfect hate object. Among the legislative items that Newt Gingrich, the Republican leader, had proposed when he introduced his so-called Contract with America in September 1994 was the National Security Restoration Act, which would have cut American spending on peacekeeping operations and prohibited the president from placing American troops under UN command save in cases of national security.

The act, like most of the contract, never became law, but by the

time Kofi Annan became secretary-general, resistance in Congress to
authorizing peacekeeping missions, and to paying both annual dues
and the separate peacekeeping assessment, had become an embarrassment for the United States, and a genuine crisis for the UN. Congress
had been periodically withholding funds from the UN since the 1980s,
demanding that the organization institute various reforms before receiving the balance. President George H.W. Bush, a committed internationalist, had managed to pay off some, but not all, of the backlog.
By 1996 the total debt had ballooned back up to $1.6 billion. That
same year Congress unilaterally declared that it would pay no more
than 25 percent of overall peacekeeping costs, rather than the 31 percent that the United States was assessed. Legislation circulating in
Congress also would lower America's overall assessment for the UN
budget from 25 to 22 percent of the total, and ultimately to 20 percent.

Annan understood that he had no more urgent task than changing
the perception of the UN among America's ruling elite. He had gone to
Washington in March 1997 on his very first trip as secretary-general,
even though doing so aggravated the impression that he was in the
American pocket. He had tried to explain why the UN was good for the
United States, how each needed the other, how deep and abiding
the American commitment to the institution had been. It had all been
very cordial, but he hadn't made much headway. "They don't understand," he had said to me at the time, "and I don't know how to explain
it to them." Annan was startled by the overt unilateralism, or even iso-
lationism, he encountered. "I know America," he said, "because I've
lived here. Americans don't like to be deadbeats. I feel frustrated and
saddened, because this isn't the America I know." Mark Malloch
Brown, a friend and former colleague then at the World Bank, had
challenged him to use his "Ronald Reagan–like ability" to go over the
heads of the diplomats and the legislators to speak directly to ordinary
people. And he had done that, giving speeches around the country. But
even the many Americans who thought well of the UN didn't care
enough to call their congressmen to account on the subject. Conservatives could beat up on the UN with impunity.

Annan said he wanted to go to Montana to talk to the Americans
who thought the UN had a fleet of black helicopters that they were using to deposit a fifth column around the country. But he probably need

have gone no farther than the House of Representatives. In the fall of 1997, the House easily approved the American Land Sovereignty Protection Act, which would have rescinded the designation of seventy-six American places as World Heritage sites or Biosphere Reserves and required congressional approval for any further designations. These essentially honorific titles had never before entered public debate; now they were seen as a threat to "sovereignty." Several months later I spoke with Roscoe Bartlett, a Maryland Republican who had served as one of the bill's sponsors. Bartlett claimed that 80 percent of his constituents opposed UN membership: "They think that our participation in the UN is infringing on our sovereignty, that it is infringing on our personal property rights. They are appalled when they go to one of our national parks and they see a sign that says, 'You are entering a UN Biosphere Reserve.'" By contrast, Bartlett solemnly explained, a group he called "globalists" "genuinely believe that our interests are best served if we become weaker and weaker and the UN becomes stronger and stronger, so they ultimately have a bigger army than we do, a bigger army than anybody has, so they can keep the world peace." Very few globalists lived in Bartlett's district. And there were dozens of Bartletts in Congress.

Not only had the American people voted into office a remarkable number of provincials who didn't own a passport and were proud of it, but very few of those who felt otherwise actually cared enough about the UN to take on the black-helicopter crowd. In late 1997, when Chris Smith, a New Jersey Republican and antiabortion zealot, drew up a bill prohibiting the United States from spending money on organizations that lobby in favor of abortion, Speaker Gingrich permitted him to attach it to the legislation withholding UN arrears absent reform. Gingrich fancied himself a worldly figure and suffered from no delusions about UN armies. The one time he had met Annan, at the annual Davos conference of the international elite, he had said, Annan recalled, "Kofi, you've got to get *The New York Times* and *The Washington Post* on your side." But Gingrich considered UN funding a small price to pay to keep the religious right happy.

President Clinton, a consummate survivor and pragmatist, made the same calculation, if in the opposite direction: choosing between outraging the pro-choice constituency and the microscopic pro-UN constituency was an easy call for him. The administration made no serious attempt to dislodge the Smith amendment from the UN funding legislation; the president never discussed the issue in public. In the fall of 1998, Clinton vetoed the UN bill with the Smith rider, thus preventing any payment on the arrears, which the United States estimated at $921 million and the UN put at about twice that figure. Those few legislators, Republican as well as Democratic, who actually cared about multilateral institutions were disgusted with the White House's passivity. Lee Hamilton, an Indiana Democrat and one of Congress's most respected voices on international affairs, told me at the time that the administration was intimidated by the spirit of truculent unilateralism and the black-helicopter paranoia, to which much of the American public had fallen prey. Hamilton wanted the United States to pay its dues on time and in full. But when I asked how many of his colleagues shared that view, he said, "It's not close to a majority."

Bill Richardson, the U.S. ambassador to the UN, had not been able to make much headway with Congress, though he was himself a former member. In June 1998, Richardson left New York to become Clinton's secretary of energy. The following January the administration nominated in his stead Richard Holbrooke, the negotiator of the Dayton peace accords that had ended the war in Bosnia and a close runner-up to Madeleine Albright in the competition to serve as secretary of state in the second term. But the nomination stalled in the Senate Foreign Relations Committee. The chairman of the committee, Jesse Helms of North Carolina, had drawn up a bipartisan arrears-for-reform bill with Democratic senator Joseph Biden, Jr. Soon after Holbrooke was nominated, Helms told the White House that he would not schedule hearings unless the administration pledged to support the legislation. Helms-Biden, as it was known, incorporated much of the earlier legislation; it was a compendium of cranky, paranoid, and, in some cases, perfectly reasonable reform proposals. The bill proposed to prohibit the full payment of dues unless the UN maintained a suffocating zero-growth budget and ended the practice of holding global conferences. And it provided for the payment of about two thirds of the $921 million in arrears over a three-year period so long as, among other things, American sovereignty and property rights were not infringed upon, the UN levied no international fees or taxes and made no effort to establish a standing army, and, most important, American dues were lowered from 25 to 22 and then 20 percent.

Helms was the kind of senior legislative figure almost unimaginable elsewhere in the West. He had been a beloved radio personality with a mass following among working-class whites and a reputation for unsubtle race-baiting. "Cousin Jesse," as he was known back home, loved to stick it to the liberals, which meant pretty much everyone to his left— which meant pretty much everyone. Once he climbed to the top of the Foreign Relations Committee, he took a special delight in kicking around the UN. Congress, he recalled in 1996, had told the institution to reform or die. "The time has come for it to do one or the other," he said. "You could flip a coin as far as I am concerned." Helms had proposed that the United States withdraw from the UN should the institution fail to adopt the congressional reform agenda; he had also suggested that beyond a core budget of $250 million, all payments to the UN be voluntary, so that countries could fund whichever programs they liked and ignore what they didn't. And this man, who knew next to nothing about the world beyond America's borders, or for that matter beyond North Carolina, held an effective veto over a significant portion of American foreign policy.

Madeleine Albright, herself no mean politician, had spent years holding Jesse's hand and appealing to his chivalrous southern impulses in hopes of persuading him to stop holding up peacekeeping missions and diplomatic postings and budget bills. Kofi Annan had made Helms one of his chief targets. "When you meet him," Annan said, "he comes across as a fragile, gentle person. He had a cane, which he didn't like to use. You sometimes wonder, 'Can this man be all that they say he is?' But then as you talk to him and try to convince him, it comes across that he's the one that did these things." Helms's manner toward Annan was always polite and even courtly, but he would not budge.

Helms-Biden could be made less toxic, but it could not be altogether neutralized. Senator Biden told me that he himself found some of its terms pernicious, but he took the view that "once you establish that the UN is legitimate, then the rationale for the conditions"— which was that the UN was anti-American, ungovernable, and so on— "begins to dissipate." The State Department was not persuaded of this logic and was loath to capitulate in order to get a nominee confirmed.

But since Helms controlled the Foreign Relations Committee calendar, and thus the Holbrooke appointment, his threats were highly effective. Albright finally buckled. In the course of negotiations, Helms agreed to stretch out some conditions to a third or fourth year and to advance the schedule of payments. Most important, he accepted that the United States could not pay less than 22 percent of the UN's annual budget. The deeper reduction in dues would have forced huge increases on other members, and also would have made the United States the second-largest contributor to the UN, behind Japan—an unthinkable blow to national pride, ironically enough. Holbrooke, who had languished in limbo for well over a year, was finally confirmed in August 1999.

Richard Holbrooke was a man in search of his moment. He had been a junior member of the best and the brightest in Vietnam, filled a backseat at the Paris peace talks, served as a very young assistant secretary of state under Jimmy Carter, and then, after waiting out twelve years of Republican rule, found in Bosnia a drama worthy of his profoundly melodramatic nature. Starting in September 1994, when he was handed the Balkans portfolio, he had infused the hesitant Clinton team with his own sense of moral urgency, thrown down the gauntlet in repeated meetings with Slobodan Milošević and the Bosnian Serb leadership, and then pushed for a major bombing campaign when the Serbs proved intransigent. In Dayton, he had bullied, wheedled, flattered, and exhausted the three ethnic camps into accepting an agreement none of them liked, an act of virtuoso orchestration that very few diplomats could have brought off. Holbrooke was, at fifty-eight, a big, broad-shouldered man with big gifts, big commitments, and big foibles, as renowned for his naked self-aggrandizement as he was for his intellect and energy. His memoir, *To End a War*, is a work of auto-idolatry; it is also a fabulous read.

Holbrooke was drawn to whatever was most dramatic, turbulent, consequential. The job of saving the UN—for this was precisely how he put it to himself—was every bit as thrilling, as worthy of his energies, as the job of saving the Balkans had been. Saving the UN did not mean ending the standoff over dues, though this was a prerequisite for doing so. Saving the UN meant ensuring that it could and did bring its unique form of legitimacy and, when necessary, force to bear in the face of aggression. Holbrooke believed that the UN would rise or fall on its performance in the most critical peacekeeping missions. The institution had made a thorough mess the first time around, in Somalia, Bosnia, and Rwanda. And when it failed, the United States had abandoned the secretary-general and the UN itself. Now there was a second round—Kosovo, East Timor, Sierra Leone. "If this second round we're in now doesn't work," he said, "if the UN fails again, I don't think the world system will give the UN a third chance." And it would fail unless the United States returned to the fold, peacekeeping was given the resources it needed, and the UN was subjected to real reform. That was why the job mattered so much.

The situation Holbrooke faced was very dire. In 1998, the United States had suffered the indignity—and the additional provocation—of being voted off the General Assembly's budget committee for the first time. And the UN's largest contributor was facing the prospect of being stripped of its vote in the General Assembly if it did not pay its back dues by the end of the year. Washington seemed intent not only on punishing the UN but on humiliating it, forcing the institution to accept the asphyxiating strictures of Helms-Biden in exchange for the payment of arrears and a *decrease* in dues payments. And even the money problem, as Kishore Mahbubani, the highly regarded ambassador of Singapore, put it, "symbolizes the real problem, which is attitude. UN-bashing seems to have become a sport in Washington." Even Madeleine Albright, once seen as a champion of the UN to Washington, had, at least in the Turtle Bay view, reversed course after Somalia went bad and joined the chorus of belittlement.

The United States, which had established the UN, now found itself virtually friendless within its precincts. At a General Assembly committee meeting that Holbrooke attended, Jeremy Greenstock, the British ambassador, said, "The United States has muffled its voice and stained its reputation"—a stinging rebuke from America's most important ally. The United States was losing its ability to do business in the UN. Nancy Soderberg, an ambassador at the U.S. Mission, said that when she proposed that the Security Council extend a peacekeeping mission, she would be told, "What do you care? You don't pay anyway."

Holbrooke hit New York like a racehorse let out of the van after a long confinement. He began his campaign by winning a symbolic victory in Turtle Bay that he could carry back with him to Washington. In the past, the United States had filled one of the two seats reserved for the West on the ACABQ, as the budget committee was known; now New Zealand filled its spot. When the European foreign ministers came to New York for the General Assembly session in September, Holbrooke "grabbed them by the throat and beat the shit out of them," according to Peter Burleigh, the number-two figure in the U.S. Mission. "I ran a campaign with the same candidate—the U.S.—and we were a complete failure," Burleigh said. But Holbrooke was able to operate at a higher level. He and Albright persuaded the Europeans to ask New Zealand to step down—which, being New Zealand, it did.

Holbrooke had far more influence in the upper reaches of the Clinton administration than Richardson had had, and he was able to persuade the president to treat the UN debt as a nonnegotiable issue rather than a minor misfortune. And with this commitment in hand, as well as his modest initial victory, he began lobbying Congress. When Kofi Annan had spoken to legislators, he had talked about mutuality and multilateralism and the benefits of global citizenship. Holbrooke had a keener sense of his audience. He would say, "It's about national security." The United States couldn't act as the global policeman; the UN could do what the United States could not. Look at East Timor, where the UN had done the right thing with no American soldiers and very few American dollars. When he testified before the Senate Foreign Relations Committee, he propped up a chart showing that only thirty-six American soldiers were serving in UN peacekeeping forces. He had a pat formulation about the UN—"flawed but indispensable." He did not use the words that got the Republicans' goat—"deadbeat," "isolationist." But he made it clear that the United States was paying a price for its dismissive treatment of the UN. As he said before the Senate committee, "We have to remove this latent, grudging anger at the U.S., which isn't just anti-Americanism."

Holbrooke started with the sympathetic Republicans, trying to peel them away from the party leadership. Then he moved on to the hard cases—the ones with the poster on the wall reading, "My President Is Charlton Heston" (and that was a Democrat). Holbrooke would loiter in the House Dining Room, on the underground trolley that connects the legislative office buildings, or in the parking lot behind the Capitol.

He invited key legislators, and even key staff members, to glamorous dinners at the ambassadorial residence on the forty-second floor of the Waldorf Towers, where they could mingle with statesmen and anchormen and plutocrats. He stalked Denny Hastert, who had succeeded Gingrich as Speaker, and finally cornered him at a White House ceremony and backed him up against a statue of Ulysses S. Grant.

Holbrooke laid siege to Chris Smith, treating with the highest regard a man he viewed as a lunatic. Toward the end of the process, with a deal finally in sight, he asked Smith to meet him at the office of Congressman Tom Lantos, a Holocaust survivor and one of the UN's strongest backers in the House. Smith was no isolationist—he just cared about abortion far more than about the UN—and Holbrooke and Lantos talked fervently of the benefits of multilateralism. "Tom and I thought we had him," Holbrooke recalls, "and he began to shake and he began to sweat. And finally Lantos said, 'Gentlemen, let us pray.' " Lantos had converted to Mormonism. "The three of us get up and stand in the middle of Tom's office holding hands while Tom leads us in prayer—'God give us the strength to find the right way to lead the UN . . .' Tom hugs Chris. After Smith leaves, Tom says to me, 'I think we're going to get this.' " An hour later Smith called Lantos. He said, "Tom, I've been praying. I can't do it."

When he first came to New York, Holbrooke says, he reached an understanding with Annan, whom he had known since his work in the Balkans five years earlier and whom his wife, Kati Marton, had known for twenty years. "I said, 'Kofi, I will speak to you always as a friend, as a brother, in private, and I will never attack you personally in public.' " He would assail the institution, observing in almost every speech that the UN employed far more people in its public information department than it did in peacekeeping—meaning that the UN was more preoccupied with bureaucratic self-preservation than with effective action. But he did not, in fact, take shots at the secretary-general. Annan's end of the bargain apparently consisted in taking Holbrooke's advice. "I would call," Holbrooke says, "and say, 'So-and-so senator is coming over.' He would say, 'I'm busy.' I'd say, 'Kofi, you have to see him.' The staff would object; they would say, 'You're spending too much time with only one of a hundred ninety members.' I would say, 'Wait a minute. We're not one; we're *the* one.' And he trusted me." Over the months, Holbrooke says,

"Kofi charmed, seduced, cajoled, and negotiated with the Congress, with a lot of coaching from me."

By early December, with the deadline for repayment only weeks away, a compromise began to take shape. Though Smith never really relented, Republicans agreed to narrow the range of activities prohibited by his amendment and to give the president the latitude to waive its strictures for payments up to $15 million, which covered virtually everything, since the amount of money involved was always trivial. Family-planning groups, and their allies in Congress, cried betrayal, and Holbrooke did his best to sweet-talk them into sullen acceptance. The bill was passed, the president signed, and the crisis was averted. Credit belonged to Albright and to centrist Democratic and Republican lawmakers—but above all, according to administration officials, to Holbrooke and, to a lesser extent, to Annan.

The ambassador's crowning achievement, or at least his most impressive act of chutzpah, came in late January, when, in his role as president of the Security Council, he invited Cousin Jesse himself to address the council. Holbrooke knew very well that he couldn't control Helms. The man had spent his career vilifying the UN, and he might well choose to cap it off by upending a vat of bile on this nest of foreigners. Holbrooke felt confident—but not very confident—that he wouldn't. And, just barely, he was right. After hobbling over to the American seat at the Security Council table, Helms spoke of Congress's "deep frustration with this institution," its anger at being called a "deadbeat," its resentment that UN human rights monitors presumed to investigate American prison care. I noticed that Jeremy Greenstock was looking studiously at his hands, while Holbrooke was listing sharply to the side, away from the senator. Now warming to his task, Helms accused the UN of undermining the "sanctity" of sovereign rights, of seeking to establish a "new international order," of imagining that only its actions could confer legitimacy on humanitarian interventions. "The UN, my friends, has no power to grant or deny legitimacy to such actions," Helms declared. "They are *inherently* legitimate." Still, at least he had said "my friends." And he hadn't actually told them to go to hell.

It was what ensued that mattered. After Holbrooke incongruously introduced the senator to each of the permanent representatives, magnifying their various virtues, the council members called on their deepest diplomatic gifts to respond to the visiting American dignitary, who embodied all that they despised, with exquisite politesse, and criticism just circumlocutory enough as perhaps to pass by the senator. Alain Dejammet of France observed that his country, too, had once been deeply skeptical of the UN, "but France, too, has many Christian people who believe in the importance of recognizing errors." On the way out, the Cuban ambassador rose and started yelling, but Helms, who was extremely hard of hearing, appeared not to notice. Holbrooke then hosted a lunch for Helms to which he invited all the leading UN officials and diplomats, as well as several conservative celebrities. As he left, the senator was heard to murmur, "Ah've met a *lot* o' nahce people."

Holbrooke had also had the brilliant inspiration to suggest that the Senate Foreign Relations Committee hold a hearing on the UN in New York. This unprecedented event took place the next day. By now Helms, whose vanity must have been tickled beyond measure, had sheathed his claws altogether. Over his bald pate he sported a blue UN cap. After the usual shameless introduction from Holbrooke—"Welcome to the city that you spent your honeymoon in"—Helms went to the rostrum and rousingly cried, "Let's have the visiting ambassadors stand, if they will." The diplomats among the spectators, utterly bewildered, looked at one another, then slowly rose to their feet, as if expecting to be cut down by incoming fire. "The General Assembly of the UN will now be in order!" called the UN's newest enthusiast. Holbrooke was himself the committee's chief witness. "It's clear that the message has gotten through," he said, looking right at Helms, "and the message is, you're not anti-UN, you have a view of the UN, and you want the UN to succeed on your terms."

Actually, it was the medium that was the message. As Annan put it, "Symbolically, it was very important. It was very important for them to sit in the council, which they see on television and they hear about, and for them to be in the chamber and be part of it. I could see that they were also moved to be there. And of course they could go back and see themselves on television in the Security Council. I think it also sent a message that the U.S. is part of the organization, and we should work together." One of Helms's aides said to me, "He knew that he was stepping into a potentially hostile audience. I think he felt that he was received very respectfully. I would say that he saw the individuals that make up the UN, countries and officials, in a way that you can't see from afar. I think this is really a new start. The running battle with the UN is over here. Now we're talking about how we're doing it, not whether we're doing it." Helms even invited the secretary-general to serve as commencement speaker at his alma mater, Wingate University. Annan was more accustomed to Harvard Yard than to lily-white Bible Belt campuses, but he knew better than to plead scheduling conflicts.

In the UN, on the other hand, the battle was far from over. Just because Holbrooke had delivered the U.S. Congress didn't mean the other members would swallow their embitterment and increase their dues payments. The Americans were promising to pay off only about 60 percent of their arrears. *And* the members would have to accept the onerous and in some cases inane strictures of Helms-Biden, including the ruinous prospect of a no-growth budget for years to come. It felt like the worst kind of bullying, as if the United States had hit on the most brutal possible reminder that it, and it alone, could defy the rules that bound everyone else. "The members hate it," as John Ruggie, Annan's adviser, said at the time. "The choice they're confronted with is: What do they hate more?"

The actual sums were ridiculously small: the difference between 25 and 22 percent of the budget was $32 million. Holbrooke went from country to country asking for another million dollars or two. "They kept saying, 'It's all about principle,'" Holbrooke recalls. "I said, 'Wait a minute, the principle is saving the UN.' And they said, 'Well, we're not going to let Jesse Helms hold us up.'" Some countries, including Japan and members of the EU, were already overpaying and were not about to absorb yet more of the burden. But when Holbrooke approached countries like Singapore and the United Arab Emirates, which had become far more prosperous since the last adjustment, in 1972, "they suddenly turned out to be very poor developing nations." Russia, which had once paid as much as 17 percent of the budget as a matter of national pride, had fallen to less than 2 percent after the breakup of the empire—and that was including all members of the Commonwealth of Independent States. After much bludgeoning, from Madeleine Albright as much as from Holbrooke, the Chinese agreed to a significant increase, the Russians held steady, and a number of smaller countries kicked in additional amounts. And so the deed was done.

Holbrooke was almost certainly the most effective American ambassador in UN history. He was also, despite his voluble and sometimes imperious manner, quite popular; the diplomats I talked to liked his blunt, unequivocating manner. Of course Holbrooke was given great credit for drawing the poison from the right-wing serpent, but he was also seen as a champion of the institution who, unlike Albright, hadn't heaped abuse on the UN in order to score points in Washington. His criticisms were harsh, but scarcely unjust. Above all, Holbrooke wanted the UN to *do* things.

The United States inherited the rotating presidency of the Security Council in January 2000, and Holbrooke declared it "the month of Africa." The very idea of a thematic presidency was novel, in part because in the 1980s the United States had insisted that the council stick to handling emergencies rather than look for problems to solve. But Holbrooke had a crucial point to make: Africa, the most desperate of regions, the focus of much of the UN's peacekeeping and humanitarian activities, offered the grossest evidence of U.S. disengagement from its international responsibilities. Holbrooke was getting pressure from administration officials to oppose the extension of a modest peacekeeping mission in the Central African Republic. Why? Because staff aides to right-wing congressmen were complaining about the $4 million cost. "I'm not going to the Security Council," he said, "and veto a peacekeeping mission even if it's not a worthwhile mission." It was hard enough as it was to counter the view of his African colleagues that the United States and the other Western powers were willing to send 100,000 soldiers to the Balkans but barely a platoon to Africa. The glaring disparity placed Kofi Annan, the African secretary-general and friend of the United States, in an excruciating position.

Holbrooke stage-managed the month of Africa with his usual combination of moral urgency and marketing genius. He dedicated one session to the crisis of AIDS in Africa. In the UN, diseases were the province of specialized agencies, like WHO or UNICEF. The Security Council deliberated on threats to international peace and security, not threats to health. But Holbrooke argued that AIDS, by crippling an entire generation in Africa, *was* a threat to international peace and security. And as keynote speaker he brought in Vice President Al Gore, a gimmick that brought great attention both to the problem and to Gore, who would be running for president later that year.

Holbrooke decided that the diplomatic centerpiece of his month of Africa would be the continent's single most intractable military and political problem—Congo. The previous summer Congo and its neighbors, who had been waging what was sometimes called "Africa's first world war," had signed a cease-fire agreement in Lusaka, the capital of Zambia. In November, the Security Council had authorized a very modest force of five hundred military observers to monitor the agreement. Here, where UN peacekeeping had been born forty years earlier, was the crucible in which, Holbrooke thought, a new generation of peacekeeping could be fired. "Congo was the graveyard of the UN, literally and figuratively," he said. (Actually, it wasn't.) "What they're doing has huge historical resonance for the UN—if we don't get it right, we're simply going to go down." The Lusaka accord was fraying; the tide of violence was rising. Holbrooke hatched the idea of inviting the heads of the states in conflict to the Security Council to sign a new document—Lusaka Plus, he called it.

Holbrooke bullied and flattered everyone in sight until, on January 24, the Security Council, in a majestic display of ceremony, welcomed the presidents of Angola, Mozambique, Uganda, and Zimbabwe, as well as Laurent Kabila, the blood-soaked insurgent who had unseated Joseph Mobutu to became head of Congo, and who was himself soon to be assassinated. The heads of state never actually signed Lusaka Plus, and a State Department official later told me that Holbrooke had, if anything, set back the cause of regional agreement by offending quite a few of them. Holbrooke conceded that it hadn't all gone according to plan. But, he added, "One thing I'm sure of—we have to make the effort. We cannot sit back and say, 'American prestige is hurt if we try and fail.' American prestige is hurt more if we ignore the problem." And that was surely true. As David Malone, a veteran Canadian diplomat and authority on the UN, put it, "The month of Africa succeeded not only in the immediate sense that it brought these heads of state to New York and made them realize that the UN was really paying attention, but also in the broader sense that it reenergized American engagement with the UN."

Holbrooke argues that Kofi Annan's great achievement came in weaving back together the ties that had once bound the United States to the UN, and that had dwindled to a filament during the era of Boutros-Ghali. That may be so, but Holbrooke would no doubt be the first to grant himself substantial credit for that achievement.

Kofi Annan was a man of the global South who had spent virtually his entire adult life in the global North. His views were fundamentally those of a high-minded and progressive European—a Norwegian, say, or a Dutchman. He believed devoutly in what he took to be the universal principles of human rights and humanitarianism and in the use of force against evil, so long as the force was mustered collectively and in conformity with international law. He also believed that the rich nations had a moral obligation to help the poor ones. He did not take it as an article of faith, as many Third World ideologues and activists did, that global capitalism was a device by which the industrialized world exploited the resources and manpower of the developing world. He did not want to overturn the system—he didn't want to overturn any system—but he did wish to see it managed, in his humane, Scandinavian way, so as to fully extend its benefits to the have-nots.

Annan had, fortuitously, taken office at a time when the debate over the role of the industrialized world in addressing global poverty had emerged from the ideological stalemate of an earlier era, when socialism still exerted a strong hold over Third World intellectuals and policy makers. Most developed countries had come to accept the inevitability of global capitalism and agitated to be let into the game. In the West, the neoliberal doctrine that poor nations simply needed to accept the global rules of the road, eliminating subsidies and barriers to trade and investment, had been chastened by the Asian financial crisis of 1997, which afflicted a number of countries that had played by just those rules. Economists like Jeffrey Sachs, Joseph Stiglitz, Amartya Sen, and Kemal Derviş argued that the West had to do more than preach the virtues of free enterprise. A new kind of contract had to be negotiated between the haves and the have-nots. Annan and his advisers believed that the United Nations, with its history of establishing global norms on the treatment of women and children, or on population or the environment, was the one setting in which this contract could be hammered out.

Annan was the first secretary-general to speak at the World Economic Forum in Davos, the annual conclave of capital and its various managers and political masters. He gave an innocuous speech in 1998. Invited to return the following year, he cast about for something worth saying. Annan came into office believing that the UN, with its relatively puny resources, had to leverage the skills and resources of the business community. First, he knew, he would have to repair the damage inflicted by one of the follies of the 1970s—a binding "code of conduct" for multinational companies that Third World diplomats had spent years devising before the Reagan administration dismissed it as presumptuous nonsense. Davos was, of course, the perfect place to begin this salvage job. He asked John Ruggie to think about how the UN could recast its relationship with the world of private enterprise.

Ruggie and his staff came up with the idea of proposing a set of behavioral principles that corporations would pledge to adopt. Annan liked this idea. "If you're going to work with corporations," he felt, "there have to be certain ground rules. If we didn't have those ground rules, we would just appear to be supporting the corporate world." In Davos, Annan called for "a global compact of shared values and principles, which will give a human face to the global market." He asked the gathered moguls to commit themselves—voluntarily, of course—to a standard of conduct on human rights, labor, and the environment. It was in just these fields, he observed, that "various interest groups" were applying "enormous pressure" on governments to act by restricting trade and investment. More than that, he said, a deep anxiety about the benefits of globalization had made many people "vulnerable to the backlash from all the 'isms' of our post-cold-war world: protectionism; populism; ethnic chauvinism; fanaticism; and terrorism." In order to respond to this deep feeling of insecurity and alienation, he went on, leaders must "find a way of embedding the global market in a network of shared values." This was the kind of formulation Annan always felt comfortable with: there need be no conflict between self-interest and collective good.

The Global Compact became one of Annan's favorite initiatives, since it answered both to his moral and to his managerial impulses. In

July 2000, he convened a High-Level Meeting on the Global Compact at which fifty multinationals committed themselves to the code of conduct. Among the ten principles of the compact, all derived from UN declarations, were acceptance of the right to collective bargaining, a commitment not to use child labor or engage in employment discrimination, the promotion of environmental sensitivity, and a prohibition on the use of bribery or extortion. Over the years, twenty-five hundred companies formally accepted the ten principles. Whether or not this new social contract actually reduced the incidence of forced labor or job discrimination, it clearly accomplished Annan's original goal of repairing the UN's relationship with the corporate world and changing its reputation as a nest of socialism. Virtually all UN agencies now work with the private sector and seek to encourage public-private partnerships.

From the time he took office, Annan had believed that the intensive focus on peacekeeping and security issues in the 1990s had obscured the role the UN could and must play on ending global poverty. Though the demise of Third World socialism, on the one hand, and neoliberal purism, on the other, had purged much of the ideological antagonism from the issue, Annan still knew that he needed to move delicately on the question of development. But by openly criticizing African leaders early in his tenure, he had given himself the space to preach to the West without being accused, as Boutros-Ghali was, of special pleading. "I speak," as he put it, "from the humanitarian point of view." Annan and his aides wanted to use the pretext of the millennium to advance the program of reform, and above all to stake out a more meaningful role for the UN on economic development. In early 1999, Annan proposed to the General Assembly that the world's heads of state convene at a Millennium Summit, to be held in September 2000, immediately before the opening of the new General Assembly. The summit would be dedicated to institutional self-renewal.

In early April, Annan released a report, written by his staff, titled "We the Peoples: The Role of the United Nations in the 21st Century." The intellectual premise of the document was that globalization, while unleashing tremendous energies of growth and change, had altered the nature of war, of economic development and competition, of threats to the environment, to public health, to privacy, and so forth. Thus, "if we are to capture the promises of globalization while managing its adverse effects, we must learn to govern better, and we must learn better how to govern together." And this "we" must, of course, signally include the UN, which would have to ensure that the benefits of globalization flowed to all, and to "broker differences among states." In the new millennium, the UN was to serve as the global referee.

John Ruggie, the report's chief author, had wanted to avoid at all costs the high-minded blather that such documents typically invited. He and his staff combed through past UN conferences, harvesting specific targets to which states had committed themselves in the past and which they could pledge to meet in the Millennium Summit. "We the Peoples" was structured as a blueprint for a new UN, covering matters of war and peace, the environment, economic development, and institutional reform. But once you got past the rhetoric, the really specific targets were largely limited to the section of the document known as "Freedom from Want."

At its core, "We the Peoples" laid out the terms of a new contract between beneficiary and benefactor countries. The report offered a series of postulates on economic success in the age of globalization: that the only long-term solution to entrenched poverty lay in income growth; that sustained growth came only with successful adaptation to the demands of the global marketplace; and that globalization favored countries with strong governance, with schools that imparted a high level of skills to the average citizen, with ample opportunities for women and girls, and with decent public health systems. The authors assumed that few poor countries could manage this transformation without a great deal of help, but they were unsparing in their description of the self-destructive policies pursued in many impoverished countries, attributing the systemic failure in much of sub-Saharan Africa to corruption, economic mismanagement, and a winner-take-all political culture. "Inexplicably, even today," the report stated, "relatively few African governments show the necessary commitment to poverty reduction."

This was new rhetoric, but it was still rhetoric. What really commanded attention in "We the Peoples" were the targets interspersed throughout the document, which Ruggie had added mostly as a device to focus attention. Most of them stipulated a development goal to be attained by 2015. Foremost among them was the target of halving the number of people living on a dollar a day or less, a pitiful figure that at that time included 1.2 billion people, or 22 percent of the world's population. The report also called for, among other targets, halving the number of people without access to safe drinking water, ensuring universal public-school enrollment, sharply reducing the rates of HIV infections, and increasing access to prevention services and information. "We the Peoples" offered an implicit contract: impoverished countries would commit themselves to good governance and to an unambiguous focus on poverty reduction, while the wealthy nations agreed to dismantle trade barriers for products exported from poor countries, to sharply reduce and even cancel the debts of the so-called heavily indebted poor countries, and to increase official development assistance.

The targets were immensely ambitious. But because, in most cases, they stipulated a desired end state without specifying a means of ensuring that one would get there, one could subscribe to them without making any real commitment. And everyone could agree that reducing poverty and illiteracy—unlike, say, interfering in the sovereign right to abuse one's own people—was a very fine thing. And so the secretary-general's report met with relatively little resistance. The Millennium Summit, the mightiest conclave of heads of state in world history, issued a Millennium Declaration that preserved much of "We the Peoples," albeit with only the most fleeting glance at good governance, a term to which the Chinese took exception, and the addition of such new beneficiaries as "small island developing states," "landlocked" developing states, and heavily indebted nonpoor countries.

But that's not to say that the Millennium Summit was all hot air and diplomatic license plates. John Ruggie says that he always saw the targets as a "social and political mobilization tool." UN norms, whether on the rights of women or on sustainable development, rarely cause anything directly; rather, they escape into the world, bearing the bright seal of legitimacy. The targets stipulated in the Millennium Declaration came to be known as the Millennium Development Goals, or MDGs; over time, they became the standard against which success in overcoming extreme poverty was judged. The World Bank and various UN agencies adopted the MDGs, as did many finance and development ministries in both the industrialized and the developing world. In late

2001, Annan asked Jeffrey Sachs, the globe-trotting economist, to head the Millennium Project, which would bring together academics and practitioners in order to map out strategies to realize the MDGs in the specified time frame. The MDGs became the UN's great contribution to the ongoing debate over poverty and development. Annan had succeeded in placing the UN at the center of an issue of the highest moral importance. And, as he had with human rights and with humanitarian intervention, he had demonstrated his gifts as a norm entrepreneur.

CHAPTER NINE

Who's Going to Run Afghanistan?

THE OUTCOME OF THE AMERICAN PRESIDENTIAL ELECTION
of 2000 turned on George W. Bush's easy amiability, or Al Gore's
fear of Bill Clinton's shadow, or the seductive lure of tax cuts as far as
the eye could see, or perhaps the simple fact that Republican nomi-
nees outnumbered Democrats on the Supreme Court, five to four. It
did not, in any case, turn on foreign affairs. For one thing, the Texas
governor knew next to nothing about the world beyond America's borders and was not very comfortable talking about it. And Al Gore, who
knew a great deal about the subject, could not gain much purchase on
it, for America was at peace, its military supremacy unchallenged, its
enemies remote. The most divisive question of foreign policy was just
what America ought to do with the immense might it had accumulated.
George Bush argued that President Clinton had used American power
promiscuously, intervening in places where America's vital interests
were not engaged. Al Gore argued that policy must be guided not just
by interests but also by values.

Indeed, one of the few issues on which the candidates held irrecon-
cilable views was the one Kofi Annan had most passionately engaged—
humanitarian intervention. Gore was for it, at least under the right
circumstances, and Bush against it. Asked what he would do should
an incident like Rwanda recur, Bush said flatly, "We should not send
our troops to stop ethnic cleansing and genocide in nations outside
our strategic interest." Bush offered himself as an unsentimental and

unambiguous defender of America's interests, a patriot who would dedicate himself to securing the nation's supremacy. But he was no isolationist: he urged congressional Republicans to continue supporting America's ambitious and expensive role in Bosnia and Kosovo (though only after Condoleezza Rice had provoked a panic in NATO by suggesting that the United States might withdraw as part of a new "division of labor" with the allies).

When Bush won the election, he appointed Colin Powell, the former chairman of the Joint Chiefs of Staff, as secretary of state. Powell's wide international experience, moderate views, and diplomatic gifts were meant to reassure allies nervous about the president's ignorance and doctrinaire tendencies. But Powell was the odd man out on the team. Condoleezza Rice, Bush's national security adviser and confidante, was a Kissingerian realist who in a widely read article in *Foreign Affairs* observed that when foreign policy is driven by values, "the 'national interest' is replaced with 'humanitarian interests' or the interests of 'the international community.' " According to this liberal worldview, she wrote, "the United States is exercising power legitimately only when it is doing so on behalf of someone or something else." Both Defense Secretary Donald Rumsfeld and Vice President Dick Cheney shared Rice's dim regard for "values," her scant faith in treaties and international law, her insistence that great powers made rules for themselves.

This was realism, but in a new key, for the United States was now in a position to dispense with the balance-of-power politics required in a world of competing blocs. Ivo Daalder and James Lindsay, two former Clinton administration national security officials, were later to describe this strain of thinking as "hegemonism," which they characterized as the belief that "America's immense power, and the willingness to wield it, even over the objection of others, is the key to securing America's interests in the world." George Bush's father and his centrist aides shared this faith in the efficacy of American power, if not the reflex of resistance to any assertion of power by allies. But the feature that really distinguished the circle of the younger Bush from that of the older was an overwhelming belief in the country's unique destiny and virtue, a sense that America was less a nation among nations than an exemplar to others. To question America's motives was a sign of bad faith—for, as

Daalder and Lindsay write of this view, "the exercise of American power would jeopardize only those threatened by the spread of liberty and free markets." This quasi-evangelical credo, which realists like Kissinger had long deplored, goes back to the nation's origins and became a governing philosophy with President Woodrow Wilson. But never before had this spirit of exceptionalism and high purpose been joined to so dismissive an attitude toward the web of institutions and agreements that bound the country to its allies, and to the rest of the world.

The foreign-policy leitmotif of the Bush administration's first eight months in office, outside of parrying gibes about how many foreign capitals and heads of state the president could name, was the blunt rejection of international agreements. Rice informed foreign ministers from the European Union that the Kyoto Protocol on global warming was "dead." Bush withdrew from the Anti-Ballistic Missile Treaty with Russia. The White House stated its opposition to a pact to control the dissemination of small arms, to a new protocol to the Biological Weapons Convention, and to the Comprehensive Test-Ban Treaty. The repudiation was most spectacular in the case of the International Criminal Court, which President Clinton had signed into law at the end of his term. Though congressional leaders had declared the court dead on arrival, Bush made a point of publicly killing the document anyway, formally repudiating the treaty in May. The administration then demanded that each of the court's signatories accept bilateral agreements exempting Americans from the court's jurisdiction. Bush and his team not only embraced the almost unarguable proposition that America's unique role in the world gave it unique interests but also believed, as a matter of principle as well as strategy, that America should not relax those interests even slightly—even symbolically—in order to find common ground with others.

The Bush team seemed not so much hostile to the UN as scarcely aware of its existence. The administration made little effort to appoint a UN ambassador, making do with James Cunningham, the highly professional career diplomat who had remained behind once Richard Holbrooke stepped down. At the same time, Bush himself established a comfortable and professional relationship with the UN secretary-general. The president invited Annan to the Oval Office on March 23, before he had traveled abroad or met with most of his chief allies. The meeting was notably stilted, with Annan ticking off the issues from note cards—Iraq, Kosovo, the Middle East, AIDS, the Millennium Development Goals. Bush, still a hopeless novice in matters of statecraft, was plainly ill at ease. But both men were skilled in the arts of putting others at their ease, even if their methods of doing so could scarcely have been more different, and by the next time they met, six weeks later, the formality had melted away. They were "Kofi"—no nickname —and "W." Annan worked hard to find a comfort zone with Powell, Rice, Rumsfeld, and Cheney. Only with the vice president did he fail hopelessly. Cheney would not be drawn out. He barely made eye contact, as if fearing that a glance might lead to seduction. Instead, he sat stolidly, staring at the floor, contributing little. Annan eventually gave up trying to charm him.

Annan's great preoccupation lay largely, though not wholly, at a tangent from the Bush administration's concerns. He spent much of the spring and summer of 2001 trying to advance the agenda first laid out in the Millennium Summit. He pushed the agenda on sustainable development, climate change, girls' education, and aid and debt relief for the least developed countries. He organized a conference, to be held in Monterrey, Mexico, in February 2002, to focus attention on the goal of halving extreme poverty by 2015. But most of all, he talked about AIDS. Ever since Richard Holbrooke had staged his AIDS extravaganza in the Security Council in January 2000, Annan had championed the idea that the epidemic was not merely a public health disaster but a threat to international peace and security. The World Health Organization had appointed a commission to examine the question of how AIDS treatment could be made affordable in the Third World; the chairman, Jeffrey Sachs, was Annan's chief adviser on the Millennium Development Goals. Sachs argued that with the cost of antiretroviral medications beginning to come down, the mushrooming population of AIDS victims in Africa could receive treatment—given a massive expansion in funding.

Annan returned again and again to the subject of AIDS. He admonished African heads of state to break "the wall of silence and embarrassment" that surrounded the issue. He called on Western nations and institutions to ensure universal access to antiretroviral therapy at affordable prices and to provide a minimum of $7 to $10 billion a year in additional funding to achieve these and other goals. And he proposed the establishment of a global fund to coordinate the vast effort to fight AIDS and other infectious diseases. But it was easier to get attention than money. The Bush administration was deeply skeptical about the idea of providing treatment in Third World countries—the head of USAID observed that since African villagers couldn't tell time they could hardly be expected to take drugs according to the prescribed schedule—and when President Bush announced in mid-May that the United States would make the first pledge to the global fund, the amount was a disappointing $200 million, rather than the $3 billion Annan had hoped for. Other major donors preferred their own bilateral efforts.

The Bush administration also made it clear that they would not participate in the fund at all were it to be housed, as planned, inside the UN. Instead, the Global Fund to Fight AIDS, Tuberculosis, and Malaria, as it was called, was established as an independent body based in Geneva and jointly chaired by Annan and Tommy Thompson, the U.S. secretary of health and human services. The fund provided assistance for countries seeking to improve their health care systems in order to effectively deliver preventive services and treatment for these three great killers. Though generally well regarded, the fund never received anything like the kind of money Annan had called for.

Annan was now at the height of his popularity, a figure with innumerable admirers and few, if any, important enemies. In *Deliver Us from Evil*, an account of UN peacekeeping and crisis management published in 2000, William Shawcross, the celebrated British journalist, breathlessly tracks Annan's interventions in hot spots across the globe; Shawcross describes the secretary-general as the incarnation of "the spirit of the international community," a "remarkable" figure with an "unusual presence" and even a "mischievous sense of fun." There was no question that Annan could have another term if he wanted it; after all, even his far less respected and effective predecessors (save Boutros-Ghali) had been routinely reappointed. President Bush had put this question to rest during Annan's initial White House visit, when he had told the secretary-general in front of the press corps that he would be working "to make sure you serve a second term" as well as "to keep the peace and to make the world more prosperous."

When Annan had first become secretary-general, he had promised Nane that he would serve one term and then walk away. Especially in the first few years, Nane had felt suffocated by the constant attention, the lack of privacy, the relentless demands on her husband's and her own time. She still wanted him to step down, though over time she had become more reconciled to her queenly status. But Annan, who recoiled from ambition but cherished the impersonal ideal of service, felt, as he puts it, that "there were quite a lot of concerns that one was engaged in that one wanted to see towards conclusion." Nane eventually agreed, as he says, "to be a good soldier."

At the end of June, the General Assembly appointed Annan by acclamation to a second term. In his statement before the General Assembly, Annan summarized the goals he had pursued in his first term: "I have sought to turn an unflinching eye on the failures of our recent past, in order to assess more clearly what it will take for us to succeed in the future. I have sought to speak out in defense of those who cannot speak out for themselves—for the right of the poorest to development, and the right of the weakest and most vulnerable to protection. And I have sought to make universal human rights the touchstone of my work, in all their aspects, because I believe they belong to every faith, every culture, and every people."

The summer of 2001 offered the usual array of local emergencies and global palaver. The Security Council tried to shore up a very leaky peacekeeping effort in Congo; the Secretariat organized elections in East Timor; the General Assembly remonstrated with the United States for failing to pay more than $500 million in past dues; and in late August, delegates from every nation gathered in Durban, South Africa, for the long-planned World Conference Against Racism, Racial Discrimination, Xenophobia, and Related Intolerance. The delegates agreed that these were all very bad things. Among their worst manifestations, of course, was "the racist policy of Israeli politicians," as the secretary-general of the Organization of the Islamic Conference put it in plenary session. Others insisted that the United States issue a formal apology and reparations for the slave trade. The Norwegians pleaded helplessly for compromise. And the low-level representatives whom Israel and the United States had sent walked out of the conference.

On September 10, 2001, the secretary-general issued a statement in advance of the International Day of Peace, September 11. The General Assembly had marked the day every year for the last twenty, but this year, Kofi Annan said, the assembly had decided to declare the date "a day of global ceasefire and non-violence." This step, he added, "promises to be more than symbolic," for "even a one-day pause in the fighting gives us something to build on in the work to end conflict."

The workday at the UN normally begins between 9:30 and 10:00. And so very few people were in the Secretariat Building when a plane crashed into the World Trade Center at 8:48 on the morning of September 11. When the second plane hit, at 9:12, Michael Doyle, a professor of international relations at Columbia who had taken over from John Ruggie the role of in-house American, discovered that he was the seniormost official on the thirty-eighth floor. Doyle recalled that the UN had been the alternate target of the terrorists who had tried to bring down the towers in 1993. But he didn't have the authority to order an evacuation. He telephoned Iqbal Riza, who could issue an order under Annan's name, and Riza initiated what turned out to be a thoroughly chaotic evacuation process.

The terrorist attacks were no less terrible for the polyglot world of the UN than for more local institutions, both because many UN officials had come to view New York as their adopted home and because the World Trade Center was almost as heterogeneous as the UN, and few countries were spared from the list of fatalities. As he walked through the General Assembly several days later, Ambassador James Cunningham was hugged by almost everyone he came across. "The sense of outrage and sorrow was palpable," he recalls.

Jean-David Levitte, the ambassador of France, which that month held the rotating presidency of the Security Council, watched the buildings burn from his forty-fourth-floor office on East Forty-seventh Street. The next day he convened an emergency meeting of the council in an unused one-story building behind the General Assembly. In condemning the attacks, the council invoked the Charter's "inherent right of individual or collective self-defense" and authorized "all necessary steps" to strike back at "those responsible for aiding, supporting or harbouring the perpetrators, organizers and sponsors of these acts." This extraordinarily broad language provided legitimacy to a military response against both the Al Qaeda forces that had planned the terrorist mission and the Taliban government in Afghanistan. That same day, in Brussels, NATO for the first time in its history invoked Article 5, declaring the terror attacks a breach of collective security.

The Bush administration immediately expressed its gratitude to the UN by promising to pay its back dues and to send to the Senate a nominee for ambassador. The candidate, who was swiftly approved, was John Negroponte, a respected and tough-minded professional, though one with very little influence at the White House. But for all the rhetoric of common purpose, the terrorist attacks had little noticeable effect on the strategic calculations of the United States or its allies. The Bush administration appeared to simply brush aside NATO's proposal for a collective response in Afghanistan—though Nicholas Burns, then the U.S. ambassador to NATO, asserts that in the weeks after 9/11, "not a single ally offered to go with us." The United States went to war in Afghanistan with only the U.K. and Australia; only once it became clear that Washington and its Afghan allies would prevail, says Burns, did other European countries propose to contribute supplies or logistical aid, though he concedes that the administration was so slow to acknowledge the offers that these would-be allies had reason to feel they were being shown the back of the mighty American hand. The Europeans were left feeling bruised by American unilateralism, while the White House concluded that it could not count on the West in the fight against terrorism.

The question of postwar Afghanistan was quite literally an afterthought for the Bush administration. During the presidential election, Bush had spoken of "nation-building" as the prime example of soft-headed misuses of American military power. And America's new reality had not yet touched this a priori view. In *Bush at War*, Bob Woodward reconstructs the following exchange from a National Security Council meeting on October 4, three days before hostilities began: "As for post-

Taliban Afghanistan, Wolfowitz and Rice talked about getting other countries to put up money for re-building.

" 'Who will run the country?' Bush asked.

"We should have addressed that, Rice thought. Her most awful moments were when the President thought of something that the principals, particularly she, should have anticipated." But there were more pressing things to think about, and five days later the principals revisited the issue with the same remarkable nonchalance. "Maybe the UN should take Kabul," the president suggested, according to Woodward's account. Secretary Powell agreed that this would be a good idea. At a press conference two days later, Bush suggested that "it would be a useful function for the United Nations to take over the so-called 'nation-building' . . . after our mission is complete." The White House seemed to view this as a bone thrown to the striped-pants set.

The UN had maintained a large humanitarian presence in Afghanistan throughout the Taliban period. Annan had also appointed Lakhdar Brahimi as his special envoy to the Taliban government, which the UN did not recognize. Brahimi traveled regularly to Afghanistan and worked with the contact group of neighbors and major powers. He had witnessed the growing radicalization of the Taliban. In September 1998, he had met Mullah Omar, the one-eyed peasant leader, whom he recalled as "a nice young man with a lopsided grin—very soft-spoken, very handsome, tall, lean, hungry. There was an air of sincerity about him, but he was totally ignorant of what a state is." Thereafter, Brahimi felt, Mullah Omar had fallen under the radicalizing influence of Osama bin Laden and the Saudi fundamentalists.

By 2000, Brahimi had wearied of trying to persuade the Pakistanis, the Iranians, and other neighbors to stop meddling in Afghanistan, backing this or that warlord for their own purposes. "I came back," he said, "and said to the SG, 'I give up.' And he said, 'No, you can't give up.' We agreed instead that I would be frozen." And so, after 9/11, Brahimi was available to be defrosted. But he was the wrong man to mastermind a UN takeover of Kabul. His generation of Algerians had come to maturity fighting the French occupation, and as foreign minister he had championed the country's vehemently anticolonial line. The Brahimi report had questioned the very idea of the transitional administration. Brahimi said that Annan had asked him in 1999 to become his first proconsul in East Timor, and he had declined. "I'm a person of my own background and experience in politics," he said. "Anything that looks like neocolonialism would be difficult for me, and is something I would not want to be involved in." What's more, Brahimi understood that the Afghans, who had sown the earth with the bones of their colonizers, would be a good deal less receptive to UN overlordship than the hapless and patient Timorese.

In the first press conference after resuming his mission in mid-October, Brahimi made a point of saying, "The UN is not seeking a transitional administration or peacekeeping or anything like that." Rather, he said, he would work to bring the various parties together, and then help the Afghans rebuild their own country. Brahimi believed that a successful resolution depended, as it had before, on the acquiescence of the key neighbors. In late October, he flew to Pakistan, whose army and intelligence service had provided crucial support to the Taliban, which they saw as a bulwark against Russian encroachment. The Pakistanis needed to be reassured that the new state would not be hostile to its interests in the region. The envoy reached an agreement with President Pervez Musharraf of Pakistan which stipulated, among other things, that any new government would "not allow its territory to be used for hostile acts against its neighbors or anybody else." Brahimi then traveled to Iran, which had supported the Northern Alliance, the chief rebel group. The Iranians needed to accept that Afghanistan would have a pluralistic government. Brahimi met with much of Iran's leadership class, as well as with Afghan expatriates. In his public remarks he stressed that the Afghans had been suffering from "foreign interference" and expressed the hope that they would soon have a chance to guide their own destiny.

By mid-November, the Northern Alliance, with considerable help from American Special Forces and American bombing, had routed the Taliban from Kabul and begun to occupy the city. No one had expected the capital to fall so rapidly; military reality had outrun the political process. The Bush administration seemed content to turn control over to the Tajiks and Uzbeks who dominated the alliance, but Brahimi understood that doing so could send the Pashtuns, the country's largest ethnic group and the major constituent of the Taliban, back to the battlefield. In a lengthy briefing to the Security Council, Brahimi proposed an elaborate political process that he had already cleared with the major actors, including of course the White House. The UN would bring together the chief Afghan factions at a neutral site. These parties would nominate members of a broad-based Provisional Council, which would in turn draw up a transitional administration to last no more than two years. A *loya jirga*, a traditional Afghan gathering, would then be convened to confer its seal of approval on the government. Later, another such gathering would approve a constitution and create a permanent state. Brahimi had, in effect, redesigned the process used in East Timor by substituting the Afghans themselves for the UN. And he had dispensed with democracy in favor of ensuring representation for each contending group. For Brahimi, political transformation ran a distant second behind political stability.

The talks among the Afghan factions were held at the Petersberg castle outside of Bonn. Brahimi, working with the U.S. State Department officials Richard Haass and James Dobbins, had invited what he called the four main Afghan factions (excluding the Taliban). This was, in fact, a convenient fiction. "Brahimi invented the four factions before he got to Bonn," says Salman Ahmed, his political adviser. He and his American colleagues recognized that they needed to balance the dominant power of the Northern Alliance without unduly fragmenting the new government. For all Brahimi's talk of placing the Afghans in the driver's seat, he wasn't about to let them make a hash of the political process. He was a very different kind of diplomat from his ethereal, impeccable, gentle, and sometimes naive boss. Brahimi was of the earth, earthy—blunt, pragmatic, wry. After forty years of refereeing tense conflicts not only in Algeria but in Lebanon, Haiti, South Africa, and elsewhere, he had the air of a man who had seen everything and was surprised by nothing. And just as Annan had his acolytes, who revered his purity and dedication to ideals, so in the UN there was a cult of Brahimi and of Sergio Vieira de Mello—of men who could be thrown to the lions and come out holding the whip. Ahmad Fawzi, who served as the special envoy's spokesman in Bonn, said, "People would say, 'Let's do a Brahimi,' or, 'Can we find another Brahimi?' I don't think Kofi Annan had that kind of reputation."

Though sharply attuned, like Annan, to the pride and sensitivity of others, Brahimi ran a tight ship. He sequestered the Afghan parties in the castle's west wing and confined the great herd of diplomats following the talks to the opposite flank, where they huddled together and drank espresso. The two sides were permitted to mingle only at mealtime, and even then only at dinnertime, since it was Ramadan and the delegates were fasting. "It was extremely important to keep the foreigners away from the meeting," Brahimi explained. "If I am receiving money from you, if I speak while you're around, I have to speak the same language as you. If you're not there, they can say what they really think." Brahimi and his aides sat at a rectangular table with the four factions, trying to fill in the details on the structure he had proposed. No one was allowed to leave the castle during working hours. After the morning session, Brahimi would cross to the east wing and huddle with the factions' various patrons. If Hamid Karzai, the elegant Pashtun expatriate who was the odds-on favorite to lead the Interim Authority, was asking for too much, Brahimi would lean on Karzai's chief backer, the Americans; or he would ask the Russians to talk sense to Burhanuddin Rabbani, a prominent warlord; or he would tell the Iranians to intercede with figures from the Northern Alliance. Sometimes the Iranians and the Americans even talked to each other—one of the very few venues in which this was possible.

The parties spent days haggling over how the posts in the new government would be divvied up. A convention of dentists was scheduled to take over the castle on December 6; on December 5, the ninth day of the conclave, Brahimi informed the group that no one was getting up until the agreement was signed. And they didn't. That evening the Agreement on Provisional Arrangements in Afghanistan Pending the Re-establishment of Permanent Government Institutions was initialed. The pact, which was to go into effect in seventeen days, called for precisely the sequence of events that Brahimi had envisioned—proof of how carefully and widely he had consulted before coming to Bonn. The Brahimi report had observed that transitional administrations needed to be founded on a preexisting body of law, and the agreement stipulated that Afghanistan's constitution of 1964 would provide a legal framework until a new constitution was devised. The Interim Authority was charged with many of the same functions that UNTAET had arrogated to itself: the printing of a national currency, the establishment of a Civil Service Commission and a Human Rights Commission. The agreement also stipulated that the Security Council would authorize a "United Nations mandated force"—a multinational force like the ones in Bosnia and Kosovo—until Afghanistan had trained and fielded its own army, and that the UN itself would continue to provide political guidance to the Interim Authority.

The UN-mandated force, known as ISAF, finally gave NATO something to do in Afghanistan that the United States was happy to have it do. But the Bush administration, still deeply wary of nation-building, never envisioned ISAF as the equivalent of the large peacekeeping contingents in the Balkans and never intended to fold the U.S. presence into the proposed NATO structure. Richard Haass says he argued for a nationwide force of twenty-five to fifty thousand but lost out to the nation-building skeptics. "The counterargument was that the Afghans would resist, and in any case it's hopeless, since Afghanistan was never going to be a real country." At the same time, according to Nicholas Burns, "We couldn't get political agreement"—with NATO—"that the alliance should have a large presence." Once again, Burns says, European allies proved reluctant to make real commitments. In the end, ISAF fielded fifty-five hundred troops serving only in and around Kabul. The eight thousand remaining U.S. soldiers confined themselves to hunting down the remnants of Al Qaeda and the Taliban elsewhere in the country.

In mid-March, Annan proposed that the Security Council authorize the United Nations Assistance Mission in Afghanistan, which the council duly did. The UN would continue to provide political advice to the Interim Authority and would direct the vast humanitarian effort of feeding the destitute, resettling 4.5 million refugees, inoculating children, and so on. But the resolution explicitly declared that reconstruction assistance, as opposed to emergency aid, "ought to be provided through the Afghan Interim Administration and its successors." UNAMA would be truly an "assistance" mission, not a semi-sovereign body. Many other crucial tasks, such as the training of the army and the police, would be left to individual nations. The UN would furnish no uniformed officials of any kind, including civilian police.

The UN's "light footprint" in Afghanistan represented the successful realization of Brahimi's principles, and of the doctrine laid out in the Brahimi report. The emergency *loya jirga* took place six months after the Interim Authority was impaneled, just as planned. This grand gathering, it's true, was more a gaudy ritual than an exercise in democracy. Brahimi even later told the Security Council that the *loya jirga* "was not designed to be, nor could it realistically have been, a perfectly democratic or representative process." But of course rituals matter, and the very sight of sixteen hundred delegates, two hundred of them women, gathering from all parts of the country to discuss Afghanistan's future, talking rather than shooting at one another, was, as Brahimi said, "a great step forward in the peace process." The delegates elected Hamid Karzai president of the new Transitional Authority and ratified the Bonn process, further erasing the traces of the country's internationally assisted rebirth.

Over the next several years, Afghanistan's political structures evolved precisely as Brahimi had envisioned. The *loya jirga* that convened in 2003 ratified a constitution that provided Afghanistan's governing foundations. After an election in October 2004, in which 70 percent of the country's voters participated, Karzai became the first democratically reelected president in Afghanistan's history. All this was quite heady. But was it a success? Twenty years of almost continuous warfare had left Afghanistan one of the world's poorest countries. The average life expectancy was barely forty years, 50 percent of children were malnourished, literacy rates outside of major cities were negligible. The UN's modest presence, and the low level of international assistance—$52 per capita over the first two years, as opposed to $814 in Kosovo—ensured that Afghanistan made only modest gains in education, public health, civil administration, the provision of electricity and drinking water, policing, and justice. There was no economy; revenue came almost entirely from foreign assistance and the export of heroin, which flourished unchecked. And with only fifty-five hundred peacekeepers—one-eighth the number that entered Kosovo, a tiny cheese paring of a place—most of the country remained off-limits to serious reconstruction activity. Only Kabul, which was protected, enjoyed any real prosperity; in the countryside, warlords and brigands preyed on ordinary Afghans as well as on aid workers.

Afghanistan's political development made it a much safer place for the rest of the world, but the lack of economic and institutional development made it only a marginally better place for the Afghans themselves. It was an example less of the "light footprint" than of nation-building on the cheap. In the words of *America's Role in Nation-Building*, a study published by RAND, "Low input of military and civilian resources yields low output in terms of security, democratic transformation, and economic development." Afghanistan represented a convergence, though not a very happy one, between the Bush administration's hostility to nation-building and the UN's discomfort with neocolonialism.

On December 10, 2001, Kofi Annan delivered the Nobel Peace Prize lecture in Oslo. Along with the UN itself, he had been named two months earlier as the recipient of the prize in its centennial year. In its statement, the Nobel committee had praised Annan for "bringing new life to the organization" and for expanding its reach by taking on the issues of human rights, HIV/AIDS, and international terrorism. The committee singled out Annan's insistence that "sovereignty cannot be a shield behind which member states conceal their violations." As great lovers of peace and international organizations, the Norwegians had over the years given out several dozen of the awards to individuals and organizations affiliated with the pre–World War I peace movement, the League of Nations, and the UN. In the first two categories at least, "the prizes do not seem to have helped much," as the chairman of the committee observed in introducing Annan.

But if there was something almost hackneyed about anointing this pious organization with this pious honor, Annan was still the only secretary-general save for the great Hammarskjöld to have been so recognized—and Hammarskjöld had been granted his posthumously. Annan had reacted with his usual superhuman display of modesty, saying that he was "humbled, but also encouraged," and when he had been greeted by a cheering crowd in the Secretariat Building—as he had been once before, on his return from Baghdad—he had emphasized the half of the award that had gone to the UN, not to him personally. But the prize was the crowning distinction of Annan's career and the most indisputable evidence that he had, indeed, brought the UN from the margins to the center of world affairs.

Annan invited the inner circle to accompany him to Oslo—Riza, Lindenmayer, Lamin Sise, Shashi Tharoor, and Fred Eckhard, as well as Nader Mousavizadeh, who had done most of the work on the peace prize lecture. Oddly enough for a man so apparently companionable, the only personal friends he invited were the Holbrookes and the Shawcrosses. He was, after all, a very private figure. The Nobel lecture is one of the world's bully pulpits, and Annan's speech had been buffed to a high sheen of eloquence and noble sentiment. "We have entered the third millennium through a gate of fire," he said. International terrorism had instilled in everyone "a new insecurity," but this shared fear had in turn instilled "a deeper awareness of the bonds that bind us all." As the threat had become collective, so must be the response, for "no walls can separate humanitarian or human rights crises in one part of the world from national security crises in another." (The speech seemed to take for granted a direct connection between poverty and abuse, on the one hand, and terrorism, on the other.) Annan's speech was, above all, a plea on behalf of the fundamental rights of each individual to peace and access to basic human goods, even against the prerogatives of the state. It would be the role of the United Nations in the twenty-first century to advance those rights by "eradicating poverty, preventing conflict, and promoting democracy." In the era of the global threat, the United Nations, so often marginalized and belittled, would at last come into its own.

CHAPTER TEN

Saddam's Pyrrhic Victory

O N SEPTEMBER 28, 2001, SEVENTEEN DAYS AFTER THE DE-struction of the World Trade Center, the Security Council, in a great show of solidarity with the United States, adopted resolution 1373 calling on all states to suppress the financial resources and freeze the assets of terrorists; to track down and deny safe haven to terrorists; and to cooperate closely with other states in the exchange of intelligence as well as in police and judicial work. The resolution also established a Counter-Terrorism Committee to monitor compliance with its provisions. The committee was initially chaired by Jeremy Greenstock, probably the most important ambassador in the UN, given the power vacuum at the U.S. Mission, and certainly one of the ablest. In the committee's first public meeting, on January 18, 2002, Greenstock explained that its goal was "to raise the average level of government performance against terrorism across the globe." He had already received reports on compliance with the resolution's provisions from 122 members; over time, he hoped to begin working with members to recommend additional legislation that might be needed, to offer technical assistance on thorny issues like the tracking of terrorists' funds, and to build cooperation among states and regional organizations.

Members of the committee from the developing world generally applauded these goals, but hastened to add that the committee must of course delve into the "root causes" of terrorism—for example, as the Costa Rican ambassador noted, "hunger, illness and the lack of adequate housing to ensure respect for human dignity in conformity with the commitments prescribed by world leaders in the Millennium Declaration." Terrorism was failed development; good development was the ultimate cure. And Middle Eastern nations wished to make another point altogether. The ambassador of Syria observed that foreign occupation was "the most brutal form" of terrorism. Who was guilty of such a crime? Israel, of course. The Israelis were committing war crimes every day against the Palestinians and must be brought to justice, and so on.

The Counter-Terrorism Committee did help some countries with important issues like tracking financial flows. But the committee, as Greenstock frequently explained, had no enforcement powers; nor did it have the capacity to alter the political calculations of states. Members who did not feel threatened by terrorism, or who resented the sudden eclipse of the Millennium Development Goals by the specter of jihad, would not throw themselves into the global campaign sought by Washington. Kofi Annan saw in the new international terrorism a global problem demanding a global solution—that is, the UN. But so long as this global threat, like others, struck countries unequally and was defined by them differently, and in any case was treated by the United States as a matter of supreme national interest, the UN would struggle to find a place for itself.

Countries could not even agree on what terrorism *was*. Yet another UN grouping, the Ad Hoc Committee on Measures to Eliminate Terrorism, had been meeting since 1996 without having succeeded in defining the problem. Twelve different treaties covered various aspects of terrorism, including hijacking, bombing, and hostage taking. The ad hoc committee was now trying to draw up an omnibus convention that would fill the gaps between them, promote international cooperation, and provide a universally accepted definition of terrorism. Most of the convention's twenty-seven articles proved noncontroversial. The problem was Article 18—the definition. Many Third World states, and above all the Arab and Islamic ones, insisted that the killing of noncombatants in the course of "wars of national liberation," such as the one Palestinians were said to be waging against Israel, did not constitute terrorism. And so the committee met in January and February, and adjourned without producing the draft of a convention.

During this same period, a different group of UN officials and diplomats worked on a document for a very different conclave—the International Conference on Financing for Development, to be held in mid-March in the Mexican city of Monterrey. The conference would be the first attempt to give real substance to the promises made, and the new bargain struck, at the Millennium Summit. Impoverished countries would vow to mobilize such internal resources as they could muster by fighting corruption, adopting sound economic policies, and moving toward more transparent and accountable systems of governance. Donor nations, in turn, would increase assistance, improve the terms of trade for poor nations, and forgive billions of dollars in debt. The White House could have scuttled the agreement, but in these early post-9/11 days the Bush administration was eager to embrace the idea, advanced by Annan in his Nobel lecture, that the war on terrorism could not be won without a commitment to improve the lot of the poor.

The Monterrey Consensus codified this new bargain. Recipient nations among the signatories committed themselves to good governance and pro-growth policies. Donor nations accepted the premise that, neoliberal doctrine notwithstanding, even the best governed of the impoverished nations could not succeed without foreign aid, known formally as official development assistance. "ODA," the final document read, "can be critical for improving the environment for private sector activity and can thus pave the way for economic growth. ODA is also a crucial instrument for supporting education, health, public infrastructure development," and the like. The wealthy nations agreed to "make concrete efforts towards the target of 0.7 per cent of gross national product (GNP) as ODA." This was an astonishing concession, since development assistance then totaled 0.2 percent of the GNP of donor nations. Aid would thus increase from $53 billion a year to $175 billion a year by 2015. U.S. assistance would increase from $15 billion to $75 billion, at least if "make concrete efforts towards" could be construed as an actual commitment.

President Bush not only came to Mexico for the signing ceremony but arrived with a "deliverable" in hand. He announced a new program, the Millennium Challenge Account, which would provide $10 billion over the next three years to highly impoverished countries that had satisfied a series of good-government principles. Here was the first major new commitment of foreign aid by the United States in several decades—and from a conservative Republican president to boot! It was a rare moment of comity and optimism in the Bush administration's relation with the international community. And it didn't last long. The Millennium Challenge Account did not spend a dollar on Third World poverty for the next two years. The administration quickly fell behind the trajectory toward 0.7 percent, and later argued that the plain language of the Monterrey Consensus did not in fact commit the signatories to any particular goal, or even fixed increments, in development aid.

The habit of seeing everything through the prism of terrorism moved the Bush administration closer to the global consensus on issues like foreign aid—second-order issues, from the administration's point of view. But on the cardinal question of national security, the fight against terrorism hardened the conviction of the people around the president that the United States had to be prepared to chart its own course. The preeminent example, of course, was Iraq, which for years had been languishing on the world's back burner. The economic sanctions had grown ever more porous, while the Iraqis had refused to permit the return of the inspectors, who had left with the Desert Fox bombing campaign in December 1998. In February 2001, Secretary of State Colin Powell had proposed replacing the comprehensive sanctions regime with "smart sanctions" narrowly focused on proscribed weapons systems. British and American diplomats won widespread support for the idea on the Security Council, but it died when the Russians, vigilant defenders of Iraq's prerogatives, vowed to veto such a resolution.

The terrorist attacks put a decisive end to American fiddling with sanctions. In his 2002 State of the Union speech, in which he included Iraq in an "axis of evil," President Bush put the world on alert that Washington would no longer accept the status quo. The president's threat had no effect on the logjam at the UN, in part because the United States had lost interest in the discussion. First in January 2002, then in March, and then again in early July, Kofi Annan and his chief disarmament officials held discussions with their Iraqi counterparts, including the new foreign minister, Naji Sabri. Annan was hoping to persuade the Iraqis to let the inspectors back in, but he had no real incentives to offer in return. The final round of negotiations was held in Vienna and was accompanied by high hopes. But after emerging from the last meeting, Annan conceded that while there had been "some movement," it was "obviously not enough."

We now know that the White House began focusing its crosshairs on Saddam Hussein almost from the moment the Twin Towers collapsed. Richard Clarke, then Bush's chief counterterrorism adviser, has written that on September 12 the president instructed him to see if Saddam was "linked in any way" to the attacks. A few days later Paul Wolfowitz, the influential deputy secretary of defense, laid out the case for regime change before a very attentive president. Perhaps most important of all, Vice President Dick Cheney came to see Saddam, more than Osama bin Laden, as the most dangerous figure in this suddenly transformed world. Defense Secretary Donald Rumsfeld soon joined the chorus. Each of these figures had a slightly different rationale for an invasion of Iraq, but collectively they made a powerful case to a president who felt that history had presented him with a supreme test. By June 2002, according to George Packer's *The Assassins' Gate*, Condoleezza Rice had told the State Department's Richard Haass, who shared Colin Powell's skepticism about the merits of war, that he might as well save his breath, since "the president has already made up his mind."

The debate would be over not whether to go to war but how. And the question of how involved, above all, whether the administration should seek the legitimacy of a resolution authorizing war from the UN Security Council, as President Bush's father had. There would be a price attached to such a decision, for the council would insist on trying to restore the weapons inspectors to Iraq; only if Saddam refused or stonewalled once again would the council have its casus belli. "The Pentagon view was 'It's not necessary, and it's not desirable,'" says Haass. "From our point of view, it was both necessary and desirable. I thought it was going to be hellacious, and I thought having the UN chapeau would make it easier for others to contribute, and might make it more acceptable to Iraqis." In early August, Powell laid out this argument in a private dinner with President Bush, and the president promised that he would use his upcoming speech to the General Assembly to seek council action.

But the hard-liners in the administration, contemptuous of the UN and fearful that the United States would be trapped in its labyrinth, continued to fight. The debate broke out in the open when Vice President Cheney gave a major speech in late August laying out a dire scenario. "Many of us are convinced that Saddam will acquire nuclear weapons fairly soon," he declared. "There is no doubt," he went on, that Saddam now "has weapons of mass destruction" and that "he is amassing them to use against our friends, against our allies, and against us." In the face of these terrifying designs, "a person would be right to question any suggestion that we should just get our inspectors back in Iraq," for Saddam would exploit their presence to stave off war. The vice president pursued his argument inside the White House as well. In the meanwhile, however, Prime Minister Tony Blair told President Bush that British support for the campaign against Saddam would be predicated on going the UN route and seeking to return the inspectors to Iraq. In a final showdown on September 6, according to Bob Woodward's *Bush at War*, Cheney argued against asking the UN for anything. But Powell ultimately carried the day once more, with the president's proviso that dithering would not be tolerated.

On September 12, a year and a day from the terrorist attacks, first Kofi Annan, then George Bush, addressed the General Assembly. Annan felt that he needed to assert the centrality of UN decision making, though of course he had to be careful not to fling it in the president's face. "Choosing to follow or reject the multilateral path must not be a simple matter of political convenience," he observed. And while the Charter fully accepted the inherent right of states to self-defense, "when States decide to use force to deal with broader threats to international peace and security, there is no substitute for the unique legitimacy provided by the United Nations." This said, he warned Iraq that should it continue to defy the international community, "the Security Council must face its responsibilities."

President Bush then echoed Cheney's dark presentiments. "Saddam Hussein's regime is a grave and gathering danger," he stated. "To assume this regime's good faith is to bet the lives of millions and the peace of the world in a reckless gamble." Saddam had ignored UN resolutions for years and gotten away with it. Now, the president asked, "Will the United Nations serve the purpose of its founding, or will it become irrelevant?" Bush left no doubt about his meaning: "The Security Council resolutions will be enforced . . . or action will be unavoidable." Legitimacy, for the president, lay in the cause itself, not in the UN Charter.

In years past, tinhorn dictators, Soviet premiers, and right-wing U.S. senators had occasionally addressed the UN in the bald language of ultimatum, but the leaders of democratic nations had typically been far more respectful. Many of the members sitting there that day bristled at President Bush's lecture. What's more, although very few of them assumed Saddam Hussein's good faith, even fewer of them considered his regime a threat to millions and to world peace, or even a grave and gathering danger. And yet for all that, the UN greeted the president's speech with some gratitude, or at least with the relief of the long-suffering spouse who finds a tongue-lashing vastly preferable to abandonment. When I spoke soon afterward with Shashi Tharoor, he said, "As a UN official, I welcome the fact that the president came to the United Nations; I welcome the fact that the United Nations is the forum in which this thing is being thrashed out. In that spirit, I actually welcome what's happened, and I would say so do a lot of the members."

The very real fear that President Bush would simply ignore the Security Council exposed the hollowness of Annan's hope that the terrorist attacks would force the world into a recognition of mutuality. They had, in fact, had the opposite effect in Washington. The tragedy had brought out in the president and his advisers a deep streak of nationalism—the "hegemonic" sense, as Daalder and Lindsay put it, that only American might could thwart the forces of chaos and disintegration. Americans felt at once uniquely vulnerable and uniquely empowered. In his long essay "Of Paradise and Power," the policy analyst Robert Kagan observed that Americans accepted the brute Hobbesian reality of international relations, whereas Europeans, secure beneath the American nuclear umbrella, pursued Immanuel Kant's vision of a "perpetual peace" among democracies. Europeans simply did not view terrorism as an existential threat, as Americans did. This view surfaced in cruder form in Donald Rumsfeld's notorious distinction between an "old Europe" that sought to block America's world mission and a "new Europe" eager to abet it.

As the terrorist attacks seemed to vindicate the administration's hegemonic impulse, so they gave scope to the sweeping idealism, the vision of transformation, that animated the neoconservatives on Bush's foreign-policy team. Paul Wolfowitz, among others, had been arguing since the late 1990s that America could not and should not accept the status quo of an authoritarian Middle East with a ferociously anti-Semitic Stalinist, Saddam Hussein, at its heart. These were "forward-leaning" activists who would never have thought to take candidate George Bush's side in the debate between "interests" and "values"; for Wolfowitz or Kagan or Bill Kristol, editor of *The Weekly Standard*, the favored publication of the neocons, America best served its vital interests by taking the fight to the "Islamo-fascists" in Iraq, and perhaps elsewhere. Many of them had opposed "containment" during the Cold War; now they opposed it in the Middle East. Writing in *The Weekly Standard*, Kagan and Kristol argued that "the failure of the United States to take risks, and to take responsibility, in the 1990s, paved the way to September 11."

The hardheaded realism that Bush had espoused during the 2000 campaign had never really suited his deeply moralistic, Manichean understanding of the world; it sounded more like something he was channeling from Condoleezza Rice. Like Ronald Reagan, Bush was a man who saw "good" and "evil" not as vague metaphorical categories but as real forces contending for supremacy. The Evil Empire has passed, he had said in a 1999 speech, "but evil remains." And that demonic force, Bush believed, had shown its face on 9/11. "Today our nation saw evil," he told Americans in his address that night. In the ensuing days, he spoke frequently of God's active role in the world, his firm hand behind those who support freedom and justice. The terrorist attacks elevated Bush's presidency, which had seemed almost vagrant at times, into the realm of the transcendent—a dangerous realm, perhaps, for a political rather than a theological leader to occupy. The terrorist attacks were, as he wrote that night in his diary, "the Pearl Harbor of the 21st century." The adversary was similarly vast and implacable—"the axis of evil." And the one member of that axis that posed the most imminent threat to the United States was plainly Iraq.

A week after the president's speech the administration published its National Security Strategy. The NSS advocated strengthening alliances, promoting global development, and using the tools of public diplomacy, but those weren't the passages that made the headlines—and rightly so. "While the United States will constantly strive to enlist the support of the international community," the document stated, "we will not hesitate to act alone, if necessary, to exercise our right of self-defense by acting preemptively against such terrorists, to prevent them from doing harm against our people and our country." Here were the two doctrines that made the NSS such a departure from its predecessors—unilateralism and preemption.

The authors rightly observed that the United States had long reserved the right to act preemptively in the face of an imminent threat; the break with the past was the conclusion that terrorism had forced a fundamental change in the calculus that governed the traditional doctrine of containment. "The inability to deter a potential attacker, the immediacy of today's threats and the magnitude of potential harm that can be caused by our adversaries' choice of weapons," they wrote, means that "we cannot let our enemies strike first." The same need for swift action meant that one could no longer afford to wait for collective action. But the Bush administration's unblushing embrace of the unilateral option was a matter not only of tactics but of philosophy: a nation that was not only unique in power but also unique in its sense of destiny and moral purpose could not allow itself to be constrained by lesser and more expedient actors. This "distinctly American internationalism" was "open to all"; but that was only to say that others could join the war on terror on America's terms. As President Bush said in his address to Congress soon after 9/11, "Either you are with us, or you're with the terrorists." The operative word was "us": it was for America to define the terms of combat.

The National Security Strategy was only a codification of principles already understood to be guiding the policy of the Bush administration, but as the worldwide debate over the document merged with the worldwide debate over the merits of the administration's case for war in Iraq, it became painfully clear that the UN was being asked to accept not merely a particular course of action in a particular conflict but a set of doctrines that appeared to be inimical to its own survival. The UN Charter acknowledged the right of *preventive* attack, which is to say the right to respond in self-defense to an imminent threat, but other forms of hostilities, including a preemptive attack intended to prevent an adversary from becoming dangerous, could be made legitimate only by a resolution of the Security Council. International law could not countenance the doctrine of "unilateral preemption." The only way to make America's war aims legitimate was thus to acquiesce in them, in the form of a Security Council resolution. But this, too, seemed unacceptable. Irrelevance seemed to beckon on every side. As Nader Mousavizadeh, the speechwriter, said at the time, "The members are facing a very difficult choice—either they go with the United States on this, and are seen to be selling out on principles of international order and international law, or they block this, provoking the U.S. to go away from the council, and maybe not return." And without American engagement and support, the Security Council might as well close up shop.

And so the sense of relief, not to mention the pride and excitement of standing at the heart of the world, as proved by the breathless media accounts and the phalanx of network satellite trucks parked out on First Avenue, was very real. But underneath it was a fear that the system was coming apart. The reason nations brought their disputes to the Security Council was that it possessed a precious good that no other institution could claim—the "legitimacy" that came with the council's stamp of approval. It was understood that great powers would settle problems with their neighbors, or their former colonies, on their own. Here, however, was a global confrontation that plainly required adjudication in the world's global body. But Washington was giving the very strong impression that it did not much need the UN's legitimacy and would dispense with it if pressed.

Indeed, the initial draft of an Iraq resolution that the United States circulated was so provocative that it confirmed the fear that the administration simply wanted to conscript the UN into its plans for regime change. The inspectors would be accompanied by armed guards, and the United States would have a right to include its own nationals on the inspection team. These terms, obvious nonstarters, had come from the Pentagon and had been included over the objections of the State Department, for the battle inside the upper ranks of the administration was still raging. American diplomats quietly dropped these demands but continued to insist that in the event of "noncompliance" with the inspection regime, the United States would be able to declare the Iraqis in "material breach" of prior UN resolutions, and begin hostilities. The French, who along with Russia and China had defended Iraq for years, refused to grant this principle of "automaticity," insisting instead that the council would have to authorize the use of force in a second resolution. This impasse stretched on through September and October, thus proving to Cheney and the other hard-liners that the UN's goal was simply to constrain American power.

And in this they were not altogether wrong. Both diplomats and UN officials were far less worried than the Americans were about the threat from Iraq, and far more worried about the threat to the UN itself, and to the principle of multilateralism, that the United States posed. Everywhere I went in the UN that fall, I heard the fear that the world would spiral into chaos should the United States set a precedent of acting in defiance of the international order. What would stop India from acting preemptively, and unilaterally, against Pakistan, or Russia from invading Georgia to root out terrorists? Diplomats are conservative by nature; they are inclined to fear action more than inaction. Gelson Fonseca, the Brazilian ambassador, cited Hegel to the effect that "order is better than justice." What he meant was that no single actor could arrogate to itself the right to determine a just order; only by subordinating each actor, even the most powerful, to a set of rules could one ensure a stable world system. This was the wisdom of the medium-power nation. "We're committed to multilateralism because the rules of international law protect us from the powerful," Fonseca said. The United States, he said, had to be "contained," just as Iraq did.

Annan's idea of containment was to lock both sides in the UN embrace. After the president's speech, he had called to offer thanks, but added, "Don't bash the UN, Mr. President; you'll find you need us later." Soon after, when the Iraqis initially answered Bush's call for inspections in vague and snippy terms, Michael Moller, Annan's adviser on politics, peacekeeping, and humanitarian affairs, gathered the Iraqi foreign minister and other officials in his office and rewrote the response to make it clear that the Iraqis did, in fact, accept the return of the inspectors. Annan tried, as he had in 1998, to push both sides into some notional middle. "If you allow yourselves to be divided," he said in mid-October while negotiations seemed hopelessly stalled, "the authority and credibility of this organization will undoubtedly suffer." But it was not 1998. The Bush administration was far less invested in the UN than the Clinton administration had been, and with war in the offing, the stakes were much higher. This battle would be conducted over Annan's head.

It wasn't only the difference between Clinton and Bush, or between a multilateral and a unilateral impulse, that made this new debate over Iraq so much more momentous than the previous one; it was the difference between the era before and after 9/11. Desert Fox had been one of the indecisive skirmishes of the post–Cold War era, a time when old threats had subsided and new ones had not yet taken shape; containing bad actors seemed well within the competence of the major states. The terrorist attacks had reversed the logic of containment, at least in the United States. Since, in this new age, catastrophe could strike from a clear blue sky, the consequences of erring on the side of patience had become unacceptably high. What's more, the enemy read containment as weakness.

But that was for Washington. A French diplomat pointed out to me that with a Muslim population of five to six million—up to 10 percent of the country—France was at least as worried about the effect back home of an American attack as it was about the Iraqis. Anything that smacked of holy war would be very bad; a Security Council resolution at least would pit the whole international community, and not just the West or the United States, against Saddam. What he did not say was that France, like Russia, might have been influenced as well by its strong and long-standing commercial ties with Iraq, and in fact had competed with Russia over the years for the role of Iraq's stoutest defender among the permanent five. Finally, the showdown over Iraq also gave France the opportunity to obstruct the will of the United States, and thus to enjoy, however briefly, a spurious sense of equality with the "hyper-power" (to use the expression of the former French foreign minister Hubert Védrine). Only in the Security Council, where it occupied the inner circle of the veto bearers, did France enjoy a status equal to its own sense of self-esteem, and there also it could exercise its talents for diplomatic subtlety.

The French and the Americans seemed to be united only in their willingness to do serious damage to the international order so as to make a point or to have their way. For many American conservatives, who had despised the UN ever since the era of "Zionism equals racism" and the New International Economic Order a quarter of a century earlier, the destruction wasn't incidental; it was the goal. Right-wing think tanks like the Project for the New American Century had begun planning for a post-UN world in which the United States stood at the lead of ad hoc coalitions, or perhaps of a new organization of democracies. They seemed not to notice that the chief opposition to the Iraq war came not from left-leaning Third World countries, of which few remained, but from America's traditional allies. And in any case, they dismissed opposition, at least in the old Europe, as mere pusillanimity. It became fashionable to detest the French; the U.S. Congress led the way by bravely rechristening "French fries" as "freedom fries." And the Bush administration was all too happy to exploit the emerging spirit of nativism.

At the outset, however, both countries had reason to want the process to work—the United States in order to rally the UN behind its war aims, France in order to bind the United States to the Security Council process. And when both parties to a negotiation have reason to make common cause, as they did here, what cannot be reconciled can always be fudged. In early November, the Bush administration agreed that the council would "convene immediately" for deliberations should the inspectors report Iraqi noncompliance, while the French agreed to delete language requiring a second resolution to authorize force. There would be a "two-step process" but not a "two-resolution process." On November 8, the Security Council unanimously, and with a great sigh of relief, passed resolution 1441, restoring the inspectors to Iraq, eliminating the special protocol for "sensitive sites" established four years earlier, and threatening "to consider the situation and the need for compliance"—the understood euphemism for force—should Iraq be found to be in "material breach" of its obligation to disarm.

The resolution had required Iraq to submit a "currently accurate, full and complete declaration" of its WMD program, and in early December Iraq delivered a whopping twelve-thousand-page report intended to satisfy that demand. Tiny needles of fresh information —none of it very revealing—were scattered through this giant haystack, as if the Iraqis were amusing themselves by satisfying the Security

Council's requirements in the most literal-minded way possible. It was a bad sign. Colin Powell declared that the omissions in the report themselves constituted a "material breach," though of course he was assuming that Iraq had weapons programs that it was glossing over. Others drew no such conclusion. The inspections, which had begun in late November, continued.

The International Atomic Energy Agency was responsible for nuclear inspections, as it had been earlier, while UNSCOM had been dissolved and replaced by UNMOVIC, which was designed with safeguards to prevent some of the problems that had dogged UNSCOM, such as the allegation in 1998 that American inspectors had channeled intelligence back to the CIA. The heads of the two groups, Mohamed ElBaradei and Hans Blix, delivered their initial report to the Security Council on January 27. By this time, the United States had already massed well over 100,000 troops in the Gulf; military planners were openly talking about the need to begin a campaign in winter, before the hot weather set in. The administration was counting on the inspectors to catch Iraq in a "material breach." But the inspectors weren't finding anything. Jacques Baute, the head of the IAEA inspection team, told me a year or so later, "It was embarrassing when we came back." Iraq's facilities seemed to be in even more of a shambles than they had been in 1997, when the IAEA had concluded that the nuclear program was finished. ElBaradei reported that he had found no evidence that the program had been revived. Blix, on the other hand, focused on Iraq's sullen intransigence and halfhearted cooperation. He said that "Iraq appears not to have come to a genuine acceptance—not even today—of the disarmament which was demanded of it and which it needs to carry out to win the confidence of the world and to live in peace."

Once again the Bush and Blair administrations jumped on this piece of news as evidence that Iraq had defied the will of the international community. But Blix had come up with nothing resembling a smoking gun, and there was no appetite in the council for immediate action. It's unlikely that the inspectors could have said anything that would have produced a consensus for or against war. The Americans were defining "compliance" as the kind of unconditional acquiescence demonstrated by Nelson Mandela when he had invited the international community to help him dismantle the nuclear program built by

South Africa's apartheid-era government. The French, on the other hand, flatly opposed hostilities. Indeed, on January 20, Foreign Minister Dominique de Villepin had declared that under no circumstances would the French authorize a war in Iraq—a position Germany had already adopted.

Both sides were now prepared to ignore the evidence, if for opposite reasons. On January 28, President Bush delivered his State of the Union speech, in which he famously alleged that Saddam had sought to buy "yellowcake" uranium from Niger. The speech convinced many listeners that war was inevitable, but not that it was necessary. A week later, Secretary of State Powell was dispatched to the UN on a rare mission to present the administration's case. Powell's careful delivery and quietly forceful manner—and the giant screens on which he offered up grainy satellite images—may have won over a few more fence-sitters. He alluded to intelligence on Iraq's mobile bioweapons units, "decontamination" trucks for chemical weapons, aluminum tubes for centrifuges to purify uranium, and a "truck caravan" near a "biological-weapons-related facility." It was all very impressive—save for the fact that the inspectors had already looked into all of these claims and found nothing to contradict the innocent explanations the Iraqis had offered. As for the tale of the yellowcake, which Powell had had the tact to omit, Jacques Baute of the IAEA quickly determined that the whole thing was based on a transparent forgery. Powell later said that he was mortified to have delivered up before the world what turned out to be a skein of falsehoods.

Iraq was looking increasingly like a poor test case of the doctrine of preemption. The administration's claims of an Iraq–Al Qaeda connection seemed tendentious and overdrawn. And two months of inspections had done nothing to advance the case that Iraq had weapons of mass destruction. The Bush administration was isolated not—or at least not only—because other nations were too pusillanimous to face up to a grave and gathering threat, but because they disagreed on the severity of that threat. By February, the administration was adopting the uncomfortable position that the means that the Security Council had chosen to ascertain the truth about Iraq's weapons programs—the inspections—should be curtailed well before the inspectors had been able to ascertain that truth.

ElBaradei and Blix returned to the Security Council on February 14. Though the administration had focused its case largely on Iraq's nuclear program, ElBaradei reported that in fact he had no "unresolved disarmament issues." In effect, nothing had changed since 1997. Blix, who had been shocked by the way the Americans had treated his first report as a casus belli, cautiously praised Iraq's cooperation with his inspectors and said that while many weapons and other items were "not accounted for," this was not proof that they existed. Both men asked for more time. Blix has since written that at this point he still believed, as did most of the officials of national intelligence services he was working with, that Iraq had concealed weapons, but he had yet to find the evidence.

Annan shared the general UN view that the Americans were exaggerating the imminence of the Iraqi threat, and thus that war was unnecessary, and he did not believe that such a war could be justified as an act of humanitarian intervention, as he had in the case of Kosovo. He also felt that, absent Security Council approval, the war would be legally indefensible—a view he continues to hold. "How can you argue that you're going to war in defiance of the Security Council," he asks, "to establish the credibility of that council?" Nevertheless, Annan's chief concern was always the integrity and relevance of the UN, and he would have accepted, and perhaps even embraced, a resolution authorizing war so long as the council was firmly united behind it. He kept hoping, to the very last, that diplomacy would save the day.

Annan spent much of January and February manning the phones in his endless search for common ground. He spoke constantly with Colin Powell and Dominique de Villepin and Jack Straw, the British foreign secretary. He often called Chirac and Blair, or they, him. Chirac talked in apocalyptic terms: "It's going to be a disaster, there's going to be chaos, there's going to be resistance, the Iraqis will shoot at everybody." (And he was not far off the mark.) Blair, like Bush, considered Iraq a grave threat, but like Chirac, he wanted to give the inspectors more time. Annan tried to find language that would give the Americans pause without angering them. At the same time, he knew very well that the Americans would not stand for another act of heroic intervention on his part. Toward the end, Nelson Mandela called to say that Richard Branson, the flamboyant British entrepreneur, had offered to fly Mandela and Annan and perhaps Jimmy Carter to Iraq to work out a last-minute compromise. Annan told Mandela to forget about it.

By mid-February more than 200,000 troops had gathered in the Gulf. The prospect of war galvanized the European public, leading to the largest mass demonstrations in memory. A sizable protest movement mobilized in the United States as well; a majority of citizens accepted that war might be necessary, though most said they would be comfortable only if the war had UN support. Blair was still trying desperately to avoid repudiating the Security Council. The British endorsed a Canadian proposal to give Saddam a set of "benchmarks" for cooperation, with the understanding that a failure to reach them would constitute a "material breach." The Americans briefly toyed with this idea, and then rejected it as new grounds for UN temporizing.

Blair was even more keen on returning to the council for authorization, as resolution 1441 somewhat ambiguously foresaw. The Pentagon and the vice president's office opposed the idea, while the State Department took Blair's side. For once, State won. The Americans and the British began counting heads in the Security Council. France did not want to have to make good its promise to veto a resolution authorizing force, and Paris instructed Jean-David Levitte, its ambassador in Washington, to quietly advise Bush administration officials to simply go to war on the basis of existing resolutions, as NATO had done in Kosovo—a characteristically crafty, if cynical, piece of diplomatic finesse. Condoleezza Rice's deputy, Stephen Hadley, explained that while the Bush administration had no need for a second resolution, Tony Blair very much did. Hadley was also convinced that the United States could win at least nine of the fifteen council members, thus carrying the motion—unless France cast a lone veto, as it had threatened to do.

The United States was accustomed to getting what it wanted in the UN, not so much by force of argument as by sheer weight. The Clinton administration's campaign to reduce American dues, which succeeded in the face of almost universal opposition and even disgust, proved, if proof were needed, that few nations would stand up to the world's superpower on a matter of real importance (as opposed to rhetorical or symbolic issues, where opposition was relatively cost-free). American political engagement had been the fuel of Security Council activism from the time of the UN's inception; no responsible actor wanted the United States to walk away from the institution. In this case, though, the Bush administration had backed even its allies into a very uncomfortable corner. The half-dozen undecided countries on the council were torn between the fear of angering the Bush administration and the fear of angering their own citizens, who opposed the war almost as one. And they shared the general UN view that the war was simply wrongheaded.

"They didn't want to choose," says a French official. "And then we had a discussion with the key actors—Mexico, Chile, and Pakistan. And the president of Mexico told us, 'Look, I want to abstain, but I don't want to be the one killing this resolution. I fear that you would shift from a no to an abstention. And if I stay where I am, I will be the one blamed, because the resolution will not be adopted, not because of a veto, but because there will not be nine votes. What I want from you is to say publicly that if there is a vote, you would vote no.' " The key moment of this whole very public drama came on March 5, when the foreign ministers of France, Germany, and Russia met in Paris and vowed that "they would not let a resolution pass that would authorize force." The fence-sitters then told the Americans that they would oppose the resolution. And that was the end of the game: the Americans and the British withdrew the resolution rather than allowing it to go down to defeat.

Given the widespread fear of crossing the United States, the failure to win a second resolution came to be seen as proof of the bullying clumsiness of American diplomacy. "If you're publicly threatened with the consequences if you don't go along," says Kieran Prendergast, Annan's head of political affairs, "then if you're a self-respecting country, you can't go along." The Bush administration had dissipated the goodwill that came with the terrorist attacks by its rhetorical bellicosity, its unwillingness to acknowledge that other nations might have legitimate interests of their own, and its bullying demand that even allies sign protocols exempting Americans from the jurisdiction of the International Criminal Court. The Americans were thus expecting other countries to do for them something the United States itself would not have contemplated doing for those others—not a good basis for acquiescence.

Annan took the view that "if a bit more time had been given, and they had tried everything and they had concluded that the inspectors had been unable to come to a conclusion, they"—the French and others—"may have joined the coalition." They might have, but logic argues otherwise. Given more time, the inspectors, as we now know, would have found nothing. The Iraqis probably would have continued to cooperate sufficiently to avoid flagrantly violating the benchmarks. Public opinion would have become, if anything, more antiwar. And so the status quo would simply have been prolonged, agonizingly, while a quarter of a million troops sweltered in the desert. The United States and its allies would have faced the same decision, only later. The Bush administration would have sent in the troops one way or another. Saddam Hussein thus made war inevitable by refusing to cry uncle, but by complying sufficiently with resolution 1441, he also ensured that that war would shatter the international community. Surely that must be the definition of a Pyrrhic victory.

Many top UN officials were furious at Bush and Blair; Prendergast describes the war as "one of the most shameful episodes in British foreign policy since Suez." Annan, however, liked both men. He felt sorry for Blair, whom he felt the Americans had hung out to dry. And he and Bush remained on friendly terms. In January, in the midst of all the turbulence, the president had invited Annan and Nane to a small dinner at the White House. Harsh words rarely passed between them. When they disagreed, Bush would say, "Kofi, you've got to do what you've got to do, and I've got to do what I've got to do."

Most men in Annan's position would have been outraged. The great powers—mostly, but not only, the United States—had trampled on the thing that was most precious to him, the principle of international order as embodied in the United Nations. They had, in a way, trampled on *him*, for he had long since merged his own sense of self into the being of the institution. But Annan wasn't angry; he was, rather, beset by a profound sense of failure, even of despair. On March 19, as the first bombs were dropping over Baghdad, he spoke to the Security Council and said, "We must all feel that this is a sad day for the United Nations and the international community."

People around Annan noticed that he was quite suddenly getting gray—not his hair, which had long gone silver, but his face, which appeared to be losing its luster day by day. He was also losing his voice, a kind of literal enactment of the way in which he had lost his voice in the councils of state. He slogged through the latter half of March and the first several weeks of April, preparing for the return of the UN to Iraq. But after he came back from a trip toward the end of April, he suffered a kind of slow-motion collapse. "He was broken," says Elisabeth Lindenmayer, who accompanied him on this last trip, as she did on all his travels. "It was some kind of personal drama." For several weeks, Annan rarely stirred from his home. He had a severe cold, but everyone understood that the problem was psychological. The Secretariat's decision-making machinery, which revolved wholly around the secretary-general, virtually ground to a halt. The UN was like a sailing ship locked in the doldrums. Then, in mid-May, Annan returned to the office. He had, through whatever means, regained his grip, and the ship sailed warily, shakily on.

The war in Iraq did not, of course, destroy the UN, any more than it destroyed the secretary-general; it did, however, seriously, and lastingly, weaken both. The Bush administration was perfectly heedless of the damage it caused. Key figures in the administration viewed Security Council deliberations, and the inspection process itself, as a trap; the administration never intended to let the chips fall where they may, unless they fell its way. Policy makers wanted the legitimacy that comes with UN backing but would not make meaningful concessions in order to gain it; they wanted the Security Council to act as a rubber stamp. Had the council meekly done the administration's bidding, that legitimacy might well have been seen as a counterfeit good. But the White House seemed to be heedless of this as well; both for the hard-headed ex–Cold Warriors like Cheney and Rumsfeld and for the sunnier Wilsonians of the right, America's interventions in the world were, as Jesse Helms had put it before the Security Council, *inherently* legitimate. The UN was not built to accommodate so intoxicating a mixture of self-righteousness and power.

But that's not the whole story. The French, the Russians, and the Germans seemed at least as preoccupied with thwarting American ambitions as they did with disarming Saddam. How else could they have unequivocally declared that they would not vote to authorize war, even though they had no idea whether or not Saddam was flouting Security Council resolutions? At the time, after all, almost all major intelligence agencies believed that Saddam *was* concealing dangerous weapons; the opponents would have looked very foolish indeed had those expectations turned out to be right. The widespread intelligence failure also had the effect of discrediting the administration's case for preemptive war. But it wasn't the doctrine that was wrong; the *facts* were wrong. The next time someone cries wolf, there really may be a wolf.

Unilateralism, on the one hand, and obstructionism, on the other, immobilized the Security Council. But underneath the ugly theatrics was a problem for which no one was to blame: the very different estimates among nations of the danger posed by Iraq, and the different understandings of what is required of the West in the face of millennial terrorism. The Cold War had the virtue, unappreciated at the time, of unifying the West in the face not only of a common enemy but of a shared perception of threat. The age of terror may well have the opposite effect. Few Third World nations—and certainly not China—treat the fight against terrorism as the organizing principle of their foreign policy. Russia has been happy to cheer on the United States, but largely in order to provide cover for its own campaign against Islamic insurgents in Chechnya. The French may have been right in fearing an outraged Muslim population at home more than they feared Saddam Hussein's designs, and thus in calculating that accommodation served their purposes better than confrontation. But the Americans also may have been right in thinking that as the acme and symbol of the West, they constitute the bull's-eye of Islamic terrorism, and thus that in their case, as Donald Rumsfeld often put it, "weakness is provocative." If these estimates are right—or in any case, if they persist—the awful deadlock over Iraq could prove to be the shape of things to come.

CHAPTER ELEVEN

"What Did They Die For?"

T HERE WAS NEVER ANY QUESTION OF REPEATING IN IRAQ the political formula that had worked so well in Afghanistan. After the swift, if grossly premature, declaration of victory in Baghdad, the Bush administration was in no mood to seek help from the UN, which had denied the military campaign its precious stamp of legitimacy. Nor would the Security Council, battered after months of bitter debate, have accepted the offer had it been made. The prevailing attitude was: Let the United States drink from its own poisoned chalice. And finally, it wasn't at all clear that even Lakhdar Brahimi himself could do a Brahimi in Iraq. Saddam Hussein had so thoroughly extirpated the opposition that Brahimi might have lacked for interlocutors, save for the expatriates who had been tainted by close association with the United States. The Bush administration, in any case, wanted the credit for liberating Iraq before returning the country to its people.

Inside the Secretariat, an interdepartmental body called the Steering Group on Iraq had been meeting weekly since November 2002, preparing for every kind of eventuality: the swift evacuation of personnel in case of war, the need to respond to a humanitarian catastrophe caused by war, the question of postwar government. Once the U.S.-led attack began, the steering group meetings focused on the question of whether, and under what circumstances, the UN should return to Iraq. Opinion tended to be determined by job description: "humanitarians," who concerned themselves with the effects of war, not its causes, were generally prepared to return to Iraq the instant the environment permitted, whereas political officials, many of whom viewed the war as a raw exercise in American power, had no wish to wrap the effort in the UN flag. But many veteran UN figures believed that their responsibility to the institution trumped personal views—that personal views could not be allowed to infect the decision process. "We always felt," as Iqbal Riza says, "that we should not be the first to leave any place and we should not be the last to return."

Kofi Annan was an extreme example of this view; for him, the wish to restore the centrality of the UN, which the war had undermined as no other single event had since the end of the Cold War, rendered other considerations irrelevant. "I told Washington at the end of the war," he says, "that we have had these deep divisions and we need to heal. And one way to heal is to come back to the UN and work with them on a program for how to stabilize Iraq. And at the beginning the attitude was 'Why should we? We fought the war; you were against the war'—as if we were asking them to help share their big victory or hand it over to us on a platter, when I thought *we* were helping *them*."

The triumphalism of the Bush administration, its overweening sense of vindication, only increased the resistance inside the UN to playing a role in American-occupied Iraq. The Steering Group on Iraq was so deeply divided that the members took several straw polls; a narrow majority favored returning to Iraq. Riza reported the results to Annan, who said that he wanted a clear policy judgment, not a vote breakdown. Riza went back to the group, and on April 28, seventeen days after the U.S.-led forces had declared victory, they agreed that the UN belonged in Iraq. A security assessment team traveled from Amman to Baghdad soon thereafter, and humanitarian officials, who had waited out the war in Jordan, began to filter back. On April 30, in one of his last appearances before disappearing into his residence on Sutton Place, Annan implored the Security Council to "leave behind earlier disagreement and find unity of purpose in the postwar phase."

But what was the UN's role in the postwar phase? The Security Council had accepted the replacement of Saddam Hussein's government by the Coalition Provisional Authority, run by the United States and Great Britain. The UN could have only the powers that the CPA was willing to grant, and the council to confirm. Both the Secretariat and most council members wanted to give the UN mission an explicit role in fashioning a future Iraqi government, but the Bush administration would have none of it. On May 22, the Security Council approved resolution 1483 requesting the secretary-general to appoint a special representative who, "in coordination with the Authority," was charged with "promoting" the return of refugees, the protection of human rights, and the process of economic reconstruction; "encouraging international efforts" in various sectors; and "working intensively" with all relevant parties, including the Authority, to create political institutions and ultimately to establish a permanent Iraqi government. The UN, in short, would have no authority of its own.

This was precisely the sort of mandate political officials in the UN feared. "The issue should have been: the UN will come back to implement a political strategy," says Salman Ahmed, a veteran of Lakhdar Brahimi's tutelary role in Afghanistan. "With no clear strategy, the UN shouldn't go back." Ahmed recognizes that the Secretariat couldn't resist a unanimous decision of the Security Council, but he says, "We could have been more aggressive about saying well beforehand that we shouldn't go in. After all, a central tenet of the Brahimi report was that we shouldn't go in where we don't have the capacity to help. Wasn't this just such a situation? I don't think we needed to be everywhere. So we're not in Iraq. What the hell?"

But after this great institutional and personal trauma, Annan was eager, perhaps desperate, to restore some version of the *status quo ante*. He asked Sergio Vieira de Mello, the most experienced crisis manager in the UN and perhaps its single most gifted official, to head the UN Assistance Mission for Iraq, or UNAMI. Many people, Annan very much included, imagined him as a future secretary-general. Vieira de Mello had just become high commissioner for human rights and had absolutely no wish to go to Baghdad, especially as a powerless version of the proconsul he had been in East Timor. But by now, after weeks of unrestrained looting and street violence had blunted the initial mood of euphoria, the Bush administration had come to see the advantages of a UN presence, which would offer some of that "legitimacy" at which White House officials so often sneered, and they wanted Vieira de Mello, whom U.S. officials had worked with in trouble spots all over the world. Condoleezza Rice asked him to come see her at the White

House, and after pressing him to take the job, she brought him across the hall to see President Bush, who repeated the request. Vieira de Mello relented. Annan asked him to serve as his special representative for six months. Vieira de Mello offered three months, tops. They compromised at four. The special representative reached Baghdad on June 1.

By this time, Iraq was fast becoming a disaster area. In one of the truly astonishing failures of the war, top administration officials, above all Donald Rumsfeld and Dick Cheney, had annulled months of planning centered on the State Department, leaving the governance of postwar Iraq to a team of retired military officers with no mandate to work with Iraqis to create a viable state, and in any case no ability to do so. Washington was full of civilian and military officials with long experience in peacekeeping and nation-building; it was accepted wisdom among them that job one was establishing security, which required a massive military and police presence, and that thereafter, "everything is politics." But all these voices had been ignored, for in its uppermost levels the administration remained deeply suspicious of nation-building. Hadn't the "light footprint" worked perfectly well in Afghanistan? What's more, Rumsfeld, Cheney, and Bush were persuaded, in part by a handpicked group of Iraqi exiles, that a jubilant population would embrace American soldiers as the French had done in 1944. After the Americans had repaired whatever was broken, they would stand up a government led by these expatriates and remove all but thirty thousand or so troops. Mission accomplished, as President Bush would famously say on May 1.

That this "plan" was in fact an exercise in wishful thinking became painfully obvious as the orgy of looting inflicted vastly more damage than American bombers had. Coalition troops, with no clear instructions on postwar conduct, stood by, infuriating and frightening the Iraqis who had celebrated Saddam's downfall. Looters stripped the power grid and oil facilities, leaving Baghdad and other major cities with only sporadic electricity as temperatures rose to 120 degrees. Even as President Bush was declaring victory, his top aides had decided to replace Jay Garner, the bluff and politically maladroit retired general who served as the head of the entity directing the postwar effort, the hopefully named Office of Reconstruction and Humanitarian

Assistance. The new man in Baghdad would be Paul Bremer, a veteran State Department official who would head up the new, more sweepingly titled Coalition Provisional Authority.

Bremer was a counterterrorism expert with no prior experience of Iraq or of peacekeeping; he arrived with all of ten days of preparation for the job of rebuilding this shattered, blood-soaked country. In his first two decisions, shaped by the Pentagon and its team of favored Iraqis, he disqualified all but low-ranking members of the Baath Party from holding jobs in the new Iraq and dissolved the Iraqi army, the nation's sole coherent institution. Bremer later explained that the army had already "dissolved itself," but Iraqi officers certainly could have reconstituted the ranks. No one familiar with the history of Kosovo or Bosnia would have considered such moves wise; one of the first decisions made by the chief UN administrator in Kosovo was to convert the KLA to an unarmed civilian force called Kosovo Protection Corps. Bremer, however, had no such experience, and White House officials had persuaded themselves that the guiding analogy should be the American postwar regimes in Germany and Japan, rather than the UN-administered missions in the Balkans. In two swift strokes, Bremer had deprived the new state of much of its professional talent, driven Sunnis deeper into opposition, and left several hundred thousand men with their weapons and nothing to do save use them.

By the time Vieira de Mello arrived with his vague mandate, the mood outside the American sanctuary known as the Green Zone was turning increasingly sour and ominous, though the insurgency had not yet formed. Vieira de Mello assigned himself the job of traveling around the country and meeting with the leadership class who had had little or no contact with the Americans. Bremer had decided to appoint an Iraqi advisory council in order to put a local face on American dominance, and he was willing to give the UN a role in recruiting its members. By this time, Vieira de Mello had come around to something like the Brahimi view in such matters. He told Bremer that legitimate Iraqi leaders would never accept so marginal a role. "You've got to give them responsibilities, even though you might be ultimately challenged," he told the author George Packer, recalling his conversations with Bremer. "Iraqis are traumatized, Iraqis feel humiliated, rightly so . . . They might be happy that Saddam is gone forever, thank God, but they're not happy with this kind of situation." Bremer never took the argument seriously.

Vieira de Mello's political adviser, Jamal Benomar, took him to meet Grand Ayatollah Sistani, the Iranian-born cleric who commanded the loyalty of millions of Shiites and who had refused to meet with any American official. Vieira de Mello listened as Sistani complained about the American scheme to convene an assembly to draft a constitution; only a body elected by Iraqis, Sistani insisted, could devise the laws under which Iraqis would live. Vieira de Mello conveyed this to Bremer, who, assuming that the ayatollah was bluffing, went ahead with his plans—at which point Sistani issued a fatwa prohibiting Iraqis from participating in the assembly and thus scuttling the idea. Vieira de Mello talked to Sunni clerics and Baathists and Communists and academics. He nodded sympathetically as they spoke of their fear and anger over the American occupation, and he addressed their feelings by speaking publicly and privately about the imperative of Iraqi "ownership" of political institutions and policy decisions. Over the course of six weeks, he persuaded reluctant leadership figures to identify themselves with the American regime, and he persuaded Bremer both to accept figures he was inclined to balk at and to change the name of the body to the more dignified Governing Council (even though it remained powerless). The council was seated in mid-July.

This was just what Annan had had in mind when he argued for a serious role for the UN. But now that Vieira de Mello had made the Governing Council possible, Bremer didn't know what to do with him. And the special representative was only halfway through his four-month commitment. He was counting the days. Every day, Salman Ahmed recalls, Vieira de Mello would say, "I'm here for four months, and that's it." He was frustrated and impatient. "Sergio had his own self-respect," says Jeremy Greenstock, the former ambassador who was soon to come to Iraq as Bremer's British counterpart. "He wanted to be part of the ruling triangle. He wanted to equate with the Americans for the dignity of the UN."

What's more, the days when Vieira de Mello could move around the country with a driver and translator were long gone. The insurgency was coalescing; the number of attacks against coalition forces tripled from May to July. And when, on August 7, a car bomb exploded outside the Jordanian embassy, killing eighteen people, it became frighteningly clear that the rules of the game—what had appeared to be the rules of the game—had changed. If Arab diplomats were fair game, then so, clearly, were any noncombatants. Several days later UN security officials learned of a planned bomb attack in the Canal Road area, where the UN mission was located.

Many of the 350-odd UN employees had become seriously alarmed. Salim Lone, Vieira de Mello's spokesman, sent his boss an e-mail immediately after the Jordanian bombing, saying that they would have to address security measures. But he was speaking to the wrong man, for Vieira de Mello, who preserved his air of immaculate elegance even in the lowest circle of hell, viewed constraining security measures as an impediment to the unhindered access to the local population that he considered crucial to his success. Visitors found it absurdly easy to gain access to the Canal Hotel, where UNAMI was quartered. And though it was regularly discussed, neither Vieira de Mello nor the mission's security head had ever ensured that the hotel's windows were coated with blast-resistant film. Vieira de Mello wrote back to Lone, suggesting he speak to the chief of security. "But I didn't talk to him," Lone says, "because I already knew that the answer would be business as usual."

At 4:30 on the afternoon of August 19, a flatbed truck pulled up directly beneath the special representative's second-story corner office and detonated a ton of high explosives. The floor of Vieira de Mello's office vaporized, and he was crushed beneath masonry. He died before medical help could reach him. Twenty-one other officials were killed in the blast, the worst disaster ever to befall UN civilians. Among them were such widely admired figures as Rick Hooper, a passionately engaged young American in the Department of Political Affairs, austere, bearded, and bespectacled. In our last conversation, in late 2002, Hooper had described the prospective Iraq war as a secular jihad by "the Washington Taliban." But Salman Ahmed, who had served on the Steering Group on Iraq with Hooper and had made a deal with him to split the job of Vieira de Mello's political adviser—Ahmed happened to take the first two months—said that Hooper hadn't been bitter about going. And I could almost believe that, because Hooper would have fully accepted the UN's responsibility to shape a better Iraq than the Americans would do on their own.

August 19 was the worst day in the history of the United Nations. Virtually everyone lost a friend, or many friends, in the bombing. And something else died that day—a faith, scarcely examined, that the UN stood apart from, and above, the violent conflicts in which it intervened. To the Iraqi insurgents, there was no "apart," and certainly no "above"; the UN served the coalition forces and was thus indistinguishable from them. Just as the Balkans shattered the old faith in neutrality, so Baghdad marked the end of a sense of privileged remove: the UN's inviolable status, once compromised, could never be restored.

The immense collective grief quickly gave way to anger and resentment. Why had these fine people been sent to die in a war that ought never to have been fought? What's more, they had gone in before a proper security assessment could be done. Why the feverish haste? "The problem wasn't just the lax security," says Salim Lone. "It was the political imperative to get back in there as soon as possible." These twenty-two UN colleagues had died, or so the feeling went, not so much in the service of Iraq as in the service of preserving relations with the White House—and this after the Bush administration had tried to bend the entire institution to its will. This was monstrous. And Kofi Annan, in his zeal to restore the centrality of the UN, had offered himself as an instrument of American power. Anger imparted a hysterical edge to the reaction; after all, UN officials serve in the world's most dangerous places and know very well that terrible things can happen. Still, even those who accepted this reality and who fully understood Annan's political predicament could not quite forgive him. "I don't question the SG's calculation that the U.S.-UN relation would have been gravely affected if we hadn't gone," says Salman Ahmed. "But could we have gone in later? Some of us wondered at the time."

Annan was in Helsinki when the bomb hit. He spoke constantly to Vieira de Mello, and the day before he had called to ask his representative to meet him in Europe a few days hence. "He was laughing," Annan recalls. "He said, 'You must remember, I'm taking the whole of October off.' I said, 'Yes, you deserve it. Lets' talk tomorrow.'" Annan was devastated by the news; few people in the UN knew these twenty-two men and women as well as he. "You live through a war that you neither defended nor supported," he says, "and then you have a mandate to do something about it in the aftermath. And I sent in some of my best people and friends and they got killed." He had persuaded Vieira de Mello, whom he had known for twenty years and whom he viewed as a kind of son, to take a dangerous job of which Vieira de Mello wanted no part. "This was quite heavy. And you said, 'What did they die for? Why did it have to be them?' I sent them in. Even if you say, 'They volunteered,' I could have not sent them in. If they are soldiers, they know there is great risk in their mission, and they are prepared to accept it. These are civilians who are there to help, who didn't have to be there." It was, he said, the most painful episode of his career.

Some agency heads, like Mark Malloch Brown of the UN Development Programme, spent hours with angry and heartsick colleagues. Annan, however, was always uncomfortable with raw emotion and shied away from direct contact. He remained in Europe for Vieira de Mello's funeral, and when he returned to New York, he went to Greentree, his lushly appointed monastery, rather than minister to his flock at Turtle Bay. He gave orders that he would receive no mail of any kind during this interval of several days. What about the letters of condolence to the next of kin that his staff had prepared? No, there would be no exceptions. And so the letters went out signed by autopen. Annan had recovered only a few months earlier from something like a nervous breakdown; some of his closest friends felt that he might not have survived, at least psychically, if the bombing had taken place earlier. Now, it seemed, he lacked the strength to be a source of support to others. The pastoral visits he made to various departments felt painfully stiff.

The mission had remained in Baghdad after the bombing. Annan's chief aides were almost unanimous in recommending that UNAMI withdraw, but he overruled them. "Part of [the rationale for the attack] was to intimidate and scare away the international community," he says, "and I felt that we had work to do, and we are going to continue our work." The UN, he said, "will not be deterred." Of course this stoic posture only deepened the anger and alienation of many staff members. And then, on September 22, a suicide bomber blew himself up outside the Canal Hotel, killing several Iraqi guards. Annan finally ordered the UN's international officials to depart for the safety of Amman.

Throughout this period, Annan conducted himself with such pragmatism and reserve that many of those who worked for him wondered if he had any deep feelings about the tragedy at all. Ahmad Fawzi had worked as Vieira de Mello's spokesman in June and July and had returned to London when his friends and former colleagues were killed. In September, he shifted to New York, and Annan invited him for what he knew would be a brief and ritualistic audience. He had been crying for the last month, but he was determined to control both his misery and his considerable anger. When he was ushered into the thirty-eighth-floor office, Annan remained seated behind his desk, as was his wont with employees. But then the secretary-general beckoned to a chair placed next to the desk. Nonplussed to find himself so close to Annan, Fawzi forgot his resolve and blurted out, "May I have a hug, please?"

"Excuse me?" Annan said, startled. Annan did not give hugs, or even much physical contact beyond the friendly touch on the arm.

"May I have a hug?" Fawzi repeated. And Annan pushed his chair back and somewhat tentatively placed his arms around his grieving employee. Immediately, Fawzi's tears began to flow.

"It's okay," Annan said. "I know how you feel." But his own manner was as cool, as gentle, as unruffled, as ever. Fawzi was now blubbering, and Annan was handing him handkerchiefs from a desk drawer.

"I don't know how you do it," Fawzi finally said. "You must have known Sergio for twenty-five years, so many of these people were close friends."

"There are certain responsibilities that come with my position," Annan answered gravely. "I have to keep control of my emotions. The only person I can share that emotion with is my wife." Fawzi says that he left Annan's office "having almost gotten over my anger." It's a very affecting scene—and yet one doesn't know whether to be struck more by Annan's stoicism or by his intense discomfort with strong feeling.

Annan responded to institutional failure as he almost always did: by assigning a report to study the problem, apportion blame, and suggest solutions. A first study, "Report of the Independent Panel on the Safety and Security of UN Personnel in Iraq," found the UN security team, the UN leadership in Iraq, and the Steering Group on Iraq, which managed policy, lax to the point of nonchalance about the threat of attack. A more extensive study, "Report of the Security in Iraq Accountability Panel," which was issued in March 2004, accused the main actors, as well as the humanitarian agencies, of having been blinded by the conviction that the UN would not be a target of attack, and of failing to respond even in the aftermath of the Jordanian bombing. It was as if UN officials, including the profoundly experienced Vieira de Mello, believed so deeply in their own special status that they simply could not accept the fact that the insurgents held all such distinctions in contempt.

Annan responded by firing the UN's chief security official, a step he had rarely taken against any member of his team. Others he reassigned or reprimanded. Louise Fréchette, the head of the steering group and thus the official ultimately responsible for the cascading series of failures that both reports identified, offered her resignation. Many UN officials felt that Annan had good reason to accept the offer, though of course they blamed the secretary-general as well. But "taking into account the collective nature of the failures attributable to the Steering Group on Iraq as a whole," he said in an official statement, he declined to accept her resignation. Annan was far more comfortable ascribing moral agency, both for good and for ill, to the institution than to individuals, including himself. Instead, he sent Fréchette a letter "expressing his disappointment and regret."

The Bush administration had initially envisioned a two-and-a-half-year transition period during which it would restore Iraq's shattered infrastructure while slowly building up the political institutions to which sovereignty could be restored—something like what the UN had done in East Timor. But the Iraqis were not remotely as patient as the Timorese. Grand Ayatollah Sistani, who had emerged as the single most influential figure in the country, insisted not only that a democratically elected body draw up the constitution but that such elections be held no later than June 30, 2004. What's more, the handpicked Governing Council was a source more of ridicule than of respect. By the fall, even the most optimistic American officials recognized the need for a change of course. In November, Bremer returned to Washington to confer with administration officials, who agreed that by June 30 the coalition would hand over power to an interim authority of its choosing.

Sistani and other leadership figures continued to demand that the new government be chosen by a national poll. No national election could be held so soon, but Sistani refused to believe it. The coalition needed an interlocutor whom the Iraqis would trust. And now administration officials began to understand the wisdom of Annan's prediction that they would be coming back to the UN for help in Iraq, whether they liked it or not. They did, in fact, need someone to do in Iraq what Lakhdar Brahimi had done in Afghanistan. And the best candidate for doing a Brahimi was plainly the man himself. The UN, traumatized as it was, could not send a mission into the maelstrom of Iraq, but it could send one person and his support staff, and Brahimi had already demonstrated that one person could constitute the ultimate light footprint. In January 2004, he agreed to return to Iraq as Annan's special adviser.

The first Iraqi official Brahimi met with when he traveled to Iraq in mid-February was Ayatollah Sistani. "The first words out of Sistani's mouth," according to Ahmad Fawzi, who had returned to Iraq as Brahimi's spokesman, were "I would like to express my sadness and condolence about Sergio. He was a man who cared about the Iraqi people; he was a great man." Sistani also flattered Brahimi by claiming to know all about him. Brahimi then began to explain to the ayatollah why elections could not be organized in a few months. According to Brahimi, Sistani then said, "Our experts say that elections are possible. If the Americans say they aren't, they must have something going on." Sistani feared that the United States was using the postponement of elections as a pretext to hold on to power, or that they would unilaterally grant autonomy to the Kurds. He told Brahimi that Shia leaders had made a terrible mistake when they had rejected offers of power sharing from the British in 1920, thus surrendering control to the Sunnis forever after. They would not make this mistake again. Sistani was surely right in thinking that he would have been wasting his breath holding such a conversation with Paul Bremer.

But the UN was different. Sistani said that if the UN told him it

truly was impossible to hold elections in a few months, he would accept it—surely the very definition of legitimacy. And when Brahimi explained the enormous procedural difficulties that, according to UN
election experts, required eight months of preparation, Sistani agreed
that power would pass to an interim government until national elections could be held in late 2004 or early 2005. With obstacles thus
cleared away, the United States and the U.K. formally blessed the UN's
growing role in shaping a political order in Iraq.

During a second trip to Iraq in early April, Brahimi met with as
many of the stakeholders in the new Iraq as he could find, often the
same people with whom Vieira de Mello had met the year before.
The trip was billed as a listening tour designed to hear Iraqi views on
the composition and powers of the transitional administration, but, as
in Afghanistan, Brahimi already had a pretty good idea of what he
wanted to hear. Upon his return, he spoke of fashioning "a government
of technocrats" that would do little beyond preparing for and overseeing the elections. Many of the figures Brahimi had in mind weren't in
fact technocrats, but the word carried a nonpartisan ring intended to
reassure the contending parties that no one of them would be granted
an unfair advantage.

On his third and final visit to Iraq, a monthlong marathon beginning in early May, Brahimi canvassed potential members of the new
caretaker government, including the interim prime minister. It was the
worst possible moment to be attempting such a delicate task. The grue-
some images of Iraqi prisoners tortured by American interrogators at
Saddam's old prison complex at Abu Ghraib had been widely dissemi-
nated. American forces had mounted a full-scale attack on the Sunni
stronghold of Falluja, outraging the Sunni leaders with whom the coalition needed to work. At the same time, the Shiite militia of the young
firebrand cleric Moktada al-Sadr had gained control over the vast slums
of Baghdad and was now seeking to establish itself in other Shiite centers. U.S. Marines laid siege to Sadr's forces in the holy city of Najaf,
provoking fierce battles among shrines and in the city's vast cemetery.
Whenever he talked to Bremer or Robert Blackwill, who headed up
Iraq policy on the National Security Council, Brahimi would ask, "How
can we conduct these negotiations while you're bombing Falluja?" The

Americans answered that they could not let the insurgency flourish in order to mollify the Sunni leadership, though they did in fact call off the assault on Falluja (a decision they were later to rue).

Washington had tried, and failed, to impose its own favorites, expatriates with long-standing CIA ties like Ahmad Chalabi. Iraqis scorned these figures as White House puppets. Brahimi was determined to find leaders who would not bear this taint, nor the stigma of having served on the Governing Council. But the leadership class he had once known had long since ceased to exist. "Saddam practiced a scorched-earth policy," Brahimi says. "If he looked at you and thought that perhaps ten years from now you may have some political aspirations, he cut your head off. Why wait? And so there weren't many people who were both prominent enough to take this mantle and acceptable to a minimum of the players inside the country." There was no Iraqi equivalent of Hamid Karzai. After weeks of shuttling among the CPA, the Sunnis, the Shia, the seculars, the expats, and so on, Brahimi proposed as president Dr. Hussein Shahristani, a former nuclear scientist who had been jailed by Saddam and yet had remained in Iraq. Shahristani was a Shiite, but no fundamentalist. He was apolitical. Bremer supported him. But the CPA had granted to the Governing Council the power to choose its own successor, and council members rejected Shahristani. "The Sunnis said, 'Shahristani—that's an Iranian name,'" recalls a bemused Brahimi. "The religious people said, 'Who is this guy?'" Brahimi kept looking.

At the end of May, the Governing Council announced the formation of an interim government with few technocrats and few "internals," and a good many faction leaders and, not incidentally, members of the Governing Council itself. The prime minister would be Iyad Allawi, a secular Shiite who had lived abroad for decades and had well-known ties to the CIA. Allawi had been a Baathist hard-liner but had broken with Saddam, and had barely survived an assasination attempt. Brahimi said that he "respected" the choice. It was widely believed that the council and Bremer had imposed Allawi on him, but Brahimi describes Allawi as, in effect, the last man standing. "Allawi was the guy who had the fewest vetoes," he says, "not necessarily the best." Sistani, the Kurdish leadership, and the former Baathists all said that they could live with him. The Bush administration was delighted to give the impression that the Iraqis had chosen their own leaders, with UN help. Asked about the composition of the interim government, President Bush said modestly that he had instructed ambassadors Bremer and Blackwill to "work with Mr. Brahimi," who served as "the quarterback" of the process.

On June 8, 2004, the Security Council unanimously passed resolution 1546 endorsing the transfer of sovereignty from the CPA to the interim government, as well as the timetable for national elections and the drafting of a constitution that Brahimi had helped broker among the various parties. Council members, many of whom had only reluctantly approved the U.S. occupation of Iraq, wanted to make sure that real, and not just formal, sovereignty would be vested in the new interim government; France, Russia, China, and several others spent two weeks tinkering with the resolution. But the United States got what it wanted: the resolution reaffirmed the authorization of the U.S.-led multinational force, noting that it remained in Iraq at the request of the interim government, and formalized the security relationship between coalition forces and the new Iraqi state. The Americans would continue to largely call the shots, but now they would do so not as an invading power but as the lead party in a UN-authorized Chapter VII peacekeeping force. Resolution 1546 also called on member states to assist the multinational force in its task of building a free and sovereign Iraq.

The resolution was surely a triumph of sorts. The UN had emerged from the abyss of irrelevance into which George Bush had cast it in March 2003. The United States had, as Annan had predicted, come back to the Security Council. But if the UN scored any more victories like this one, it might collapse altogether. The United States had gotten what it wanted without paying any real price: fifteen months after trying, and failing, to bully the Security Council into supporting a war virtually all of its members opposed, the Bush administration had nevertheless won the UN's coveted stamp of legitimacy. It was the UN that had paid the price. It had returned to Iraq on American terms and given its imprimatur to American rule. Twenty-two civilian officials had died in the scramble to reestablish a UN presence in Iraq. Annan had earned the scorn first of the Americans and then of his own staff. Both he and the institution he led seemed diminished and enfeebled. And the Bush administration seemed to like it that way.

Annan, however, could not bear or accept the marginalization of the institution in which he had reposed all his deepest ideals. His impulse was always the same: if something is broken, it must be recognized and then fixed. As far back as May 2003, at a Security Council retreat, he had pushed the members to discuss the doctrine of "preventive war" that the Bush administration had cited as justification for the invasion of Iraq. Over the next few months, Annan came to feel that the breach could be healed only by thinking anew about the whole question of threats in the post–Cold War world. And he believed that the moment for this rethinking was ripe. "The world's attention has never been on us so much even when things were good," he said at one point. "Let's take this attention and make something of it."

Annan and his team came to feel that reform would succeed only as a "package" in which all members could find something that they cared about deeply enough to swallow whatever they found objectionable. The Human Rights Commission had become a toothless embarrassment; the failure to agree on a definition of terrorism had immobilized the UN on a subject central to its future; the nuclear nonproliferation regime was teetering on the brink of collapse; and while everyone agreed that the Security Council represented the vanished world of 1945, all attempts to make it more representative had degenerated into a zero-sum standoff. And representatives from the Group of 77 told Annan that he could not count on their support for reform on collective security and human rights issues unless questions of development were treated with equal importance. Annan had already commissioned a highly ambitious report on the progress of the Millennium Development Goals, to be delivered in 2005. But that would not be enough. His report on threats to collective security would also have to recognize that underdevelopment was as great a threat as terrorism or nuclear proliferation.

On September 23, 2003, Annan delivered his annual address to the General Assembly, a speech that was always closely watched and drafted with minute care. "Excellencies," he said, "we have come to a fork in the road. This may be a moment no less decisive than 1945 itself, when the United Nations was founded . . . Now we must decide whether it is possible to continue on the rules agreed then, or whether radical changes are needed." Annan directly addressed the American argument that states—or at least the United States—must have the right to act preemptively when menaced by weapons of mass destruction. Were such a principle to be adopted, the secretary-general said, it could lead to "a proliferation of the unilateral and lawless use of force, with or without justification." On the other hand, he said, "it is not enough to denounce unilateralism, unless we also face up squarely to the concerns that some states feel uniquely vulnerable." Moreover, the "soft threats" of poverty, disease, and climate change must be taken as seriously as the "hard" ones.

Annan announced that he would establish a "High-Level Panel of eminent personalities" to study these problems and to deliver answers. A groan went up from many a UN expert, for the Secretariat Building could have been wallpapered with the pages of reports by high-level panels that had, in years past, been written by eminent persons and acted upon by no one. But if the UN really had reached a fork in the road, this report would have to be different. The institution's future, and perhaps also the secretary-general's historical reputation, depended on this rash and profoundly ambitious bid for renewal.

PART II

CHAPTER TWELVE

The Security Council Fiddles While Darfur Burns

O N THE MORNING OF JULY 1, 2004, KOFI ANNAN, ALONG with aides, security staff, and a dozen or so reporters, flew from Khartoum, the capital of Sudan, to El Fashier, one of the chief towns of the western province of Darfur. He was precisely halfway through his second term in office; his star, which had shone so brightly a few years earlier, was looking tarnished and wan. The UN had endured and finally concluded the long siege of helplessness over Iraq. Now, in Sudan, it faced a supreme moral challenge: exactly a decade after Rwanda, and almost five years since Annan's forthright defense of humanitarian intervention before the General Assembly, organized ethnic slaughter had returned to Africa. The Sudanese government had equipped and organized a force of nomadic Arab tribesmen, known as Janjaweed, to crush a revolt by the region's "black" pastoral tribes. (Both groups are in fact black-skinned.) With the help of bombing from government planes, the Janjaweed had put the area to fire and sword, wiping hundreds of villages off the map and uprooting hundreds of thousands of farmers, who now faced starvation and disease. Yet reports of this brutal campaign of ethnic cleansing had provoked only the mildest reproofs from the Security Council. Annan was hoping somehow to prevent the guilt-stricken "never again" that had emerged from the ashes of Kigali from disintegrating into a ghastly mockery of UN impotence and of his own brave words.

When we landed, a caravan of white UN Toyota Land Cruisers was waiting for us on the tarmac. We were driven to a house near the airfield. Annan was received in a hot, darkened room crowded with local notables. A magnificent functionary in a navy robe with a red sash covered with Arabic script stood silently in one corner; his role seemed to be strictly decorative. Annan was seated between Othman Mahmoud Yusuf Kiber, the provincial governor, or *wali*, and the federal minister of the interior, Abdulrakim Mohemed Hussein, resplendent in sky blue fatigues and matching beret and with a carved walking stick. The *wali* dispensed with the usual courtesies and instead embarked on a lecture, addressing the crowd rather than the secretary-general. "This is a local conflict which has been going on for many years . . . The government has been working very hard to negotiate with rebel groups for more than eighteen months . . . We have directed police officers to take care of all of the violations which have taken place."

Annan listened quietly, barely moving; the collective body heat had begun to overwhelm the feeble efforts of a ceiling fan, though Annan, in a suit and tie, seemed perfectly composed. At last he gently interrupted. "How many policemen are there in Darfur?" he asked.

"Three thousand," said the *wali*, and then he resumed his monologue. He had compiled a list of atrocities committed by the rebels that he wished to present to the secretary-general. Annan said, "May I ask a few questions?"

The *wali* listened to the translation and snapped, "I prefer to finish." Cars had been stolen, hospitals destroyed, children kidnapped . . .

The filibuster threatened to consume the remainder of his visit. Annan's store of patience was not, in fact, illimitable, and he said, "What about the Janjaweed?" It was, he noted, widely believed that the government was acting in concert with the Janjaweed.

Now an elegant gentleman in a gray suit and neatly clipped mustache piped up from amid the crowd. This was Ibrahim Mahmoud Hamid, Sudan's minister of humanitarian affairs, who had accompanied us on the trip. The minister politely explained that the rebels were spreading lies to discredit the government. Annan recognized that his message was not making much headway, and he repeated himself, a bit more firmly this time. "Why should the government fight side by side with the rebels [that is, the Janjaweed]? They should be *confronting* the rebels."

Now it was the interior minister's turn, for as the official directly responsible for security he could not, presumably, let this misconception go uncorrected. "Sometimes the Janjaweed attacks the same area after the government attacks the area," he asserted. "There is no connection. We are fighting all the militias in the area."

Annan politely pretended to agree. He then seized on a patently insincere commitment made by the interior minister in order to offer a closing benediction: "I am happy today that you say that the government accepts that it is a government-responsibility to ensure law and order." This was a subtle bit of diplomatic phraseology in which an admonition was rendered tolerable by being presented as praise; you had to wonder if such delicacy had been lost on the audience.

We emerged from our stifling cave into blinding sunlight. Our caravan snaked over the baked, arid ground to Zam Zam, one of Darfur's show camps—large, relatively well organized, and close to an airfield. Even so, none of Zam Zam's eleven thousand refugees lived in a tent, much less a solid dwelling. Shelter meant an enclosure of thorn branches on a hillside; the lucky ones had plastic sheeting to keep out the windblown sand. The aid groups who ran the camp had food. enough for only thirty-seven hundred people; those who had arrived later had to beg or, if they had any money, buy from the others. Annan was beckoned to join a circle of elders who had been gathered beneath the shade of one of the few trees in the area. The secretary-general kneeled uncomfortably on a rush mat. The humanitarian affairs minister wedged himself next to Annan and proceeded to rectify translations he deemed inexact or inopportune. Annan asked the elders what they needed. They needed everything—food, plastic sheeting, health care, schools. "Even the donkeys are suffering and dying," said one. Did they fear for their safety? No, no, everything was fine. Perhaps it was so, or perhaps no one was foolish enough to complain about security in front of a government minister.

Most of the refugees were women, for the menfolk had been hunted down by the Janjaweed or had survived to join the rebels. It was hard, at first, to recognize just how miserable the refugees' situation was because there was something gaudy about their billowing robes of ocher, purple, or parrot green. But there was nothing festive in the half-naked children who clung to their legs or had been tucked in behind, their tiny feet sticking out at their mothers' hips. One of the bolder women, Khalza Abdul, a thirty-five-year-old mother of eight, spoke up from the crowd. "Our whole village"—Tabet, to the south—"was destroyed by the Janjaweed," she said. "We fled from this place, and then we walked for seven days and nights to come here." All the stories were variations on one another: the attackers came on horses and camels or by car; they ran through the village, setting huts aflame; at the same time, planes—government aircraft—dropped bombs on those who ran.

After a few hours in Zam Zam, our caravan set off again along the dusty swales. After several miles, we halted in the middle of nowhere. We walked up to the front and found a knot of officials milling around the secretary-general's car. Something bizarre had happened—an entire refugee camp had disappeared overnight. To our right was a broad plain empty save for piles of trash and some dead donkeys. The night before, it had been Meshtel, a squalid and makeshift camp holding at least a thousand people. The UN official who had arranged the trip was reduced almost to tears of frustration, while the lone Sudanese administrator who had remained behind insisted, with an impressive show of indignation, that for fear of flooding the entire population had been moved to another camp—a much better camp, which we could visit this very moment. In an astonishing triumph of logistics, the authorities had contrived to move hundreds of families over a trackless road in the middle of the night, leaving no trace of their existence behind. Here was a regime prepared to go to truly extraordinary lengths to disguise the truth—no matter how ludicrous their impostures. Perhaps they didn't care whether we believed them or not. You couldn't help wondering how much the vaunted moral authority of the United Nations, or of its secretary-general, mattered to them.

The problems of Darfur were the problems of Africa—ethnic rivalry, resource scarcity, desertification, gross neglect, failed or absent governance. In this immense region, invariably described as "the size of France," farmers and nomadic herders had been skirmishing for generations over access to land, water, and cattle. The two groups are physically indistinguishable, at least to outsiders, but the herders, who originally migrated from the Maghreb, thought of themselves as Arab, while the indigenous farmers considered themselves African and black. (Both practice Islam.) A conflict over resources had thus played out in ethnic and racial terms. And as arable land and water had become more scarce, the conflict had become more violent. In addition, the African farmers felt increasingly marginalized by the Arab Islamist government in Khartoum, though in this they were not much different from a number of other ethnic and regional groupings in Sudan. Indeed, the country was effectively split in half between the Christian south and the Muslim north; the civil war between the two sides had dragged on for twenty years and resulted in an estimated two million deaths.

In early 2003, insurgents announced the formation of the Sudanese People's Liberation Army to fight for the rights of African tribesmen in Darfur. On April 25, the SPLA seized the airfield in El Fasher, killing one hundred Sudanese soldiers, destroying planes and helicopters, and emptying an arms warehouse. This was a declaration of war, and the government responded in kind. Khartoum had long fought insurgencies by proxy; in Darfur, this meant exploiting the nomadic Arab groups who were at odds with the African tribes. In this case, the government had little choice, because about half of the country's army was drawn from the area and could scarcely be expected to attack their own people. The rebellion in Darfur was, in fact, a greater threat to the state than was the endless civil war, because it threatened to divide not just the territory but the ruling class. The killings at El Fasher appear to have panicked Khartoum, and over the summer the government began to provide money and weapons to Musa Hilal, the most notorious of the Janjaweed leaders, and authorized him—how explicitly it is not clear— to lay waste to the African tribes of Darfur.

The UN had long maintained a large presence in Sudan, as it did in many desperately poor nations. The UN spent $300 million a year in humanitarian assistance, employed ten thousand people, and maintained a vast fleet of aircraft. But most of the resources were concentrated in the south or the east; Darfur was almost terra incognita. And since few NGOs ventured into the region, either, there were few international eyewitnesses to the burgeoning violence. Throughout the spring of 2003, the head of the UN mission, Mukesh Kapila, a medical doctor with long experience in conflict areas, heard reports of ethnic violence in Darfur, but he knew that in Sudan these insurgencies had a way of flaring up and then abruptly disappearing. In the summer, though, tribesmen and women from Darfur began appearing in the UN's office in Khartoum to report organized atrocities and mass flight from villages under assault. In September, Kapila tried to send in some of his officials, but the Sudanese government, ominously, kept canceling UN flights.

By late November, it had become clear that something terrible was happening. Officials from Amnesty International interviewed refugees who had fled across the border to Chad, and learned that Arab militias on horseback or camelback were storming villages and burning them to the ground, killing the men and raping the women. Government planes dropped bombs on the survivors. This wasn't the usual Sudanese spasm of violence; it was an organized campaign of ethnic cleansing. On November 30, Kapila sent a memorandum to UN headquarters describing the massive humanitarian crisis provoked by the militia attacks. International pressure, he noted, had induced Khartoum to sign a cease-fire agreement with the Darfurian rebels, but the Janjaweed had continued to prosecute its reign of terror. Six hundred thousand Darfurians had become refugees, many of them far beyond the reach of aid organizations. "It is, therefore, imperative that the international community exert the strongest possible political pressure on the Government to take urgent steps to reduce violence and killing in Darfur," Kapila wrote.

Kapila was one of those humanitarian nomads who had found himself in the middle of almost every humanitarian catastrophe of the previous fifteen years—Kurdistan, Sarajevo, Rwanda, Angola, Liberia, Afghanistan. He was a talkative, excitable man; inside the UN, he had a reputation as something of an alarmist and a melodramatizer. Now, however, he faced a calamity for which alarmism seemed the only honest response. In a conversation a year later, he said, "One thing I remembered from the Rwanda report and the Srebrenica report was the doctrine of personal responsibility: If you are confronted with crimes against humanity, it's not sufficient to write a paper to your boss, and to have him pass it on to his boss. Every single person has a personal responsibility." Kapila felt that his responsibility lay in forcing diplomatic actors to face the truth. Starting in October, he made the rounds of the major capitals: Washington, London, Paris, Oslo, Copenhagen, Stockholm, Rome, Brussels. His message was simple: "The situation in Darfur is deteriorating very fast, it's approaching the world's greatest humanitarian crisis, and the government in Sudan is responsible." And almost everywhere he went the response was the same: "We're equally concerned, but don't rock the boat. The problems of Darfur will be sorted out once we get a north-south agreement."

This was hardly a trivial argument. The Sudanese civil war had been one of the world's most destructive conflicts, and by the end of the year it appeared tantalizingly close to a solution. American evangelicals had long taken an interest in the plight of the beleaguered Christians of the south. In January 2004, President Bush asked the former Missouri senator John Danforth, who had been helping guide the talks for three years, to return to Naivasha, in Kenya, where the talks were being held. Danforth was fully expected to come back to Washington with President Omar al-Bashir and John Garang, the head of the southern rebels, for a signing ceremony and a choice seat at the State of the Union address. The conventional diplomatic calculus was that denouncing the Sudanese over Darfur would topple this delicate house of cards (though Kapila says that American officials, despite their lead role, were more willing to take that risk than any others).

As the talks dragged on inconclusively, it became clear that the government was exploiting the West's eagerness for a settlement of the civil war in order to give it a free hand in Darfur. Indeed, a study commissioned by the British House of Commons concluded that "the government used that lack of resolve to slow the [negotiation] process, while its army, air force and allied Janjaweed militia jointly bombed, raided and burned to the ground hundreds of villages." Jan Egeland, the UN's humanitarian coordinator and thus Kapila's boss, believed only real international pressure would stop the killing. "I felt in my gut that we were front-row witnesses to ethnic cleansing of the worst kind," Egeland says. A former politician who understood very well the uses of the media, Egeland had been speaking out publicly on a range of humanitarian issues since he had taken over, three months earlier, from a press-averse Japanese diplomat. On December 5, he called a press conference to dramatize the issue, describing Darfur as "one of the worst humanitarian crises in the world" and blaming both the rebels and the government for blocking access to the affected population. Four days later Annan himself said that he had received reports of "killings, rape, and the burning and looting of entire villages," and called on "all parties" to give humanitarian workers unhindered access to the area.

But the Secretariat itself was deeply divided over the issue. Tom Eric Vraalsen, Annan's special envoy for humanitarian affairs in Sudan, generally stuck to the most anodyne language, both in conversations with Khartoum and in his public statements, to the despair of many of his colleagues. "At the time the reports were describing Darfur as one of the worst situations in the world," says Brian Grogan, a public-affairs officer who worked for Egeland, "Mr. Vraalsen would say, 'It's a very serious situation.'" Sudanese authorities could have been excused for concluding that, Kapila's protests notwithstanding, they had nothing to fear from the UN.

Even more important, Kieran Prendergast, the head of the Department of Political Affairs and one of Annan's most trusted confidants, did not view Darfur as a particularly grave or even abnormal situation. Prendergast was a diplomat of the old school, a British foreign servant who had served as high commissioner in Zimbabwe and Kenya as well as ambassador to Turkey. An Anglo-Irishman of aristocratic lineage, a wag, and a bit of an intellectual snob, loomingly tall with a great pink balding head, Prendergast was a kind of lord chamberlain of the UN, a majestic servant of the cause of international law. He had been thoroughly disgusted by the willingness of the European powers to ignore the UN Charter, at least as he understood it, in Kosovo. The Charter was his rock. But he was also a man temperamentally skeptical of intemperate enthusiasm and moral passion; he would take the fine-grained judgment every time. East Africa was his specialty, and he had scant regard for the Johnny-come-latelies on the subject. In Darfur, Prendergast saw yet another of the episodic struggles over access to resources in Sudan, complicated by drought. The solution, he thought, was to persuade the Sudanese government to call off the Janjaweed, and then to work patiently on a more equitable distribution of resources and political power. A solution to the north-south problem, Prendergast argued, would offer a template for all of Sudan's regional disputes.

Prendergast was disinclined to credit information that did not suit his views. Isabelle Balot, a UN official in Khartoum who drew up many of the reports sent under Kapila's name in late 2003, says, "We kept sending these reports back to headquarters, and then there was a terrible silence. We were under great pressure from the Sudanese government, and we received no political guidance from headquarters." When I asked Prendergast about this terrible silence, he gave me an astonishing answer: "There was never as I recall a request for us to exercise our good offices." Darfur, so far as he knew, was not on anyone's agenda in late 2003 and early 2004. What about the frantic requests from Kapila? "I don't remember seeing anything," Prendergast said. Not a single document? No. The problem, as he understood it, was humanitarian access, not ethnic cleansing. "It was obvious," Prendergast said, "that most people were dying of malnutrition, not being killed." In fact, villagers were being murdered and driven from their homes, where they died of exposure, disease, thirst, and starvation. It is not easy to fathom how Prendergast could have remained ignorant of these conditions—especially since his immediate subordinates were well aware of the scale of the violence.

Kapila was in an almost impossible position. As head of the mission, he was responsible for humanitarian and developmental projects that required the government's cooperation. At the same time, he had to confront government officials with evidence of state-sponsored atrocities. The Sudanese were outraged by his claims, and they had little reason to feel that either senior UN officials or diplomats shared his view. On December 10, Kapila instructed staff members to evacuate Geneina, the capital of West Darfur, owing to ongoing violence. The minister of humanitarian affairs reminded him that his predecessor had been replaced not long after he had ordered a similar evacuation. "Pressure from GoS [the Government of Sudan]," he wrote in a note to Egeland, "is considerable." And the more Kapila pressed the UN's concerns, the tighter the pressure became. On January 22, when Kapila told the minister that refugees were fleeing from one large camp being terrorized by armed militia, he was sharply rebuked, "hinting at the fine line the UN was treading," as he wrote Egeland, "in terms of what was acceptable in our relations with the Government."

By this time, the UN's humanitarian teams, as well as NGOs, were being blocked from virtually all of Darfur. The World Food Programme was instructed to stop submitting requests for access to the northern areas. Whatever the army and the Janjaweed were doing, the government did not wish it seen. And then, on February 8, the humanitarian affairs minister informed Kapila that, the government having now "gained control" over Darfur, his teams would be free to visit selected areas as of February 16. "Of course," Kapila says, "that meant that they would be finished with their work by then. They could even tell us to the day when to come back—and they were true to their word." The UN team returned to find empty, burned-out villages, and refugees huddling in makeshift camps or simply out in the open. There could be no more doubt about the scale or nature of the atrocities: aerial photographs showed villages burning across the region; a staff member had seen Janjaweed fighters rape 120 women, one by one; others had seen government helicopters drop off reinforcements and pick up wounded militia. In mid-February, a delegation consisting of Western diplomats and UN officials toured the area by helicopter and counted seven villages either in flames or freshly reduced to ashes.

Back in New York, Egeland and his staff were receiving Kapila's feverish dispatches with a mounting sense of horror. Egeland appealed to the ambassadors of the United States, the United Kingdom, and Norway—the troika who were handling the north-south peace process—to try to get Darfur put on the Security Council agenda and to let him brief the council on the situation. But each of them turned him down flat. "The three were so obsessed with getting a north-south agreement," Egeland says. One Western ambassador says that he sent a cable back to his capital saying, "Some people think we're making too much of north-south and ignoring Darfur." He received, he says, a blistering response. Egeland went to the Pakistanis, who would be president of the council in March and thus could determine the body's agenda. But the Pakistanis objected in principle to discussing any issue that was directed against a specific member state, especially an Islamic one. He tried, unsuccessfully, to engage Prendergast on the subject. "It was very clear that the Department of Political Affairs would not help me with this," he says.

In mid-March 2004, Kapila left for a brief and much-needed vacation at the Windsor Golf Hotel, a supremely gracious resort on the outskirts of Nairobi meant to evoke the apex of colonial glory. When he arrived, he took a long walk around the Windsor's fastidiously barbered grounds. "At this point," Kapila says, "I felt that I had made the diplomatic démarches, I had reported to the Sudanese government, I had exhausted the normal channels of communication." Was that enough? Kapila believed that by knowingly unleashing a monster fueled by ethnic hatred, the Sudanese government was guilty of genocide. He thought of the Rwanda report and knew that he could not simply discharge his professional responsibility and walk away. And so he decided on an act of insubordination, if a characteristically self-dramatizing one: he instructed his press aide to arrange an interview for him with the domestic service of BBC television, to be aired live on the 8:00 a.m. news, which Kapila had heard that Prime Minister Tony Blair listened to. He knew that the Sudanese government would have his head; perhaps the UN would, too, since he hadn't cleared his comments with anyone. But on March 21 he went on the air and described the violence in Darfur as "an organized attempt to do away with a group of people." He compared the situation to the early stages of the bloodshed in Rwanda—not yet a genocide, but a genocide in the making unless the world intervened.

Kapila had said the terrible word—"Rwanda"—and he had said it only two weeks from the tenth anniversary of the beginning of that nightmare. His accusations were flashed around the world, just as he had hoped. On April 1, the European Parliament, citing Kapila's claims, condemned the Sudanese government's support for the Janjaweed and called for the establishment of a no-fly zone over Darfur, to be monitored by the UN. The reaction inside the UN itself was far more equivocal. Kapila was considered a poor administrator, and he was due to be relieved the following month. But he was also understood to have violated the peculiar protocol that attaches to all things at the UN, even those involving moral urgency. Prendergast says that he found the episode unpleasant and bizarre. "I was very surprised when Mukesh rent his garments," he recalls. He says that he thought, "What's he been doing the rest of the time?"

Annan was due to deliver a speech before the Human Rights Commission in Geneva on April 7, the tenth anniversary of the beginning of the Rwanda genocide. After hearing Kapila's remarks, Edward Mortimer, Annan's chief speechwriter and the principal author of the doc-trine of humanitarian intervention, rewrote the address. Annan de-scribed his "deep sense of foreboding" about the current of events in Darfur—a reference to Rwanda that could scarcely be missed—and said that should the Sudanese government remain intransigent, "the in-ternational community must be prepared to take swift and appropriate action." Annan then parsed his own meaning by saying that he was re-ferring to "a continuum of steps, which may include military action." We must, he concluded, "be serious about preventing genocide." This was the first time any prominent diplomatic figure had broached the possibility of a humanitarian intervention. It was also the first time he had invoked the moral imperative he had laid down in his 1999 speech.

In April, the presidency of the Security Council had passed to Ger-many, which was eager to place Darfur on the council agenda. But this would have provoked too much resistance from council members who had no wish to raise the issue. Instead, working with the British and the French, German ambassador Gunter Pleuger invited Jan Egeland to give a "humanitarian briefing." On April 2, Egeland came and talked about food shortages in Africa and then worked his way around to Su-dan, and thus to Darfur. Then he spoke bluntly of the Sudanese gov-ernment's collaboration with the Janjaweed. Egeland emerged from the council to give a press conference in which he accused government forces and their accomplices of "scorched-earth" tactics and a cam-paign of ethnic cleansing. He felt that he had finally broken through the crust of apathy. Prendergast felt that his colleague had sunk to puerile "sloganeering." And the Sudanese canceled an invitation they had extended to Egeland to visit Darfur.

And then . . . nothing. After Egeland's testimony, the council issued a toothless "presidential statement" expressing "deep concern" about the crisis and calling on "the parties concerned to fully cooperate in or-der to address the grave situation prevailing in the region." The Chi-nese and the Pakistanis had insisted on the watered-down language. The Pakistanis objected to Western meddling with the internal affairs of a fraternal Muslim state; the Chinese purchased 40 percent of Su-dan's oil production, and were eager to ingratiate themselves with Khartoum. At the same time, the Human Rights Commission in Geneva was considering a motion, introduced by the United States with backing from the European Union, condemning the killing in Darfur and demanding full access for aid workers. The United States had already imposed bilateral sanctions on Sudan; the human rights resolution was one of the few forms of punishment still available to it. But the Sudanese, who, grotesquely, had just been voted onto the commission, refused to accept any criticism, and their African brethren rallied to their side. The commission, like the council, issued a weakly worded statement instead.

Improvement came slowly. In April, the Sudanese permitted a delegation from the UN High Commissioner for Human Rights to visit Darfur, and the subsequent report suggested that the government might be responsible for war crimes. Annan continued to bring high-level officials before the council, which in mid-May finally issued a much tougher statement condemning attacks on civilians, sexual violence, and forced displacement in Darfur. Annan himself spent hours dickering with Sudanese officials over access for humanitarian workers and relief supplies. Access improved, but the killing and the displacement continued. The international community was now, finally, engaged with Darfur, but there was no collective attempt to force the Sudanese to change their ways. It was under those circumstances that Annan made his trip to Sudan at the end of June.

The day after the visit to Zam Zam and to the phantom refugee camp of Meshtel, Annan and his retinue climbed back on their plane and flew to Chad, Sudan's neighbor to the west. Unlike an actual head of state, the UN secretary-general does not have a plane of his own, and Annan was traveling across Africa in a jet lent by the emir of Qatar; the plane's carpeted stateroom and first-class seating almost certainly made it the most luxurious conveyance in this vast, arid, and dismal region. Chad was a hopelessly impoverished desert nation that could scarcely care for its own people, much less the hundreds of thousands of refugees from Darfur who had fled across the border rather than face the Janjaweed. Annan flew to the capital, N'Djamena, a crumbling ex-colonial outpost with hardly a building taller than three stories. The Chadians were at daggers drawn with the Sudanese and were widely believed to be sponsoring several of the rebel groups. They worried about cross-border attacks by the Janjaweed; UN officials in Chad worried that the camps could become recruiting centers for the rebels. (Both concerns proved to be justified.) Annan spent the day conferring with government officials; that night, President Idriss Déby welcomed him at a lavish state dinner at his palace, where gazelles and zebras wandered the manicured lawns.

The Sudanese, who were on hostile terms with much of the world, had been no more than correct with the secretary-general. But the Chadians laid on the royal treatment for Annan, a son of Africa who had risen to the world's most prestigious, if scarcely most powerful, position. The following day we were to fly back across the country to the border with Darfur in order to visit a refugee camp on the Chadian side. While Annan sat in the airport's VIP lounge, workers rolled out an endless red carpet, and then a shorter one stretching from the carpet edge to the foot of the plane's staircase. Impoverished, authoritarian African nations seem to specialize in splendid honor guards, and now ten tall Chadian Beefeaters in royal blue capes with gold braid and epaulets emerged to line the long carpet on either side. As Annan and his party filed past, the guardsmen removed their swords from their scabbards and raised them aloft, the blades reflecting the brilliant early-morning sun. Ramrod stiff they stood. Then Annan climbed aboard his upholstered jet, the soldiers melted away, and the workers rolled up the carpet. And once again the N'Djamena airport was a dinky little depot where hours passed between takeoffs and landings.

The plane put down at Abéché, Chad's second-largest city, a mud-walled backwater with a population of 200,000; from there we boarded helicopters to fly farther east, close to the border with Sudan. Eastern Chad is one of the planet's least hospitable regions: in the course of about seventy minutes we passed over only five or six hamlets, each a tiny cluster of huts surrounded by a berm to keep out wild animals, and perhaps also to stand between man and the vast ocher nothingness of the desert. We touched down at the edge of the Iridimi camp and emerged into sheer nullity—soft yellow sand, stunted shrubbery, rocks split by the remorseless sun. You couldn't help feeling that mankind had never been intended to inhabit such a place.

All fifteen thousand of Iridimi's inhabitants had formed into a giant semicircle in the midst of this lunar wasteland to welcome the secretary-general. They carried signs in English: "Disarm the Janjaweed and Bring Them to Justice." Annan was hoping to talk to refugees, but instead he was forced to sit beneath a green canopy in the stultifying heat to hear speeches, songs, tributes to the glory of the United Nations, and so on. I wondered whether he was ever able to gain a purchase on unvarnished truth. The Iridimi narrative was even more searing than what we had heard in Zam Zam: the woman who lost her brother, husband, parents, and four of her six children; the woman who walked for twenty-five days, drinking from puddles, eating almost nothing, leaving behind children, first the little ones, then the bigger; the junior-high-school teacher who woke to an aerial bombardment and then run straight into an artillery attack. This last, Omar Suleyman, had been a man of means, and even this morning he had a fresh shave and a perfectly starched white robe. In quite presentable English, he complained that while he was in no danger of starvation, he got no sugar, no meat, no milk. Was there a school in the camp where he could teach? No. What did he do with his time? "We sleep all day," said Omar Suleyman.

After sitting stoically through his endless welcoming ceremony, Annan had time for only a brief tour of the camp, and then a press conference in a roped-off square of sand, where he spoke so softly that few of the reporters, leaning over from the far side of the rope, had the faintest idea what he had said. Fortunately, he was immediately followed by Jan Egeland, who talked in booming tones about Khartoum's "hideous campaign of terror." Annan then returned to Abéché and flew back to Khartoum.

Annan did not really take these detours through the inferno in order to "see for himself," any more than other statesmen did. He did so in order to focus press attention on a problem, to ratchet up public pressure on intransigent actors, and to engage in quiet diplomacy. Indeed, U.S. secretary of state Colin Powell was traveling through Sudan at the same time and for very much the same set of reasons, though the trips did not appear to have been coordinated. Annan had begun negotiating an agreement with Sudanese president Omar al-Bashir several days earlier, and discussions had continued in his absence. The secretary-general had been trying to persuade Bashir that Sudan would remain an international pariah unless it stopped abusing its own citizens; nor would it be able to enjoy the economic benefits of a peace treaty with the south. But the agreement also mattered greatly to Annan, who was already being accused of allowing another genocide to occur on his watch. The secretary-general was loath to leave Khartoum without a tangible sign of progress.

On July 3, Annan and Bashir issued a "joint communiqué" in which the government of Sudan promised to lift all restrictions on humanitarian aid and aid workers; to "ensure that all individuals and groups accused of human rights violations are brought to justice without delay"; to "train all police units in human rights law and hold them responsible for upholding it"; to disarm the Janjaweed; to welcome cease-fire monitors from the African Union; to resume talks on a comprehensive settlement. It was a fine agreement—at least if you thought the government intended to honor it.

I had been told that rather than threaten the Sudanese, Annan had adopted a more "African" approach, emphasizing the country's special responsibility as the geographically largest nation on the continent, in addition to warning of the economic consequences of continued turmoil. On the flight back to Abu Dhabi to return the emir's jet, Annan confirmed that that was so, and added that he felt that he had gotten through. "That's why in the discussions I had with Bashir," he said, "he seemed to understand that if he wants to come out and join the family of nations and open up to investments he needs to gain the respect of the international community." I asked if he really thought the Sudanese cared enough about joining the family of nations to call off the Janjaweed and to extend protection to the very citizens they had been busy uprooting and exterminating. "I think so," Annan said. "I think that financial pressure is very important, maybe even more important than the sanctions on travel," which constituted an implicit threat in the case of failure. It sounded utterly naive. But Annan had realized after long and painful experience that nothing good would come of issuing threats he couldn't back up. He was offering a carrot not so much because he didn't believe in sticks as because he didn't *have* a stick. "I don't," he said wearily, "see anybody rushing in with troops."

In fact, the Sudanese put so little store by the pledges they had made that government forces bombarded several rebel-held cities in North Darfur as soon as Annan left the country. For good measure, government officials beat up and arrested several of the community leaders who had spoken with Annan in Zam Zam. The Janjaweed assaults continued apace; in late July observers from the African Union reported that a contingent of men on horseback had ridden into a town, plundered the market, chained up a number of the townsfolk, and set them on fire. The Sudanese were thumbing their noses at "the international community" that Annan purported to represent. If there was, indeed, such an entity as the international community, now was the time to demonstrate that it could act.

Days after Secretary of State Powell returned from his trip to Sudan, the United States introduced a resolution threatening sanctions should Khartoum fail to meet the commitments it had undertaken in the joint communiqué. On July 9 the U.S. Congress upped the ante considerably by passing a resolution declaring the violence to be a form of genocide—though the outraged legislators offered no troops, no money, and no guidance at all as to what action, if any, should be taken in the face of the Sudanese atrocities. Nor, for that matter, did they offer any evidence that the government had, in fact, undertaken a systematic campaign to wipe out Darfur's African pastoralists. A more practical suggestion came from General Mike Jackson, the former force commander in Bosnia, who suggested that Britain send a force of five thousand men to quell the violence; the British government, however, showed no sign of interest in the idea.

As the violence continued, and the Sudanese made it plain that they would not be deterred either by condemnation or by appeals to economic self-interest, the Western media began to echo the call for intervention. Sudan was increasingly coming to be seen as the new Rwanda. This was too simple: the increasingly provocative behavior by the rebels blurred the moral clarity of the situation; the dispersed and episodic nature of the attacks would have made it extremely difficult for a small force to quell the violence; and the peril, post-Iraq, of sending Western troops into an Islamic country would have made such a mission far more dangerous than it would have been in Rwanda. Still, there were many options short of the Marines. Annan urged the council to pass the toughly worded measure that the Americans had drafted. But despite his entreaties, the Third World nations on the Security Council—China, Pakistan, Algeria, Angola, Brazil, and the Philippines—

warned that they would not vote for any resolution even threatening sanctions, much less imposing them; nor would Russia. The Arab League cautioned the council to "avoid precipitate action" (though portions of the Arab media poured scorn on this timidity). The African Union would not condemn Sudan, though it volunteered to send troops to enforce a cease-fire. The U.S. resolution could not pass as written, and the Americans were compelled to amend it to threaten unspecified "further actions" under Article 41 of the UN Charter, which describes forms of punishment short of military action that the council may impose. Even so, China and Pakistan abstained.

Resolution 1556, which passed on July 30, gave the Sudanese thirty days to comply. During August, the UN and aid groups continued to report incidents of mass rape, of terror in the camps, of the forcible return of refugees to ruined villages menaced by the Janjaweed, though the scale of violence seemed to have diminished slightly. The rebels, emboldened by the international action against Khartoum, increased their attacks, further muddying the picture. And Khartoum shrewdly allowed the spigots of humanitarian aid to open wide. More food and medicine reached the displaced people of Darfur, though because of the ongoing violence and threats, the number of people who had abandoned their homes continued to swell, so that by September about 1.7 million people, almost a quarter of Darfur's population, had fled to a camp inside Sudan or in Chad.

In fact, when I went to see Annan to talk about Darfur in mid-September 2004, the *New York Times* columnist Nicholas Kristof had just written a column in which he observed that as many people were dying every week in Darfur as had been killed in the World Trade Center attack. Kristof meted out blame to the Bush administration and its chief allies, to the Islamic world, and to the secretary-general. "I hate to say it," Kristof wrote, "but the way things are going, when he dies his obituary will begin: 'Kofi Annan, the former U.N. secretary general who at various points in his career presided ineffectually over the failure to stop genocide, first in Rwanda and then in Sudan, died today.'" That was quite a blow. I asked Annan whether he felt that he had, once again, failed to shout from the rooftops in the face of atrocities. He didn't so much as flinch. He said, "What I find is the worst situation for me is to get up and threaten that we'll send a force to Sudan, and it doesn't happen. It weakens the council even more. To throw ideas out, and then the council gets hopelessly divided, and the Sudanese know nothing is going to happen . . ." There was no need to finish the sentence.

The council was just then debating another resolution threatening sanctions against Sudan, and the Chinese had vowed to exercise their veto to block the measure. "I had the Chinese ambassador here this morning," Annan said. "He said, 'We want to see progress, we want the government to take action, but we have difficulties with the resolution as it is currently presented, and my government cannot go along with that.'" This was the reality Annan had to live with. He suggested I read an Op-Ed piece written by Samantha Power, author of a highly regarded book on American responses to genocide, and Morton Abramowitz, head of the International Crisis Group, which reports on, and sometimes seeks to mediate, civil conflict all over the world; the piece had appeared that very morning in *The Washington Post*.

The authors traced the failure to act decisively in Darfur to a straightforward political calculation: "Major and minor powers alike are committed only to stop killing that harms their national interests." The very existence of the Security Council, they argued, allowed nations to "do something" without incurring any real costs—simply "throw the problem into the labyrinth of U.N. deliberations." Only when the "righteous clamor" for action became intolerably loud would leaders in democratic states accept the perils entailed by intervention. This was Annan's view as well, absorbed over a decade of painful experience. But he also knew from those same episodes that when member states looked for cover, it wasn't just "the UN" they would blame, it was him— the scapegoat in chief. "When Darfur happened," he said, "somebody raised the question 'Is the secretary-general going to let this happen?' And I said, 'How many times are they going to hide behind the secretary-general as an alibi for their inaction?'"

CHAPTER THIRTEEN

The Gentle King and His Court

S O FAR AS MOST OF THE WORLD KNEW, THE UN CONSISTED of one man—Secretary-General Kofi Annan. This was a very strange irony, for Annan's temperament was not only bureaucratic but communal. He wasn't much more gregarious than Dag Hammarskjöld had been, but unlike Hammarskjöld, so radically autonomous and self-reliant, Annan seemed almost incomplete without others. He relied on those around him to give voice to his intuitions, to read his moods and know his wishes, to deal with unpleasant things he would sooner avoid. He and his chief aides were linked by deep bonds of trust, earned over years of shared experience; they functioned almost as a distributed intelligence, like a flock of birds. Perhaps this explains why, almost eight years into his tenure as secretary-general, Annan had kept around him virtually everyone who had first accompanied him to the thirty-eighth floor. They were, in some deep way, *him*.

Immediately adjacent to Annan's office lay a suite of rooms occupied by the *chef de cabinet*, Iqbal Riza, Annan's friend of many years and campaigns. The chief of staff was a figure of mystery. Tall, spare, elegant, as slow and watchful as a lizard on a riverbank, Riza was Kofi Annan's vizier. He knew much, said little, pondered deeply. Few professed to fathom his depths. He was a master of paper flow, of procedural arcana, of diplomatic nicety. He claimed to remember almost nothing, but he knew the history of everything. Riza and Annan had met in 1978, when they were both mid-level officials; Riza described

Annan as "my first friend at the UN." They had worked together since 1993. The relationship between the two was a subject of endless fascination inside the building. "It's like a tribal chief with his elderly adviser," said Wegger Strømmen, a Norwegian diplomat. At the monthly lunch with the Security Council, Riza would sit silently, but if he gave any sign of wishing to express an opinion, Annan would instantly call on him.

Annan consulted widely, inside and outside the UN, before making important decisions, but in the end he decided either by himself or with Riza. Annan rarely announced a decision in the course of a meeting. He would take home a thick sheaf of papers, and then, it was assumed, talk to Riza, and Riza would announce the decision. The two men appeared to have a perfect intuitive understanding of each other. Riza may also have been the one person who was as dedicated to the UN and its ideals as Annan; a widower, he seemed to have little life outside the thirty-eighth floor. But Annan also understood something that many outsiders did not: beneath his minutely calibrated circumlocutions, Riza had a deep sense of conscience. Riza had given up his diplomatic career in an act of protest; he had enraged Boutros-Ghali with his critique of UN neutrality in Bosnia; he had beaten back all attempts to soft-pedal the horrors of Kosovo.

When Annan became secretary-general, Riza had said to him, "You're just too soft on people. And in this position, you will have to be hard." If Annan had to choose between keeping a mediocrity in place and firing or transferring him, he would inevitably choose the first option. If someone did have to be told that he or she was to be fired, or even not hired, it was Riza who did the dirty work. And nothing had changed; when Riza told me, in the late fall of 2004, of the advice he had given Annan, he conceded that it had apparently fallen on deaf ears.

Across the hall from Annan and Riza was a warren of offices; in one of those offices sat Lamin Sise, a sweet-natured, ruminative, ironical lawyer from the West African country of Gambia. He had gotten a Ph.D. in international affairs at Johns Hopkins and a law degree at Cambridge before joining the UN. Few people outside the UN, including some of the most knowledgeable reporters, had any idea who he was or what he did. He was the secretary-general's counselor, but his real job was to handle all sensitive personnel matters, whether hiring or firing. The filing cabinets on one wall of his small office held the files of virtually every high-ranking official in the Secretariat. But he handled other sensitive jobs, too. When the Oil-for-Food scandal hit, it was Sise who dealt with investigators, and it was Sise who dealt with Annan's wayward son, Kojo. Like Riza, Sise had worked with Annan since 1993, and, like Riza, he was a man whose loyalty to both the secretary-general and the institution was beyond question. Annan's own staff had long since lost patience with Sise's inveterate wool-gathering, but his position was understood to be unassailable.

Down the hall and to the other side was Elisabeth Lindenmayer, the assistant *chef de cabinet*. Within the inner circle Lindenmayer was first among equals, not in influence but in service and proximity. She had first met Annan in the late 1970s, when he was deputy chief of personnel, and with every promotion thereafter Annan had taken her with him as his special assistant. She had been by his side on almost every trip he had taken for the previous quarter century, and she spoke of him with a combination of reverence and mock exasperation, like a nun whose brother has grown up to be archbishop. She loved to talk about the argument they had waged over twenty years. "He always says, 'You are free to choose.' And I tell him, 'You're bloody arrogant to say so.'"

At the opposite end of the thirty-eighth floor from Annan were the offices of the deputy secretary-general, Louise Fréchette, who had previously served as Canada's ambassador to the UN and as its deputy minister of defense. The office had been established, with vaguely delineated responsibilities, in Annan's initial reform effort. Fréchette occupied the position immediately below Annan in the UN's formal hierarchy, and she officially had jurisdiction over a wide range of substantive issues, including Iraq, but her influence did not rival Riza's. The official hierarchy, in fact, was an almost meaningless guide to real status. Annan may have been the first secretary-general ever to have received a management degree, but his own office resembled the court of a benevolent Renaissance prince, governed by ancient ties of kinship and an acute sensitivity to the sovereign's mood. Scarcely anyone ever left. Annan's spokesman, Fred Eckhard, was another veteran of the peacekeeping office. Michael Moller, the special adviser for peacekeeping, political affairs, and humanitarian affairs, had known Annan for twenty years and described him as his "mentor." The only member of the inner circle who had even moved was Shashi Tharoor, who a year earlier had accepted a promotion to become under secretary-general for public information, though he and Annan still spoke often.

When I asked these people, who had known Annan so long and who admired him so deeply, what it was about their boss that made him so special, they rarely mentioned the conventional attributes. Few, for example, thought him brilliant or intellectually curious or even contemplative. Annan's observations, in casual conversation or formal settings, were never scintillating and often enough banal. He seemed to be so devoid of intellectual vanity as to preclude the normal desire to be found original or even interesting. He was quite content to deliver speeches written wholly by others. Annan's mind was pragmatic; he was interested in understanding a set of facts only in order to work on it. He was said to have a tremendous memory for particulars. He could sit through a dozen consecutive "bilaterals" with heads of state, and it afterward describe the nuances of each. And he was a dogged worker: each night he took home a great stack of paper and plowed through it.

People often spoke of Annan's "charisma." And yet, seen from close up, that didn't feel like the right word at all. Annan was handsome and amiable and exquisitely polite. He was sincere; more than that, he was a person of great moral seriousness. But the electric current he generated was too mild and too intermittent to qualify as charisma. Even the lesser term "charm," with its implication of suppleness, seemed misleading. Annan was palpably uncomfortable in impromptu social settings where most diplomats would have been thoroughly at their ease. His Christmas parties for his staff were famously starchy; everyone, Annan included, seemed relieved when the time had come to go. His socializing often seemed dutiful. One evening during the trip to Sudan, Annan decided that he should socialize with the reporters who had accompanied him. He joined us in a conference room in our hotel in N'Djamena. Rather than invite us into the bar next door, he stood in the room, while the reporters and photographers formed an arc at a respectful distance of four or five feet. He asked them how they had enjoyed the trip, they asked him the same, and he responded with a string of warm platitudes. Within minutes, everyone seemed to be at a loss for words. It was so exquisitely awkward that I finally left.

Annan's great gift, at bottom, was his temperament. He had, as Riza put it, "this ability to connect." How could you not like Kofi Annan? Whoever you were, he seemed more interested in you than in himself. He had no discernible ego at all; he was artless, open, honest, and kind. He looked for the good in everyone. There was, it was true, something undiscriminating and faintly vapid about this sunny receptivity. One of his aides once described him to me as "the perfect foreign exchange student." But it was a far more effective disposition than Boutros-Ghali's imperial condescension, especially when you were trying, for example, to seduce the U.S. Congress. And because Annan's dedication to principle was so sincere, and so selfless, people wanted to help him succeed, to vindicate his faith in them and in the world.

And he had a *feel* for things. Lindenmayer liked to say that he had a sense of timing, a sense of when things were and weren't ripe. He would say, "I'm hanging pegs," when he was methodically laying the predicate on some large and difficult question; this was what John Ruggie meant when he called Annan a "norm entrepreneur." The secretary-general's inner compass seemed very sound, so that when he ignored advice, it usually turned out that he was right and his advisers wrong. He was famous for his patience and calm endurance; Shashi Tharoor liked to describe him as "a yogi." Annan wasn't really as serene as advertised; he had, after all, been shattered by the events of 2003. And yet he had an inner core of self-confidence—perhaps because he had experience of the rightness of that inner compass. Fred Eckhard remembered going to see Annan in his first weeks as secretary-general— the walls of his office still bare—and thinking that he could smell the fear. "He felt that he was completely unprepared for this job, he had never sought the job, and he just didn't know what to do. And then everything he did was right." Soon, he said, Annan realized that he could trust his instincts.

And yet this worldless communing with himself sometimes made Annan seem ever so slightly extraterrestial. There was something uncanny, even a bit weird, about the perfect equipoise he maintained in all settings. "Does he ever raise his voice?" a bewildered UN official once asked me. "Does he go home and beat his wife?" The answers were no and no. The emotions, such as they were, stayed inside; you had to be one of the adepts to recognize anger as it flickered across Annan's features. Indeed, nobody, not even his closest friends, could say for sure whether there was "another side" to the secretary-general, some deep pool of judgment or disaffection or ironic amusement— *something*. Kieran Prendergast once compared Annan to Ronald Reagan: "He's friendly and cordial to everyone, but he doesn't have many close friends, so his thoughts are known to him alone. He's very close to Nane, and he has a somewhat remote relationship to his children." And Nane presented to the world much the same gentle, shy, kindly, and benevolent demeanor as he. They were like a couple in a fairy tale, or in a crystal bubble.

In the late summer and early fall of 2004, Annan was preoccupied with the ongoing catastrophe in Darfur, the terrifying prospect of civil war in both Congo and the Ivory Coast, upcoming elections in Iraq, and his high-level panel of eminent personalities. He seemed to be staking his legacy on the outcome—not that he would ever admit to so grossly personal a motive—but students of UN history were offering obsequies in advance. In one study of a dozen blue-ribbon panels, for example, Edward C. Luck, a professor of international relations at Columbia and an authority on UN history, concluded that "there has been an inverse relationship between how ambitious a report's proposals were and how likely they were to be adopted." Nor, he observed, did "having the blessings of the Secretary-General" increase the likelihood of success.

The composition of the panel was not considered terribly encouraging, either. One of the members told me that the panel had been "put together in a fit of absentmindedness"; another attributed the composition to Annan's depressed state of mind in the summer of 2003. The eminentoes had obviously been chosen with the usual concern for representing all regions and viewpoints, but Annan also seemed to have selected for devitalization. The panel's chairman was Anand Panyarachun, an elegant and genteel—and elderly—former prime minister of Thailand. The panel also included Yevgeny Primakov, the former foreign minister of Russia; Amr Moussa, the head of the Arab League; and Satish Nambiar, a retired Indian general. The panel's only really active members were Gareth Evans, the former foreign minister of Australia; David Hannay, the former British ambassador to the UN; and Gro Harlem Brundtland, the former prime minister of Norway.

The panelists' views of what needed reforming were shaped almost entirely by national background. Evans and Hannay, as well as Brent Scowcroft, the first President Bush's national security adviser, focused on the use of force. For Evans, the catastrophe of Iraq was that it had discredited the doctrine of humanitarian intervention, which he played a central role in formulating. The expression was now being treated as a mask for the cynical pursuit of national interest. Evans was eager to enshrine "the responsibility to protect" in UN doctrine. For Hannay, one of the architects of the Security Council's policies in Bosnia, the central post–Cold War, post-Iraq question was "Can we produce a new consensus on security policy for the UN which will include the U.S.?" Nambiar, however, hailed from a country that did not accept the responsibility to protect and that was more concerned with constraining American power than with accommodating it. Nambiar took the G77 view of reform. "There is," he said to me in the summer of 2004, "an excessive focus of the developed world on these security issues, as if the panacea for everything is the use of force."

Throughout the first half of 2004, the panel flailed around in displays of posturing and speechifying; Panyarachun seemed to quiver with unease whenever an argument was seriously joined. Evans warned Annan that the whole thing would flop if he didn't intervene. In July, at the tail end of the Darfur trip, Annan had stopped in Baden, where the panel was meeting. There he had delivered a pep talk, whose essence, according to Evans, was, "I want to bring this discussion to a head, I want an explicit recommendation, and I want something that can be voted up or down." Evans had the feeling that Annan himself wasn't quite sure what he wanted, but that he knew he wanted something specific and bold. The talk, Evans said, "completely turned the atmosphere around." By the end of the session, the group had moved toward agreement on such deeply contentious issues as the responsibility to protect and a blanket prohibition of terrorism.

At the end of September, Annan met in his office with Stephen Stedman, a Stanford academic who was the panel's staff director; Kieran Prendergast; and Robert Orr, a former Clinton administration official who was formally the head of strategic planning, and informally the American responsible for explaining the UN to Washington and vice versa—an indispensable position in the regime of every secretary-general. Stedman ticked off the issues. Security Council reform was proving as contentious as expected. Nonproliferation was stalled, because Brazil did not accept the idea of surrendering its enriched uranium to a multilateral body; the Brazilian panel member was receiving instructions from his country's Foreign Ministry, which on one occasion he had absentmindedly transferred wholesale, in a separate typeface, into his own position paper. The panelists had agreed to kill the embarrassingly vestigial Military Staff Committee and Trusteeship Council.

The talk returned to Security Council reform. This was easily the most vexed of all the issues the panel faced. It was obvious that Germany and Japan had a greater right to membership than, say, France and Russia; Third World powers like India and Brazil had a strong claim as well. But no permanent member would voluntarily leave, and proposals to add others provoked opposition from second-tier neighbors. Council expansion had become the third rail of UN reform; a committee of the General Assembly had been debating innumerable formulas for over a decade without making progress. The panelists had initially supported a variant on a familiar reform proposal, in which the council would admit a "third tier" of semipermanent members, who would serve four-year terms rather than the two years now given nonpermanent members and would be eligible for reelection. But when news of the plan leaked, public opinion in the countries aspiring to permanent membership had been outraged, and the panel had relegated the three-tier plan to one of several options.

Bob Orr observed that the Germans and the Japanese had presented permanent membership to their publics as the sine qua non of great-power status. Should failure loom, Annan might have to devise some means to let them extricate themselves without losing face; otherwise, they could sink the whole reform process in a fit of resentment. Annan said, "The next six months we'll use to build consensus, so when they come in September, they're prepared. Germany and Japan can tell their publics they tried hard for permanent status, but they failed; the best they can do is wait five or six years." But Annan agreed that the two countries seemed to have chosen what Prendergast called "the kamikaze option"—succeed or crash. "I intend to work the capitals," he said. "I can use the members of the panel." Prendergast then suggested that some of the reforms could be broken off and given to Security Council members to chew over, but Annan disagreed: "This is a very important issue, and I don't think the capitals want it to be seen that the decisions are going to be made by their perm reps. My inclination is to go to the key capitals to build up support."

Annan believed—indeed, took it as an axiom—that "the collective interest is the national interest," as I once heard him put it. But he was not so naive as to think that merit alone would carry the day. The whole exercise had been provoked by the fear of American unilateralism, and it was hardly clear that reform of any kind would persuade the Bush administration of the UN's merits. Annan had placed Brent Scowcroft on the panel because Scowcroft was as close as he could get to the inner circle of Bush *fils*—which wasn't close at all, since the former national security adviser was a pillar of the party's internationalist wing and had opposed the Iraq war. Annan worried about the reports he had been getting of Scowcroft's diffidence during the panel's debate. "Was Brent Scowcroft there at the last meeting?" he had anxiously asked Stedman.

"Yes, and he was much more constructive and engaged than he had been before," Stedman reassured him.

In fact, when I spoke to Scowcroft soon thereafter, he said, "Given my expectations, if anything comes out of this, I'll be happy." Scowcroft hoped that the panel could devise meaningful guidelines for the use of force, and also rationalize the system of peacekeeping and nation-building—"this continuum of states under stress, and then states in conflict, and then states being reconstructed." And he did feel, he said, that "we're starting to talk to each other now instead of preaching." But he saw no evidence that the Bush administration was even paying attention. "Washington is supremely uninterested in this whole thing," he said. "Next to France, the UN is the whipping boy of the moment."

CHAPTER FOURTEEN

Two Cheers—If That—for Diplomacy

I n late October 2004, John Danforth, the new U.S. Ambassador to the UN, won agreement from the other members of the Security Council to hold an extraordinary session of the council in Nairobi, several weeks hence, in hopes of concluding the so-called Naivasha process to end the north-south civil war in Sudan. Annan had already planned to be in Dar es Salaam several days later for a conference, which he himself had put in motion, designed to engage the problems of Congo on a regional basis, and then in Ouagadougou, the capital of Burkina Faso, for the annual conference of French-speaking nations, which was the kind of gesture that pleased the French. And then the Egyptian government, eager to play a peacemaking role in Iraq, decided to hold a summit in the seaside resort town of Sharm al-Sheikh. No one knew what the Meeting of the Neighboring Countries of Iraq, the G8, and China, as it was gracefully titled, was supposed to accomplish, but Annan would be in the neighborhood, and so he would go to that one, too. It would be ten days of transcontinental conference barnstorming.

Danforth's bid to move directly to a resolution of the north-south problem constituted an implicit admission of the Security Council's failure to address the mayhem in Darfur. Danforth had been compelled to soften, and then soften once again, the language of the resolution on Darfur that the United States had submitted to the council a month before. The measure that the council finally passed repeated the threat

of sanctions which an earlier resolution had already made, and established a commission of inquiry to look into allegations of genocide.
Even this was too much for China, Algeria, Pakistan, and Russia, all of
whom abstained. The commission, in any case, would not report until
the end of the year. It had become increasingly clear that the only response that would enjoy consensual support was to send in troops from
the African Union. The Sudanese had already accepted a token force
of 385; on October 1, the government agreed to allow 3,500 troops to
deploy in and around Darfur's refugee camps.

The AU had no experience fielding a peacekeeping force, and no
funds with which to equip, transport, feed, or house them; it would
take several months at least to find and field 3,500 soldiers, in itself a
tiny number for so vast a region as Darfur. Annan did not delude himself about the motives of the Security Council members. "It turns out
to be a rather cynical game," he said soon after the vote, "where everybody is coming to the African Union knowing full well they don't have
the capacity, but at least your conscience is clear that someone is doing
it. There's another cynical part of it, when you hear the Sudanese say,
'We'll accept these African troops,' knowing delay is in order." The
agreement was, in fact, hailed by one and all as a pathbreaking act of
regional self-reliance, "an African solution to an African problem." For
the Africans themselves, this formulation had a particularly chauvinis-
tic, anticolonial appeal. In a regional meeting in mid-October, the
heads of state of Sudan's most important neighbors—Nigeria, Chad,
Egypt, and Libya—strongly endorsed the Sudanese government and rejected "all foreign intervention in this purely African question."

Meanwhile, Darfur continued to disintegrate. In a November 4 report to the Security Council, Jan Pronk, Annan's special representative
in Sudan, said, "Darfur may easily enter a state of anarchy; a total collapse of law and order. The conflict is changing in character. The government does not control its own forces fully. It co-opted paramilitary
forces and now it cannot count on their obedience. The spirit is out of
the bottle and cannot be pushed back. The borderlines between the
military, the paramilitary and the police are being blurred. Within the
rebel movements, there is a leadership crisis." With this war of all
against all looming, Annan, unlike Danforth, could not afford to focus
just on the north-south process.

The weekly meeting of the Senior Management Group on November 9 was devoted to Sudan. The Department of Political Affairs had distributed a paper as the basis for discussion. The document plainly bore the authorship of Kieran Prendergast and Haile Menkerios, the head of the Africa division. Sudan's underlying problem was that power had been monopolized since independence by "a small elite of riverine 'Arabs.'" Darfur was a symptom, one of several. The solution was a "comprehensive approach" leading to a more just distribution of power. A north-south settlement could be followed by a national conference that would use Naivasha as the basis for an overall agreement. The AU force was the only plausible solution in Darfur, since a "non-AU international military intervention . . . would be likely to exacerbate the conflict rather than expedite its resolution."

Prendergast began the meeting by briefly presenting the paper's conclusions. He compared Sudan to "a complex piece of clockwork" that could be repaired only by getting the sequence exactly right—first Naivasha, then Darfur—the view that he had long held, but that others blamed for the failure to act in the face of atrocities. Others disagreed. Shashi Tharoor said, "The grand narrative in the Western media is that something like genocide is happening, and the UN hasn't been able to do anything about it." How would it look if they went to Nairobi and ignored Darfur? Yes, but could they, on the other hand, afford to alienate Khartoum? James Morris, head of the World Food Programme, reported that his agency was now feeding more than 2 million people in the south, and over a million in Darfur; the latter number was projected to climb by April to 2.3 million.

Annan said nothing—not a word—for the first hour. Finally, after listening to all sides, he said, "The council is in a very difficult situation. If they focus on Naivasha, and not on Darfur, they'll be accused of fiddling while Rome is burning." And would the AU troops be sufficient to bring the violence under control in Darfur? Experience suggested otherwise. "What if we come to the conclusion that something more needs to be done? How do we engage the international community?" The meeting reached no conclusion on these hard questions.

Annan and the Security Council ambassadors left for Nairobi on November 16. The council session was held on the eighteenth at the UN's beautifully manicured and graciously landscaped compound. The diplomats, the UN officials, and the principal figures from Sudan and its neighbors gathered in the auditorium—a hundred-odd people in a space built for ten or twenty times that number. The African politicians gave long, hortatory speeches. Sudanese vice president Ali Osman Taha said all the right things about regional autonomy and the sharing of national power and resources. President Yoweri Museveni of Uganda, one of Africa's great pedants, delivered a stem-winder accusing the UN of failing Africa since the days of Lumumba, and then tracing the rise of the region's chief language and ethnic groups. From the balcony where the local press was quartered, I had an excellent view of the council members sleeping off their jet lag. The secretary-general's speech would not have jolted any of them awake. He focused on Naivasha and on "the general issue of governance." He did say, "When crimes of such a scale are being committed, and a sovereign State appears unwilling or unable to protect its own citizens, a grave responsibility falls on the international community, and specifically on this Council." Annan did not, however, explain what that responsibility might entail.

After a closed session that afternoon, Danforth and Annan emerged to announce that John Garang, leader of the southern forces, and Vice President Taha had signed a memorandum of understanding promising to reach a peace agreement by the end of the year. The council then passed a resolution affirming its support for the peace effort, holding out the promise of increased aid and trade, and demanding that all parties, rebel and government, in the south and in Darfur, "immediately cease all violence and attacks." Khartoum and the Christian forces did, in fact, conclude a historic agreement bringing the rebels into the government as equal partners and establishing a system for sharing the oil resources in the south. Ultimately, the Security Council mandated a peacekeeping force to enforce the agreement, and international donors began to target the pitifully underdeveloped bottom half of the country. By separating the north-south problem from Darfur, Danforth achieved his long-sought goal of ending the civil war.

But this also meant allowing Darfur to fester. On Darfur, the council resolution was all carrots and no sticks. When Danforth was asked about this at a press conference, he bridled genteelly, saying, "I would say that we're *increasing* the amount of pressure. We put Sudan and the problem of Sudan right at the center of the world stage." But the world stage didn't want the problem of Sudan at its center. Six days after Danforth's fine words, African countries prevented the General Assembly's human rights committee from voting on a resolution, sponsored by virtually every Western country, that called for a cease-fire and political settlement in Darfur and demanded that all parties stop committing "cruel, inhuman or degrading forms of treatment or punishment." The African group complained of a "double standard" in which abuses in Third World countries, but not in the West, were singled out for condemnation. The normally diplomatic Danforth blew his stack, sputtering, "One wonders if there can't be a clear and direct statement of principle. Why have this building? What is it about?" He was scarcely the first person to ask those questions.

The International Conference on Peace, Security, Democracy, and Development in the Great Lakes Region opened November 19, the day after the Nairobi conference. Considered strictly as a matter of spectacle, the Great Lakes conference was much superior to the rather desultory Security Council session. Annan's special representative had spent the last two and a half years working with the Democratic Republic of the Congo and its neighbors to establish talks that would culminate in the two-day session at the Golden Tulip hotel in Dar es Salaam. It was, for the participants, a far more climactic and consequential event than the snoozy session in Nairobi had been. The lobby of the hotel, the hallways, the little coffee shop, all were thronged with African and international officials. A tent had been pitched in the Golden Tulip's garden, which looked out over the sea. The weather in Dar es Salaam is never exactly temperate, and the hundreds of delegates jammed together under the tent fanned themselves in the still, steamy air.

The Great Lakes region was almost certainly the most tormented place on the planet. The Rwandan genocide of 1994 was only the most sickening example of a recurring phenomenon: In neighboring Burundi, mass killings had accompanied each swing in power between Hutus and Tutsis over a quarter of a century. And Congo was hell on earth: a savage war in the late 1990s had taken the lives of as many as 4 million people, chiefly through displacement, hunger, and disease.

And each of these conflicts had fed into the others, ensuring an end-less supply of provocations for new rounds of bloodshed. Clearly the Great Lakes needed a regional solution.

But it wasn't easy, from the outside, to understand what the confer-ence could contribute to this solution. The conference opened with the Tanzanian Police Band tootling up a processional tune, and then seven-teen heads of state, or their surrogates, marched in stately fashion up to a dais. Among their number were not only the presidents of the Great Lakes nations but the world-class villain Omar al-Bashir of Su-dan, who had no apparent connection to the problems of Central Africa but who was obviously happy to share the stage with so distin-guished a cast. Many speeches were delivered, including one by Kofi Annan congratulating the leaders for having made "a strategic decision to pursue peace." The heads of state then went into closed session, where they approved, with very few changes, a document that had been drawn up several weeks earlier. The signatories expressed their deep awareness of, and concern for, the catastrophes that plagued the region, including genocide and crimes against humanity; recalled that the causes of conflict were rooted in "pre-colonial, colonial, and post-colonial eras"; owned up to "the lack of full application of essential le-gal instruments," "the degradation of the ecosystem," "unsound policy choices" in matters of economy, gender discrimination, and so on; and resolved to act collectively in order to "transform the Great Lakes Re-gion into a space of sustainable peace and security." And that was it.

An ignorant outsider might well suppose that an astonishing amount of time and effort had just been wasted. I was assured by sev-eral officials that I was quite wrong. Hamuli Kabarhuza, the head of the Congolese delegation that had worked on the draft document, ex-plained to me that it was the very fact of the meeting that mattered rather than the purely rhetorical commitments in the final statement. "For the first time," he said, "the presidents of the region sat together." For the last decade they had been deviously plotting against one an-other; now they had committed to speak regularly. Their aides had come to know one another, and one another's countries, over the two years of planning.

I left feeling that I had at least witnessed a single moment of a slow, organic process of knitting together what had been violently torn apart.

And then, three days later, Rwandan authorities announced that they were preparing to send troops across the border into Congo to prevent incursions by Hutu *génocidaires* who had fled to eastern Congo. This was not the form of communication envisioned in the Dar es Salaam process. Ten thousand Rwandan troops massed at the border, though it was never altogether clear if they crossed into Congo. Perhaps Rwandan president Paul Kagame only wanted to remind everyone that he reserved the right to retaliate against the Hutu militias. Or perhaps he feared that amid all the attention to Congo, people would forget his own country's martyr status. Or perhaps Kagame, who coveted the farmland and the fabulous mineral resources of eastern Congo, was just trying to keep the pot boiling. Whatever the explanation, Kagame had demonstrated how little store he put by agreements, no matter how grandly they were solemnized.

The third stop on Annan's mad dash was Sharm al-Sheikh, a beach resort bordering Israel, where the international conference on Iraq was to be held. Iraq was a different order of problem from Sudan or the Great Lakes. On the one hand, in Iraq the UN played second fiddle to the United States, which had led the coalition that fought the war and that continued to dominate the affairs of the country. Resolution 1546, passed the previous June, had spelled out the areas in which the UN was to play a "leading" or a supporting role in Iraq, though the only one that was central to the country's future was the organization of national elections scheduled for the following January. But Iraq was also, of course, an area of overwhelming sensitivity between the UN and the United States. The mutual resentment over the collapse, in March 2003, of negotiations on a resolution authorizing war still burned bright, though principally in the White House. And the suicide bombing in Baghdad that had killed twenty-two UN employees in August 2003 had left the UN's rank and file with a profound sense of embitterment both at the Bush administration and at Kofi Annan, who had agreed to send the mission there.

Annan had made two very uncharacteristic gaffes over Iraq, which revealed the intensity of the pressure he was under. In the summer of 2004, an interviewer from the BBC had pressed him as to whether he

considered the war in Iraq "illegal." This was a word Annan was careful
never to use; instead, he described the war as "illegitimate," because it
violated the prohibition in the UN Charter against wars fought (save in
self-defense) without the approval of the Security Council. But after
being repeatedly badgered, Annan had slipped and agreed that the war
was, indeed, "illegal." This concession infuriated leading officials both
in Washington and in London and provided choice ammunition to
those who considered the UN a nest of anti-Americanism.

The second mistake had been much worse. In late October, U.S.
forces were preparing to storm the Iraqi city of Falluja, which had become a citadel for Sunni insurgents. Annan and his advisers were
united in considering the impending attack a disastrous miscalculation
that would broaden and harden Sunni opposition to the American-
backed state without dealing a decisive blow to the insurgency. Annan
spent the last weekend in October at Greentree, where he was holding
the annual session of the "executive committee" of the heads of all the
UN agencies. On the morning of October 30, a Saturday, he called
Kieran Prendergast to talk about Falluja. Prendergast had vehemently
opposed the Iraq war and believed that the Americans were about to
burn the bridges to influential Sunnis that the UN, among others, had
been building. Prendergast says he suggested that the secretary-general
call Secretary of State Colin Powell and British foreign minister Jack
Straw, but Annan said he feared Powell would interrupt him before he
had explained himself. He wanted to send a letter. Lakhdar Brahimi,
whose antipathy to American foreign policy was equal to Prendergast's,
agreed.

The text of a letter then went back and forth between New York
and Greentree. On Sunday, Annan sent the letter to Bush, Blair, and
Iyad Allawi, Iraq's interim prime minister. "I wish to share with you my
increasing concern at the prospect of an escalation in violence," Annan
wrote, "which I fear could be very disruptive for Iraq's political transition . . . The threat or actual use of force not only risks deepening the
sense of alienation of certain communities, but would also reinforce
perceptions among the Iraqi population of a continued military occupation." It would seem foolhardy even at the best of times for a UN
secretary-general to admonish a U.S. president to call off an impending
invasion, but the letter arrived in the White House—and then was in-

stantly leaked—two days before a bitterly contested presidential election in which the conduct of the war in Iraq was a central issue. Administration officials took it for granted that Annan was trying to swing the election to the Democrat John Kerry, an act, in their view, tantamount to betrayal.

The thought appears not to have crossed Annan's mind, though it's easy to see why it might have. One of the few things that united people from the top of the UN to the bottom was an intense hostility to the policies of the Bush administration, which gave every indication of holding multilateral principles in contempt. Kerry, on the other hand, was almost a caricature of Democratic internationalism, with a high regard for Europe and an excellent command of French. Kerry held out the promise of deliverance. And few UN officials were sufficiently well versed in the dynamics of American politics to recognize Kerry's downward spiral. Bob Orr, the head of strategic planning, walked into the UN lobby the morning after the election to see Bush giving his acceptance speech. "There must have been 140 UN employees there," he recalls, "all in their various native dress, staring up at the screen, looking utterly numb. Every meeting I was in for the next several days, people seemed almost clinically depressed." Perhaps Annan, too, had persuaded himself that Kerry would win.

But since it was Bush who won, Annan was in a deep hole thanks to "illegal" and the Falluja letter. Several weeks later, when I asked him why he had sent the letter, he said, "I was genuinely concerned about a possible boycott of the election. I'm worried that if the process is not inclusive, and the Sunnis get a very small representation in the National Assembly, which is also going to write the constitution, that could fuel more alienation, and the violence is going to escalate further." Annan's analysis of the situation, which he had absorbed from Brahimi and Prendergast and Ashraf Qazi, his special representative in Iraq, was perfectly accurate. He was right about Falluja. But Annan knew very well that being right does not, by itself, constitute effective diplomacy. I asked if he actually thought the letter might affect American and Iraqi military plans. He said he had been hoping it would "trigger some reflection." And it simply had not occurred to him that the letter could leak before the election.

Or perhaps Annan didn't want to think about it. UN officials had come increasingly to view the Iraqi elections as a futile errand that the United States had assigned to them in order to use the organization as a convenient scapegoat. Annan himself was free from such conspiratorial views, but he was increasingly frustrated and worried about the prospects for the election, and he felt that Washington had locked him in a crushing vise, with angry UN employees seeking disengagement on one side and administration officials demanding greater engagement on the other. Annan never consulted Iqbal Riza, his closest confidant, before sending his momentous letter. "It was uncharacteristic," says Riza delicately. Annan called him only to say that the letter was being sent. Riza instantly recognized the danger: "The election is two days from now. Why can't it be held up?" But Annan said, "No, it's urgent."

It was in this atmosphere of deep anxiety, almost of helplessness, that Annan prepared for the summit in Sharm al-Sheikh. A week before flying to Nairobi, he met with his chief aides in the conference room next to his office; Qazi was on the speakerphone from Baghdad. Prendergast sketched out the UN's objections to the American course of action. "We agree that we need to drain the swamp," he said, "but the question is how to deal with the mosquitoes. We're not pacifists, but we want to divide the mosquitoes between nationalists, who can be encouraged to join in a political dialogue, and jihadists, who are beyond political dialogue. We'd like to see more outreach, more time, more effort." But neither the Iraqi government nor the Americans wanted the UN to use its "good offices" to reach out to these nationalist Sunnis; the Iraqis had barred a UN official with broad ties in the country from joining the UN mission. Sunni participation in the election seemed to be hanging by a thread.

Now conversation turned to a very worrying cable from the mission in Baghdad, reporting that the Fijian contingent that was to protect UN officials in the Green Zone seemed poorly equipped and prepared. Annan was exasperated. "Why did we even bring them to Kuwait?" he asked. But he knew the answer: the Bush administration was applying intense pressure on the UN to supply its own security in order to release American troops from the job, as well as to enable an increase in the size of the UN mission, which then totaled thirty-five. Resolution 1546 had called for a four-thousand-man security force, but none of the signatories had any intention of sending their own soldiers into the Iraqi cockpit. The Koreans had made some vague promises, but, Prendergast said, "They don't want to touch this with a barge pole." Georgia had spoken of sending troops, but they weren't materializing. The Romanians had promised a hundred soldiers. The Fijians, who were in fact highly professional peacekeepers, had offered several hundred. The Americans had asked allies to pitch in, but found no takers. "I must tell the Americans," Annan said, "if they don't have a viable alternative, and can't do it, then I have no basis to send in the staff." This was a message he knew he didn't want to deliver.

Soon after reaching Sharm al-Sheikh on November 22, Annan met in the living room of his hotel suite with Brahimi and Qazi. He asked the latter how voter registration was going. "Nothing in Anbar or Nineveh," Qazi said, mentioning two Sunni strongholds. "Baghdad is not good, and has every indication of getting worse. There's no activity at all in Mosul"—a major city besieged by insurgents. The UN had arranged a simplified election along national rather than regional lines, and it was now facing an unforeseen consequence: if turnout varied by ethnicity, the election could produce a deeply unrepresentative assembly. Annan and Qazi now discussed just how grave this outcome would be. Should the UN call for a postponement? Brahimi said, "In Iraq, you can't talk about not holding the election—you will be said to be playing into the hands of the insurgents. But holding the election may cause more problems than it solves. At some point, we may have to face up to the responsibility, and it may be up to the UN to say no. And we need to prepare ourselves for that eventuality."

Qazi said, "The Americans argue that the analysis you are hearing from me and from Mr. Brahimi is too pessimistic." Brahimi laughed into his fist.

The conference accomplished virtually nothing beyond giving the various players the opportunity to meet quietly "on the sidelines," in diplomatic parlance. This seems to be the chief practical virtue of most of these stultifying confabs. The whole affair made me wonder if Annan wouldn't have been better off with a body double to deliver his speeches in hotels and conference rooms, freeing him to attend to the world's business on the telephone in his office. But Annan always seemed to find a plausible reason why his attendance was required at such events, especially in Africa, where it was expected as a matter of pride.

Annan's final stop on this weirdly ritualistic tour of Africa would be Ouagadougou, the capital of Burkina Faso, where he would attend Francophonie, the most content-free of his stops. For some reason, we were scheduled to spend three nights in Ouagadougou. But soon after our plane left Egypt, Annan's aide Elisabeth Lindenmayer came to the back of the plane, where the staff was sitting, and said, "There has been a change of schedule." Lindenmayer, never a calm figure, now seemed as taut as piano wire. "The secretary-general has urgent business to attend to," she told us, obviously trying out a line that was soon to be offered to the press, not to mention to our hosts in Ouagadougou. Whatever that urgent business was—and not a word of it could be coaxed from Lindenmayer's tightly compressed lips—it would cause us to leave Ouagadougou for Paris, and thence New York, the following morning.

Lindenmayer's cryptic message launched Annan's staff into a frenzy of speculation. What could that urgent business be save the burgeoning scandal over the Oil-for-Food Programme in Iraq, which now seemed to be engulfing Annan's son, Kojo, and thus perhaps Annan himself? Later in the flight we learned that in a conversation on the sidelines, Colin Powell had handed Annan a letter rebuking him for failing to find the troops to defend the UN team in Baghdad. This was very bad, since until that moment Powell had been Annan's staunchest—indeed, only—defender in the upper ranks of the Bush administration. And still later—it must have been the next day—we discovered that Nane, deeply upset and frightened about the abuse being ladled on her husband in New York and Washington, had been calling constantly, asking him to cut short his trip in order to defend himself. Some terrible new phase in Kofi Annan's history, and perhaps also in the history of the institution, was about to unfold.

But first he would have to endure diplomatic hell. The other heads of state would not arrive in Burkina Faso until the following day, so Blaise Compaoré, the country's dictatorial leader, had arranged a state dinner in Annan's behalf. The dinner was held outdoors, in a plaza behind the rather modest presidential palace. There was a buffet and plenty of wine, and a performance by singers, dancers, and musicians on a stage up in front. It was, for those of us in Annan's entourage, a lovely evening. But our glances kept being drawn to the long dais at the rear of the plaza, far removed from the music and the lights, where the secretary-general had been seated between the president and the first lady. Annan could not talk policy in such a setting, and he had little talent for small talk. Perhaps the Compaorés were accustomed to being entertained by others. Whatever the case, long minutes passed in which the three peered across the vast intervening space at the performance and at the happy spectators, without exchanging a word. Annan's mind was surely on the troubles that awaited him back home, and on his distraught wife. And he was exhausted from the travel, the mental effort, the tension. But a secretary-general can't excuse himself from a state dinner in his honor. And so he sat there, in shadow and in ponderous silence. I had never felt so sorry for the man.

CHAPTER FIFTEEN

Oil-for-Food: The Witch Hunt

I N FEBRUARY 2004, AN IRAQI NEWSPAPER PUBLISHED A document that had emerged from the great mass of material uncovered after the fall of Saddam Hussein. The document was, or in any case purported to be, a list of people whom Saddam had selected as recipients of oil vouchers that could be sold for a profit under the Oil-for-Food Programme authorized and managed by the UN. The vouchers were understood to be bribes paid in reward for, or expectation of, the use of influence on Iraq's behalf. The alleged recipients included prominent Middle Eastern journalists, Western business figures, leading politicians in Great Britain, France, and Russia—and Benon Sevan, a career UN employee who had managed the Office of the Iraq Programme, which oversaw Oil-for-Food. This would have been a very grave matter at any time, but given the bitterness toward the UN that many Republicans continued to nurse after the failed debate over war in Iraq, the allegation that Saddam Hussein had corrupted the manager of Oil-for-Food was a disaster. Several congressional committees and several prosecutorial jurisdictions began to investigate the $64 billion program. And Kofi Annan, recognizing the perilousness of the situation, asked the Security Council to establish an independent investigative body. In April, he announced that Paul Volcker, the highly respected former chairman of the Federal Reserve Board, and, not at all coincidentally, an American, would lead the investigation.

The Volcker committee got off the ground very slowly. The UN was not in the habit of investigating itself, and certainly not at the behest of Americans who wished the organization no good. The ACABQ, as the General Assembly committee that holds the UN's purse strings is known, informed Volcker that it would be unable to fund his inquiry, since the UN's budget cycle wouldn't begin until October. Meanwhile, leaks from the other investigations made their way into the press: the Iraqis were extorting money from the suppliers of humanitarian goods that they purchased under Oil-for-Food; Annan's son, Kojo, had worked as a consultant for the firm that inspected those incoming goods, leaving the very month it won the contract to do so. In July, William Safire, the conservative Op-Ed columnist of *The New York Times*, published a piece under the ominous headline "Kofigate Gets Going." Having thus enrolled Oil-for-Food in the semiofficial scandal register of "-gates," he melodramatically characterized it as "the largest financial rip-off in history." That got the UN's attention. Soon Volcker had the $30 million he needed; and now, in addition to all the other threats, a glittering sword of Damocles hung over the institution's head.

The Oil-for-Food Programme, like the safe havens policy in Bosnia, was a stopgap measure prolonged to the point of disaster; it was prolonged, as the safe havens were, because the major powers could not or would not agree on a lasting solution. Oil-for-Food was a giant patch applied to the crumbling regime of sanctions that the Security Council had imposed on Iraq in the aftermath of the Gulf War, a policy which itself was supposed to expire when a crippled Saddam lost his grip on power. Of course no such thing happened; instead, the sanctions dragged on for years, magnifying the suffering from an already shattered economy. By 1995, Iraq's GDP per capita had dropped to $495 from $2,304 six years earlier. Large numbers of children were dying from malnutrition and disease. Saddam, who never lacked money to build more palaces for himself, shamelessly exploited his people's suffering in order to discredit a policy designed to keep him in his cage.

The sanctions had become a political as well as a humanitarian disaster. And yet if they were eliminated, Saddam would lose all incentive to submit to the highly intrusive weapons inspections he had accepted at the time of his surrender. In early 1995, the Clinton administration, trying to shore up support for the sanctions, dispatched UN ambassador Madeleine Albright to Europe with intelligence photos showing (or apparently showing) that Saddam was clandestinely rebuilding his weapons capacity; nevertheless, when she came back to Washington, she reported that the sanctions could be saved only if the harm they did could be mitigated. In 1991, the Security Council had in fact passed a resolution permitting Iraq to sell limited amounts of oil in exchange for food and medicine. But Saddam had balked; the system was to be controlled by the UN, and he would not accept a program he could not manipulate.

Now, with the sanctions looking more and more like a terrible victor's justice exacted on the Iraqi people, the Americans and the British, who had dominated UN policy on Iraq since the Gulf War, were willing to accept what they would not accept before: Saddam would be permitted to control the distribution of goods within the country and to choose buyers for Iraqi oil. Diplomats did not delude themselves about the consequences of this concession. According to Jeremy Greenstock, then a leading official in the British Foreign Office and later his country's UN ambassador, "It was realized that a certain amount of misbehavior was going to happen on the Iraqi side if they were going to accept this. But the Iraqi government had to agree, or it wouldn't work."

In December 1996, the Iraqi government began to sell oil under the terms of the program; humanitarian goods, purchased with the proceeds of the oil sales, began arriving the following March. In the Kurdish areas of northern Iraq, where the UN controlled the distribution of humanitarian goods, health and nutrition returned over the next several years to prewar levels. The effect was less dramatic elsewhere in Iraq, because Saddam used his control over distribution to siphon off the supplies to enrich himself and his coterie. Nevertheless, the threat of starvation and epidemic receded—as did the political threat to the sanctions.

The Oil-for-Food Programme not only succeeded in humanitarian terms; it also made it possible to preserve the inspections program, with all its limitations, until the inspectors were withdrawn immediately before the American and British bombing campaign in December 1998. And for the ensuing four years, the sanctions, which remained in force, deprived Saddam of the revenue he needed to rebuild his military and threaten his neighbors. Kenneth Pollack, a former official in President Clinton's National Security Council who helped persuade many wavering Democrats to support the 2003 war by arguing that sanctions had given Saddam cover to reconstitute his WMD programs, later conceded that "the combination of inspections backed by powerful sanctions worked in disarming Iraq."

Oil-for-Food worked, but it didn't work very well. In 1996, the UN had almost no experience managing large-scale financial transactions. The Oil-for-Food Programme was bigger by many orders of magnitude than anything the UN had undertaken before, but no one seems to have recognized the need to bring in new kinds of expertise or create new kinds of organs. The program was run simply as a supersized version of a conventional sanctions regime. As in all such cases, the Security Council appointed a committee, consisting of all fifteen of its sitting members, to oversee the process. The 661 Committee, as it was called, was a classically dysfunctional UN body. Since the committee operated by consensus, all fifteen of its members, rather than the usual five on the council itself, effectively wielded a veto. Peter van Walsum, the Dutch ambassador who chaired the committee in 1999 and 2000, has written that "a little bit of arithmetic teaches us that a sanctions committee must be about three times as inflexible and irresolute as the Security Council itself." Normally a sanctions committee has relatively little to do beyond trying to prevent illegal trade; in Iraq, it had to monitor billions of dollars of transactions both in oil and in humanitarian goods.

But as was almost always the case with the UN, administrative problems were really political problems in disguise. The Americans and the British wanted to keep Saddam in his box; the Russians, the Chinese, and, increasingly, the French wanted the sanctions relaxed and ultimately ended. What this meant in practice is that the Americans, and to a lesser extent the British, used their position on the committee to ensure that Saddam did not sneak in military items under the guise of peaceful use; a team of analysts at the State Department pored over contracts for imported goods for signs of such "dual-use" items. The Americans often placed a hold on contracts for months, sometimes preventing Iraq from receiving crucial humanitarian supplies. This infuriated the Iraqis and their allies on the Security Council. And so France, Russia, and China devoted themselves to keeping supplies flowing through the pipeline as single-mindedly as the Americans did to preventing abuse. This combination of structural and political paralysis often immobilized the committee for months on end.

Since the Security Council has no staff of its own, the 661 Committee turned to the Secretariat for the day-to-day management of Oil-for-Food. In March 1997, Kofi Annan established the Office of the Iraq Programme and appointed Benon Sevan, a Cypriot and career UN official, as its executive director. It was UN operatives who actually set the price of oil sales, reviewed contracts and contractors both on the oil and on the humanitarian sides of the program, issued approvals, disbursed funds to the Iraqi government from an escrow account, and the like. These officials thus had a far closer view of what was actually happening in Iraq than the diplomats on the 661 Committee could have. By 2000, if not before, many of them had heard stories of widespread corruption both in the sale of oil and in the pricing of contracts for humanitarian goods. It was widely rumored, for example, that the Iraqis were demanding that contractors add 10 percent to the actual purchase price; once the sale of, say, a water-purification plant had been completed, the contractor kicked back the surplus by wiring it to an Iraqi-controlled bank account.

How could such systematic cheating have gone undetected? The answer is that it didn't. UN officials saw the privations inflicted by the sanctions and heard the incessant complaints of Iraqi officials about the American holds. Few believed that the imperative of restraining Saddam could justify such suffering. In 1998, in fact, Dennis Halliday, the head of the UN mission in Iraq, quit in disgust over the stranglehold he felt the Americans had placed on the disbursement of humanitarian goods. Most UN officials felt far more passionately about mitigating the effect of the sanctions than they did about preventing Saddam and his circle from profiteering.

The kickbacks were, in any case, small change compared with the illegal smuggling of oil. Jordan and Turkey, two key U.S. allies in the area, depended heavily on Iraqi oil and would have suffered serious economic damage had they been deprived of it. But they weren't: throughout the 1990s, well before the Oil-for-Food Programme permitted limited Iraqi oil sales, a continuous caravan of tankers filled with oil crossed from Iraq to the two neighbors, as well as to Syria. Oil-for-Food officials had no jurisdiction over this trade, though of course it was an open secret. And in any case they understood that U.S. policy was to prevent collateral damage to its friends. "We were not going to address the Jordanian smuggling," says Kenneth Pollack, who oversaw Oil-for-Food for the White House from 1999 to 2001. "In the case of Turkey, we tried a couple of times, but the Turks made a horrific stink."

Oil-for-Food was, in short, just the kind of ugly compromise diplomats craft because they have some larger good in view. It had been created for legitimate, if arguable, political ends, and then sustained by the failure to arrive at a preferable solution. It is true that as the program grew to immense proportions once the cap on Iraqi oil sales was raised from $4 billion to $10.5 billion a year, and then eliminated altogether at the end of 1999, the scale of the theft grew commensurately, for the Iraqis were skimming 10 percent of a very large total. Nobody took responsibility for it, because control over the program was diffused among so many bodies and individuals that nobody felt accountable, but it is also true that it didn't seem all that important at the time. "A degree of corruption is quite normal," as a leading British diplomat blandly puts it. "I don't think the UN did much better or worse than most companies do when doing business in Iraq."

This, in any case, was the internal understanding of the Oil-for-Food Programme and its role in sustaining the frayed consensus on Iraq in the Security Council. And then suddenly it was . . . *Kofigate*. Had Benon Sevan looked the other way on the extortion and kickbacks because Saddam was paying him off? And what about Annan's son, Kojo? He had worked at Cotecna, a Swiss firm that in December 1998 had won the contract to inspect goods arriving overland to Iraq. In January 1999, *The Sunday Telegraph* of London had disclosed the relationship. Annan, who apparently hadn't known that his son's employer had become an important UN contractor, had ordered a cursory investigation, which had concluded that nothing untoward had occurred. Cotecna had said that Kojo had had nothing to do with that side of its business—he was working on deals in Nigeria, his mother's native country—and in any case had stopped working for the firm in late 1998.

Then, in October 2004, six months or so into the investigation, came a godsend for conservatives looking for a cudgel with which to whack the UN: Kojo turned out to have continued to receive monthly "non-compete" payments of $2,500 for months after he had allegedly severed ties with Cotecna. Had Kojo lied to his father? Or had his father swept the truth under the rug in a hurried inquiry? William Safire asked whether Sevan had known about Kojo's fees, or Kojo about Sevan's under-the-table payments from Saddam, leaving the clear implication that he could have blackmailed the head of the Oil-for-Food Programme—though there was no evidence that the two had ever met, much less confabulated. But no matter: Safire predicted that the scandal would not end "until Kofi Annan, even if personally innocent, resigns—having, through initial ineptitude and final obstructionism, brought dishonor on the Secretariat of the United Nations." Until that moment Safire had not been known to have harbored such concern for the Secretariat's honor.

And now the allegations took yet another turn, one all too familiar to American readers: it wasn't the crime; it was "the cover-up." Kofi Annan would not permit UN officials to testify before the congressional inquiries, though this reflected long-standing policy at the institution, which is, at least formally, equally answerable to all 191 of its members. Paul Volcker had refused to turn over documents from the Oil-for-Food "procurement" firms, as the inspection companies were called—though Volcker took the view that it would be an abuse of his position to turn over documents he had received in his capacity as the UN's appointed investigator. Was a desperate UN resorting to obstruction of justice?

In mid-November, a few days before Annan left for Nairobi for the Security Council session on Sudan, Norm Coleman, chairman of the Senate Permanent Subcommittee on Investigations, which had been conducting a particularly zealous inquest into the Oil-for-Food Programme, held a press conference to announce that Saddam Hussein's illicit gains from Oil-for-Food amounted to $21.3 billion, double previous estimates. Perhaps it really *was* the largest financial rip-off in history. But who, exactly, had Saddam ripped off? Senator Coleman neglected to mention that fully two thirds of the total came from the smuggling of oil, which three successive U.S. administrations had chosen to overlook.

Oil-for-Food, all by itself, would have been a catastrophe for the UN and for Annan. But Annan was already under siege when Kofigate blew up. In the fall, news of widespread sexual abuse in the UN's mission in Congo began to appear. Both civilian staff and troops from a number of national contingents had hired child prostitutes, preying on the desperation and hunger of the population they were supposed to protect; one headquarters official was said to have trafficked in child pornography over the Internet. Senior officials were said to have brushed the whole thing under the carpet. And this willingness to turn a blind eye to abusive behavior seemed to be systematic. A year earlier, half a dozen UN employees had accused Ruud Lubbers, the UN high commissioner for refugees, of making unwanted advances. Annan, a very proper and even prudish fellow, had been shocked at the allegations and had ordered the UN's Office of Internal Oversight Services to conduct an investigation.

The inquiry had largely vindicated Lubbers's accusers, but the investigators had done such a shoddy job that Annan's lawyers warned him that he lacked the grounds to fire the official. Annan believed in due process; he would not be a hanging judge, even at risk to himself and the UN. And having the decision overturned on appeal would hardly be good for the UN. In November 2004, Ralph Zacklin, the deputy head of the UN's Office of Legal Affairs, says he and others suggested that Annan send Lubbers a strong letter of reprimand that would compel him to step down on his own. "Instead," says Zacklin, "they talked on the phone, and the SG never asked him to step down. We were all quite dismayed." This was what Iqbal Riza had had in mind years earlier when he had warned Annan of the danger of being too soft on people. (Lubbers angrily denied the allegations.)

During this same period, a number of allegations were lodged against Dileep Nair, the chief, inconveniently enough, of the Office of Internal Oversight Services. Anonymous complainants accused Nair of promoting favorites, of mishandling Oil-for-Food funds, and of sexual harassment. The charges were potentially serious, but flimsier than those that had been made against Lubbers. Given Nair's position, Annan couldn't order an internal investigation, but he could have referred the Oil-for-Food claim to the Volcker panel, established an external inquiry, or issued a mild reprimand admonishing Nair for failing to guard against the appearance of impropriety. Instead, on November 16, Annan issued a statement concluding that "no further action was necessary." Several days later the UN Staff Council, which had been in a state of permanent inflammation since the suicide bombing of UN headquarters in Baghdad, passed a vote of no confidence in Annan—the first such resolution in the UN's history. This may have been a hyperbolic reaction and a calculated stunt, but the message it sent to the larger world was that even UN insiders were fed up with a culture of fecklessness, denial, and impunity.

It was yet another gut-wrenching revelation that had impelled Annan to cut short his trip to Africa: investigators had learned, and then told reporters, that Cotecna had continued sending Kojo monthly checks until early 2004—until, that is, the Oil-for-Food inquiries had begun. The press was waiting for Annan when he returned to the Secretariat Building on November 29. Annan's speechwriters had prepared an apologia for him, which he duly recited: "First, naturally I have warm family relations with my son, but he is in a different field. He is an independent businessman. He is a grown man and I don't get involved with his activities, and he doesn't get involved in mine."

Had he been surprised to learn that Kojo's payments had continued so long?

"I had been working on the understanding that it ceased in 1998 and I had not expected that the relationship continued . . .

"Did you get in touch with your son upon hearing this? What did you say to him? What did he say back?

"I did talk to him, but I don't really want to get into this. I did talk to my son about it.

"Are you disappointed? Are you angry with him for putting something away for four years?

"Naturally I was very disappointed and surprised, yes."

Even a man less given than Annan to tortured circumlocution might have had difficulty formulating a clear answer to such a question. What do you say about a son whose self-serving lies threaten to destroy your career and profoundly damage the institution you love? Annan had, in fact, been completely blindsided by the story. "Quite frankly," he said to me several weeks later, "I didn't see how he could even conceivably continue working on this if the company said it had stopped. I didn't even bother to talk to him about that company anymore." Cotecna had stated in writing that Kojo had stopped working for the company at the end of 1998; Lamin Sise, who handled discussions with the company, says that the senior executive who had made that assertion had been unaware of the non-compete payments. Whether or not that was so, Kojo himself had simply lied to his father. Annan was surprised, yes, and certainly disappointed, but he seemed, above all, to feel humiliated.

Kojo and his older sister, Ama, had been toddlers when Annan and his wife had separated. Never one to shirk a burden, Annan had been a dutiful father, taking a job in Geneva to be near the children, leaving work early to spend afternoons with them. But in 1984, when Kojo was eleven and Ama fifteen, he had moved back to New York while they remained in London with their mother, and he had stayed in New York while they had stayed abroad. And he had been too busy saving the world to spend large amounts of time with them. He did not seem very close to Kojo. Kieran Prendergast was struck to see Annan shake hands with his son rather than embrace him when Kojo came to see his father at Claridge's hotel in London. But Annan rarely embraced anyone; proximity made him uncomfortable.

Kojo had absorbed little of his father's grave and measured demeanor. "He's a big, overt personality," says James Goodale, who had known Kojo for many years and was very fond of him. "Kojo is a salesman kind of guy—he has that type of personality." The position at Cotecna, which his father had helped him get, was the only full-time job he ever held. He was sent to the Lagos "liaison office" in the hopes that he would bring in deals in a country where his mother's family was well known. In fact, he appears never to have made a dime for his employers. The corporate memo traffic turned over to investigators shows the young man to have been a good-natured layabout. A senior executive admonished him to give advance notice before granting himself a vacation; another official wrote, "It's important that KA respect the hours and rules of the liaison office," since "laxity on his/our part" would inevitably lead local staff to ask, "Why him and not us?"

There was only the flimsiest evidence connecting Kojo to Cotecna's successful bid for the inspection contract in Iraq or its subsequent work on it (though the evidence was to become more suggestive over time). But that didn't stop the conservative media from connecting imaginary dots. "Annan's son was in on the scam," an editorialist on Fox News flatly asserted. And Kojo was, in turn, a symptom and a symbol. "It is an enormously corrupt bureaucracy up there," said Brit Hume, Fox's anchor. "It's a world unto itself. Self-dealing, I think, is rampant."

The dam finally broke on December 1, when Senator Coleman wrote a *Wall Street Journal* Op-Ed piece whose first sentence read, "It's time for U.N. Secretary-General Kofi Annan to resign." Annan, he said, must "be held accountable for the U.N.'s utter failure to detect or stop Saddam's abuses." Since the stolen funds "may be funding the insurgency," Coleman wrote, without furnishing any evidence that this was so, one could conclude that "our troops would probably not have been placed in such danger if the U.N. had done its job in administering sanctions and Oil-For-Food." The senator was holding Annan responsible for the death of American troops. He also claimed that the Volcker committee lacked the investigative powers to get to the truth, and that in any case Annan could decide "what, if anything, is released to the public." The whitewash was all but foretold.

Coleman's allegations were so scurrilous that the following day Senator Carl Levin, the Democratic co-chairman of the investigations subcommittee, appeared on CNN in order to rebut them. "There's no evidence that our subcommittee has seen that shows any impropriety on the part of Kofi Annan," he said flatly. But evidence had nothing to do with it; now the knives, sharpened on the whetstone of Iraq, began to glint. And the Bush administration was not about to intercede on Annan's behalf. A State Department spokesman would only say that Annan's resignation "is not something, frankly, that is in front of us." Ambassador Danforth, widely considered one of Annan's admirers, merely called for the investigations to proceed. Bush refused to answer questions about the secretary-general's tenure, saying only that he favored "a full and fair and open" investigation of Oil-for-Food. Annan had long planned to go to Washington to present the high-level panel's report, and to meet with Bush and Condoleezza Rice in order to discuss a range of issues, above all the upcoming elections in Iraq, and perhaps to make amends for "illegal" and the Falluja letter, but nobody in Washington was prepared to meet with him. Perhaps he would scrub the whole trip.

The atmosphere on the upper floors of the UN was compounded of bewilderment, panic, and impotent fury. Had the UN's allies all gone to ground? "Norway was the chair of the 661 Committee," Michael Moller, one of Annan's chief aides, said to me. "Where are they? Where is Blair? He needs to call Bush and say, 'We've got to prop up Kofi.' But everyone's afraid to speak up against Bush." But that pattern was all too familiar. The more painful question was "Where is the UN?" Or, rather, "Where is Kofi?" Why had Annan gone silent in the face of calumny? He had started losing his voice in Africa, the way he had after war broke out in Iraq. I had used a notebook rather than a tape recorder during a conversation on the plane, since I knew the tape would barely pick up a sound. As he was racing back to Paris, plans were being formulated to have the secretary-general of the United Nations defend himself on . . . C-SPAN. Annan's media and communications aides seemed to have no idea how to wage this battle. One of the staff members on the plane, remembering Bill Clinton's first great test, said, "This is his Gennifer Flowers moment. He's got to come out fighting, and he's got to go on *60 Minutes* with Mike Wallace. But *can* he fight?"

Can he fight? This was the question that consumed everyone around Annan during the first two weeks of December. Of course he could fight for the UN; he would grind himself to a powder for the UN. But could he fight for *himself*? Did he believe in himself enough to fight? Did he believe in fighting enough to fight? His Christlike forbearance, which had felt like heroic self-restraint back when Jesse Helms was tearing the leather off him, now played out in public as enfeeblement. No one would rally to his side, and thus to the side of the UN, if he couldn't speak with passion and conviction. Mike Wallace, a member of the Kofi Chorus since the trip to Baghdad in 1998, was ready to do a profile, but Annan declined; he just wasn't up to the tough questions that Wallace would feel obliged to put. He canceled some minor event, then at the last minute said he would appear only for the beginning, then instead showed up at the end. He was calling heads of state to ask all too plaintively for a public show of support. He was tentative, irresolute, passive. Kieran Prendergast had been shocked that he had cut short his trip. "The word that comes to mind is 'panic,'" he said. "He's markedly lost the grip he had." His voice had gone, and his skin had gone matte, the way it did at the very worst moments.

Everyone around Annan was frightened by the sense of drift; some were angry as well. The secretary-general seemed not to recognize that the reservoir of goodwill he had always been able to count on in the past had dried up, at least in the United States. On November 29, a Monday, Shashi Tharoor, among the most loyal of the loyalists, sent Annan a memo, which he also circulated to senior aides, laying out just how dire the situation was. Tharoor said that he had been speaking to "well-placed figures in the American media"—something he had been doing for years—and they had made it plain to him that the UN should not expect sympathetic treatment on Oil-for-Food, that the whole thing looked terrible, that writing letters to the editor objecting to errors was a waste of time, that "the mood in Washington is as bad as it has ever been during your tenure." And the first Volcker report, scheduled for the following January, "will certainly prompt another round of attacks on the UN."

That Thursday evening Annan was asked to come to a nighttime meeting with his senior aides at the home of deputy secretary-general Louise Fréchette. A wag on the thirty-eighth floor referred to it as "the pajama party." Tharoor and others spoke to Annan more harshly than they ever had before. He had to lead; he had to pull out of his apathy. He needed to make the staff changes that had long been urged on him. Collectively, they needed to address the deep demoralization of the staff; to devise a media strategy; to find a way of talking about Iraq that would mollify the Americans; to raise the profile of the issue of reform. And Annan sat quietly, writing notes on a yellow pad. At the end of the conversation, he finally spoke up. "Thank you all for what you had to say," he said softly. "We're in this for the long haul—but I'm not sure how long the haul is going to be." There was a moment of collective shock. How could they stand up for him if he was preparing to throw in the towel? Edward Mortimer filled the silence by saying, "The purpose of this whole thing is exactly the contrary."

The following Monday, I went to see Michael Moller, the melancholy Dane of the thirty-eighth floor. Moller had known Annan for a quarter of a century and viewed him as a mentor, but he was a man of deep and rather unforgiving convictions, and now he was descending into a kind of prophetic disgust. When I asked him about Annan's behavior at the pajama party, he said, "He was not showing any willingness to respond to anything. He was his usual sphinxlike self." And in the ensuing four days, Annan had agreed to only one of a long list of suggestions—that he personally present the first draft of the high-level panel report to the General Assembly in order to receive a carefully arranged standing ovation. "He's not a fighter," Moller said bitterly. "He's *never* fought." And neither had the institution itself; that wasn't its nature. Annan, and the people around him, had sailed into the doldrums; now they rocked slowly back and forth, waiting for a freshening breeze from they knew not what quarter.

But it wasn't just weakness and despair that kept Annan from getting up on his hind legs. In a staff meeting, Bob Orr, the implacably levelheaded director of strategic planning and the liaison to the Bush administration, said, "Everyone wants to hit back. The feeling is understandable, but is it effective? The calls for resignation haven't spread. If we had hit back, we'd have eighty-some senators calling for the end of the UN." You couldn't hit back at Washington, no matter how satisfying it would be. But neither could you put the blame for Oil-for-Food on the members, where it belonged; a chief executive can't afford to finger his own board of directors.

An outsider to the UN and an American, Orr was not about to fall prey to the conspiracy theories gripping many of his colleagues, according to which Norm Coleman, William Safire, Karl Rove, and representatives of the Heritage Foundation met over Scotch and cigars to plot the downfall of the UN—though he did believe that conservatives had seized on Oil-for-Food in order to discredit an institution they loathed. For Orr, the whole sorry mess recapitulated the UN's fundamental and recurring weakness. "There's a confusion between the UN as a stage and the UN as an actor," he said in late November. "As an actor, there's so little we can do, and often the people accusing us are the same ones who prevent us from being able to act." He had, he said, once asked a UN veteran, "How deep can the secretary-general fire people?" And the answer had been, "They have to have 'SG' in their title"—meaning, no lower than assistant secretary-general. The Secretariat and the secretary-general had so little real power, and yet when anything went wrong, they suddenly became "the UN." "The crisis is an existential one," Orr said. "It has relatively little to do with the institution, and everything to do with its limitations as an institution."

The only consolation for Annan was work. He could leave behind the vitriol and the painful self-reflections by focusing his attention on his program of reform, which could, he believed, or fervently hoped, finally lift the UN out of the agonizing predicament of being asked to do so much with so little authority and so fitful a commitment from its members. The high-level panel was to deliver its report in the first days of December, and for weeks Annan and his staff had been preparing to herald its delivery with suitably epochal fanfare. Planning began in a meeting on October 22. Steve Stedman relayed a suggestion from the South African ambassador that Annan travel to "manufactured regional meetings"—African Union "special summits" and the like—to present the report. Edward Mortimer had been talking to *The Economist* and *Foreign Affairs* about running pieces by Annan, or under his name. Richard Haass, the former State Department official and now president of the Council on Foreign Relations, had promised to do a major event with Annan and Brent Scowcroft in Washington. Bob Orr warned that "opinions are going to form very quickly in Washington as to whether this a good thing, a bad thing, or an indifferent thing." At the moment, he said, key members of the Bush administration "have no clue what's in this."

Now Iqbal Riza spoke up from his perch at the end of the conference table. The Washington event sounded like a fine idea, he conceded. "But how will it be perceived in the G77 and even in Europe if the first event is in Washington?" Riza worried that Annan, forever placating Washington, was losing his bona fides with the Third World. It was agreed that an effort would be made to schedule events on different continents simultaneously.

There was a deeper problem that marketing alone could not solve: the G77 countries, for the most part, wanted the opposite of what the West wanted—more on development, and less, or perhaps nothing at all, on human rights and collective security. Most took the view that the Secretariat and the Security Council had accumulated too much power at the expense of the General Assembly; the goal of reform must be to strengthen the more "representative" institutions. How were the developing nations to be mollified? Mark Malloch Brown pointed out that the high-level panel report would offer little on development beyond hortatory language; the real pledges would come as a result of the "Millennium Plus Five" report being prepared under the leadership of the economist Jeffrey Sachs.

Not altogether, said Shashi Tharoor: "The win for the G77 is Security Council reform." The developing world would accept reform on human rights and collective security in exchange for a seat at the table. The rhetoric of the G77 did, in fact, suggest that a more representative Security Council would constitute a resounding collective victory. But would it really? Would Malaysia or Colombia or Mozambique so rejoice in the enhanced power of India or Brazil or South Africa that they would accept the collective security agenda? Or would both Washington and the G77 find reasons to sink the whole thing?

The report, titled "A More Secure World: Our Shared Responsibility," was issued on December 2, the day after Senator Coleman had publicly called on Annan to resign, thus ensuring that it would be swallowed up in the maelstrom swirling around the UN. The report rested on the premise that in a world transformed by technological and political forces, collective thinking and collective action had become matters of dire necessity, not merely noble aspirations. "Today, more than ever," the report declared, "threats are interrelated and a threat to one is a threat to all." An epidemic in a country with a shattered public health system could spread almost instantly, through air travel, to the wealthiest nations; failed states could be incubators of terrorism; the breakdown of the nonproliferation system in one state menaced all others. Here was the dire evidence for Kofi Annan's lofty view that "the collective interest is the national interest."

The report was an omnium-gatherum of reform, with 101 specific recommendations listed in a twenty-page annex. The panelists proposed, among other things, major new investments in the development of the poorest countries; strengthening the UN's capacity in peacekeeping and nation-building; the establishment of guidelines for the use of force, including an obligation of humanitarian intervention; the creation of a new body to control worldwide stocks of nuclear fuel; the replacement of the enfeebled Human Rights Commission with a more forceful and focused Human Rights Council; and management reforms that would allow the secretary-general "to do his job properly."

That morning Steve Stedman spoke at the weekly gathering of the senior management group, stressing the large themes that leading UN officials would need to hit as they went out into the world to sell this astonishingly ambitious package. Annan rushed into the conference room only at the end of the session, apologizing for his lateness. His mind, it seemed, was elsewhere. "I'm sure," he said in his husky whisper, "you're all feeling concerned about the criticism of the UN, and the criticism of myself, that you've been hearing." They would have to hang on until the Volcker committee issued its first report next month. "In the meantime, we have to carry on with our work. It's a shame that the press has become so focused on this at a time when we are coming out with the report. It's important that we not be consumed by the negative impact of the Oil-for-Food issue. I know that that is something that is bothering all of us." Annan ended this demoralized would-be pep talk to total silence. At last he said, "Are there any comments from anyone?"

Malloch Brown waited a beat. Then, with a nervous laugh, he said, "I'm glad I'm not in your shoes."

The onslaught from the American Congress and the American right-wing media inevitably produced a furious reaction elsewhere in the world—not only in defense of the widely admired Annan but in outrage at Washington, which seemed prepared to defenestrate a highly popular secretary-general after having terminated the career of his predecessor. On December 4, the very centrist *Financial Times* ran an editorial stating, "The witch-hunt against Kofi Annan and the United Nations over the Iraq oil-for-food scandal is, quite simply, a scandal all its own. The leaders of this lynch mob in the US Congress and the rightwing commentariat are not gunning for Mr. Annan so much as aiming to destroy the UN as an institution." World leaders finally began to respond to Annan's entreaties to speak up. On December 7, Tony Blair said, "I believe Kofi Annan is doing a fine job as United Nations secretary general, often in very difficult circumstances. I very much hope that he is allowed to get on with his job without criticism that, I think, if people analyze it for a moment, they will see that it is unfair."

On the eighth, Annan played his role in the coup de théâtre to which he had agreed several weeks earlier. Speaking in his usual gentle monotone, he delivered the initial report of the high-level panel to the General Assembly. The television cameras were trained on the front of the hall, so viewers were spared the great sea of unoccupied blue seats in the rear, signifying an event of no great moment. When Annan finished, he was met with gentle applause—there must have been panic in the wings—and then the Swedish ambassador, by prearrangement, rose up from his seat, and then others did, and then finally the American representative, and Annan received what was no doubt a soul-restoring forty-five-second standing ovation.

Annan held a staff meeting the following day. The terrible tension that had gripped the office for the previous two weeks had begun to subside. Bob Orr, who had been trying to contain the hemorrhaging in Washington, said, "The tone began to shift sometime late yesterday after I think the word went out from the White House that they're going to shift the tone." Important Republicans like John McCain had refused to join the campaign for the secretary-general's head; the Democrats had held fast. And Annan had made it clear that he would not accommodate his critics by resigning. Both the State Department and the National Security Council had said that they wanted to talk to Annan about Iraq during his planned visit to Washington on December 16. Annan's spokesman, Fred Eckhard, reported that Ambassador Danforth, who had recently announced that he would be leaving his post, "will go to the stakeout"—the hallway area where the press waited—"and will express his confidence in you and in your integrity." Annan himself finally spoke: "We seem to be doing better, but let no one think that the right wing will go away." And then he turned the discussion to Iraq, and after that to the reform process.

Whatever lingering fears Annan had that the administration, if not prepared to push him off the cliff, was still hoping that he would fall of his own accord were put to rest during his meeting with Rice, the secretary of state–designate, on the sixteenth. I spoke to Bob Orr the next day, and he was euphoric, if in a levelheaded sort of way. "She's always polite, seldom warm," he said of Rice. "She was very warm yesterday. She didn't do any of this cheap kind of distancing—'We're going to let you hang a little bit.' She said, 'We appreciate everything you're doing in Iraq. Negroponte'"—John Negroponte, American ambassador to Iraq—" 'has called your efforts on the election heroic. And we really appreciate everything on Haiti; there are six thousand Brazilian troops, and if there weren't, there would be six thousand Marines.' It was thank you, thank you, thank you, not a push in sight." And then, in what no one was supposed to mistake for a coincidence, the president had called from the economic summit in Évian, France. Rice reported that he said, "Please give my greetings to the secretary-general." It was only a scrap, but Annan wasn't refusing scraps at the moment.

Rice herself disputes the idea that the administration was letting Annan dangle over the abyss. "I don't remember a particular hesistancy about coming out and saying that we support him," she says. The Falluja letter, she insists, was already a nonissue. And while she concedes that the administration was feeling frustrated about the size and limitations of the UN mission in Iraq, Rice says that she and others ascribed it to the post-traumatic reaction to the August 19 bombing rather than to resistance on the part of the secretary-general. "I don't think relations with Kofi ever got to a place I would even call difficult," she says. "We always had a very warm relationship, a very easy relationship." At times, she says, "there's a kind of disconnect about what's really being thought inside the administration." Or perhaps there was more than one thought being thought inside the administration.

The secretary-general was still very shaky. He entered meetings unprepared, an almost shocking failure for one so punctilious as he. He had not scheduled his annual end-of-year press conference. Perhaps he was too fragile to survive a pummeling from a suddenly aroused press contingent, but omitting the press conference would send an unmistakable sign of weakness. Annan agreed to schedule the event, but he seemed terribly apprehensive at a "murder board" held to prepare him for the ordeal. When I spoke to Kieran Prendergast on the sixteenth, he said, "I still have the feeling that if the Volcker report is tough, he might go." The threat had receded, but the sense of drift remained. "I have no appetite for two years of wounded bird," said the always declaratory Prendergast. "And he's going to be a lame duck. I guess he'll be a wounded lame duck."

Annan endured his trial by reporter on the twenty-first. He began by enumerating the UN's achievements in Afghanistan, Iraq, Congo, and Sudan. He spoke of the reform document and the next year's summit. And then he took questions. "I am," he conceded, "relieved that this annus horribilis is coming to an end." He would not take the bait on whether he was the victim of "an organized campaign." And "of the question of my resignation, let me say that I have quite a lot of work to do." It was a notably unemphatic response. A phalanx of cameras flashed every time he lifted his hands from the podium to make a gesture, and amid the noise and light Annan gently turned aside all provocation, picking his way with his usual infinite care through one minefield after another.

I spoke with Annan in his office that afternoon. We sat on the black leather couch beneath the serene pastoral of forest and river bend. He told me that Tony Blair had called with a consoling message. His friend David Rockefeller had offered the kind of sympathy that only one Olympian can offer another: "There are people in this world who, when they think someone is on a pedestal, make it their business to cut him down." The British prime minister and the world's most famous tycoon were his confessors in times of trial. All was wood-paneled, upholstered understatement. When I asked Annan how he was bearing up under the onslaught, he said, "It breaks one's stride." When I said that that seemed rather mild, he added, "It can be pretty upsetting and depressing."

Annan would not say, and perhaps did not acknowledge to himself, how deeply abandoned he felt. "When this whole thing started," he said, "the governments who were so intimately involved with the running of Oil-for-Food—not a word out of them." Chirac had called. "He was appalled by what was going on and offered support, but he didn't say, 'We are responsible.'" And it wasn't just the permanent five. "When you look at the number of countries that went through the council from the time Oil-for-Food was set up, you have about sixty-six, seventy countries"—someone had obviously done some counting—"who for two years or more were in there approving these contracts. And then they say it was a secret operation."

Annan felt, at bottom, that he had done nothing wrong, and yet he saw his world crumbling. "You do get mad sometimes," he conceded—not "I get mad"—"and what has been particularly difficult about this one is not just that they're coming at me, attacking the UN through me, but the link with my son." Kojo may have caused him infinite pain and humiliation—though he wouldn't say so—but he felt sure that the allegations against his son were preposterous. Another man would have been tearing his hair out—or somebody else's—but not this man. His anger disappeared inside him, and took away his voice and the luster of his skin. Perhaps it wasn't even anger that he felt, but demoralization. Why *couldn't* he show any fight? I asked him for the last time. "Probably," he said, "I don't show it in an explosive sort of way." And then he changed the subject.

CHAPTER SIXTEEN

Kofi Briefly Rescued by Disaster

W HETHER, WHEN, AND WHERE KOFI ANNAN WOULD BE
taking a vacation was a matter of great mystery and confusion during the nerve-racking weeks of December 2004. Annan had unusual resources in this regard, for he moved in a circle of immensely wealthy
men who were eager to have him as their guest, and as he seemed to
enjoy the combination of luxury and seclusion available in the homes
and compounds of the great, he often took up such offers. And so, immediately after his year-end press conference, he and Nane left for the
Wyoming ranch of James Wolfensohn, president of the World Bank.
There he would take the long walks that provided him both relaxation
and exercise. And he needed both, for he had exhausted his stores of
physical and mental energy. But his annus horribilis was not quite over:
On December 26, four days after he arrived, an earthquake off the
coast of Indonesia sent a tidal wave thousands of miles to the north
and the west. In a few minutes, the tsunami killed more than 200,000
people and obliterated coastal areas in Indonesia, Sri Lanka, Thailand,
and as far away as the eastern coast of Africa.

Disaster relief is, of course, one of the UN's core functions. The actual work on the ground—the delivery of food, the pitching of tents,
the purification of drinking water—is increasingly the province of organizations like the Red Cross or Oxfam or Doctors Without Borders and innumerable smaller NGOs. But UN agencies, including

the World Food Programme, the World Health Organization, and UNICEF, play a critical role in delivering matériel, disseminating intelligence, informing the public, and coordinating the activities of the private actors. Overseeing what is inevitably a chaotic and disjointed rush to bring aid is the Office for the Coordination of Humanitarian Affairs, a body inside the Secretariat that emerged from the 1997 reform program when Annan abandoned the idea of a "lead agency." And since the tsunami, spread across countries and continents, posed unprecedented organizational and logistical problems, it was plain that the UN would have to play a central role in the response.

But in the immediate aftermath of the tsunami, Annan was nowhere to be seen. He issued a statement but made no public appearances. To all intents and purposes, he was continuing his vacation. He tried to reach the heads of the affected countries by phone but made contact only with the president of the Maldives. Colin Powell called to ask what he was doing; so did Tony Blair. The answer was that he seemed still to be stricken with irresolution. The UN's humanitarian machinery was clanking into motion, but since Annan was the visible symbol of the institution, the UN itself appeared to be disengaged. Horrible though it sounded, the tsunami offered the perfect cure for an institution that seemed, at least to the public, to have been exiled to the sidelines of history. Finally Annan roused himself, flying back to New York on December 29, two days earlier than planned. He would not, however, go to the affected area, he said; he could be more effective organizing the response from New York.

By the time Annan convened a staff meeting the morning of the thirtieth, the tsunami had already become yet another source of contention between the UN and the United States. After the Bush administration had authorized a paltry $15 million as its initial contribution to relief, Jan Egeland, the humanitarian coordinator, had the temerity to characterize the offer as "stingy." Diplomats and aid officials were thrilled to see a high-ranking UN figure stick his head so fearlessly in the lion's mouth; what's more, even as it growled, Washington made haste to up the ante. It was a satisfying, if minor, confrontation for a psychically battered institution. That morning, while several of us were in the waiting room outside Annan's office, Iqbal Riza told Egeland, " 'Stingy' has gotten their attention more than 'illegal.' "

"I wasn't talking about the tsunami response," Egeland protested. "I was just commenting on ODA [official development assistance.]."

"You don't have to explain it to *us*," Riza said with a smile.

Nevertheless, Egeland knew that he had to do some explaining to the boss. Once the meeting began, he told Annan that he had been assured by Marc Grossman, the assistant secretary of state working with the UN on the response, that Washington was "way beyond" any pique over Egeland's barb. "Anyway," he added, "the military and civilian assets they're bringing are really large." The United States already had cargo planes and warships converging on the disaster area. Egeland also had far more pressing things to worry about. "We cannot start working in Banda Aceh, because there's *nothing* there," he said. Banda was the province at the western tip of the island of Sumatra that had been the epicenter of the tsunami. "The team that went in said, 'Where's my food? Where's my shelter?' So now we're sending in a fully equipped camp." Meanwhile, humanitarian organizations—the NGOs—were pouring into Indonesia and snarling the response. Egeland asked Annan to call the big aid organizations and tell them to stanch the flow of people until the UN could begin coordinating them.

Here, at last, Annan and his staff seemed to have a strictly logistical problem to deal with, even if one of towering dimensions. But, no; politics proved irrepressible. A few days earlier the Bush administration had announced the formation of a "core group" consisting of itself, Australia, India, and Japan. The administration explained that each of these countries had major assets in the area and thus could profitably work together. But the organization felt more like an exclusive club than a coalition. Around the UN, the core group was taken to be the Bush administration's bid to export the idea of the "coalition of the willing" into the terrain of humanitarianism. In the privacy of his staff meeting, Annan had said that he wanted to understand why the core group existed and whether others could join. For once, China wanted to participate in a global relief effort; could they join? What about Singapore, with major maritime and civil defense assets? But when Carol Bellamy, the head of UNICEF, asked whether the core group would "marginalize the multilateral system," Annan blandly said, "The group will work in support of the UN and international efforts. I think we should welcome it." What else could they do?

The interagency meeting was followed almost immediately by a videoconference with Secretary of State Powell and his staff. Powell was already seated on the stroke of 11:00. Annan, meanwhile, had gone off to make a phone call, leaving Mark Malloch Brown to desperately attempt idle chitchat. Malloch Brown swiftly lost altitude, and an increasingly uncomfortable silence settled over both rooms. Annan's spokesman, Fred Eckhard, dashed in to whisper, "He's not coming yet," to which Malloch Brown said murderously, "He's *got* to come." Eckhard dashed out. Powell wore a look of barely suppressed impatience. Finally Annan rushed in, pulled back his chair with a haste wholly out of character for him, and threw himself down. Only when he looked up did he see that Powell and his staff were seated and silent—at which point an expression of utter horror crossed his face.

Powell instantly put the secretary-general out of his misery by getting down to business, explaining that the United States understood very well that far more money would be required to finance the relief effort. Annan thanked him rather formally. They made a very unlikely pair, for Powell spoke in bristlingly short and crisp bursts, while Annan, perhaps rendered uncomfortable by the other man's air of martial authority, delivered windy sermonettes. I had heard that Annan was much more comfortable with Bush than with Powell, and I could see why. Marc Grossman now spoke up to reassure the UN officials that the core group would not compete with the UN or "siphon off resources" from the multilateral effort, but rather "reinforce" that effort. But when Annan asked about expanding the membership, Grossman cited Powell to the effect that the premise of the core group would be "no bureaucracy, no committees, no meetings." Grossman's point was that countries would be added only in order to help the effort, not to smooth ruffled feathers. It also couldn't help feeling like a rebuke to the UN.

Egeland now piped up for the first time. "The four countries in the core group have been among the most generous—"

"You all heard that," Annan interrupted, reaching for a joke. "He said, 'You have been generous'—and you can quote us on that."

Egeland had prepared a mea culpa, and he was not to be deterred. "I'm sorry that I was misunderstood when I commented on the overall trend in the past year."

Powell was apparently not in a mood to be indulgent. "The more serious it gets, the more hysterical the press gets," he said sharply. "They're looking for things to criticize us on." Then he told Annan that the following evening he would be in New York to drop the New Year's Eve ball in Times Square.

"I hope that provides a much better year for 2005," Annan said forlornly. "This has been an awful one." This transparent bid for sympathy shattered against Powell's granite surface. "That's all we have here, Kofi," said the secretary of state, who then pushed back his chair and left.

Secretaries-general had not traditionally made themselves the face of emergency relief as they had with diplomacy or peacekeeping. Annan had kept a low profile, for example, in the aftermath of the earthquake that had leveled the ancient Iranian city of Bam. Perhaps he simply wasn't comfortable in physically chaotic environments; he would say, "I'm such a burden to the people on the ground." But Jan Egeland worked hard to persuade him to go to the tsunami area, and thus to assert the centrality of the UN's role in coordinating the relief effort. After a few days back in New York, Annan capitulated. A conference of regional governments and major donors to be hosted by the government of Indonesia on January 6, 2005, provided the perfect vehicle.

Speaking at the conference, Annan said that while billions would ultimately be needed for long-term reconstruction, the UN and aid organizations would be spending $977 million over the next six months for water, food, shelter, sanitation, and the quick restoration of shattered livelihoods—to repair fishing boats and nets, for example. Donors had already pledged $4 billion, but Annan said that those lofty vows had to be made good with cash right away. And in a later press conference, he spoke pointedly of the "gaps" that all too often appear as the immediate emergency ebbs. "We trust that the world community . . . will stay with us for the longer term," he said. "And I look to you, the media, to hold them to that commitment." After years of watching donors abandon disaster areas as soon as a new one appeared on the horizon, he had learned that the prospect of public embarrassment was one of the very few weapons he had at his command.

No less important, Colin Powell announced at the conference that the core group would no longer be needed and would "fold itself into the broader coordination efforts of the United Nations." Annan told me later that the Bush administration had been surprised by the outcry against the impromptu body; even the Japanese, ever wary of giving offense, had been extremely uncomfortable with their own membership in the club. The Jakarta conference became a forum to reassert the primacy of the UN in the face of the perennial threat of American unilateralism. In the press, expressions of relief combined with fear that the magnitude of the catastrophe would overwhelm the UN and expose the limits of its painfully rule-bound bureaucracy. Already there were reports that NGOs in Banda Aceh were bypassing UN officials in order to keep from being bogged down. The UN's humanitarian coordinator in Indonesia complained that "utter confusion" reined among humanitarian actors.

The following day Annan and his entourage flew to Banda, and then boarded helicopters to survey the wreckage. More than 100,000 people had died in the region's coastal towns and villages. The view from several hundred feet up was astonishing. In the sharply folded green hills that tapered off a few hundred yards from shore, the rice paddies and the few houses were unscathed, but the coast itself was so comprehensively flattened that sometimes you couldn't be sure whether it had been inhabited at all. One square pillared structure—a temple, perhaps—sat alone in the midst of a flooded plain; a road rounded a curve, and then vanished into a lagoon, emerging a mile later on higher ground; palm trees lay fanned out and flattened like matches shaken from a box.

As the helicopter dropped a bit lower, we could see white rectangles set into the earth with tiny flakes sprinkled on top—the foundations of homes, along with the few fragments of building material that had not been swept by the wall of water into the hills beyond. The glorious green Andaman Sea, discolored by household or factory chemicals, turned the sickly color of dried blood along the shore. After about half an hour we reached the city of Meulaboh, where about forty thousand people had died. Along the water, the city had been reduced to piles of rubble; half a mile or so inland, cars moved along an undamaged four-lane road. You couldn't help thinking, "It's as if a bomb hit it."

But what kind of bomb could obliterate everything in its path, and then leave barely a mark a few feet up the hill?

Nane had accompanied her husband, and they made for exquisitely gracious and compliant guests on their various guided tours through the wreckage. When they were brought over to little children, as they inevitably were, they would get down on ground level like the good grandparents they were and smile sweetly. Annan was most comfortable meeting officials and asking about desalination and the like. Even in the apocalyptic wreckage of Meulaboh, he had been driven down the main street between towering piles of rubble to a refugee center, where he spoke briefly and consolingly to a woman who had lost her entire family, then had gotten back in his car and returned the way he had come. It was as if his empathy were so universal as to be remote from all particulars; or perhaps he was simply more comfortable with people who spoke the technocratic language that is the lingua franca of international organizations.

That evening Annan and his party flew to Colombo, the capital of Sri Lanka, where thirty thousand people had perished in the tsunami—a far higher fraction of the national population than had died in Indonesia. Sri Lanka had been tormented for years by a civil war pitting ethnic Tamils in the north, almost all of them Hindus, against the predominant national group, the Sinhalese, largely Buddhist. The tsunami had struck Sri Lanka's eastern coast, whose northern regions were controlled by the Tamil Tigers, a militia that enjoyed the dubious distinction of having pioneered the suicide bombing. (A Tiger had murdered the former Indian prime minister Rajiv Gandhi more than a decade earlier.) Annan had hoped to visit both government- and militia-controlled areas, but President Chandrika Bandaranaike Kumaratunga had refused, fearing that such a visit would afford the Tigers a propaganda victory.

After another round of visits to devastated areas, Annan was taken the next evening to the presidential palace, a splendid seventeenth-century Dutch residence with high, airy galleries beneath an elegantly inlaid wooden ceiling. President Kumaratunga greeted Annan in a sitting room dominated by a large oil painting depicting harmonious relations between Dutch colonists and Sri Lankan natives. Annan went straight to the point, saying that in a humanitarian crisis "we need to be able to go everywhere where people are in need . . . I talked to the minister of foreign affairs in Jakarta, but he said no." Now, he said, the press was having a field day with the controversy. All of this, of course, Annan delivered in his characteristically gentle and deferential tone.

President Kumaratunga, an impatient, fast-talking woman, looked distinctly cross. She had bent over backward to help the north, she said. "Government has done maximum for them." The real problem was that political representatives from Tiger-controlled areas had refused to cooperate in the relief effort. "We concluded that it was not advisable for the world's topmost diplomat to go." James Wolfensohn could go, but Annan could not. The Tigers, she said, would exploit such a visit to advance their political goals. "The talks would have been embarrassing for the government." President Kumaratunga now embarked on an extensive monologue on the government's relief efforts, while Annan waited patiently for an opening. When she finally ground to a halt, Annan said that he hoped the relief task force she had assembled would be "inclusive," for the effort could serve as a model for a broader program of national reconciliation.

"The opposition is working with us," President Kumaratunga snapped. "We have sixty-eight parties, and we can't be talking to all of them."

The secretary-general and his aides then moved to another gallery, whose walls were lined with long, swan-necked cast-iron fans, like something out of *Beauty and the Beast*. This was a meeting with key legislators. I wasn't technically supposed to be present, but I stayed with the group moving from the talk with the president. Annan went down the long table introducing each of his aides; when he unexpectedly got to me, he quickly improvised. "This is James Traub, who has come with us from New York." Nice piece of diplomacy, I thought.

After President Kumaratunga opened the meeting by saying, "We have had no political difficulty in resolving this problem," the representative of the Tamil National Alliance launched into a long and bitter plaint about the systematic neglect and mistreatment of Tamils and excoriated the president for refusing to let the secretary-general visit the area. Other lawmakers spoke. Then the representative of the Sinhalese nationalist party embarked on an even more ferocious and long-winded attack on the Tigers. The president finally dispatched an aide to go down the table and instruct the man to finish his harangue and let the secretary-general leave. Defeated, the Sinhalese representative flourished the printed text of his speech at me and insisted I make sure it was delivered to the secretary-general. It struck me as unlikely, on reflection, that Sri Lanka's political leadership would seize the opportunity of reconstruction to end the politics of ethnic rivalry.

Annan hoped otherwise. He had a little sermon, which he preached to me several times during the trip, about the kinds of reckonings forced upon people in the aftermath of catastrophes. A disaster revealed the common humanity of its victims; the conflicting ambitions and identities that had once seemed worth fighting and dying over were now exposed as petty and overblown. Catastrophe, in short, could be the gateway to reconciliation. In a press conference in Colombo, Annan had said, "The ordinary people of Colombo have come together on an extraordinary scale to meet the needs created by the emergency. I fervently hope that their political leaders will do the same."

This all seemed terribly naive, and in fact Colombo was awash in rumors of Tigers seizing control of relief sites. Neither side was willing to give ground. In the spring, after the rebels assassinated Sri Lanka's foreign minister, a presidential election brought to power a hard-liner who insisted on extending the country's state of emergency. The tsunami had, if anything, made matters worse. On the other hand, Annan's faith was vindicated in Aceh, Indonesia, where an independence movement had been flaring on and off since the 1970s. The Acehnese fighters had been decimated by a long military campaign, while the national government was looking for a peaceful resolution of the dispute. The tsunami gave both sides the pretext to negotiate that they had been looking for; they signed a peace agreement the following August. A fair conclusion was that the revelation of common humanity through disaster could alter the trajectory of conflict only if the two sides were already looking for a way out.

CHAPTER SEVENTEEN

Nice Guys Get Crushed

I N THE SUMMER OF 2001, WHEN IT HAD BECOME CLEAR that Kofi Annan would serve a second term as secretary-general, Iqbal Riza asked Annan to let him retire. Riza believed that no one should serve beyond the age of seventy, and he would be turning seventy in 2004, in the middle of the second term. In that case, Annan said, why not serve until the beginning of 2004? Riza agreed, but when the date approached, Annan implored him to remain one more year. Annan might have found it almost unbearable to dispense with the reassurance of Riza's presence. But by the fall of 2004, the tables had turned, for Riza felt that if he stepped down amid the furor over Oil-for-Food, it would create the impression that he was in some way responsible for the scandal. Annan agreed that Riza would remain until after the Volcker committee had published its first report, in late January.

But events were already flying out of control. The calls for Annan's resignation, the growing disaffection of the Bush administration, the casual scorn with which the institution was coming to be treated in Washington and in the mainstream press, and the sense of drift and despair inside the UN—all had created a deep sense of crisis not only among Annan's colleagues but among the circle of outsiders and ex-insiders to whom he often turned for advice. The fact that Annan himself seemed to have little clue about the gravity of his situation only made the situation more grave. While he was in Africa in late November, this group, which included the former UN ambassador Richard Holbrooke; John Ruggie, the former under-secretary-general for strategic planning; and Timothy Wirth, a former U.S. senator who ran the United Nations Foundation, planned a secret meeting in which they would confront Annan with the truth.

Holbrooke had been growing increasingly incensed as he had watched the UN flounder over the previous weeks and months. The Falluja letter that Annan had sent days before the presidential election struck him as an act of incredible stupidity—"a declaration of war on an administration which was leading in the polls." He blamed the affair on Kieran Prendergast and, more broadly, on the UN moralists around Annan who viewed the United States as an unprincipled bully. "They think that if they issue something on a letter which says 'Nations Unies,' that somehow that has standing in the world," Holbrooke fulminated in the first days of December. "The UN is not *ever* going to succeed without American support."

The UN, Holbrooke argued, had succeeded in the past because American presidents had been willing to make "a trade-off between total autonomy and giving up a little bit of our freedom of maneuver for collective security." For all its impossible demands, the United States had kept the UN focused on the core issue of sustaining the global order. "Kofi doesn't have a guiding purpose anymore," Holbrooke said. "I don't want to be self-serving here"—a caveat he was wont to insert before saying something that to the naked eye appeared grossly self-serving—"but I did that." They had had a partnership back in 2000. "He'd use me in a good-cop, bad-cop way. When my role as the bad cop, the heavy-breathing, tough-love guy, was eliminated and no one took its place, Kofi fell into the clutches of the bureaucrats." There was a corollary to this theory. "When the U.S. withdraws from the terrain"—as it had done ever since George W. Bush had become president—"the bureaucrats go to work turning the UN into an anti-American organization, a bureaucratic organization." The permanent UN, in Holbrooke's view, was driving the institution over the cliff. He had been the prime mover of the secret meeting, which was held at his large and elegant Upper West Side apartment overlooking Central Park.

The meeting was convened on Sunday, December 5, 2004—three

days after the "pajama party" at Louise Fréchette's house. Bob Orr was the only UN official present besides Annan; the others at the UN knew nothing about the meeting. According to accounts from several of the participants, Holbrooke called his confederates together at 2:30; Annan, in blazer and charcoal gray turtleneck, arrived at 3:00. The tone of the conversation was deferential, at times painfully so. "We're all here as friends," each said in turn. "We don't want you to resign." But for three and a half hours, a man who lived inside a crystalline sphere of euphemism and high-minded sentiment was forced to face ugly facts. Holbrooke said, "You're going to have to live with the Bush administration for the next four years, and they think you ultimately supported Kerry. You're in an incredibly dangerous situation, and the future of the UN is at stake." Leslie Gelb, the former head of the Council on Foreign Relations, had been dispatched to Washington to take the temperature of the Bush administration. When he had asked, "Are you going to push the secretary-general over the cliff?" the dismaying answer he got back was "You won't see our fingerprints on it." (Gelb's conversations occurred a week or two before the abrupt change in tone signaled by John Danforth's public support for Annan.)

And so it went, around the room. Tim Wirth spoke of the way Oil-for-Food was sapping the UN's reputation for integrity. "If you don't make major changes," he said, "the institution is going down." Nader Mousavizadeh, the former speechwriter, said that the budding sexual abuse scandal in the peacekeeping operation in Congo, and above all the way the problem had been swept under the rug, offered the perfect proof for UN critics that the institution was "out of control" and unaccountable. The staff was demoralized. "They think there's a double standard at work. They feel like they're shut out of decision making." John Ruggie said that people in the building wanted to stand up and fight back—but for what? For whom? There was, he said, "a leadership vacuum."

Annan filled page after page of a yellow pad with notes. What was he writing—"going over a cliff," "leadership vacuum"? How did he feel about being told that he had lost his grip—that the problem, ultimately, was him? It was impossible to know. Annan remained eerily silent, just as he had in the meeting four days earlier. When the subject of his upcoming trip to Washington arose, Annan said that since Bush wouldn't

meet with him, perhaps he would decline meeting with other administration officials. Holbrooke, who was getting more and more agitated,
burst out, "That's the most solipsistic piece of crap I've ever heard!" It
sounded, at least to the unsentimental Holbrooke, like Annan was being consumed by self-pity.

After having anatomized the situation, the group turned to the
question of what to do. A few days earlier Annan's own colleagues had
urged him to seize the initiative, but these outsiders wanted him to do
something that went much more sharply against the grain of his nature:
change the inner circle. Iqbal Riza had to go, and sooner rather than
later, even if that left the unfair impression that he had been jettisoned
owing to Oil-for-Food. The problem wasn't even the scandal so much
as the inability to recognize the danger it posed and the failure to respond to it in a way that inspired trust. The thirty-eighth floor could no
longer operate like the Vatican, shrouded in mystery and occult ritual;
Annan needed a campaign manager, not a vizier. He needed someone
who could think strategically and who could speak the language of the
larger world, very much including the language of Washington. Virtually everyone in the meeting agreed that the only figure in the UN who
could mastermind such a campaign was Mark Malloch Brown, the administrator of the UN Development Programme.

Of British and South African background, Malloch Brown had
served with Annan in the Office of the UN High Commissioner for
Refugees in the late 1970s; worked as a journalist at *The Economist*;
helped found Sawyer Miller, a major player in the world of political
consulting and public relations; and then moved to the World Bank,
first as spokesman and then as vice president, in 1999. It had taken
some political courage for Annan to bring him to UNDP the following
year, for the top job was understood to "belong to" the European
Union, which had supplied a Dane for the job. But Annan hadn't liked
the candidate, and after a brief stalemate he had named his own candidate. What's more, he had been drawn to Malloch Brown's critique of
the agency, which was essentially that it was, like so much at the
UN, noble rather than actually effective. The UNDP had far too little
money to make a difference on a national scale and was too tied to recipient governments to do anything innovative. Malloch Brown proposed instead that the agency use the goodwill it had built up over the

years to help states make their civil service and ministries and legislature more accountable and transparent—precisely what big donors had
begun to demand. Many of UNDP's beneficiaries viewed this doctrine
as the new face of colonialism, and they did everything they could to
block it. But Malloch Brown persisted, and Annan supported him, and
UNDP became a model of UN reform.

John Ruggie sorted UN officials into two groups: "traditionalists,"
who believed that the institution's legitimacy came from fidelity to its
own rules and viewed the Charter as the final arbiter in questions
of justice; and "modernizers," who looked to outcomes rather than
processes and were ready to change whatever obstructed the achievement of good outcomes. In this typology, Malloch Brown was an ur-
progressive. He couldn't abide the institution's obsession with process.
Soon after he had taken over at UNDP, he had sent his country officers
a form asking them to explain exactly what they were doing. Several
months later he had to send an addendum: "When describing a UNDP
program, consultations held and publications issued do not themselves
count as an action." He made use of management tools considered
outré in the UN's archaic culture, for example, sending out annual sur-
veys to determine how employees felt about their work and about the
UN. Malloch Brown had no use for the UN's suffocating ideological
propriety. In 2002, the UNDP produced a study called the "Arab Human Development Report," written chiefly by Arab scholars. The report
provoked a sensation by openly blaming development failures on poor
governance, authoritarian rule, and intellectual close-mindedness.

In the muffled, stifled world of international civil service, Malloch
Brown was brash, peremptory, and demanding. And he was glib and
prolix, and on suspiciously good terms with the press—which also recommended him for the job of chief of staff. Holbrooke, who spoke with
the UNDP administrator regularly, viewed him as one of the very few
people in the upper echelons of the UN who shared his own understanding of the institution and had the toughness and political savvy to
take on its entrenched culture. Ruggie thought of him as "a magnet in
a field of iron filings": someone who would demand coherence and
clarity, who would unambiguously say yes and no.

At the same time, it was understood that the rules of "equitable national distribution" dictated that if a British citizen became chief of

staff, one could not have another Brit as head of the Department of Political Affairs. Kieran Prendergast, in other words, would have to go. From Holbrooke's point of view, of course, this made the appointment of Malloch Brown a twofer: The UN would get a forceful hand at the tiller and shed an official who reinforced the UN-above-all mentality. For Annan, on the other hand, the prospect of losing Prendergast might have been reason enough to find a candidate other than Malloch Brown. In any case, he and Riza had been talking about the succession for eighteen months now, and the candidates they considered looked very much like Riza himself: UN lifers who were past masters in the arcane processes of the institution. Annan now understood, however, that such a choice would carry a serious political, and perhaps practical, cost.

After the meeting, John Ruggie moved back into the UN in order to talk with senior officials and plan specific changes. Holbrooke says that he undertook "a brutal two-week campaign" to force the reluctant Annan to hire a new chief of staff. When he saw the secretary-general a week or so after the meeting, he said, "Please give us a Christmas present"—that is, Riza's head.

"I'll make the announcement after I get back from vacation," Annan said.

"You've really got to move as fast as you can," Holbrooke rejoined. "It doesn't matter when he goes; what matters is that you announce it soon."

On December 14, Malloch Brown, who knew very well that he was being touted for the job, was asked to come straight from a flight from South Africa to the SG's residence to meet with Annan and Ruggie. There, Annan offered him the job of chief of staff. Malloch Brown asked for time to mull over the offer; he wanted to remain temporarily as head of UNDP, and he understood what a staggering burden he would be shouldering in holding two more-than-full-time jobs. He also knew very well how demoralized and embattled the upper reaches of the Secretariat had become. But the chance to ride to the UN's rescue fired his ambition, and he accepted the offer. On the twenty-second, as Annan was preparing for vacation, he called Holbrooke and said, Holbrooke recalls, "I have your Christmas present." Annan then informed a shocked Riza that he would be announcing his retirement within the hour. Until now Riza had always known everything, but he knew nothing of the December 5 meeting, and he had little idea that his fate had been batted back and forth like a shuttlecock. Fred Eckhard then went before the press to announce that Riza would step down as soon as a successor could be named. The chief of staff scarcely deserved such brusque treatment after his long career of selfless service; one of the harsh consequences of being too soft on people is that you often end up being too hard on them.

The announcement set off a frenzy of speculation, of wishful thinking, of fear. Eckhard told me that he dreamed that the secretary-general would appoint Bob Orr, who was now handling the reform process, relations with Washington, the response to Volcker, and pretty much everything else that was urgent. "Everyone's turning to Bob," Eckhard said. "He's the kind of person who says, 'Okay, here's what we need to do—these three things, bop bop bop.' We don't *have* people like that in the UN." Michael Moller said he had been trying to persuade Annan to ignore the unspoken rule that dictated that neither the secretary-general nor his chief of staff would come from one of the permanent members. Moller was hoping Annan would give the job, ironically, to Prendergast.

But Moller had also come to conclude that Annan himself, whom he otherwise much admired, was part of the problem. "Right now," he said, "if you screw up, you don't pay a price." Ruud Lubbers hadn't paid a price; nor had officials in Congo; nor had some notorious mediocrities whom Annan had appointed and sustained. "If we had true accountability and meritocracy," Moller went on, "people would be able to do their job, and in time we'd attract large numbers of high-quality people. This is a great place to work, but it's great only because of the nature of the work, not because of the environment of the place. Unless you're incredibly strong and you can see the big picture, you're going to get worn down, and you'll leave." Moller himself had one foot out the door; his plans, he said, would hinge on Annan's choice as chief of staff. If it was one of the Riza clones, he would leave.

Annan did not accept the idea that the UN's crisis caught him unawares; nor did he feel in any way responsible for his staff's sense of demoralization. "Nobody wants to work for an organization that is being battered, that is being discredited, day in and day out," he told me in January. "And nobody seems to be out there to stem the hemorrhage. It's been relentless, and it takes a toll on everybody, myself included." Annan conceded that the UN had been slow to respond to the allegations on Oil-for-Food and thus had "left the field" to its detractors, but at bottom he felt that he was a victim, not the cause, of the crisis. How could he feel otherwise? He was the same man, behaving in the same way, as always. The salient fact to him was that he was now being attacked rather than celebrated for what he was, and his friends were abandoning him. The underlying narrative was a narrative of American antipathy and power. "When I deal with other governments," he said, "they are quite focused on reform." And so he would focus on reform.

Annan says that he had always liked the idea of making Mark Malloch Brown his chief of staff but that he had assumed his colleague would refuse to take a step down in the formal hierarchy from a program administrator. Malloch Brown himself was willing to drop a notch in the pecking order, for he understood the powers that would come of stepping into the breach on the thirty-eighth floor, but he was loath to surrender control over UNDP with the cultural revolution he was fostering there still half finished. When Annan offered him the post, he agreed to take it so long as he could temporarily retain his current position. The decision was announced January 3, just before Annan left for Jakarta.

Malloch Brownism had begun seeping into the thirty-eighth floor even before the man himself arrived there. Earlier in the year, with Oil-for-Food just beginning to loom on the horizon, he had prevailed on Tim Wirth to hire Robert Mead, a specialist in "crisis management and change management," to help the UN navigate its crisis. What this meant, in practice, was that Mead offered advice on how to talk to the outside world about fiascoes like Oil-for-Food and the sexual abuse scandal in Congo, as well as about major campaigns like the reform effort. Mead said that he had counseled against hitting back on Oil-for-Food and in favor of transparency on Congo. The UN struck him as bizarrely undisciplined. "It's a very interesting organization," he said with some care. "Anyone is entitled to an opinion, and anyone can talk to the press." As a result, the organization projected no coherent sense of purpose. But that, he said, would change once Malloch Brown settled in.

In late January, I visited the new chief of staff in Riza's old office. Over the last several months, Malloch Brown's eyes had grown baggier, and his gut had swelled. The few people who actually work effectively at the UN wind up doing almost everything, and Malloch Brown looked like a victim of his ambition and decisiveness. The few weeks he had spent on Annan's staff had only lowered his already low regard for UN work habits; he suggested I read *Defeat of an Ideal*, Shirley Hazzard's evisceration of the UN. "She gets at the sheer inertia of the place," he said. "We're organized around process. And I'm still struggling with where in that context do you find the levers to transform it into a more performance-oriented, result-oriented culture." He had been, he said, "struck by the way people tiptoe around and this extreme deference and courtesy and civility, and where the hell is the work being done? And I do think that's the other side of the Oil-for-Food failure, the lack of any real sense of executive management. I just am struggling with that." Perhaps he was struggling as well to find a way of characterizing this failed culture without pointing at its fountainhead, the secretary-general.

For all the time he had spent in the UN, Malloch Brown was seeing its executive culture through a stranger's shocked eyes. There was, for example, the all-important question of paper flow. According to Malloch Brown's chief aide, Mark Suzman, another South African and also a former journalist—with the *Financial Times*—"You have these really trivial pieces of paper that are expected to be signed by the *chef de cabinet*, like people's leave plans. And after you're finished with it, you have to deliver each piece of paper yourself, it has to circulate around to everyone on a checklist, you don't get to keep a copy, and then it returns to a central registry. And everything has to be signed, because verbal agreements aren't enough. 'The secretary-general welcomes X' has to be signed. And Mr. Riza never used an autopen."

Malloch Brown had plans. He was planning to scrap the senior management group, a baggy gabfest, in favor of two smaller, more tightly focused bodies, one on policy and the other on management, whose meetings would conclude with both decisions and assignments for the various members. He wanted to institute the kind of "options-paper discipline" taken for granted in the White House, so that the secretary-general could reach decisions based on a concise and explicitly articulated set of options, rather than on whoever happened to get in the door last, or on a private huddle with the chief of staff. He wanted to bring in McKinsey, the management consultant, to help restructure the executive office. But beyond all that, he viewed as a central aspect of his job something Riza would have found unfathomable and possibly abhorrent: talking openly, to the press and to critics in Congress and elsewhere, about everything that was wrong with the UN—though also, of course, about why the institution was so very much worth saving and fixing.

Malloch Brown also referred to himself, only half mockingly, as "Kofi's friend on the dark side." If the thirty-eighth floor was to function like a rational and effective organization rather than a Renaissance court, some of the courtiers would have to go, and Malloch Brown was quite prepared to be the bearer of bad tidings. One of the first people he targeted was Elisabeth Lindenmayer, the most scrupulously loyal of all the retainers, a charter member of Annan's inner circle. When a management consultant had reported a year earlier that Lindenmayer was considered neither collegial nor particularly effective, Annan had reluctantly agreed to do something about it, but when Lindenmayer emerged from his office, she had been promoted to become deputy chief of staff, a startling and unwelcome piece of news to the chief of staff, Iqbal Riza. Malloch Brown did not want her as his assistant, either.

At the end of January, Annan made a brief trip to Nigeria and Cameroon. On the way back, his party changed planes at Charles de Gaulle airport. While they waited in the large and dismal VIP lounge, Annan beckoned Lindenmayer over. Both were exhausted from jet lag; Annan was also depressed and devitalized, as he had been for the previous two months. With no warning or preamble, he said, according to Lindenmayer, "I must tell you that some colleagues feel that you are difficult to work with." Lindenmayer, who apparently had no inkling of the truth, was astounded to hear so harsh an assessment from her boss and friend of twenty-five years.

"Who are these people?" she demanded.

"Mark and the DSG"—Deputy Secretary-General Louise Fréchette. "But what about *you*?" Lindenmayer asked. "What do you think?"

Annan fell into a painful silence. Then he said, "I want you to talk to Mark when we get back." Apparently, Malloch Brown was to be the executioner. Lindenmayer stumbled away in a daze; the solid foundations of her life had suddenly dropped away. Back in New York, she approached Annan, who said once again, "Talk to Mark." Instead, she wrote out a letter of resignation, gave it to Annan's personal assistant with instructions to make sure he received it, and then waited. If he really expected her to leave, she reasoned, he would find an appropriate post for her elsewhere in the organization. Lindenmayer heard nothing that evening, and nothing the next morning, at which point she sent an e-mail to colleagues announcing her resignation. Then Malloch Brown hurried over, but made no attempt to dissuade her, and a few days later Lindenmayer was gone.

The incident, and indeed the whole ugly narrative, quickly became a cause célèbre. Lindenmayer wasn't simply another member of Annan's inner circle. She was the conduit from the ambassadors to the secretary-general, and thus indispensable to them. She was widely admired, whatever her flaws, for her devotion to the institution and above all to Annan, whom she seemed genuinely to worship, even after all these years. "She carried his flag into every battle," as one of her admirers put it. It was unimaginable, in a velvet coffin like the UN, that such a person could be unceremoniously bounced from office without so much as a face-saving alternative.

Annan hadn't meant to humiliate Lindenmayer. But as with Riza, his horror of confrontation—his cowardice, really—had first postponed, and then unnecessarily exacerbated, the inevitable pain. Here his friend on the dark side came in handy. Though it was noble Othello who had decreed the murder, the blame naturally fell on his Iago. Wasn't he already steeped in blood, as he eliminated first one loyalist and then another? And for whose benefit? The insatiable Americans, of course. They had, through the instrument of Malloch Brown, reduced Annan to their puppet. This, in any case, is how the reasoning ran. Annan may even have convinced himself of some portion of this account. Lindenmayer says that when she finally answered one of the secretary-general's phone calls weeks later, he first consoled her as if she had fallen victim to some affliction, and then, when she pointed out that he was himself the author of her demise, insisted that some unspecified "they" had demanded her head.

Kieran Prendergast, stout defender of the Charter and of the royal and ancient British virtues of sportsmanship and fair play, watched this spectacle unfold with a gathering sense of embitterment. The rise of Malloch Brown had meant his eclipse. Annan wanted to make him the UN's Middle East negotiator. One day in late January I was talking to Annan in his residence on Sutton Place, just north of the UN, when a phone call came in that he had to take. When he returned, after several minutes, he said that Condoleezza Rice had called to say, among other things, that the Israelis were blocking Prendergast's appointment. Annan had, however, recently talked to the Israelis, who assured him that they had no problem with the proposed envoy. Annan assumed that the problem lay with the White House, which may have considered Prendergast anti-American. Perhaps they blamed him for the Falluja letter, as Holbrooke did. Or perhaps they just didn't like him. Prendergast was a seigneurial figure, a Shavian wag given to erudite spoofery of those he deemed less subtle, less deeply versed, than he; cocky Americans particularly excited his ridicule. "I can see how his delivery can grate on some Americans," Annan conceded.

Prendergast wasn't anti-American, but he was a leading exponent of the view that the UN had to "contain" the United States. He viewed American unilateralism as the single greatest threat to the UN, and he bridled at the unfairness of having to pretend otherwise for fear Washington would exact revenge. He had urged Annan to outface his critics, to tell off the Americans, to speak truth to power. But instead Annan had made the Americans' fair-haired boy his chief of staff, and Malloch Brown, or so Prendergast believed, had shown his colors by "flagellating the UN" in almost American terms. Prendergast felt a cult of Malloch Brown aborning. "A lot of Mark's stuff," he said to me in the aftermath of *l'affaire Lindenmayer*, "was, 'He's a modernizer, the Secretariat is full of traditionalists, there's been no reform but he's reformed UNDP, now he's coming to clean the Augean stables.' We've had several rounds of serious reform in the last few years, but I guess they just didn't count." Prendergast was only too happy to reel off for my benefit the nicknames for the chief of staff making the rounds of the building—"Rasputin," "the regent," and, most telling, "the real SG."

I heard a lot of that, but I heard the other side as well. Michael Moller, the secretary-general's special adviser for practically everything, was no longer talking about quitting. Moller still worried that if the Volcker panel didn't swallow the UN whole, the looming sex scandal in Congo would. He continued to assume, as he had from the outset, that the reform agenda would fail. And of course he was deeply troubled by all the talk about Malloch Brown as Washington's lickspittle, and Malloch Brown of vaulting ambition. But he no longer felt that the UN was spinning down a funnel of its own devising. Moller took heart from Malloch Brown's crispness and clarity, his calls for renewal; the chief of staff had, in fact, asked him to serve temporarily as his deputy. And when the endless bull sessions of the senior management group gave way to the much smaller and tighter policy group sessions, Moller was delighted to discover that the thirty-eighth floor could consider options and make decisions, just like organizations in the outside world.

Nothing brought home the precariousness, as well as the unfairness, of the UN's relationship with Washington like the elections in Iraq, scheduled for January 30, 2005. The crucial role the Americans had agreed to give the UN in organizing the elections felt more and more like a poisoned chalice; but drink they must. In early December, Lakhdar Brahimi had gone off message, publicly calling for the elections to be postponed in order to marshal support among disaffected Sunnis. Annan immediately distanced himself from the comment, even though he thought that Brahimi was right on the merits. In a meeting a few days before his planned trip to Washington in mid-December, he said of the administration, "They've been so focused on elections. There's no mileage in suggesting that it might be a good idea to postpone the elections." The message should be: "We're on the ground, doing lots of work." Don't get fixated on the size of the mission.

Prendergast still balked at the sharp limits the Americans had placed on the mission. "We can reach people that the Americans can't

talk to and that Allawi"—the interim prime minister Iyad Allawi—
"can't talk to."

"Kieran, we *told* them all this," Annan rejoined wearily.

"But we haven't told the president, and we haven't told Condi."
Prendergast did not tiptoe around the secretary-general, as others did.
The UN, he said, must use its "good offices" to bring the parties together. (Rice disputes the notion that Washington received, or spurned,
any such offer from the UN.) Ashraf Qazi, head of the Iraq mission,
added that the Iraqis now seemed eager for the UN to involve itself in
the political process. But this would require time. "If we're being asked
to be active in the process, in order to fulfill the task, we may find it a
contradiction to keep to the January 30 deadline."

To all of which Annan said no. He understood more clearly than the
others that the UN could not wish away its political limits.

Throughout this period, the UN's electoral experts kept working
with the Independent Electoral Commission of Iraq on registration, on
the establishment of polling sites, on the logistics of securing and
counting ballots—all, of course, in the midst of a terrifying war zone
into which foreigners could venture only with the most elaborate precautions. At another meeting on January 20, Qazi reported, from Baghdad, that registration activity had come to a full stop in the Sunni
hotbeds of Mosul and Anbar province, and that Sunni turnout was unlikely to top 40 percent, raising the likelihood of a post-electoral political crisis. The UN would have to help mediate that crisis. But the UN
could do nothing in Iraq unless the Americans wished it, and while
Washington was eager for the UN to help with the constitution-writing
process—a good sign—political arbitration remained beyond the pale.
For the moment they had to focus on the election. Prendergast re-
marked that it was too bad that as a matter of policy, the UN could not
pronounce on the merits of elections that it had a hand in organizing.

"I think we will find it extremely difficult not to make an exception
in this case," Annan said. "We'll be seen as too bureaucratic if we don't
pronounce on the elections." This, too, was a matter of political reality.

I spoke with Annan a few days before the election—and a few days,
as well, before Hurricane Volcker was scheduled to make landfall. He
had been speaking regularly with Secretary Rice, but he hadn't talked
to President Bush since December 23, when they had simply ex-

changed holiday greetings. Annan said he didn't worry about the president, who understood that Annan had an audience of his own to speak to. But, he added, "I don't think everyone around him understands that"—code for Vice President Cheney and his ilk. Annan felt that Iraq would soon force a moment of truth in U.S.-UN relations. Low Sunni turnout in the election could raise the level of violence; further down the road, the rejection of the constitution would threaten civil war. No matter what, he said, "They're going to want to work with the allies, and the allies like to work with the UN. It gives them protection; it's not one-on-one." More than that, the various Iraqi parties would exploit divisions in the Security Council, just as Saddam had done. "I've always maintained that when the international community speaks with one voice," he said, "they have greater impact. So when I stress unity, it's not about form, it's substance."

The election turned out to be an inspiring event, if a transitory one, for both Iraqis and the American-led coalition. Though Sunni turnout was even lower than Qazi had predicted, producing precisely the power imbalance he and others feared, there had been far less violence than expected, and the Shiites and Kurds had voted in great numbers and with great passion. The voters' thumbs, stained with indelible purple ink, became the election's iconic image. The UN had produced a logistical masterpiece. President Bush called Annan to say, "You guys did a great job." After the terrible agony, first of the Security Council debate over the war, then of the August 2003 bombing, Iraq had, in some small but significant measure, repaid Annan's persistence, his slightly unseemly courtship of the White House. First Vieira de Mello, then Brahimi, and now the elections had demonstrated the UN's irreplaceable political capacities. Of course, the institution could have proved its mettle perfectly well without the suffering.

The first report of the Volcker committee had been hanging over the UN for months. The committee finally issued the document on February 3. Because many questions remained about Kojo Annan, and about whatever role Kofi Annan might have played in regard to his son, the entire subject was put off to the next report, thus both sparing Annan immediate damage and ensuring that the sword would continue to hang over his head. The star, or villain, of the first interim report was Benon Sevan, the career UN official who managed the Oil-for-Food Programme. The committee concluded that Sevan had engaged in "a grave and continuing conflict of interest" by directing millions of dollars' worth of oil contracts to AMEP, a trading firm whose principals he knew; in one instance, the Iraqis granted the requests immediately after Sevan talked to them about his hopes to expand access to spare parts for their oil industry. The committee also found that Sevan had reported receiving $160,000 in cash during this period. Sevan insisted that the money had come from his aunt, a woman of modest means who lived in Cyprus; the investigators cautiously wrote that the claim was "not adequately supported" by the documents he had furnished, and noted that it would continue to investigate the source of the funds. Such overtly self-dealing behavior was so obviously disgraceful that many of Sevan's colleagues could not bring themselves to believe he had done it. On the other hand, if it were to turn out that UN officials had stolen all of $160,000 from a $64 billion program, the evidence would point more toward heroic self-restraint than toward rampant theft.

The Sevan narrative, though mortifying, involved only one man. And indeed, in the press conference at which he presented his findings, Volcker made a point of saying, "We have not, repeat, *not*, found systematic misuse of funds dedicated to the Oil-For-Food Program." What he had uncovered, however, and exposed with unprecedented clarity, was the profoundly politicized process by which the UN reached supposedly impartial and merit-based decisions—in this case the selection, in 1996, of procurement firms and of a bank to hold Iraq's oil revenues in escrow. The committee noted, in fairness, that the UN's existing procurement process "was strongly tested by the need to quickly obtain qualified contractors to implement an urgent, complex and unprecedented program." At the same time, it observed, "formal financial regulations and rules set out by procurement officials were repeatedly and knowingly short-circuited and violated, without a clear and consistent written rationale." Political calculations, investigators concluded, consistently trumped considerations of merit.

Procurement officials, for example, drew up a list of sixteen banks qualified to perform escrow duties. Separately, however, and un-beknownst to administrators, Boutros Boutros-Ghali, then secretary-general, had gone to the French ambassador with a list of three French banks that the Iraqis would accept. One of those, the Banque Na-tionale de Paris, had not made the initial cut. But when procurement officials subsequently drew up a shorter list of six banks, BNP was in-cluded. Only four of those banks chose to bid for the contract—BNP, Chase Manhattan, and two Swiss banks. The Iraqis had made it clear that they would accept French or Swiss banks, but not American or British ones. U.S. Ambassador Madeleine Albright had told Boutros-Ghali that Washington did not want a Swiss bank, owing to Swiss banking secrecy laws as well as to the fact that Switzerland did not serve on the Security Council. Accordingly, the UN chose BNP, a bank that had not even been deemed qualified for the job.

This decision was "political" in precisely the sense that the entire Oil-for-Food Programme was political: it was guided by larger diplo-matic considerations before which issues of merit might have to give way. Giving Iraq some say over the choice of a bank was, after all, triv-ial compared to the willingness to give Iraq control over the distri-bution of humanitarian goods—a necessary precondition to gaining Saddam's acquiescence to the program. And the same was true of sat-isfying American concerns about Swiss banks. This is presumably why Boutros-Ghali entrusted these decisions not to UN bureaucrats but to an Iraq steering committee composed of his top officials. To be "apolit-ical," in this regard, was to be naive; the UN always had to be sensitive to the political surround in order to have room to operate.

But how far could you take this sensitivity before it began to cor-rupt basic principles of managerial competence, accountability, and transparency? Once BNP won the contract, members of the steering committee concluded that it would be "unacceptable" to award the contract for goods inspection to a French firm as well, even though a French firm was the lowest bidder. Joseph Stephanides, one of the top officials of the nascent Oil-for-Food Programme, had already informed a British diplomat that the UN wanted the contract to go to Lloyd's of London; when the bid from Lloyd's came in 25 percent higher than that of the French competitor, Stephanides told him just how much

Lloyd's would have to reduce its bid, and Lloyd's adjusted its figures accordingly. This proved to be too gross a breach of process. Instead of declaring Lloyd's the winner, the steering committee put a stop to the process of competitive bidding and awarded the contract to Lloyd's by invoking a clause allowing merit considerations to be overruled by the "interests of the Organization." In this case, however, the interests of the organization had nothing to do with preserving sanctions on a dangerous country and everything to do with the imperative of keeping important members happy.

The officials who guided the process were under no illusions about where their ultimate responsibilities lay. In minutes of the meeting of the Iraq steering committee from August 13, 1996, Chinmaya Gharekhan, Boutros-Ghali's senior political adviser, was quoted as saying, "Everything about implementation of 986 [the resolution establishing the program] was 'political,' and no aspect could be assessed purely on its merits. The Secretariat had come under terrible pressure from the member-states; the selection of [oil] overseers and the bank, and the firm to supply oil inspection agents has all been political."

What Gharekhan is saying is perfectly plain: It's not our fault. Yes, in each case we violated our own procedures and chose a less-qualified candidate; but the member states left us no choice. The Secretariat was only an instrument; it could not be held accountable. This is evidence not of corruption—no one involved was seeking personal gain—but of a set of reflexes so deeply ingrained as to appear inevitable. The UN had to operate within political limits; it was foolish to think otherwise. And so, over time, the wiser heads in the institution had internalized those limits, had learned to act without having to be prompted. Of course, since the outcome of this overtly political process could look quite ugly, the reasoning behind the selection of the firms could not be explicitly stipulated, much less publicly discussed.

At the UN press briefing held after Volcker released the report, Malloch Brown read a statement by Annan accepting responsibility for the failures the investigators had identified and stating that he had "initiated disciplinary proceedings" against Benon Sevan and Joseph Stephanides. The chief of staff then took questions. The fact that the secretary-general himself did not appear only deepened the sense that he had become too frail to stand up to further battering. Annan, however, had none of his new aide's artfulness in such a setting. Malloch Brown deftly skated around every patch of thin ice, never once falling in; he was even bold enough to try to redirect the press's attention to "the much bigger story" of oil smuggling, over which the UN had no control. But Malloch Brown was also willing, at least when it suited his purposes, to speak about the institution in ways that Annan could not or would not do. Asked if the Volcker report should be read as "an indictment of United Nations culture," he went the reporter one better by aptly describing the institutional mind-set as "the culture of political complicity," in which all parties conspired to evade accountability. Malloch Brown proposed a solution in typically blunt terms: members, he said, should "back off and let us manage the organization."

But the new chief of staff did not understand Oil-for-Food exclusively in cultural terms. The moral he drew from the overall revelations about the program, and from the onslaught the UN was now enduring, had more to do with the larger political surround. When we spoke soon after the press conference, Malloch Brown talked about "a failure to manage constituent relations" going back to the early days of Boutros-Ghali. "When I look at Rwanda," he said, "what I see is a period of erosion of Washington-UN relations leading to a general erosion of UN relations with the leading powers. You had this huge piling on of peace-keeping missions with none of the commensurate political support, let alone military muscle and financial muscle. We just lost the political commitment. When you get a telegram from Dallaire saying, 'Help,' even if you have a desk officer who takes the cable, what's completely severed is the political support network of governments to do something about it. And even when it's in place, the UN is lazy and ineffective at mobilizing it."

The habit of deference to members was sapping the UN of its vitality. The institution was trying, not very effectively, to be something else, and something more. "What you get is this odd sort of half-pregnant character of the UN," Malloch Brown said, "still stuck in its diplomatic, convening, consensus-seeking roots." What the UN was becoming, or wanted to become, was more of a "stakeholder organization" that would embrace, and seek to advance, substantive views on development, the use of force, terrorism, and the like. No more tiptoeing around, no more endless noodling with issues of process. Malloch

Brown envisioned a more muscular and assertive institution, but he also envisioned one that gave far more care to constituent relations. How could the institution be less deferential but also more assiduous about cultivating political support? It was, after all, those very constituents to whom the UN was accustomed to deferring.

CHAPTER EIGHTEEN

"They're Laughing at Us in Khartoum"

I N EARLY DECEMBER 2004, THREE WEEKS AFTER THE SE-
curity Council session in Nairobi designed to provide a comprehensive solution to the civil conflicts in Sudan, Jan Pronk, the head of the
UN mission in Khartoum, told Kofi Annan and members of his policy
coordination group on Sudan that the situation in Darfur was deteriorating. Two humanitarian workers in the region had just been shot.
"When the Security Council drew up the resolution in Nairobi," Pronk
said, "they deliberately decided to come out weak on Darfur. So the
rebels interpreted that to go on all-out attack, while the government
has mobilized the capacities of the so-called lawless elements. I don't
understand it. The Americans were always tough on Darfur, talking
about sanctions. And then, in Nairobi, it was all carrots. Now we have
to get tough again." And the problem was no longer limited to the Janjaweed; now tribal militias, operating beyond the control of the government, were fighting running battles with the Darfur rebels. The failure
to confront the situation head-on had simply bred chaos.

What could be done? Pronk said that the troops of the African
Union had proved surprisingly intrepid, but there weren't enough of
them. He proposed that the Security Council authorize a no-fly zone to
keep government aircraft from bombing villages. This had become an
increasingly popular idea, but Iqbal Riza, with his gift for bone-dry understatement, said, "I don't think you can assume unanimity among the
P5 in terms of granting a no-fly zone." What about an arms embargo?

Pronk pointed out that the Security Council had already imposed an arms embargo, but it wasn't being enforced. Could you threaten to haul government officials before the International Criminal Court? "You can't put that in a resolution," Annan said. "The Americans"—who vehemently opposed the court—"wouldn't stand for it." Jan Egeland noted that the rebel army, the SPLA, had killed seventy policemen over the previous two weeks. "Three, four, five killings more," he said, "and we're out of there."

"Doesn't the SPLA leadership care about this?" Annan asked.

"No," said Pronk.

Egeland was getting more and more exercised. "The whole world declared this to be the world's number-one priority April first," he exclaimed. "Now it's December. And right now we have 600 soldiers, 220 observers, and 5 police trainers. It's incredible, and I think we should say so." Egeland wanted to push the Americans to put pressure on the rebels, and the Chinese to squeeze Khartoum. Louise Fréchette, pragmatic and plodding, pointed out that, come what may, the UN still had to rely on the AU forces. Donors were willing to give more money, but the AU didn't seem to know how to use it. "We need to persuade the AU to not be too proud," Kieran Prendergast added. "They want to do it, they can't do it, they won't let us do it."

Now Pronk said that the AU planned to have 4,000 troops on the ground by February. Hedi Annabi, deputy head of the peacekeeping department, had spent half his career trying to drag such dreamy best-case scenarios back down to earth. Annabi began shaking his head vigorously. "That's what they *promised*," he exclaimed. "But they've only *proposed* 2,200 troops." And only half of that commitment was solid. The AU had also promised to field 800 policemen, but no one had the faintest idea where they would come from. And since the AU wouldn't accept help, there was very little the UN could do about it.

The discussion seemed to hit a wall in every direction. Pronk spoke in a thick Dutch accent, and the others sometimes strained to decipher his English. Annan spoke in his velvet whisper, and Pronk, who appeared to be hard of hearing, often seemed at a loss. Neither seemed able to understand the other. When Annan spoke, Pronk would knit his thick, sprouting eyebrows. "What?" he would say. And then Annan would raise his voice almost to the level of normal speech and repeat himself.

On January 25, the International Commission of Inquiry, established by a Security Council resolution the previous September to determine whether acts of genocide had been committed in Darfur, delivered its report. The debate over how to characterize the monstrosities inflicted on the people of Darfur, which had been provoked the previous summer when the U.S. Congress had passed a meaningless and self-congratulatory resolution describing the attacks as "genocide," had grown increasingly theological and self-defeating. Genocide was determined not by a certain quantum of acts but by a scope of intentions, and, Mukesh Kapila notwithstanding, the government of Sudan seemed no more intent on exterminating the "African" tribes of Darfur than Slobodan Milošević had been on wiping the Kosovars off the face of the earth. In both cases, murder was not an end so much as an instrument of terror. But the very act of defining a category of evil of which the Sudanese regime fell short had the effect almost of exonerating it. "Ethnic cleansing," a better description of both Serbian and Sudanese policy, may have been less wicked than the Hutu or Khmer Rouge campaigns of obliteration, but it was more wicked than almost everything else—far more, certainly, than the mere abetting of ancient rivalries, as the UN's Department of Political Affairs would have it.

The commission rightly concluded that "the Government of Sudan has not pursued a policy of genocide," but that it was guilty of "crimes against humanity and war crimes." Far from having tapered off as a result of international pressure, the report noted, the "killing of civilians, rape, pillaging and forced displacement have continued during the course of the Commission's mandate." The commissioners called for "urgent action" to end these abuses. They also compiled a list of fifty-one Sudanese government officials and Janjaweed leaders responsible for the atrocities. But where would these figures be tried? The obvious answer was the International Criminal Court, which the UN had established in 1998 for just such a purpose, but the United States, as Annan had observed, would not permit the court to be legitimized. The Bush administration thus found itself in the bizarre position of accusing Sudanese officials of plotting genocide, but proposing that they be brought to justice in an ad hoc tribunal that no other nation saw any reason to create. The UN human rights commissioner, Louise Arbour, complained that a wholly new court would be "unduly time-consuming and expensive," especially when the UN had a court of its own with nothing yet to do.

On February 8, Pronk delivered his biennial report to the Security Council. While he celebrated the finalizing of the peace agreement between the government and the rebels of the south, he described a "dismal picture" in Darfur, with an increasingly fragmented and chaotic form of conflict threatening to reduce the region to the Hobbesian condition of Somalia. He had just returned from a tour of Darfur, where, he said, "I saw the dramatic consequences of tribal or ethnic cleansing of dozens of villages, carried out by the militias during the month of January." He told Annan and his aides that the Sudanese army seemed to be feeding lies to President Bashir, who was quite convinced that he was complying with the UN's terms. What's more, government officials, like Serbian officials a decade earlier, had learned to discount threats from the Security Council, none of which ever amounted to anything. "You need a solution in February," he said. "Otherwise, they're laughing at us in Khartoum."

At a meeting later in February, Jean-Marie Guéhenno, the under-secretary-general for peacekeeping, a tall, pale, ratiocinative Cartesian to Prendergast's epigrammatic Oxbridge wag, presented four alternative security options in ascending order of muscularity and unlikeliness. The first was to continue strengthening the AU force by providing ground and air transport, communications equipment, food, water, fuel, engineering, and so on. "We have strong doubts that the AU will have the capacity to pull this off," he said. "But politically, it's the easiest." Next was a combined AU/UN force. This would encounter objections from the Sudanese and some council members, and the command and logistical problems of two forces sharing the same theater could make it "an even greater mess than the first option." Option three was replacing the AU with a UN peacekeeping operation, perhaps drawing on the peacekeepers being sent to the south. But troop contributors might not accept the change of mission, the operation would strain UN capacities, and both the Sudanese and the AU would strongly object. Finally, Guéhenno said, was the establishment of a multinational force, or MNF, approved by the Security Council, like the Australian-led contingent that quelled the fighting in East Timor. Guéhenno conceded that the Sudanese government would never submit to such a force absent tremendous political pressure. Moreover, he said, "There is no obvious Australia." But this was the only option that could quickly stabilize Darfur.

Annan said, "We would have to seek government cooperation, and otherwise threaten Chapter 7"—that is, a forcible incursion. "Who would lead a Chapter 7 mission?"

"The choices are not that many," Guéhenno conceded. "In Europe, there are only two countries which have the capacity to mount this kind of operation—the U.K. and France. The U.K. has its hands full in Iraq right now, and France might not like the idea of this mission." Perhaps it could be an EU mission, or an EU/NATO mission. European public opinion was growing increasingly aroused by the continuing atrocities.

"I wish I could believe it's a viable solution," Prendergast said, "but I'm afraid it's a desert mirage. Britain was a colonial power in the Sudan; you can imagine what the government of Sudan would say about that." The Sudanese government had, in fact, adroitly manipulated public opinion—and not only in Sudan—so that any Western engagement in Darfur would be seen as another campaign in the Christian crusade against Islam. Moreover, Prendergast added, while the AU would be hard put to step aside for a UN force, it would absolutely balk at doing so for "a European invasion."

But Annan was not prepared to surrender without firing a shot. "We need to look at a UN solution *and* the MNF," he said. "We've been looking at the prospect of genocide for a long time."

Mark Malloch Brown now spoke up. Unlike Riza, who was wont to play the ever-cautious balance wheel in such public sessions, Malloch Brown rarely hesitated to give his own point of view. "The missing element in the paper," he said, "is this enormous sense of urgency, the Jan Egeland position. There's a need to focus the heads of government on an action plan. We've all been distracted by problems not of our making, and I think we have to come roaring out of the box on this one and come up with a clear strategy. We all know by now the nature of the problem. What's been missing is the credible political threat to *do* anything about it."

On February 28, Annan and his aides met with Alpha Konare, the secretary-general of the African Union. Konare was an enthusiast who had convinced himself that the AU was already prepared to serve as the United Nations of Africa. He had grandly informed UN peacekeeping officials that a South African contingent was ready to go to Congo to forcibly disarm the ex-*génocidaires* who had crossed the border from Rwanda. Annan had then called South African president Thabo Mbeki, who said that his soldiers would do no such thing. Konare was going to send soldiers, from who knows where, to the Ivory Coast, to Somalia. The one thing he would not do is withdraw troops from the only place where they had actually been fielded.

In the meeting, conducted in French, which always put Annan at a slight disadvantage, the secretary-general tried to gently persuade Konare that the AU simply could not muster a force large enough to protect the civilians of Darfur. Konare demurred; if the West would send him equipment, and provide housing and food and so on, he would find all the soldiers and policemen he needed. Annan ran through the four options. He recognized, he said, that the Sudanese might not accept a multinational force. No, they wouldn't, Konare said. Annan raised the possibility of a joint UN/AU force. It was unnecessary, Konare said. The AU was prepared to "readjust and augment" its mission so long as the EU was prepared to pay. The AU would not agree to be sidelined, even for the UN. And Konare transmitted the same message to Security Council members; this was, of course, exactly what they wanted to hear.

In early March, Annan called the council to his office for a highly unusual meeting. The Americans were still unwilling to grant jurisdiction to the ICC, thus holding up a resolution that would authorize a peacekeeping mission to enforce the north-south accord. Annan was asking the council to amend the resolution to include some kind of enhanced force in Darfur. He laid out the four options in the same order Guéhenno had, making it plain that he believed that the council should be prepared to tell the Sudanese, as they had the Indonesians in East Timor, that if they couldn't handle the situation, they should in-

vite the UN to come in and do it for them. This plea was met with perfect silence. Indeed, none of the members showed any interest in any
option save the first. U.K. Ambassador Emyr Jones Parry said that he
understood that his country would be expected to lead the multinational force; it wasn't going to happen, he said. Annan had come roaring out of the box, just as Malloch Brown hoped—and the council had
stuffed him back into that box.

Several days later I went to speak with Jones Parry. He admitted
that there was something awkward about the council's current approach to Sudan: "If we pass this resolution we're working on now, we'll
put eight thousand men where there isn't violence, and not one additional soldier in the area where there is violence." But the troops were
needed to enforce the peace agreement. And a military intervention in
Darfur would require a "huge force," Jones Parry said, and would
scarcely help the north-south problem. The ambassador had, in fact,
taken umbrage at Annan's interference in council deliberations.
"The whole meeting," he said, "seemed to be designed to present the
secretary-general as a toughie standing up for what was good against a
Security Council which had refused to do the right thing. He was lecturing the council like a schoolmaster." Nor did Jones Parry share the
Secretariat's sense of urgency. "The AU was doing rather well," he said.
"The problem is they don't have enough troops. When you've been encouraging the AU to do this, do you want to say, 'You guys are screwing
up, we're going to take over'? Had we done that, it would have been
counterproductive to the AU operation." And so what was meant to be
a desperate plea to come to the aid of defenseless civilians had been
understood as a petty act of moral one-upmanship.

That was the end of any discussion of forceful alternatives. And it
was easy to see why: the political stars were perfectly aligned for the
least effective solution. An AU-only force gave the officials of this budding regional organization a chance to show their mettle; satisfied the
continental demand for "an African solution to an African problem"; assured the government of Sudan that it would not have to contend with
a serious fighting force; and allowed the Western powers to say that
they were addressing the problem without having to commit anything
save money. The only losers were the people of Darfur, who continued
to spin down the funnel of catastrophe.

During the last week of March, the Security Council devised its own version of a comprehensive solution to the problems of Sudan. On March 24, the council passed resolution 1590 establishing a ten-thousand-man peacekeeping mission to govern the north-south agreement. On the twenty-ninth, it imposed a travel ban and an asset freeze on those found guilty of fomenting violence in Darfur and demanded that the government of Sudan stop sending aircraft into the region. And in resolution 1593, signed March 31, the council agreed to refer cases from Darfur to the ICC. The Bush administration had surrendered reluctantly, having failed to convince anyone of the merits of an ad hoc tribunal. According to Nicholas Burns, who had just taken office as the under-secretary of state for political affairs, "We felt that if the ICC is the only institution that can be the court for war crimes, should the U.S. veto a resolution that would have prevented the international body from adjudicating war crimes?" Nonetheless, Washington had insisted on language exempting American citizens from the jurisdiction of the court for any acts arising out of the mission in Sudan, and sparing itself the costs of the operation. This had consumed weeks of debate. Of the urgent need to supplement or replace the AU force, nothing was said.

I often asked people, as a threshold question, whether any of the reforms contemplated in the report of the high-level panel would prevent another fiasco like Darfur. When I posed this to Abiodun Williams, who worked for Bob Orr in the Office of Strategic Planning, he put the matter plainly: "People ask if the lesson of Rwanda has been learned. The answer is no." So long as nations did not consider even genocide reason enough to shed the blood of their soldiers, no guidelines on the use of force, no abstract commitment to "the responsibility to protect," would make a real difference.

But the UN policy officials who were working to adapt the panel's report into a document issued under the name of the secretary-general felt that reform could do a great deal to rescue the institution from the doldrums into which it had sunk. "Right now," said Thant Myint-U, head of the small policy planning staff of the Department of Political Affairs, "we're focused on places like Iraq and Palestine, which are dead ends for the UN. What about bio-security? What if the Ebola virus is approaching a refugee camp with a million people? We have no way of getting troops there to remove the people in the camps." This might be the kind of task to which the UN was peculiarly suited. "We want to lift the secretary-general and the whole institution out of the little box that we've gotten stuck in," as Thant put it.

The most energetic and self-critical people in the UN understood that the ultimate object of reform had to be the institutional culture itself. A decade earlier Thant, a Burmese with a Ph.D. in history, had gotten himself kicked out of his job as spokesman for the peacekeeping force in Bosnia when he refused to parrot the company line that the UN was doing all it could given the constraints of the mandate. Now he took the view that none of the reforms would matter unless the member states agreed to give the secretary-general the freedom to hire and fire, to move officials as needed, and to deploy resources according to need. People who had spent time inside the glass box of the UN understood something that few outsiders did: if you deprive an institution of real authority, you will remove the incentive to develop real professionalism.

Stephen Stedman, the panel's chief of staff, began working directly with the thirty-eighth floor once he had finished writing the report. The experience proved as revelatory for him as it had for Malloch Brown. "If a crisis erupts," he said, "nobody will start the day knowing how a decision will be reached. It's all ad hoc. A meeting will be called but without an agenda. They *never* have an agenda. Decisions aren't really taken, or someone is out to undermine them. No one is really confident that their voice will be heard." People like Stedman or Thant or Williams cared very much about the structural changes the secretary-general would propose in peacekeeping, in nonproliferation, in the enforcement of human rights violations, and in other areas. But they also recognized that the UN would never regain its lost legitimacy unless the Secretariat, its operational arm, could be seen as an effective and modern organization—which it plainly wasn't.

This is what reform looked like from the inside. From the outside, though, it was something else altogether. In the world's major capitals, there was very little talk of the Peacebuilding Commission or the Human Rights Council or the responsibility to protect, and none at all of the pathologies of UN culture. There was, in fact, one subject and one subject only: Security Council "reform." Germany, Japan, India, and Brazil, widely accepted as the likeliest beneficiaries of expanding the council, banded together to advance their collective case. The Gang of Four, as they quickly came to be called, began to line up support in capitals across the globe. Among the current permanent members of the Security Council, only France and the U.K. endorsed the four-nation package. Russia backed the candidacy of India; China, the self-appointed voice of the developing world among the P5, made vague gestures of support to India and Brazil, but vowed to block Japanese aspirations, and then encouraged a fiercely nationalistic campaign of opposition to its Asian neighbor and rival; and the United States said as little as possible, while quietly talking up Japan. Other rivals of the aspirants, like Italy and Spain, championed a plan that would create a new class of longer-term members, but no new permanent ones. And the Gang of Four itself was split, with India's foreign minister, Natwar Singh, insisting that his country would never accept a permanent seat without a veto, a position the others had long since given up as hopelessly quixotic.

Annan met regularly with both the Gang of Four and the "Coffee Club," the innocuous-sounding name for the advocates of the three-tier alternative. He always remained scrupulously neutral, ignoring fervent pleas for support from each. Both sides insisted that they enjoyed overwhelming support from the members; an ambassador from one of the aspirants for permanent membership earnestly informed Annan that in the current General Assembly session, 166 of the members had spoken in favor of council reform, with 120 endorsing some version of the two-tier plan. The Gang of Four wanted to separate out council expansion from the rest of the reform package in order to hold a General Assembly vote within the next few months, rather than in September. Even now, at this early stage, the issue had provoked appalling displays of pettiness and rancor, not only between rivals like China and Japan but between allies like Germany and Italy. A vote could produce a donnybrook that would doom the rest of the reform package—an outcome that did not seem to perturb the four aspirants. Annan told them that the Coffee Club had issued just such a threat. "Are you talking to them," he asked, "or are they talking to you, or are you passing like two ships in the night?"

"We're talking to them individually," said one of the ambassadors, "not as a group. Many are sympathetic to our position."

"They have to have the sense that this issue has been discussed exhaustively," Annan rejoined. Exhaustive discussion was a good way to kill an issue, but also to draw its poison.

"This point is well taken," said the ambassador. But the two ships would continue passing in the night.

Annan and his aides feared above all the "train wreck" scenario, in which the entire reform program stalled behind the shattered remains of Security Council reform. But even this assumed a readiness, not much in evidence, to move ahead on other difficult issues. At a meeting in early February, Steve Stedman reported that both the Americans and the French opposed any sort of guidelines on the use of force. This was precisely the issue that had first presented the institution with its "fork in the road," for the United States had gone to war in Iraq according to a doctrine of preemptive warfare enshrined in its own national security strategy but unacceptable by the terms of the Charter. Absent guidelines of some sort, every state would be free to make a similar choice. And yet the proposal had been dead on arrival. The Americans would accept no such constraint. And the French, Stedman explained, had said, "Why should we have to explain why we're taking action according to some checklist?" Mark Malloch Brown, who instinctively opposed anything that sounded like procedural pettifogging, said, "They have a point." Why should "technicalities" be permitted to block what might be necessary action?

Now Bob Orr, always acutely aware of what the White House market would bear, spoke up. "It really depends on how you want to handle the U.S. in this whole exercise," he said. "Here you've stepped over a screaming red line, and they will fight this one." The staff had presented Annan with two options, one that stipulated that in any debate over the use of force the Security Council "should address five guidelines," and a watered-down one that stated that the council "can enrich its debate by referring to" the guidelines. After Orr had finished speaking, Annan said, "We have told everyone to give us bold proposals, and they rose to the challenge. Here I'm the one that gave them that challenge, and I'm pulling back." What's more, his report would inevitably be judged against the language of the high-level panel; he couldn't be seen as buckling before American opposition. The choice between a clear statement of principle and a politically attuned compromise came up on issue after issue. In each case, Annan chose the tougher option.

But it wasn't just the Americans. The high-level panel had proposed that member states condemn terrorism in unambiguous terms, with no exception for "people under foreign occupation"—the formulation perpetually advanced by the Palestinians and their allies. Stedman reported that Middle Eastern states remained adamant on the subject, even though Amr Moussa, head of the Arab League, had served on the panel and endorsed the report. "You have to stick closely to this definition," said Malloch Brown. "It goes to the heart of what you've been as secretary-general." Annan agreed. He was scheduled to talk about terrorism in Spain the following month. "I cannot go to Madrid and not say anything," he said.

On a less magisterial note, Orr reported that it might prove difficult to eliminate the Military Staff Committee, one of the very few organs of the UN that the panel had proposed to abolish. Of all the hollowed-out vestiges at the periphery of the institution, none was quite so vestigial as this body, which had been designed to coordinate military planning among the P5 and had ceased to function with the onset of the Cold War, in 1947. Ever since then, the military attachés of the five had gathered once a month, as required, declared the meeting opened, and then instantly adjourned, allegedly to reconvene over a drink at the Delegates' Lounge. "The Russians want to protect the Military Staff Committee," Orr said. "Their attitude is 'It works perfectly well.'" The meeting ended, for once, with Annan issuing explicit instructions—this option for this subject, that for that. In almost every case, including on issues sensitive to Washington, Annan made the bolder choice.

If the United States was a problem, then so were Russia, China, and the Middle East. But so was the entire Third World bloc. They thought of the high-level panel report, for all that it called for increases in aid, debt relief, and the like, as the reform document of the North. The South had a report of its own: "Investing in Development: A Practical Plan to Achieve the Millennium Development Goals." This was the "Millennium Plus Five" document produced by a team of economists working under Jeffrey Sachs. The report concluded that while "the world has made significant progress in achieving many of the goals," some areas, above all sub-Saharan Africa, were actually retrogressing, and some goals, such as gender equality, seemed little closer than they had five years earlier.

The authors of "Investing in Development" noted that poor nations had to overcome the habits of arbitrary rule and to focus their own resources on proven antipoverty strategies. But the chief cause of failure, they argued, was not poor choices but inherent disadvantages: low rainfall, poor soil, high incidence of infectious disease, lack of access to efficient transport, and, crowning everything, soaring incidence of HIV/AIDS. The "poverty trap," as Sachs called it, prevented nations from mustering the internal resources needed for sustained development. The only way out was "to raise the economy's capital stock to the point where the downward spiral ends and self-sustaining economic growth takes over." And that capital stock would have to come from Western nations, the World Bank and IMF, and private investment. In short, most of the Millennium Development Goals would not be reached absent a major commitment of funds, as well as debt relief and more favorable terms of trade. "Investing in Development" had been scheduled to appear in March 2005, but was hustled to completion in January so as not to be overshadowed by the more celebrated report on threats to peace and security.

"In Larger Freedom," the secretary-general's version of the high-level panel report, was released on March 21. The expression came from the Charter and reflected the idea that economic and political freedoms were intimately bound up with each other. But it was also, unmistakably, a nod to President Bush, who in the aftermath of 9/11 had taken to describing the spread of freedom as America's transcendent mission in the world. Those of Annan's aides who couldn't abide the perpetual accommodation to Washington's impossible demands loathed the title. Kieran Prendergast told me that G77 countries had taken the phrase to mean that the report would be an American product; he himself saw it as yet another symptom of the America-first mentality of the Malloch Brown era. Others, especially Orr and Malloch Brown, took the view that this was a small price to pay for engaging Washington; anyway, Kofi Annan had been talking about the spread of freedom long before George Bush had.

The preamble to the document advanced Annan's claim that development, security, and human rights—the UN's three great areas of activity—had become indissoluble: "Even if he can vote to choose his rulers, a young man with AIDS who cannot read or write and lives on the brink of starvation is not truly free. Equally, even if she earns enough to live, a woman who lives in the shadow of daily violence and has no say in how her country is run is not truly free." In fact, the report's opening section focused on development and largely incorporated the language and recommendations of "Investing in Development." Recipient nations would draw up detailed long-term plans to achieve the Millennium Development Goals, while donor nations would agree to provide "a sufficient increase in aid, of sufficient quality and arriving with sufficient speed to enable them to achieve" the goals. "In Larger Freedom" called for the immediate funding of what Sachs called "quick wins"—the distribution of antimalarial bed nets, the elimination of school fees, the incorporation of women into decision-making processes (a not-so-quick win)—as well as a major increase in funding to stop the spread of AIDS. Global warming and desertification were not forgotten.

In matters of collective security, Annan's report was largely faithful to the panel's recommendation, but with important changes in tone and nuance dictated by political consideration. The panel report blamed "lacklustre disarmament by the nuclear-weapon States" for weakening the entire regime of nuclear nonproliferation—an obvious jab at the Bush administration, which had restarted research on tactical nuclear weapons. The Annan report praised the United States and Russia for dismantling thousands of warheads, but said that nuclear-weapon states "must do more" to ensure irreversible disarmament. Both reports called for the enforcement and entry into force of various pacts governing nuclear, chemical, and biological weapons. But while the panel report called for granting control over the export of nuclear fuel for civilian uses to the UN's International Atomic Energy Agency—a proposal that was anathema to the United States as well as other current suppliers of nuclear material—the Annan report described such an arrangement as "one option." Here was a screaming red line that was better not crossed.

"In Larger Freedom" courted criticism from the G77 bloc by recommending a straightforward prohibition of terrorism, with no exceptions for "wars of national liberation." The report was similarly unwavering on humanitarian intervention, of which Annan (or rather, Orr and his fellow scribes) wrote, "While I am well aware of the sensitivities involved in this issue . . . I believe that we must embrace the responsibility to protect, and, when necessary, we' must act on it." On the core issue of the legitimate use of force, Annan observed pointedly that "the task is not to find alternatives to the Security Council but to make it work better." He proposed that the council adopt a resolution stipulating that in deciding whether or not to authorize the use of force, it would be "guided" by such criteria as the seriousness of the threat, the likelihood of success, and the availability of nonlethal alternatives. He had, in the end, gone with the more palatable formulation. The criteria themselves were unexceptionable; it was the very idea of stipulating criteria that the United States and France viewed as constraining, and that many G77 countries viewed, contrariwise, as a license to intervene.

On human rights, the third of the UN's three pillars, the report proposed that the Office of the High Commissioner for Human Rights receive a major increase in funding and importance, with the commissioner working directly with the Security Council to implement the relevant provisions of council resolutions. More radically, the secretary-general proposed the abolition of the Human Rights Commission, a toothless body on which the worst abusers typically sought and gained a seat in order to block any form of censure; for many American conservatives, the commission ended all discussion about the UN's moral position. The panel had proposed to spoil the spoilers by making membership universal; Annan took the opposite approach, proposing a smaller body whose members would be elected by a two-thirds vote of the General Assembly, rather than the current system, whereby regional groupings put up whatever members were most eager to sit. The proposal was widely praised by human rights organizations that had despaired of the endless charade of the commission, and quietly opposed by many Third World countries.

On peacekeeping, the report sought to remedy the recurring problem of slow response to urgent situations through the establishment by troop-contributing countries of "strategic reserves" of soldiers available for swift deployment. Annan also adopted the panel's proposal for a

Peacebuilding Commission, a body designed to address the tendency
of peace agreements to fray and then collapse, returning countries to
violence and anarchy and wasting the hundreds of millions of dollars
poured in by the international community. The commission would
bring together all of the key international actors in any given conflict
situation, including troop contributors, donors, financial organizations,
neighboring countries, regional organizations, and key Security Council
members as well as national authorities to plan and coordinate post-
conflict strategy.

Annan finessed the impossible question of Security Council reform
by offering two alternatives, as the panel had. Model A proposed six
new permanent seats (including two, as yet undesignated, for Africa),
and three additional two-year seats. Model B would establish eight
seats in a new "four-year renewable" category, as well as one new two-
year seat. In a different universe, neither model would have been as
consequential as the report's proposal that decision-making authority,
whether in regard to peacekeeping, dues payments, or development assistance, be vested only in states that "contribute most to the United
Nations financially, militarily and diplomatically." In the unseemly
scramble for position, however, the clause was altogether ignored.

And finally, Annan made the case for reform of the Secretariat and
of his own position. "The secretary general and his or her managers,"
he wrote, "must be given the discretion, the means, the authority and
the expert assistance that they need to manage an organization which is
expected to meet fast-changing operational needs in many different
parts of the world." He recommended a review of all mandates more
than five years old and a "sunset law" for an organization that never
eliminated anything—not even the Military Staff Committee. He
asked for the authority to arrange a onetime staff buyout to dispose of
the vast stacks of deadwood, and to conduct a "comprehensive review"
of activities that would allow him to move staff to the places they were
actually needed.

"In Larger Freedom" was without question the most sweeping program of reform ever proposed by the UN itself. More important, the
entire process, including the deliberations of the high-level panel, had
been shaped by sustained and serious thought, consensus seeking
among a very heterogeneous group, and a great many sorties along the

skirmish line of the possible. It was, taken all in all, a very impressive document, a testament to Annan's commitment to change and to the analytical skills of his staff, above all of Steve Stedman and of Bob Orr, the document's actual draftsman. It was generally well received on the world's editorial pages and in the major capitals. Orr had been regularly briefing officials in the State Department and the National Security Council. Their general position, he said, had been, "Give us a warning if there's something we're really not going to like." Orr's typical response had been "There are some things you're not going to like, but there's nothing gratuitous." And when they saw the final product, Orr said, they had agreed.

In its second term, the Bush administration had begun speaking in a distinctly different tone of voice, even if the message was generally a familiar one. Colin Powell had championed the virtues of pragmatism and diplomacy, but had lost almost every important battle he had fought. Condoleezza Rice, who was assumed to share Powell's secular if unsentimental outlook, had been widely criticized in foreign-policy circles for essentially taking the side of Cheney and Rumsfeld once it became clear that the president was inclined that way, rather than playing the role of honest broker. But Rice was no longer in the White House, at the president's side, and she began immediately to move toward Powell's territory. The president's great trust in her meant that she could defend her turf far more effectively than Powell had been able to do.

In her confirmation hearings Rice pointedly announced, "This is the time for diplomacy." And she filled the top ranks of the foreign policy apparatus, both in the State Department and at the National Security Council, with professionals and diplomats rather than true believers. Nicholas Burns, the new under-secretary for political affairs, had served as a spokesman in the Clinton State Department. "We had a very unusual first term," Burns said. "We had fought two wars in four years. We had to make a special effort to be diplomatically active in 2005 so that we could make sure the major multilateral institutions that are really important to international stability were strong, and that there was American leadership. Her instructions to me were to make a major effort to promote reform at the UN."

But did those dispassionate professionals really speak for the administration? It was hard to know. The administration had dithered for months over the naming of a new UN ambassador to replace John Danforth, who had retired in January. President Bush was widely known to be considering giving the post to John Bolton, the assistant secretary of state for arms control. Bolton was a longtime champion of American unilateralism, a contemptuous critic of the UN, and a graceless and abrasive figure with a gift for making enemies. To appoint Bolton was, in effect, to endorse his well-known views. The thought so sickened Annan that during a conversation in late November 2004 on the way back from Africa, when he was at his lowest ebb, he told me, as if it were the final insult, "And you see who they've nominated as ambassador!" Annan had apparently heard a groundless rumor, and believed it—because it was so fittingly awful.

But the report was only premature. In late January, when I was at a symposium on reform, the news suddenly flew around the room: "Bolton's been nominated!" It felt like the kind of terrifying report that might whip through a bivouac of jittery soldiers: "The tanks have just pulled up on the far side of the bridge!" The UN haters had their man in Turtle Bay.

CHAPTER NINETEEN

Oil-for-Food: The Nightmare

O N THE ELEVATOR RIDE BACK UP TO THE THIRTY-EIGHTH floor after Kofi Annan had presented "In Larger Freedom" to the UN press, Shashi Tharoor made a point of turning to his boss to tell him what a fabulous job he had just done. Tharoor had never before felt that he needed to buck up the secretary-general, whom he was inclined to view as a man of deep and unshakable poise—"a yogi." Now, however, he was desperately hoping that Annan's siege of ill fortune had bottomed out, and that Annan could go back to the job of repairing the institution and, not incidentally, his own legacy. The very next day, March 22, the press reported that the UN had been paying the sizable legal fees run up by Benon Sevan, and had continued to do so until Mark Malloch Brown had ended the arrangement three weeks after the Volcker committee had accused him of accepting payoffs from an oil broker. The day after *that*, the *Financial Times*, which had conducted an extensive investigation along with the Italian news program *Il Sole 24 Ore*, revealed that Cotecna, the company that had employed Kojo Annan, had paid almost twice as much as previously believed as a result of the non-compete agreement and that executives of the company had met with Kofi Annan on three occasions. Annan's legacy was suddenly a distant dream; it was his survival that was once again at issue.

The thick cloud of dread that had settled over the upper floors of the Secretariat Building late the previous year had never fully lifted. It had, in fact, been growing notably heavier as the Volcker committee prepared to publish its second interim report, at the end of March. The report would assess Kojo's role, and the extent to which he had embroiled his father in the business affairs of a UN contractor. Everyone on the UN's upper floors understood perfectly well that if Volcker found that Annan had intervened in any way in the process of selecting the firm that employed his son, or that Annan had not been forthcoming about his role, the secretary-general would have to step down. It was unthinkable, but, of course, everyone thought it, and feared it.

Thanks to the Sevan story and the *FT* investigation, the hammer had dropped even before Annan's aides had braced themselves. Malloch Brown himself appeared at the spokesman's daily press briefing in hopes—futile, as it turned out—of containing the damage. He pointed out that Annan's meetings with the Cotecna executives had been disclosed to Volcker's staff and insisted, to great skepticism, that none had anything to do with the company's bid for Oil-for-Food business. Malloch Brown defended the institution with his characteristic mix of sportive zest, mockery, high principle, and ingenious, if perhaps too ingenious, logic-chopping. He had a gift for meeting reporters halfway by ascribing to incompetence what they wished to characterize as duplicity. But the press corps, which was accustomed to treating the secretary-general and his representatives with quite a bit of deference, was no longer willing to believe what it was told. Annan was plainly losing one of his most important constituencies, the medium that shaped perceptions of the institution all over the world. At the end of this long and bruising encounter, a reporter asked if the allegations had done irreparable damage to the secretary-general and his hopes for reform. "You will all be the judge," said Malloch Brown, by now observably weary. "It does make me realize that this story is firmly manacled to our ankles and it's hard to escape from, and that there are many who will continue to make sure we don't escape from it."

A week later the awful clank of those manacles drowned out every other sound emanating from the institution. The second interim report was published on March 29. In the course of discussions with Volcker and his staff over the previous week, Annan's aides had learned, to their immense relief, that the report would clear the secretary-general of serious wrongdoing in regard to Kojo. The committee concluded that "there is no evidence that the selection of Cotecna in 1998 was subject to any affirmative or improper influence of the Secretary-General in the bidding or selection process" and that the evidence that Annan even knew of Cotecna's bid was "not reasonably sufficient." The report did find that the cursory internal investigation that Annan had ordered after a news story revealed that Kojo had been working for Cotecna was "inadequate," but even this was scarcely a harsh rebuke.

Volcker had, in fact, agonized over the language in which the report would couch Annan's actions. He was fond of Annan, he was a committed internationalist, and he saw his role as saving the UN from itself, as well as from the wolves howling for blood. The day before the report was published, I went to see the chief investigator, Reid Morden, and Volcker, massively tall, stooped, lugubrious, lumbered into the committee's little conference room like a giant Eeyore. Morden had just finished saying that while he faulted Annan for failing to hear any "alarm bells" when he had learned that Kojo worked at the firm that had just won a major Oil-for-Food contract, he viewed the failure as "an all-too-human conflict of his role as SG and that of a father." I asked Volcker how he would characterize Annan's oversight, and this circumspect old banker said, in his peculiar basso mumble, "I turn it over and over in my mind. What's the right word? 'Terrible'? 'Awful'? 'Minor misdemeanor'? I guess it's someplace between those two extremes. I was thinking about the word 'dereliction.'" But that was too harsh. And in the end he had dispensed with the adjectives altogether, choosing to let the facts speak for themselves—which, in such intensely political cases, they never can.

Volcker handed the report to Annan at 9:00 a.m. on the twenty-ninth; Malloch Brown, Bob Orr, Edward Mortimer, and John Ruggie, who had come down from Harvard to help with the damage control, adjourned to a small conference room to pore over it. Only then did they realize that the meaning of the report was not in its bottom line—"Annan exonerated"—but in its accumulation of ugly detail, most of it involving Kojo. The son had plainly made a living by exploiting his connection with the father. He had billed Cotecna for his work cultivating connections at the nonaligned summit and the UN General Assembly meeting in the summer and fall of 1998. He had told Iraq's ambassador to Nigeria that he and a Lebanese colleague wanted to do business through the Oil-for-Food Programme and admitted that he had not told his father of his plans. When Annan called his son in January 1999 after learning of his connection with Cotecna, Kojo swore that he had left the company. In fact, Cotecna continued to reimburse Kojo for expenses in addition to the monthly retainer, but began funneling the money through various intermediaries. Worst of all, Kojo had refused to cooperate with the investigators.

Other details touched more closely on Annan and his administration. Kojo had arranged a lunch at which the Lebanese partner had, or so he claimed, told the secretary-general that he and Kojo planned to do work under the Oil-for-Food Programme—a claim that Annan denied. Annan himself had at first told investigators that he had not met with Cotecna executives and only recalled the meetings later, though the committee found no evidence to contradict his assertion that neither Oil-for-Food nor Cotecna's business plans came up during any of the conversations. Michael Wilson, an old family friend who was an executive at Cotecna and had been instrumental in hiring Kojo, initially stated that he had talked to Annan in mid-November or so of 1998 and had spoken of Cotecna's hopes to win the procurement contract. Fifteen or twenty minutes later, Wilson had called investigators back to say that he realized that the discussion had in fact taken place in early 1999, after Cotecna had won the contract. Several months after the second Volcker report was published, investigators discovered a memo in which Wilson described talking about Cotecna to "the S.G. and his entourage" in November 1998 and being told that the company "could count on their support." Wilson himself said that no such discussion had taken place; nor was there any record that it had.

Most bizarre of all, the committee discovered that in April 2004, the day after the Security Council authorized the creation of an inquiry into Oil-for-Food, Iqbal Riza had approved a request to shred backup files. Ten days earlier Riza himself had instructed agency heads to preserve files relating to the program. Riza told investigators that it had never occurred to him that his "chron" files, which were routinely shredded for space reasons, had anything to do with the inquiry. The report did not dispute his motives, but said that he had "acted imprudently," which seemed like a fairly modest way of putting it.

Volcker presented the report to the press at eleven o'clock that morning. That afternoon Annan made an appearance in room 226, the press briefing room. He still believed, as, to varying degrees, did the people around him, that the report left him in the clear. In a prepared statement, he asserted that his "exoneration . . . obviously comes as a great relief." He said that he accepted the criticism on the 1999 inquiry, but then added that "the steps I took were fully consistent with UN regulations"—which called into question what he meant by "accept." He then added, in lines that had been excruciatingly crafted by his staff, "I love my son and I have always expected the highest standards from him. I am deeply saddened by the evidence to the contrary that has emerged, and particularly by the fact that my son has failed to cooperate fully with the inquiry." When Annan was asked what Kojo had said when he had implored him to cooperate, he said, "He is reconsi— I have asked him to reconsider. He couldn't—he didn't give me an answer immediately by the phone, on the phone." His agony was palpable. Here was a moment of public humiliation at which only Annan's most pitiless enemies could have rejoiced.

Then came an odd moment. A reporter asked, "Do you feel it's time, for the good of the organization, to step down?" And Annan said, "Hell, no." Not "*Hell*, no!"—just the words themselves, uninflected, unemphatic, almost disembodied. Annan had obviously listened to all the people who were urging him to show the world that he was mad, that he cared. But the effect was the exact opposite of what he had intended. It was as if he had put on a ten-gallon hat and the brim had fallen over his eyes. And then, after three questions, he turned the press conference over to Malloch Brown, as if he had taken all the pasting he could bear. The chief of staff explained that having "exposed himself to many hours of cross-examination" by the Volcker panel, Annan "does not think it necessary to re-subject himself to a further trial in room 226." This was like much that Malloch Brown said to the press, true enough to pass muster but too incomplete to be called the truth. Malloch Brown later said to me, "We also felt that if he had to go out there and answer questions about tiny details from the past, with only two hours of preparation, it would be just an impossible assignment."

"But that's exactly what *you* did," I pointed out.

"Yes, well, we did also feel that he was brittle. Maybe we were unduly protective." Or maybe they were right to fear that Annan would crumble before the kind of press barrage that until now his prestige, and the deference of the beat reporters, had shielded him from. Malloch Brown now tried to persuade the press of what he and the others had believed, at least until that morning: that "the ground had shifted" from "There was corruption in this by the secretary-general" to "Was the management effective enough?" He never had a chance. The press seemed to be suffering from a collective case of buyer's remorse: embarrassed at having been too willing in the past to take the institution at its word, now they would assume the worst. According to the instantly hardening conventional wisdom, Volcker was unwilling to go where the evidence led him. "There's a lot of skepticism over the findings of what Volcker put out today," one reporter said. "There's a context of secret payments, meetings, stunted internal investigation. How would the UN . . . publicly, declaratively, and definitively say that the secretary-general was not involved in what he was alleged to be involved with in a manner beyond simply saying that the Volcker committee has cleared him?" There was, of course, no answer to this question.

This time all five permanent members immediately rallied to Annan's defense. Even the White House was supportive, thanks both to the successful elections in Iraq and to the new moderate tone of the second term. But the report was a public relations disaster. Oil-for-Food had begun as a uniquely American obsession, but by now the revelations were damaging Annan and the UN all over the world. In a comment that was widely reprinted, Mark Pieth, one of the chief investigators, said, "We did not exonerate Kofi Annan. A certain mea culpa would have been appropriate." Conservative editorial pages called for Annan to step down, but even the more sympathetic described him as "wounded," "weak," or "naive." And just to make matters yet worse, that same day an internal review of the UN's electoral division, one of the most highly regarded units of the Secretariat, had been released; the review found that the group's head, Carina Perelli, had fostered an "abusive" environment full of sexual innuendo, crude jokes, harassment, and unprofessional behavior. The inference seemed clear: now that we've started turning over rocks at the UN, we're going to find nothing but worms.

When I spoke to Annan in mid-April, I found that he did not in fact feel that a mea culpa was in order. He believed, as he had implied in the press conference, that he had followed proper procedure. But the Volcker panel had to fault him for *something*. Annan thought the whole thing was trumped up: "Everyone here said, 'It's the Murdoch syndrome.' " He meant that pressure from right-wing outlets like Fox News had forced Volcker to look tough. "They're exposed to public scrutiny, and they need to find things."

But Annan's self-assurance vanished when I asked about Kojo's refusal to continue meeting with investigators. "I told him that I have insisted that the UN staff cooperate, and I myself am cooperating. And I cannot apply different standards to my son. He said his lawyers told him they are fishing, and they have given them all the documents they need, and on advice of his lawyer he shouldn't do anything further." Annan and his attorney, Gregory Craig, had held a conference call with Kojo and Kojo's lawyer. "We asked them to reconsider and go back and indicate that they will cooperate, but they wouldn't do it." Now Annan, who showed so little emotion, looked genuinely crestfallen. "It caused me lots of grief," he said. "For a father, you can imagine, and for a secretary-general." When I asked Annan whether he felt that he and his first wife had somehow failed in Kojo's upbringing, he said, "I don't know if it's mistakes we made, or the environment in Lagos," where Kojo had lived much of his life. The feckless child of a powerful, distracted man is, of course, a staple of life, literature, and TV movies, and one could hardly blame the father for the grown-up son's transgressions.

What emerged, rather, from this latest full-body scan was the striking blitheness of both the secretary-general and his then chief of staff. Annan had been perfectly content with the perfunctory review of Kojo's activities that he had received. He had followed the traditional process and thus considered his behavior irreproachable, even though the process had failed to get at the truth. He knew that he was blameless and assumed that Kojo must be, too. Riza had treated the review as a minor nuisance. And it had never occurred to him that shredding files at the outset of a vast investigation that was bound to include his own activities would look bad. Riza did not quite acknowledge the category "look bad," because it required that one take seriously the views of outside constituencies—the press, American politicians—who did not understand the institution or have its best interests at heart. Riza treated

these noisy disputants with impeccable politesse even as he regarded
them with lordly indifference and perhaps a little fear. Like Annan, he
knew that he was a selfless servant of a noble institution, and that was
enough. Or, rather, it had been enough until just the other day. And
now, quite suddenly, it wasn't. And that was why Riza was gone and Annan, for all that he was a more worldly figure than his old vizier, was a
wounded lame duck.

By the spring of 2005, it had come to seem more and more that there
were two UNs—the traditionalist one, defensive and enfeebled,
headed by Kofi Annan; and the progressive one, unsentimental, results-
oriented, pro-American, headed by Mark Malloch Brown. The people
around Annan, and people throughout the institution, heard Malloch
Brown's blunt criticisms of the UN and smoldered at the implication
that he and his allies had ridden to the rescue of an institution on its
last legs. When I went to see Lamin Sise, Annan's consigliere, hidden
at the back of the warren of offices across the hall from the secretary-
general, I found him uncharacteristically ill-tempered. "The appointment of Mark comes from this feeling that we have a communications
gap," Sise said. "For me, it's hyperbolic. People say we need to sell our
message better. But who are we selling it to? Are we trying to convince
people who disagree with us vehemently because we didn't support
their position on the Iraq war?" Sise viewed the sense of crisis that had
enveloped the institution, the supposed urgency of reform, as a form of
panic induced by fear of Washington, and Malloch Brown as Washington's tribune. It pained him that his friend the secretary-general had to
endure such belittling criticism in the final years of an admirable term
in office. "I get the feeling that it's as if we're going to redo everything,
and for me that's a tacit admission that nothing we were doing was
right before."

It was in just such tones of frustration and resentment that Sise
and Shashi Tharoor and Kieran Prendergast and the other defenders of
the old order spoke to one another. Was this how their years of dedication and hard work, and above all Kofi Annan's era of deep moral engagement and sacrifice, would be recalled? "This is the man who won
the Nobel Prize in 2001," as Tharoor said to me incredulously, "and

now he's in the doghouse? This is ridiculous." He had even reminded Annan himself: "You've got an eight-year record to stand on." Prendergast felt that Annan was coping with his own sense of demoralization by handing all the tough jobs to Malloch Brown. Some of the mid-level staffers I knew seethed with resentment at the *chef de cabinet*'s growing primacy. A sense of usurpation was in the air. Edward Mortimer told me that a number of ambassadors had approached him to ask if it was true, as they had heard, that Malloch Brown was actually American.

When I spoke with Malloch Brown in mid-April, he said that he knew very well how disliked he was. But he felt that he had had to make a zero-sum choice: mollify the insiders by protecting the institution from criticism, or infuriate them by conceding the validity of much of the critique, thus affording the UN the legitimacy to deal with the critics. "I felt if I had to offend somebody," he said, "I would rather offend the internal constituency."

"But they feel you're saying their work is crap."

"Well, the fact is, I do think what a lot of people do here is basically crap. Being in this position, I've discovered how bad things really are. I'll give you one example: There is absolutely no constituency for personnel reform. The countries don't want it, because for them it's a pension system for retired diplomats. The staff union doesn't want it. Senior management doesn't want change." Malloch Brown took the view that if the Oil-for-Food scandal didn't kill the UN, it would make it stronger, for members might now be willing to accept the kind of management changes they had always resisted in the past. As a practical matter, he also understood that internal disaffection was not nearly so great a threat to the UN as the hostility of the U.S. Congress.

Henry Hyde, a doyen of congressional conservatives, had introduced legislation threatening to reduce dues payments to the UN unless the institution implemented dozens of reforms—a kind of Helms-Biden II. As a compromise measure, in December Congress had established a bipartisan task force to examine the UN and publish a report of its own, though how the other 190 members of the organization were to incorporate it into their deliberations was never specified. The task force was chaired by the former Democratic senator George Mitchell and Newt Gingrich, the firebrand ex–House Speaker and conservative Robespierre. Task force members had begun visiting the

UN early in 2005. The more conservative among them seemed most interested in the question "When is Kofi going to step down?," though others raised far more pertinent issues. Malloch Brown understood that a hostile report from the task force would put wind in Hyde's sails, which the UN could ill afford. He instructed staff members to cooperate as far as humanly possible, and in general to draw on their diplomatic skills.

In mid-April, Annan and his chief aides met with the task force. Gingrich was strikingly deferential—a reminder of the force field of charisma and grandeur that hedged the secretary-general. But Gingrich had never been a member of the party's know-nothing wing; he was a product of the Kennedy era, an internationalist with a weakness for visionary schemes. The UN officials present tried to explain the institutional obstacles that so frequently led to failure. Malloch Brown, as usual, was the most blunt. "When the field commander calls New York," he said, "there's an in-house institutional self-censorship that says, 'We can't do anything about it, because we know the council won't support it.' If we don't fix the UN, there will be more Rwandas." One of the members said that the failure to act in Darfur had deeply damaged the UN's credibility. Why couldn't someone tell the AU to step aside and let UN peacekeepers do the job? Annan said, "On Darfur, I share your frustration." He did not tell them that Alpha Konare, president of the AU, had refused to budge on the subject. But he did say, "The AU is the only game in town as far as the Security Council is concerned. Everyone is hiding behind the AU." As the meeting drew to a close, Gingrich suggested that what the UN really needed was a "comprehensive rethinking" and volunteered himself for such a venture. No one was so foolish as to point out that the reform document was intended to do just that.

At a press conference afterward, Gingrich was effusive. "We could not have asked for more candid, more open private discussions or a more serious commitment to getting the UN to work better," he said. When he and Mitchell were asked if they felt that Annan should step down, the Democrat cautiously opined that he had seen "no basis" for such a move. Gingrich then grabbed the microphone to add, "We've been very pleased with the level of openness we've had all day, the level of candor, and the very serious intention to develop real reform." Many people in the UN so deeply resented the fact that a conservative American ex-congressman could exercise real sway over the institution that they did not recognize what a crucial ally they had just won. Malloch Brown, however, understood that Gingrich's gratitude was pure gold, and he quite rightly gave himself credit for having helped tame the dragon.

More important, relations with the Bush administration were better than they had been since before the run-up to the war in Iraq. "The administration has been embracing the SG so fully that it's almost embarrassing," the unsinkably optimistic Bob Orr reported in early April. "They have so little credibility on all the issues they're trying to make forward motion on that the only way they can make any progress is through Kofi Annan, and they know that." Rice had been talking to Annan regularly about Iraq, Sudan, and other issues. Bush had called three times in recent weeks. When Annan had issued "In Larger Freedom," Bush had called to congratulate him and to say, Orr recalled, "There must be some things in here that we'll have to look at, but overall, this is a very serious package." You could almost forget, at such a moment, that this same president had nominated John Bolton to be the new UN ambassador.

Orr felt that after months of distraction, the administration was finally focusing on reform. Rice plainly took the issue seriously. She regularly lobbied the diplomatic community in Washington on the key elements of the package. She had appointed as special envoy for UN reform Shirin Tahir-Kheli, a former NSC official of Indian (and Pakistani) background who had spent years working with the UN and fit comfortably in its culture. Tahir-Kheli had delivered a speech before the General Assembly laying out U.S. areas of interest in the reform package. The White House strongly supported the Human Rights Council, the Peacebuilding Commission, a terrorism convention, and a proposed fund to promote democracy. It did not want to see any reference to bodies or treaties it opposed, like the ICC or the Kyoto Protocol; would show very little give on nonproliferation issues and use-of-force guidelines; and would not reiterate the pledge it had made in Monterrey to move toward giving 0.7 percent of GNP for development assistance, though the issue seemed susceptible to fudging. Washington supported Japan's candidacy for the Security Council, knowing full well that no one country—especially one chosen by the White House—could be admitted. Officials were quietly hoping that the Chinese would block the whole thing, thus saving the White House the diplomatic discomfort of doing so.

The more that countries began to focus on reform, the clearer it became that the process would be driven by calculations of national self-interest, not by the sense of the collective good that reigned in and around the thirty-eighth floor. In early April, I attended a two-day symposium on reform that brought diplomats from key states, current and former UN officials, scholars, and a few journalists to an extremely charming chalet, now a resort hotel, outside of Toronto. At the first session, several experts explained cogently why expanding the Security Council was actually a bad idea. Edward Luck, historian of the UN and skeptic of reform, noted that in the final meeting of the League of Nations, in 1946, delegates looked hopefully to the UN precisely because, unlike the League, it made no pretense of democracy or representativeness, for U.S. power was embedded at its core. Security Council "reform," he said, "goes in the opposite direction." Expansion would be inversely correlated with efficiency. David Malone, a Canadian diplomat and one of the UN's shrewdest and most incisive critics, argued that the real problem with the Security Council was a growing "flight from responsibility" that would only deepen with the addition of new members.

I noticed that three members of the Gang of Four were seated together at one end of the long table, as if to acknowledge that they constituted a bloc. (Brazil was absent.) And now they joined the battle, though without bothering to refute the points Luck and Malone had made. For them, Security Council reform was a matter of national prestige, though of course they couldn't say that. Gunter Pleuger, the German ambassador, said that the growing power of the council made it even more imperative that its membership be diversified. Kenzo Oshima of Japan noted that 160 of the 191 members of the assembly had spoken up in favor of Security Council reform. Ambassador Nirupam Sen of India opened his remarks with something abstruse about dialectical thinking, and then came to the point: "The question I'm most likely to be asked is 'Why is the UN so completely under the sway of the U.S.?'" People all over the world were growing alienated from the UN; representativeness was, in fact, the only way to ensure effectiveness. Had South Africa been a permanent member of the council in 1992, perhaps the Somali warlords would have behaved themselves. What's more, the UN's true source of legitimacy was not the elite council but the universal General Assembly. "If you strengthen the General Assembly," said Ambassador Sen, "you will strengthen the Security Council. This is where dialectics is a better way of looking at it."

At the end of the conference, I shared a car to the airport with an Egyptian and a Saudi diplomat, a pair of hale and friendly fellows. Talk turned to the conference, and both explained to me that reform was, of course, impossible so long as the United States behaved with contempt for the rules that governed others. I asked how they felt about the resolution that the Security Council had just passed demanding that Syria cease its meddling in the affairs of Lebanon. The Saudi diplomat said that in fact he violently objected to the resolution as an infringement of Syrian sovereignty. And then, when we talked about terrorism, the conversation grew quite heated, for the Saudi affirmed that since Israeli civilians were complicit in the oppressive policies of the state, killing them could not possibly constitute an act of terrorism. And then our limo reached the airport, and both men said that they hoped I hadn't taken offense at their passionately expressed convictions. None taken, I said. We agreed that politics was terribly divisive, and we parted with smiles and handshakes and hopes for future meetings.

But the biggest problem, in the spring of 2005, was not hostility but apathy. Very few members seemed to believe, or perhaps care, that the UN had reached a "fork in the road." At a meeting in mid-April, Annan said that he had just met with a group of African ambassadors and discovered that few even knew what was in the report. The Asians, he said, were "subdued." Louise Fréchette described the overall mood as "lethargic." No one was taking ownership of the reform agenda. When Annan met later that day with a group of former heads of state and foreign ministers whom he had appointed as his lobbying team, he complained that non-Western countries seemed interested only in economic development. What about human rights? "When we fought the colonialists," he said, "we shouted about these rights. Now that we're masters of our own fate, you don't hear so much about it." (This was, of course, a figure of speech; Annan *hadn't* fought the colonialists.) He had begun to worry that time was running short. Since August was, by immemorial tradition, the diplomatic *grande vacance*, the re-form package would have to be substantially finished by mid-July in order to be sure that it would be ready when the heads of state arrived in mid-September. And the spoilers, he knew, would try to stall the process until it was too late.

The Oil-for-Food scandal, meanwhile, kept getting in the way of high-minded debate. Two weeks after the second Volcker report, the federal prosecutor in Manhattan indicted Tongsun Park for acting as an unreg-istered lobbyist for the government of Iraq. Here was a name from the distant past: the Korean fixer who in the mid-1970s had allegedly bribed congressmen on behalf of the Korean CIA. And now, like a bad penny, he was back. Along with Samir Vincent, an Iraqi-American busi-nessman, Park was said to have reached a $15 million agreement in 1996 to exercise his influence-peddling gifts on behalf of the Iraqis. Vincent said that they were to "take care of" a high-ranking UN offi-cial, later identified as Boutros Boutros-Ghali, then the secretary-general. Boutros-Ghali had, in fact, been a good friend of Park's in the 1990s, a startling revelation given that Park's name was almost synony-mous with graft. And in 1997, the Korean businessman had befriended Maurice Strong, a longtime UN official and friend and adviser of An-nan's, and invested $1 million in an oil company in which Strong and his son were major investors. No evidence emerged either that Park had bribed Boutros-Ghali or that Strong had interfered in Oil-for-Food. But the indictment coated Oil-for-Food in a new layer of sleaze.

And then, as if that weren't enough, the manacles rattled once again the following week, when news broke that two of Volcker's inves-tigators had quit in disgust over the "soft" treatment the panel had meted out to Annan. Though they did not publicly detail their differ-ences with Volcker, the lawyer for Pierre Mouselli, Kojo's Lebanese would-be business partner, explained to the press that Robert Parton, one of the two, had accused the Volcker panel of "engaging in a de facto cover-up, acting with good intentions but steered by ideology." It was Mouselli who had claimed that he and Kojo had spoken to Annan in the summer of 1998 about their plans to do business under the Oil-for-Food Programme. Presumably the investigators believed, as did many journalists, that Volcker had been far too willing to credit Annan's innocent explanation for the meeting. The divide within the committee only further undermined Annan's claim that the interim report had "exonerated" him.

In early May, the House International Relations Committee, which had been conducting an investigation of its own into Oil-for-Food, subpoenaed Parton's documents. Parton complied, delivering several boxes of material to the House committee. This prompted Volcker to write a severe letter to the congressional chairman of the committee, protesting that panel members had made pledges of confidentiality that could not be unilaterally abrogated. What's more, he said in a separate press statement, the difference of view covered only "a single point," and on that point "our report contains all the relevant factual information gathered by my investigative team concerning Secretary-General Annan and his son." The documents, in short, would reveal nothing. Parton had simply given Mouselli more credibility than others on the panel had. The standoff continued for several weeks, until finally the House committee agreed to return the boxes to the Volcker panel.

Nevertheless, the damage had been done. The "Kofi must go" chorus swelled once again, and now came to include some centrist editorial pages. Mark Lagon, the State Department official responsible for the UN and one of the few representatives of the hard right at Foggy Bottom, said that "while we aren't calling for the resignation of the secretary-general," it was probably "an exaggeration" to suggest that the Volcker report had cleared him of wrongdoing. Even those who had no wish to see Annan step down agreed that his ability to drive the reform process to a successful conclusion—the issue that, at this late stage in his career, he cared about most of all—had been gravely, and perhaps irreparably, undermined.

CHAPTER TWENTY

The Black Hole of Kinshasa

T HERE WAS NO BETTER, OR RATHER WORSE, EXAMPLE OF THE kind of intractable problem that the UN got sucked into simply because no one else wanted to deal with it than the Democratic Republic of the Congo. Congo had been intractable for all forty-five years of its independence. Still, Richard Holbrooke was wrong in saying that UN peacekeeping had tragically miscarried there in the early 1960s; in fact, peacekeepers had smashed a rebellion with such violence that peace-loving supporters of the institution reeled in horror and vowed, "Never again." The UN kept its distance from Congo until the mid-1990s, when the flight of the Rwandan Hutus in the aftermath of the genocide produced one of the most violent and anarchic refugee situations in a generation. When Katangese rebels began to advance on Kinshasa, just as they had in 1961, nobody even dreamed of interceding with a peace-keeping force; Rwanda and Bosnia had taught the major powers lessons they would not soon forget.

The DRC, as it was known, was now a country of more than fifty million people with no functioning government or national institutions, a vast territory contested by tribal and ethnic forces, foreign armies, regional satraps, private militias, warlords, brigands, and black marketeers. Congo seemed just about as hopeless as any place on earth. But even though peacekeeping-as-salvation was a forgotten dream, it was also true that countries no longer slid quietly into oblivion, as they had during the Cold War. The UN was expected to *do something*. And so it had. In 1999, the principal parties to the monstrous civil war that had been shredding what remained of the country's economy, society, and infrastructure signed a cease-fire agreement for which the UN was to serve as monitor and guarantor. And so the UN returned to Congo—as to a maelstrom that might well suck in the whole peacekeeping apparatus and reduce it to so many splinters.

In February 2000, with Holbrooke pushing hard, the Security Council authorized a force of fifty-five hundred troops to monitor the cease-fire. Eight months earlier, when Serbian forces had withdrawn from Kosovo, the council had authorized a NATO force eight times as large to secure a region about one-sixtieth the size of the DRC. But MONUC, as the new mission was called, was not expected to stem the violence in Congo. The council mandate stipulated only that troops "may take the necessary action," should it fall within their capacities, to safeguard the mission's officials and facilities and to protect civilians "under imminent threat of physical violence." Troop-contributing countries felt no more enthusiastic about the operation than UN diplomats did; with the exception of small detachments of soldiers from Ireland and Sweden, the troops came from countries with scanty or undistinguished histories in peacekeeping—Uruguay, Morocco, South Africa. Most of them were lightly armed and modestly trained. This was the same moment when the council sent a ragtag collection of regional battalions into the chaos of Sierra Leone.

It was only a matter of time before the madness returned to Congo. In the northeastern province of Ituri, on the border with Uganda, the fighting had never really stopped. Since 1999, sixty thousand people had died, and more than half a million had lost their homes, in raids and outright massacres among half a dozen different forces. In January 2003, two tribes began to wage a war for control of the region. But the only stabilizing force in the area, the Ugandan army, had vowed to withdraw in order to comply with the terms of the peace accord. In late April and early May, the Ugandans abruptly abandoned Bunia, the provincial capital, leaving a vacuum that was instantly filled by tribal warfare. Panicked civilians sought refuge at the UN compound and at the airport. The Congolese government sent seven hundred policemen, but the force almost instantly disintegrated, in many cases allegedly selling their weapons to the insurgents. MONUC officials dispatched an Uruguayan guard unit to Bunia in order to protect UN personnel and facilities—but not Congolese civilians. Though the Uruguayans were able to save the thousands of civilians who reached the compound or the airport, they would not venture out into town, and an estimated 420 Congolese were murdered, some in plain sight of the soldiers.

The siege of Bunia was lifted only when Kofi Annan persuaded French president Jacques Chirac to send one thousand heavily armed soldiers under the umbrella of the European Union. Operation Artemis, as it was called, offered a rare example of the kind of "rapid reaction" capability that Annan and others had long argued for. The EU force was authorized by the council on May 30 and deployed a week later, disarming local fighters and securing the airport. But like the British paratroopers in Sierra Leone, Operation Artemis was only a stopgap. The French were not about to get bogged down in Congo, and the council had authorized a three-month mission, to be relieved by a beefed-up UN force. In July, the council raised MONUC's authorized strength to 10,800, with the express goal of establishing an Ituri brigade to ensure a permanent presence in the region.

Congo's capacity to generate chaos seemed vastly greater than the UN's capacity to contain it. In late May 2004, a renegade officer formally serving in the Congolese army but still deeply tied to Rwanda and a Rwanda-backed political party began to advance southward from Ituri toward Bukavu, a major city located on the border with Rwanda. Once again, the burden of defending a city fell on Uruguayan peacekeepers, who were ordered to take up blocking positions at the airport north of town. Most of the Uruguayans were not professional soldiers; they had signed up for peacekeeping duties and received hasty training. They had little desire to stand up to a Congolese rabble. According to a senior DPKO official in New York, the force commander called his superiors in Montevideo and complained that he was being asked to exceed his mandate. With backing from his capital, he refused to implement the order—an act of gross insubordination in a normal military setting. On June 2, peacekeepers surrendered the airport to the rebels, who then poured into Bukavu, where they engaged in a four-day orgy of rape, pillage, and murder. As in Bunia, the Uruguayans protected the thousands of citizens who took shelter in their compound, but refused to venture outside.

Officials in New York were less inclined to blame the peacekeepers than their civilian masters. A report produced by the peacekeeping department's Best Practices Unit found that William Lacy Swing, the veteran American diplomat who headed MONUC, along with his chief aides had failed to recognize the gravity of the situation despite repeated warnings, excluded advisers who advocated a tough response, and overruled military officials on the ground who were prepared to use force. Swing had threatened to pound the rebels with attack helicopters if they took the airport, and then rescinded the order at the last minute. While recognizing that Swing had reason to worry that escalating hostilities might provoke the Rwandan army to join the battle, thus triggering yet another war, the report concludes with a series of stunning allegations: "MONUC's failure to use force during the Bukavu crisis smeared the Mission with the taint of impotence and cowardice. It made UN military and civilian personnel objects of contempt to the Congolese people they were supposed to be helping. It emboldened potential enemies of MONUC and of the Transition."

MONUC was vindicating every fear of the UN officials who wished it had never been formed in the first place. The taint went well beyond impotence and cowardice, for it was also at around the time of the fall of Bukavu that news of rampant sexual abuse by MONUC troops began to circulate. There were cases involving child prostitution, rape, the exchange of drugs for sex, and other forms of exploitation. The Uruguayans were among the most notorious abusers, along with South African, Moroccan, and Nepalese forces, among others. Nor was the problem limited to troops in the field. In late October, Congolese police officials in Goma, the capital of North Kivu, raided the home of a French civilian official and found him with a thirteen-year-old Congolese girl with whom he had just had sex; in the hard drive of his computer they found pictures of him and others having sex with girls as young as eight. It seemed that he was a longtime pederast who had been caught before, but released unpunished. By late 2004, with the UN already reeling from the Oil-for-Food scandal and with anger in Washington over Kofi Annan's Falluja letter, the lurid tales of sexual exploitation in Congo applied the coup de grâce. An article in *The Economist* asked, "Is this the world's least effective UN peacekeeping force?"

Some UN diplomats were every bit as disgusted as the right-wing critics. In January, a leading DPKO official said to me, "The mission is completely out of control. We talked to the contingent commanders in Kinshasa, and we got nowhere. The line was 'You can't prove any of these allegations.' " The response from the top civilian officials, including Swing, was "We didn't do anything about this for two years, so if we do something now, it will look bad. So let's let it go away on its own." When allegations had begun to appear in early 2004, Swing had approached the contingent commanders; when he was stonewalled, he had dropped the subject. And the abuses had continued, if sometimes more circumspectly.

The Congo sex scandal was the UN in miniature. The peacekeeping contingents were not ultimately answerable to the mission's force commander, or to the civilian head of mission, or to DPKO, or to the secretary-general. That was why the Uruguayans felt free to ignore an order they didn't care to execute; South American contingents tended to be "Chapter VI absolutists" who did not accept aggressive peacekeeping and often would not respond when instructed to take a more robust posture. The UN had no power of discipline over individual soldiers, or over their commanders. The strongest action they could take was to send the individuals, or even a whole national unit, back home. In the case of countries that did not take seriously allegations of sexual abuse, at least when committed elsewhere, this was not much of a deterrent. The peacekeeping department could refuse to deploy ill-trained or abuse-prone troops, but whom would they replace them with?

Since few SRSGs had the stomach for a confrontation with their generals, it had become common practice to look the other way and leave the matter to individual contingent commanders. But there had been important exceptions. When Sergio Vieira de Mello had learned of incidents of abuse in East Timor, he had immediately sent home the Jordanian troops involved. Nikki Dahrendorf, who had served with Vieira de Mello and had been sent in early 2005 to head up a new sexual exploitation and abuse unit in the DRC, told me, "I was amazed at

how little was done when I got here." Swing, she said, "had been rely-
ing on the system to deal with it." And this passivity, this sense that real
authority lay elsewhere, had become the norm, just as for years it had
governed the Secretariat's relationship with the Security Council. "Nobody's accountable," as one furious peacekeeping official said to me in
New York. "I'm not accountable, Guéhenno's not accountable. Is Swing
accountable? When are people going to get fired? Until people get
fired, nothing's going to change."

Swing was the likeliest candidate. When we spoke in Kinshasa in
May, he delicately admitted, "When you have a problem this serious,
you always wonder later what you could have done and what you
should have done. And perhaps one wasn't as aware or as sensitive to it
as one ought to have been." Swing was seventy and thus well beyond
retirement age. And asking him to step down would show that the era
of impunity at the highest levels of the UN had finally come to an end.
But Swing was also a deeply experienced diplomat who enjoyed the
confidence of both Washington and the key players in Kinshasa. And
the reason he was still around in May was that after a meeting with the
secretary-general in early March, Annan released a statement saying
that Swing "evidently had his hands full" with Congo's political and security problems as well as with the "strong counter-measures" against
abuse he had adopted, and "would need to show strong leadership."
Given the "urgent agenda" in the DRC, "this was not the moment for a
sudden change of SRSG." When the situation "stabilised," Annan
would "initiate an orderly transition." Two years after this statement,
Swing was still in Kinshasa.

The fall of Bukavu recalled the most sickening chapters of UN
peacekeeping, like the slaughter in Srebrenica; indeed, the whole mission, with its failure to come to grips with a chaotic and brutal environment, felt very much like Bosnia redux. But here there was no NATO
to save the UN with a bombing campaign. The only real alternatives
were turning over the job to the hapless Congolese army, whose members were often forced to sell their shoes to keep from starving, or
sending in more and better peacekeepers, as the UN had successfully
done in Sierra Leone. The first option would almost certainly plunge
the DRC back into utter chaos, possibly dragging the whole region
along with it. The UN had little choice but to deepen its already heavy

commitment to Congo. In October, the Security Council agreed to Annan's request to strengthen the mission, adding fifty-nine hundred troops (half the number he sought). The mission would add a new Kivu brigade to go along with the Ituri brigade it had established in the aftermath of the fiasco in Bunia. No less important was the fact that the peacekeeping department had been able to replace a patchwork of national contingents, none very effective, with brigades of Indians and Pakistanis, among the most professional armies available to the UN.

I had been present at a meeting of Annan's senior staff in January 2005, when Jean-Marie Guéhenno had laid out the rationale for the new forces. The chief danger in South Kivu came not from free-booting soldiers, he explained, but from the twelve thousand or so members of the Democratic Forces for the Liberation of Rwanda, or FDLR—the name that the ex-*génocidaires* had adopted to burnish their image—who were camped in the province's dense forests. Ideally, he said, the Congolese army should confront and disarm the Hutus, but "the military capacities of the state are quite limited." The army consisted of the various factions and militias who had been fighting one another only a few years before; most remained loyal to faction leaders and were as likely to join local insurgencies as to suppress them. The UN, Guéhenno said, didn't have the capacity for forcible disarmament, either, but all that would begin to change as the new contingents arrived. The Indians, he noted, were coming with a fleet of helicopter gunships. And in order to show he meant business, Annan was sending as deputy force commander his military adviser, Patrick Cammaert, a general in the Dutch Marines who had served in Cambodia, Ethiopia, and Bosnia, at one point working with Special Forces teams to extract war criminals from the Balkans. The UN would finally fight fire with fire, as the Brahimi report had long ago said it must.

The commitment just kept growing. The UN was now spending a billion dollars a year to keep the world's biggest basket case from disintegrating altogether. The peacekeeping contingent had grown to more than fifteen thousand. And the UN was playing a political role that was every bit as central as its peacekeeping one, though here it worked with the DRC's chief allies, the European Union, major donors, and NGOs. UN civilian officials in Kinshasa had helped to cobble the various fighting forces into an interim government and then to keep this jerry-built structure afloat, and were beginning to organize the first meaningful national elections most Congolese had ever known. But the warlords who filled the government's upper ranks were stealing funds as fast as the international community could deposit them in Congo's treasury, sacking the country's fathomless trove of natural resources, and ensuring that their militia fighters remained loyal to themselves rather than to the nascent national army.

In early May 2005, I flew from Kinshasa to Bukavu, the capital of South Kivu and the scene of MONUC's great fiasco. South Kivu is one of the most heartbreaking regions of what is surely one of the world's most ill-starred nations. It's a startlingly lovely spot, more Hemingway than Conrad—green hills fading into distant dark ridges; glossy cows grazing on the upper slopes; fields planted with corn, beans, cassava, banana. South Kivu has abundant water and timber, gold and diamonds, copper and coltan (the mineral from which cell phone chips are made). And yet it's a far better place to be a cow than a human. The province has few passable roads, few functioning hospitals, and few postprimary schools and offers few sources of legitimate income beyond subsistence farming.

The eastern frontier suffered the same neglect that almost every part of Congo endured during Joseph Mobutu's thirty-two-year kleptocracy, but the region was subjected to an extra measure of pain owing to its proximity to Rwanda. The Hutu *génocidaires* who fled across the border along with innocent civilians settled in the rural areas of South and North Kivu, living off smuggling, "taxes" on local markets, kidnapping, and plunder. In 1998, at the outset of Congo's civil war, the Rwandan army poured over the border and massacred their Hutu adversaries as well as thousands of civilians. The army remained long after the Hutu threat had been suppressed, turning much of eastern DRC into an economic protectorate. And though the Rwandans, like the Ugandans, had eventually withdrawn, as the 1999 cease-fire agreement required, they still viewed the Hutu force as a clear and present danger, or claimed they did; this was why President Paul Kagame had sent his army to, or perhaps over, the border as soon as he had returned from the Dar es Salaam conference the previous November. But the ten to fifteen thousand members of the Hutu militia remained in the eastern jungle, terrorizing the local populace.

I had, in fact, come to South Kivu to see what the three-thousand-man Pakistani brigade could accomplish that their feckless Uruguayan predecessors had not. I was taken by helicopter thirty or so miles northeast of Bukavu, an area the FDLR had been terrorizing with almost complete impunity despite the presence of an Uruguayan contingent. The field in which we landed was five or six miles below Walungu, the town that served as the Pakistanis' base of operation. Pakistani engineers had rebuilt the road to town, so it took only about an hour to jolt our way up the steep, rutted track. We passed columns of women with branches on their heads, and half-clad little children, and goats. At one point a soldier nudged me in the ribs and said, "Look, an ambulance." And there, momentarily stopped on the side of the road, were four weary men bearing on their shoulders a wooden cradle that held a women wrapped in a thin blanket. It would be hours before they reached the nearest clinic, which was unlikely to have any medicine.

At company headquarters, an island of immaculate landscaping in the midst of dusty squalor, I was greeted by General Shujaat Ali Khan, the brigade commander. General Shujaat, a bluff, garrulous character with a thick black mustache set in a round, pudgy face, gave the impression that, nationality aside, he would have been quite happy serving under Dewan Prem Chand, the Indian general whose UN peacekeepers had smashed Moise Tshombe's secessionist bid in 1962. He took as dim a view of the Uruguayans whom he had replaced as the locals did. "Never was a shot fired by blue helmets in South Kivu until we arrived," he said contemptuously. Indeed, General Shujaat bridled at the restrictive rules of engagement that governed the mission. "We are not permitted to fly the attack helicopters at night, we cannot fly with the doors open, and so on," he complained. He could not just go and shoot bad guys.

General Shujaat was prepared to forcibly disarm the FDLR, but both the rules of engagement and political considerations dictated otherwise. This was to be a job for the Congolese army, though Shujaat knew very well just how unequal a fight that would be. For one thing, the general knew his adversary: In an act of bravado that had earned him a dressing-down from his civilian masters, he had taken a helicopter and dropped down unannounced in the dense forest of Nindja, where a thousand or so FDLR soldiers were quartered. He had come away much impressed. "These fellows have a very strong command structure, they're very disciplined, they keep their weapons spic-and-span," he said. "I would compare them to our own soldiers." The Congolese army, by contrast, was barely a fighting force. The troops who had been initially assigned to work with the Pakistanis had instead devoted themselves to plunder, frequently in collaboration with the FDLR. General Shujaat had reached a deal with the regional commander in which his men would transport all twenty-two hundred government soldiers out of the area in exchange for troops actually willing to fight. "Now," he said, "it is as per our desire."

For all his bluster, General Shujaat understood that his job was not to fight the FDLR troops but to suppress their brigandage, so that life could return to something like normal. He appeared to be succeeding: since the Pakistanis had arrived, the population of a camp in Walungu for "internally displaced people" had dwindled from twenty-five hundred to eight hundred. The ultimate goal was to make life so uncomfortable for the Hutu rebels that they would go back home (though it was plain that the hard core of *génocidaires* would never leave without a fight). Here it was harder to be optimistic. The good news was that at the end of March, in a major breakthrough, the FDLR's political arm had pledged to end the armed struggle and return to Rwanda so long as they were guaranteed "political space." President Kagame had promised them a safe homecoming, but not the political space, a commodity almost unknown in Rwanda. General Shujaat, a worrier as well as a blunt realist, found the whole enterprise doubtful. "These fellows are having an excellent life raping the women and so forth," he told me. "Why should they go back and go to prison?"

Later that afternoon I drove out with a squad of forty-five to fifty soldiers in open transports with machine-gun mounts. We stopped at a plateau ringed by steep green hills. Here the men would stay for the next twelve hours: if word of an attack came from any of the detachment of government soldiers they had posted in the local villages, they would bounce down the rutted lanes and commence firing. Major Mohammed Younis, the commanding officer, pointed out the local villages along the ridgelines and said, "When we first began, in late March, we had three to four incidents every week." An FDLR raiding party would wait until nightfall, and then attack a village, stealing food and raping women; they frequently kidnapped villagers, took them back to Nindja, and threatened to kill them if relatives didn't come up with ransom. But Operation Night Flash, as the Pakistanis called their nocturnal vigil, had at least temporarily closed down the crime wave. Major Younis said there hadn't been an incident for close to a week. The Pakistanis seemed to have reduced the crime rate by flooding the bad neighborhoods.

It wasn't only in South Kivu that peacekeepers had taken the fight to the enemy. In Ituri, scene of MONUC's other great failure, peacekeepers in armored personnel carriers had conducted "cordon-and-search" operations that had led to the disarming of twelve thousand of the estimated fifteen thousand militia members in the area. Violence continued in both provinces but was no longer likely to lead to another war or to derail the peace process. MONUC's performance argued that peacekeeping really was a progressive enterprise. DPKO had learned something from the failures of the past, not only in Congo but elsewhere; and for all the shortcomings, it had applied that knowledge profitably. Disciplined soldiers equipped with helicopter gunships and armored personnel carriers, or sometimes just with guns they were willing to use, had taken the fight to the bad guys, demonstrating that robust peacekeeping could accomplish a great deal that timid peacekeeping could not. They had established an environment sufficiently stable for institution-building; that was about as much as you could ask of peacekeeping in a place like Congo.

Peacekeeping made political progress possible, but it was no substitute for politics. As Hedi Annabi, the deputy head of peacekeeping, put it, "We're getting much better at putting out the fire, but somebody else has to rebuild the house." As in East Timor and Kosovo, the UN, and the international community, had to use the space created by the more secure environment to construct the rudiments of such a state and to help local people learn how to operate it. Annabi had another saying: "Every crisis needs a godfather." The Balkans had Europe; Sierra Leone had the British. Congo had a lot of help, but no godfather. The country may have been just too big, too corrupt, and too hopeless for even the most benevolent patron.

Congo's great problem was the same one that plagues so many African countries—poor governance. But this technocratic term scarcely did justice to the self-perpetuating machine of immiseration that one Congolese leader after another had operated for over a century. Belgium's King Leopold II put the machine in motion in the 1880s, when he reduced the myriad tribes of the region to so many employees, and often slaves, of companies devoted to sucking up Congo's bottomless treasures, principally ivory and rubber. The Belgian colonial administration bequeathed the country a decent infrastructure, though they left it ludicrously unprepared for self-government. (At independence in 1960, none of Congo's fourteen million citizens—zero—had university degrees in law, medicine, or engineering.) Five years after independence, Joseph Mobutu toppled Congo's only elected president in a coup and instituted a homegrown version of King Leopold's monumental rapacity. Mobutu stole billions over the years, while the roads and hospitals and schools the Belgians had left behind disintegrated into the bush. Unlike the Belgian king, Mobutu lavished Congo's bounty on his collaborators, some of whom left a presidential audience with $5 or $10 million in their pocket. Kabuya Lumuna, a former World Bank official who served as Mobutu's deputy chief of staff in the last years, said to me, "Mobutu created an image for the Congolese people that enrichment through the state was normal practice. Now we feel that the only way you can raise your status is through politics. It is normal for a person to say, 'I have finished my studies. If I can't get a government post, I will live my entire life in poverty.'"

The function of the state was to organize plunder; an effective civil service, or for that matter a private sector, only made the job harder. What the DRC lacked was thus not only the machinery of state— customs officials, tax collectors, policemen, and so forth—but a legitimate conception of the state. But in this it was not very much different from Sierra Leone, Liberia, Somalia, Haiti, or the other failed or quasi-failed states that had become wards of the UN's peacekeeping and nation-building apparatus; it was just a very great deal bigger. The general record of failure in these places argues that even the most benevolent and effective actors cannot create functioning institutions when state power rests with people hell-bent on abusing it for their own purposes. For this reason, some of the most thoughtful people I knew at the UN argued that Congo needed less help, not more, in order to learn how to fend for itself. But would it? The rewards of corruption were arguably too lavish to permit a legitimate politics to arise on its own. And the designs that neighbors like Rwanda had on the DRC's abundant land and resources almost guaranteed that the country would be plagued from the outside as well as from within.

By the time the UN returned to Congo, an informal protocol of regional intervention had been established in Africa. A senior statesman like Nelson Mandela would convene a peace conference at a neutral site, bringing together combatants, neighboring heads of state, and various international bodies, including the UN. The warring parties would sign a cease-fire in the solemn presence of the statesmen, and then begin negotiations toward the formation of a transitional, power-sharing government that would, in the fullness of time, yield to a democratically elected state. Such a process was already under way in Sierra Leone—thus Foday Sankoh's brief reign as government minister—and Burundi, a nation with a ghastly history of politics-by-genocide.

Congo became the latest laboratory of political intervention when African leaders stepped in to put a halt to the war of all against all that pitted the government of Laurent Kabila and tribal allies against rebellious warlords backed by Rwanda and Uganda. Kabila was murdered by one of his own bodyguards in 2001, and the Katangese entourage who had come to power replaced him with one of his sons, Joseph, then twenty-nine, a feckless character who had worked as a cabdriver in Tanzania but, because he had no blood on his hands, was considered acceptable to the outside world. Soon afterward, Thabo Mbeki, Mandela's successor as president of South Africa, convened a gathering of Congolese parties in Pretoria in hopes of putting together a transitional government.

Haile Menkerios, an official in the political affairs department, was sent to South Africa as an adviser to the UN representative to the talks. The parties in Pretoria drew up two documents, one to specify the power-sharing arrangement and the other to lay out broad principles for the new state. The second document, Menkerios says, was magnificent. " 'Women's rights? Okay, fine. Sensitivity to the environment? Done.' Because nobody had the slightest intention to uphold them; all they cared about was power sharing." And here the jockeying was fierce. Because the world had recognized the Katangese rabble that overthrew Mobutu as Congo's legitimate government, and Kabila as head of state, the transitional government was shaped around young Kabila and his entourage, who had grandly dubbed themselves the People's Party for Reconstruction and Development. Through what was widely described as an adroit combination of horse-trading and bribery, Kabila managed to exclude from the government Congo's one legitimate political party, which had openly and bravely opposed Mobutu. In the arrangement that finally emerged in late 2002, known as "one plus four," the PPRD would hold the presidency, while vice presidencies went to the two main rebel parties and two parties almost wholly answerable to Kabila. In other words, the men who had provoked Congo's unspeakable civil war would now be rewarded by sharing the spoils of statehood.

The major donors were not about to trust the rogues they had just empowered with the hundreds of millions of dollars they planned to spend to rebuild—or, rather, build—state institutions during the transitional period. And so the five governing parties reached an extraordinary agreement to make a committee of diplomats from the chief donor nations as well as neighboring countries "co-responsible" for the transition. The UN played an especially important role on this body, known as CIAT, because, while the ambassadors generally pursued parochial interests dictated from capitals, the UN was there to represent the interests of the Congolese people, a concern that the five ruling parties barely deigned to address. And this status forced the UN, in the person of William Lacy Swing, to confront the political equivalent of the helicopter gunship question: How much force do you bring to bear in the face of recalcitrance?

And the resistance was unremitting. Kabila's party had gained control over the public companies that operated the DRC's crumbling infrastructure—electricity generation, local trains, and the boats that plied the Congo River, the closest thing in the country to a highway.

The revenues disappeared, presumably into the pockets of *la famille Kabila*, as the ruling clique was known. Authority in the army, as in other key institutions, had been carefully divided among the various parties, but real control rested with a parallel structure known as the *maison militaire*, a PPRD organ. Foreign donors had supplied $100 million to pay soldiers in the Congolese army. The head count was said to be 350,000, a figure inflated by at least a factor of two in order to justify exorbitant demands for funds. But it scarcely mattered, because few soldiers were actually paid. Money was deducted from a soldier's pitiful salary of $10 a month to pay for the alleged cost of floating the cash downriver, and most of the funds disappeared before the boats arrived. And so the soldiers made a living as unpaid soldiers always do: by using their weapons to steal from the citizens among whom they were quartered. Many units of the army were all but useless because, like the regiment initially assigned to the Pakistanis, they would collaborate with whomever they were sent to fight.

What could the international community do to prevent the government from sabotaging the institution-building process for which the major donors were paying? Not much, it appeared. When Ross Mountain, a tough-minded New Zealander, was moved from Iraq to become deputy SRSG in Kinshasa, he went to all four vice presidents and said, "Why haven't the soldiers been paid?" None professed to know. Swing viewed the problem in technocratic terms. "They need help," he told me, "on how do you establish a foolproof salary system." The CIAT, which met amid the rare opulence of the presidential palace, focused on formal procedures and mechanisms in a way that seemed as remote from the welfare of the desperate Congolese people as the palace itself, or as the ruling elite that occupied it. "There are so many mechanisms," as Haile Menkerios puts it. "But if there's no political will to make them work, you can have a hundred of these mechanisms." A European diplomat who occasionally attended these sessions compared them to "an afternoon tea." The problem, in short, was not that the international community had no helicopter gunships at its disposal but that it was unwilling to use them.

Swing was a genuine enthusiast, and his enthusiasm helped reassure foreign capitals that Congo was on the right track. The SRSG was a classically optimistic American abroad, a calm veteran of innumerable African upheavals who stayed in improbably wonderful trim despite his seventy years. With his elegant white mustache and his double-breasted suit, buttoned even in the blazing heat, Swing was a character out of Graham Greene. He focused on the DRC's vast potential—the unharnessed hydro power, the unforested hardwood. The big picture looked bright to him, and the country could get there so long as it stuck to the process. "Frankly," Swing said, in his big, bright office atop the UN mission, "I've been through half a dozen of these transitions, and I don't see anything there that is particularly surprising."

Swing considered Joseph Kabila a decent young fellow who had begun getting a grip on the business of governing; I met very few others who shared this sunny assessment. The politicians, journalists, and civic leaders I spoke with viewed Kabila as either a witting or an unwitting tool of his father's cronies—either a knave or a fool. Mbusa Nyamwisi, leader of a party affiliated with Uganda and a member of the new government, told me that Kabila had agreed to the transitional process only in order to continue plundering the state treasury, and to gain the political advantage that would come with the appearance of statesmanship. Kabila made little attempt to use his position to pass legislation, to broker compromise, to build bridges with the country's neighbors. *"L'espace présidentiel est absent,"* as Azarias Ruberwa, one of the four vice presidents and by far the most respected, put it.

The question of Kabila's intentions, and of the honesty and transparency of the political process, was consuming the diplomatic and political community in Kinshasa when I arrived. A committee of foreign and Congolese experts had drafted a new constitution and submitted it to Parliament, as the transitional process required. But legislators in the Senate, which Kabila controlled, kept changing the document to transfer more and more power to the office of the president, including the right to unilaterally dissolve the Parliament. According to the UN official monitoring the process, "Kabila's people go back to him every day and say, 'I got this power for you, I got that power for you.'" I had been told repeatedly that Kabila's party had bribed legislators to, in effect, surrender their own powers. Azarias Ruberwa said, "The corruption in our country has become so pervasive that these legislators were paid five hundred dollars to change their votes—not five thousand dollars, five *hundred* dollars." Ruberwa was outraged not so much at the sale of votes as at the willingness to subvert the nation for peanuts.

The French, who were Kabila's most important source of diplomatic support, had taken the position that the provisions of the constitution should be left to the Congolese; or, as the outraged UN official put it to me, "If they want to paint the house green, let them paint the house green." Others, however, were not so nonchalant. The UN was then gearing up for a staggeringly expensive and complex national election process, and the prospect of collaborating in what looked like constitutionally sanctioned Mobutuism appalled a number of officials. "We could spend three hundred million dollars to elect a dictator," as Ross Mountain said. "Normally you can get a dictator cheaper than that." But neither Swing nor the major diplomats made any serious attempt to block the process.

In late April, Jean-Marie Guéhenno went to the Security Council to alert it to this looming catastrophe. This proved to be a waste of time. "The response," Guéhenno said bitterly, "was very weak." The nearly unanimous view was that the Congolese should be free to write their own constitution; it was a matter of sovereignty. Guéhenno, deeply alarmed, then spoke to senior diplomatic officials in Europe. A few days later Javier Solana, the European Union's foreign-policy chief, came to Congo to personally deliver the message that the constitution was unacceptable. Diplomats in Kinshasa finally bestirred themselves to drive home the same point. Swing sent Kabila a five-page letter outlining his problems with the document, and the CIAT met with the political leadership to warn them that the constitution could ultimately provoke a new civil war. Kabila smiled gently and said nothing. But the president knew he could not survive without international support. He finally relented, and on May 14 Parliament adopted a new, more democratic constitution.

Congo needed robust political oversight every bit as much as it needed robust peacekeeping. The only way to rein in Congo's innumerable militias was to give their political masters an incentive to stop fighting; this was the premise of the power-sharing arrangement, which gave the major rebel bodies a place at the table. But the problem was that, once there, they had continued to play the game of every man for himself. The militias were supposed to disarm and then either return to civilian life or enter the new army. Many had in fact disarmed, but *brassage*, the process by which the militias were to be assimilated into the army, had been a failure. Ross Mountain, who had visited a *brassage* center, said, "There was nothing—and that's not a figure of speech. There were no buildings, no water, no tents, no weapons. And there were 1,600 people." The Belgians had trained one regiment, which was considered combat-worthy. Most of the Congolese army, however, consisted of fully intact units from the various militias who owed their loyalty to their political bosses. The warlords were not inclined to give up the leverage of their ragtag soldiers, who could prove indispensable at election time. And the international community had not found a means of loosening their grip.

And this, in turn, was why General Shujaat had not been able to move against the FDLR. The "Global Agreement," as the power-sharing pact was called, had stipulated that disarmament was to be left up to the army. The plan was to have the peacekeepers available over the horizon. But both Shujaat and General Cammaert, who commanded the forces in the east, knew very well that the FDLR would cut the Congolese army to ribbons in such an engagement. Of course the FDLR knew this, too. Repatriation of the Hutu foot soldiers, a prerequisite for achieving stability in the turbulent east, had ground to a halt. Nor could MONUC do the job by itself. Shujaat had boasted to me that the jungle-hardened Guatemalan special forces being sent to Walungu would be able to flush the guerrillas out of the Nindja forest, but he may have just been trying out his bluff on me. In fact, he had neither the mandate nor the capacity to squeeze the FDLR.

In late May, eighteen people in a village in a remote area of Walungu province were murdered and hideously disfigured, their chests opened up and their hearts removed. This kind of ritual defilement was unheard of. Perhaps the FDLR was sending a message to the UN: Don't mess with us. Nobody knew. Back in New York, Guéhenno concluded that if he increased the pressure, the FDLR might well respond with another massacre. This was not a problem for which there was a military solution. And in the absence of a political resolution, MONUC officials settled on a policy of containment, keeping the

FDLR bottled up in Nindja and harassing them enough to discourage rapine and pillage.

In the end, it all came down to politics. The object of the whole peace-keeping/nation-building exercise was the creation of a legitimate political order; the fundamental problems were those of political legitimacy. Though Kofi Annan was calling for more troops to patrol additional trouble spots in the country, virtually every Congo expert in the UN felt that peacekeeping had already reached the point of diminishing returns. Ugo Solinas, a political affairs officer who had spent several years with MONUC before returning to New York, said, "You're never going to have enough troops in the Congo. You can't even protect the borders; it's just so porous, and there are so many points of entry. There are no military solutions to this problem; there are only political solutions." When I asked Solinas whether the country would be better off with fewer peacekeepers rather than more, he surprised me by saying, "The logic is sound. The ruling elite is sitting back and expecting the international community to do it for them."

The international community, with the UN at its core, had to rise to a level of intervention equal to the magnitude of the problem, as the peacekeepers, after their humiliating failures, ultimately had done. But in many ways it was harder to be aggressive in political matters than it was in military ones, even though diplomats were in no danger of dis-embowelment. The UN and its international partners were all too well versed in the evils of colonialism, the tutelary relationship between governor and governed. You couldn't write a country's constitution for it, no matter how much you knew about constitutions. "People want to run their own affairs," as Guéhenno, a partisan of the light footprint, put it. And the light footprint, for good reasons and bad, was very much in vogue.

All true; but it was not "the people" who were running things in Congo, but a tiny and corrupt elite that could barely be troubled to acknowledge the people. "Sovereignty" was the catchphrase of the rogues; civic-minded folk wanted the international community to demand more of the Congolese, no matter how neocolonial it sounded. A light footprint was not the same thing as a light hand; one meant "do fewer things," the other, "show more deference." MONUC could not afford deference; and William Swing's gentility, his guileless faith in his fellow man, plainly drove Guéhenno and his chief aides, anticolonials all, around the bend. As one of them said to me, "We're spending a billion dollars, and these people are a bunch of crooks who are stealing the country blind. We have a responsibility to be pushy."

CHAPTER TWENTY-ONE

America's Interest in UN Reform Is ...
What, Exactly?

I N THE BEGINNING OF JUNE 2005, THE DRIVE TO ASSEMBLE a broadly acceptable reform document kicked into gear. Jean Ping, the ambassador from Gabon and the president of the General Assembly, was meeting regularly with permanent representatives to test the initiatives of "In Larger Freedom." He had already put together a first draft of the document that the heads of state were to adopt in September. His staff began to work closely with Bob Orr and with Orr's team. Ping had also appointed fourteen "facilitators," ambassadors who had agreed to lobby their colleagues and to take their temperature on the four "clusters" of issues. Annan continued to travel to regional confabs and conferences on this and that in order to meet with heads of state individually and in bulk. His five "special envoys" pressed the case in their own regions. Orr consumed a steady diet of ambassadors, trying to nail down pledges of support from people whose chief professional gift was avoiding irrevocable commitment. Mark Malloch Brown spoke to officials in the National Security Council and the State Department. The full-court press, in short, was getting under way.

On June 2, Annan met with his envoys: Joaquim Chissano, the former president of Mozambique; Ernesto Zedillo, the former president of Mexico; Dermot Ahern, the foreign minister of Ireland; and Ali Alatas, the former foreign minister of Indonesia. (Vaira Vike-Freiberga, the president of Latvia, hadn't been able to come.) He ran down the list, most of it grim; there were big problems with terrorism, the Human

Rights Council, the responsibility to protect. Nonproliferation looked dead; climate change was running into stiff resistance from India, China, and Brazil, not to mention the United States. Ping's first draft was a Christmas list, laden with impossible goodies. European Union development ministers had just pledged to reach the target of 0.7 percent of GNP by 2015, so that was encouraging. There was talk of a one-euro levy on air tickets to raise money for HIV/AIDS. "But you mustn't use the word 'tax,' " Annan said. "If you call it a tax, it will never fly in this country. I remember Jesse Helms saying, 'It's only Uncle Sam that has the power to tax in this country.' "

The envoys all had the same message: away from New York, in the capitals, the only issue anybody wanted to talk about was Security Council expansion. Perhaps it would be best to accept an immediate vote, just to end the paralysis. Quite the contrary, Orr responded. "Right now, everyone has an incentive to be cooperative on the other issues. Once either side loses, that incentive is gone." President Chissano reported that the Africans, who according to Model A were to be allotted two permanent seats on the council, were hopelessly torn. All agreed that South Africa would get one slot, but Egypt and Nigeria were fighting over the other. And now Senegal, Kenya, and Tanzania were insisting that they, too, should be eligible. There were rumors that Ping would put off the tough issues until after the heads of state had gone home. "Once you've opened that door," Annan said, "you've lost it." The only thing impelling recalcitrant members to reach an accord was the awful spectacle of their presidents leaving New York empty-handed.

On June 8, Annan met once again with the Gang of Four. They were confident, one explained, that in a vote between the two options they would get 150 votes. But rumor had it, he said as bashfully as he could, that Annan had agreed with the Americans to put off a vote until after the General Assembly meeting. "This is disinformation, I hope?"

"The question is," said Annan, without actually addressing that particular question, "what is the optimal time? At what point do you decide you have had an exhaustive discussion? Are you convinced that the members feel that by the end of June they will have had enough discussion? Have you consulted delegates who are not part of either group on the timing? How comfortable are they with this?" Annan always took this position, and equally with both sides. He wasn't convinced that either would carry two thirds of the members, and he was concerned less about Security Council expansion than about preventing a train wreck. A premature vote could embitter not only the losers but other members who felt the issue was being forced down their throats. The UN's penchant for endless debate opened it to ridicule, but sometimes indecisiveness was to be preferred to irresolvable conflict. Annan ended with another habitual message: "That's why in our previous discussions I encouraged you to make progress on the other clusters. If you had already advanced on the other issues, that would show you had paid attention to the concerns of others."

The G4 bid was, in fact, losing altitude, as the diplomats themselves knew. Back in April, the Chinese had announced that the issue of expansion should be determined by consensus—an impossibility— and that in any case it was not ripe for decision. The Russians had taken a similar view. The Bush administration had avoided the question for as long as possible, but that very day Secretary Rice had confirmed to her German counterpart, Joschka Fischer, that the United States would not support the German bid. A week later, perhaps feeling some pressure to demonstrate sympathy for Third World aspirations, the White House staked out a new position, asserting that it was prepared to offer permanent membership to Japan and an unspecified developing country—presumably India—but no one else. Since this was plainly untenable, it amounted to nothing more than a gesture.

Nevertheless, the pragmatists were plainly in the ascendancy at the White House. Not only Rice and Burns, but Stephen Hadley, the national security adviser, and the deputy secretary of state, Robert Zoellick, were, as Mark Malloch Brown said, "serious, professional American diplomats who fully buy into the basic pragmatic vision of Roosevelt and Truman that you need a UN to help you manage a world in which you're the dominant power." When any of them called, Malloch Brown said, "it's always because there's a problem that needs to be solved that day—Lebanon, Iraq, personnel appointments. And it's a very professional thing. They're not bullying, demanding, or unreasonable." But at the end of most conversations they would ask, "Anything new on Oil-for-Food?" Whatever it was, they knew they'd have to answer for it in front of Congress.

This administration was, not surprisingly, no more willing to spend political capital defending the UN from Congress than the Clinton administration had been. Henry Hyde's legislation, which would cut in half the United States' $400 million in annual dues, was moving toward a vote. Bob Orr had been telling his contacts that if the Hyde bill passed, the mood in the UN would revert back to March 2003. "We'll be outvoted 190 to 1 on everything we want." But he hadn't made much headway. "Had the administration wanted to," Orr said to me in early June, "they could have killed the Hyde legislation in its crib." Finally, in a June 15 interview with *The New York Times*, Nicholas Burns said, "We are the founder of the UN. We're the host country of the UN. We're the leading contributor to the UN. We don't want to put ourselves in the position where the United States is withholding 50 percent of the American contributions to the UN system."

Here was an almost startlingly passionate endorsement of the UN, as unfamiliar, in this administration, as a plea for solar power. In fact, Burns's views of the institution were indistinguishable from those of, say, Richard Holbrooke. "You have two choices with the UN," he said later. "You can basically say it's worthless and cast it aside, or you can say we recognize it for what it is, which is a highly imperfect but very important institution. And so we wanted to put our best foot forward." And to the administration's credit, they did just that. The bill passed anyway, but the White House opposition ensured that it would die in the Senate.

But the administration's attitude toward the UN could not have changed so much had the UN not become a good deal more accommodating toward the administration, and more broadly toward elite opinion in the United States. Further evidence came with the report of the Gingrich-Mitchell task force, which appeared on the same day that the White House declared its opposition to the Hyde bill. Though bluntly titled "American Interests and UN Reform," the report was not at all what UN officials had feared or conservatives had hoped. In an introductory passage the document noted, "For many of the world's people, the United Nations has carried the stamp of legitimacy and consensus." Thus, even if many Americans have "differing views" about the merits of this stamp, "in certain instances a decision by the United Nations . . . may be more acceptable to other governments than pressure from any single nation or group of nations." This was, itself, an important concession. The report was severely critical of the UN, but no more than the high-level panel had been. The Gingrich-Mitchell panel endorsed many of the secretary-general's recommendations for reform. With the exception of passages seeking more managerial latitude for the secretary-general, demanding the end of the longtime marginalization of Israel, and suggesting that lasting change would require "consistent and concerted action by the world's genuine democracies"—one of Gingrich's own articles of faith—the two documents were highly compatible.

Nicholas Burns praised the report, but so did the *New York Times* editorial page, long a source of aid and comfort to the UN. The document, the *Times* observed, "offers constructive recommendations on mobilizing Washington's powerful influence to promote urgent and necessary reforms." A post-ideological moment seemed to beckon.

Over the summer of 2005, I held my exit interview, so to speak, with my chief sparring partner, Kieran Prendergast. He and I disagreed about a great many things, and we often disagreed vehemently, but there were few people at the UN I so looked forward to meeting, for Prendergast was a pungent talker who dispensed with the ritual pieties that so often clotted conversation at the more rarefied levels of the UN. And the manner of his leaving loosened whatever inhibitions remained. He had been forced to step down when Malloch Brown's appointment had produced a glut of Brits at the top; the Bush administration had scotched his hopes of serving as Middle East negotiator; and though he would continue to serve as an envoy in the never-ending talks over Cyprus, his contract had been invalidated, and with it his salary and benefits. And why? Because, he believed, Malloch Brown had "made some Mephistophelian deal with this administration to ease out the troublemakers." And Annan had been too weak to resist. Prendergast had, in short, been laid low by the same forces that in his view were destroying the institution.

Prendergast interpreted the surprising air of comity around the Gingrich-Mitchell report very differently from Malloch Brown or Bob Orr. As he gazed through the dark lens of his own fate, Prendergast saw an institution terrorized into meek submission. "Everything is a genuflection to Washington," he said, nursing a cup of tea. We sat on either side of a narrow table on which were ranged a group of Masai clubs he had bought while high commissioner in Kenya. "And that's foolish. He's going to be judged before the court of history, isn't he? There's a real danger of frittering away the achievements of the first seven and a half years." Prendergast loathed Malloch Brown in a distinctively British way, speculating in a bemused manner about the man's schooling and family background; Annan, however, he seemed rather to pity, comparing him to "a rabbit in the headlights." But even Prendergast's most self-serving views were always shot through with cool insight. "There's a lot of evidence that courage is a finite quantity," he said. "I think he has been brave over a lot of issues over a lot of time, but if you get really beaten up, and you came from a background that has not thickened your skin and coarsened your sensibilities in that respect, it's very understandable if you don't want to subject yourself to that again."

Several weeks later, the Volcker committee delivered its third interim report, which dealt principally with the allegations against Benon Sevan, the career UN official who had directed the Office of Iraq Programme. Though Sevan had long since ceased cooperating with the inquiry, investigators had traced the flow of cash from AMEP, the firm to which he had directed the Iraqis to steer oil contracts, to the Swiss bank account of Fred Nadler, a friend of Sevan's. Nadler had in turn made large cash withdrawals during periods when he and/or Sevan were in Switzerland and about to go to New York. And immediately afterward, Sevan had made large cash deposits ultimately totaling at least $147,000. The committee now dismissed Sevan's story about his aunt, asserting that in fact he had "corruptly derived substantial financial benefits by soliciting and receiving oil allocations for AMEP from the Government of Iraq." Sevan continued to loudly protest his innocence. He was now the subject of criminal investigations in New York, though he had returned to Cyprus, presumably hoping to avoid extradition.

And now, as if to vindicate Prendergast's dire views of the *liaison dangereuse* with Washington, the awful shadow of John Bolton fell over

the UN. Bolton was the UN's bogeyman, its nightmare, its Tonton Ma-
coute. This fierce character with the bristling white mustache, which
looked like a dime-store disguise beneath his barely groomed thatch of
brown hair, was a subject of obsessive speculation in and around the
UN. Was it really true that in 2001, as under-secretary of state for arms
control, he had brought representatives of the National Rifle Association onto the floor of the General Assembly? (Almost—at the UN Conference on the Illicit Trade in Small Arms and Light Weapons, where
he had announced that the White House opposed any form of regulation that would "abrogate the constitutional right to bear arms," he had
been accompanied by several NRA members.) Was he really so un-
couth, so vehement, a character? (Yes, sometimes. Edward Luck, the
UN historian, had often been pitted against Bolton as a debating partner, and he had told me, "You can tell when he gets tense, because his
hands stiffen up, then his arms stiffen up, then his shoulders, and then
something incredibly harsh comes out of his mouth.") Was his brief to
fix the UN or to wreck it? You couldn't be sure.

I had first spoken to Bolton when I was writing an article on Kofi
Annan in 1998. In those days, if you wanted someone to say that the
UN was dangerous to American interests, Bolton was your man. In articles and speeches throughout the 1990s, he had argued that the UN,
and international law generally, were tools that had turned on their
master. He described treaties as "political obligations" rather than legal
ones, in no way binding on their signatories. When the United States
fell so far behind in its dues payments to the UN that it was in some
danger of losing its vote, he said, "Many Republicans in Congress, and
perhaps a majority, not only do not care about losing the General Assembly vote but actually see it as a 'make-my-day' outcome." Ideally, he
said, "nothing should be paid to the UN system." In our conversation,
he was scornful of Annan's last-minute dash to Iraq, saying, "When you
have a secretary-general that is so visible, I don't think you can put him
back in the closet when it's inconvenient." And he was equally contemptuous of President Clinton for offering the secretary-general that
latitude, saying that the administration acted "as if it sees the UN as
having a life or existence outside of what the U.S. wants it to do."

Bolton could be found wherever ideological armies clashed by
night. As assistant attorney general in President Ronald Reagan's sec-

ond term, he had worked with Attorney General Ed Meese to salt the ranks of career Justice Department lawyers with committed conservatives. He had guided the failed nomination of the deeply conservative and confrontational Robert Bork to the Supreme Court. Under the first President Bush he was appointed assistant secretary of state for international organizations, where he became deeply versed in the UN and its peculiar folkways. With the onset of the Clinton years, he became a member of the conservative shadow government, employed as a scholar at the American Enterprise Institute and actively involved with the Federalist Society, the Manhattan Institute, and the Project for the New American Century, the center for neoconservative thinking on America's role in the world. When George W. Bush's presidential candidacy hung by a chad in Florida, Bolton, summoned from South Korea, strode into the Tallahassee public library and famously announced, "I'm with the Bush-Cheney team, and I'm here to stop the vote." Bolton's pugnacity distinguished him even in this very combative environment. After George Bush became president-elect, a grateful Dick Cheney said, "People ask what [job] John should get. My answer is, 'Anything he wants.'"

As undersecretary of state, Bolton was respected for his grasp of highly technical arms-control issues and his exacting, not to say remorseless, negotiating style. He specialized in extricating the Bush administration from treaty obligations it had no wish to honor, including the Anti-Ballistic Missile Treaty, the Biological Weapons Convention, the small arms pact, and the International Criminal Court. When Bolton signed the document formally repudiating the Clinton administration's acceptance of the court, he called it "the happiest moment in my government service." He was far more given, by temperament, to drawing bright lines between truth and falsehood than to blurring those lines in order to find common ground. As he was preparing to negotiate with North Korea, the most dire and difficult issue within his domain, he called the country's president a "tyrannical dictator" who managed an "evil regime." The North Koreans, who cannot be bested in matters of political invective, returned the favor by describing Bolton as "human scum" and forcing the State Department to remove him from the talks. Bolton trumped his own boss, Colin Powell, in making the hard line on North Korea administration policy; the policy proved to be an unmitigated failure.

Bolton was something like a fifth column in Powell's internationalist State Department. When I was writing an article in early 2004 about the International Atomic Energy Agency, I asked to speak with Bolton but was informed by a State Department spokesman that he would not be available. Then Bolton's office called to say that he *would* be available, so long as it was off the record and I kept it a secret from the media folks at State. An aide brought me up to Bolton's office and then escorted me through a series of locked chambers, which imparted a slightly paranoid feel to the ensuing encounter. Bolton himself was perfectly pleasant and forthcoming, though wholly devoid of the graciousness that is second nature to most diplomats. His sense of the world seemed altogether dark. He was certain, though without any hard evidence, that the Iranians were developing nuclear weapons, and he spoke slightingly of both the IAEA and the effort by France, Germany, and England to negotiate an agreement with Iran. Bolton had been waging a campaign inside State to deny the IAEA's widely respected director, Mohamed ElBaradei, a third term, and he now told me that ElBaradei was soft-pedaling the Iranian threat—because he was a UN bureaucrat and "a man of the Third World," and because he had "higher ambitions," including the Nobel Peace Prize. (ElBaradei ultimately won both the third term and the prize.)

Throughout the first half of 2005 Bolton's nomination was tangled in controversy, not so much because he held the institution where he was to serve in such contempt as because the innumerable enemies he had made inside the Bush administration began to surface. He was said to have browbeaten and threatened lower-level officials. He was accused of trying to fire an intelligence analyst who in early 2002 had had the temerity to disagree with assertions Bolton planned to make in congressional testimony that Cuba was seeking to develop and market biological weapons. When Bolton was blocked from making these claims, he advanced them anyway in a speech to the Heritage Foundation. He also believed that Syria already possessed WMDs. No significant evidence ever emerged to support either of these claims.

As a matter of both temperament and belief, Bolton seemed completely unsuited to the moderate and pragmatic team that Condoleezza Rice had assembled. He had wanted to serve as the State Department's number-two official, but Rice had refused; the assumption around Washington was that the UN position was a consolation prize upon which Vice President Cheney had insisted, and that Rice had considered it a fair price to pay to get Bolton out of Washington. But as the hearings dragged on over the summer, Bolton lost not only every Democrat on the Senate Foreign Relations Committee but several of the moderate Republicans. President Bush, who rarely backed down in personnel matters, refused to abandon his nominee, and on August 1, rather than prolong the agony, he made Bolton a "recess appointment," allowing him to serve until the end of 2006.

Over the previous several months, Jean Ping and his staff had been drafting and redrafting the various reform proposals that had originated with the high-level panel and the Sachs report on development. These drafts were produced within a General Assembly culture far more attuned to the wishes of the majority of members than was the Secretariat. Ping 3, the working draft during much of the summer, was a thirty-five-page document that reproduced virtually every proposal contained in the Sachs document and proposed repositioning the UN as the coordinating body for international development policy; in the human rights and security agenda, the draft soft-pedaled several issues distasteful to the G77 and added others obviously unacceptable to the United States.

Most Western countries were willing to indulge the G77 on issues like aid and debt relief because they recognized that the commitments were chiefly rhetorical, and because they believed that this was the price to be paid for progress on security issues. But when U.S. diplomats in New York sent the Ping drafts to be run through the interagency vetting process in Washington, they met with stiff resistance. "We were surprised at the level of angst and concern at the development portions of the draft," says one. "We had a position in Washington that was not sustainable." The Bush administration felt proud of the commitments it had made on aid and debt relief and was not about to sign off on a document that blamed the North for the poverty of the South. And the language on issues like nuclear disarmament and the International Criminal Court was plainly unacceptable.

The interagency critique of Ping 3 had left almost nothing standing, but seasoned diplomats assumed that Washington was simply staking out a maximalist position. Over the summer American diplomats had treated most issues as negotiable, and Bob Orr's contacts in the administration continued to assure him that they wanted a positive outcome, and were on board with most of the collective security and human rights agenda. And then the Bolton era began—with a bang. On August 2, the day after Bolton's appointment, Anne W. Patterson, a career diplomat who had been serving as interim ambassador, went to the General Assembly to deliver a remarkably, and uncharacteristically, harsh assessment of the prospects for reform. She described President Ping's draft as too long, poorly worded, badly organized, too preoccupied with development, too focused on disarmament rather than nonproliferation, and, in general, at odds with American priorities. There was merit in each of her claims, but the tone was very different from the one that Washington had adopted in private conversations and that Shirin Tahir-Kheli had used in her speech several months earlier. The administration had made very little effort to shape the outcome document, and this vacuum had been filled, as such vacuums often were, by the ideologues of the developing world. The train had pulled out of the station, and now the United States was saying it wanted a new destination.

The following day, August 3, the grand inquisitor himself arrived in Turtle Bay. He startled Ping by saying, as he later told Bob Orr and Mark Malloch Brown, "I know you and your staff have worked very hard on this document, but it just won't do. We're going to have to start from the beginning." Bolton explained that he would be going through the thirty-five-page document line by line, and then working with his fellow ambassadors to come up with a document of their own. In effect, he was unilaterally dismissing Ping from the process. That afternoon Bolton met with Orr and Malloch Brown and told them about his conversation with Ping. Malloch Brown was inclined to dismiss the rhetoric as new-ambassador-in-town swagger, but Orr was appalled. He knew that the other members would go ballistic when they heard the news. "This approach will lead to disaster," he recalls telling Bolton. "One hundred and ninety countries already think they have a document. How are you going to start this process all over again with the summit three weeks away?" (Actually, it was five weeks away.)

"We have a strong preference for a G8-type approach," Bolton re-joined. The G8 summit in Gleneagles, Scotland, had concluded with a relatively brief summation of common ground. If the ambassadors proved unable to agree on a wholly new document among themselves, Bolton said, perhaps they could issue a one-page communiqué and four or five one-page statements on the main issues. Bolton also made it clear that his red lines, which had to do above all with any endorsement of the kinds of arms-control treaties he had spent the previous four years wrestling to the ground, mattered far more to him than substantive progress on human rights or terrorism or peace-building. Orr listened with growing amazement: this wasn't the Bush administration's agenda Bolton was propounding, but his own.

As soon as he got back to his office, Orr telephoned Shirin Tahir-Kheli, Rice's adviser on UN reform, and said, "Does Bolton have the secretary's support on this?"

"Tell me what he said," said a stunned Tahir-Kheli. Orr recounted the meeting, and Tahir-Kheli said, "I'll get right back to you." Shortly thereafter, Orr received a message: "We're working with the Ping document. Tell Orr, 'Stay cool.' " This was reassuring, but Orr knew, from talking with staff members of Republican congressmen, that the Hyde legislation would prove unstoppable if the summit failed to produce a document the administration deemed acceptable.

A number of Western diplomats were happy to see Bolton interrupt what had come to feel like an ineluctable process; they had begun to worry that while they were making important concessions on the development issues the G77 cared about, the G77 wasn't really coming around on terrorism, the responsibility to protect, the Human Rights Council, and the like. These issues would have to be negotiated among the members, or they would never pass and the "package" would disintegrate. It was all rather inchoate; no one could be sure what anyone had truly accepted. Bob Orr took the view that "as long as development was perceived to be moving well, attitudes towards the other issues were much softer, and accommodation could be found." Others were much less sanguine and felt that it was time to talk turkey.

Still, virtually all the negotiators felt that dismissing the facilitators and starting from scratch was a recipe for disaster; with everything open to debate, everything would unravel. The only advocates for this approach were John Bolton and the representatives of "the spoilers," as they were called, who were as single-minded about preserving their red lines as Bolton was. This group included countries like Cuba, Venezuela, and Iran, which flaunted their outlaw status in the West, as well as others, such as Algeria, Jamaica, Malaysia, and Egypt, who had made themselves Third World champions by opposing virtually everything the United States wanted and loudly demanding virtually everything the United States opposed. Washington thus found itself with some very strange, and very unsavory, bedfellows.

Bolton had made another apparently maladroit move in his first days in New York. He had met with the Chinese ambassador and agreed, as the latter immediately announced to the press, that the United States would be joining China in blocking Security Council expansion. Bolton appeared not to understand that Security Council reform was already effectively dead and thus did not require further killing. At a recent AU meeting, African countries not only had failed to choose two candidates for permanent membership but had passed a resolution insisting that the new members have the same right of veto as the current members—a demand that even India had agreed to drop. The Gang of Four thus could not count on Africa to vote as a unit for their own resolution, which did not include the veto.

On August 10, the Gang of Four gathered once again in Annan's conference room, and they were a very deflated lot. "Perhaps we made a mistake in judging Africa as a bloc," said Ambassador Ronaldo Mota Sardenberg of Brazil. Annan, who knew very well that everyone is in favor of your plan until it comes time to vote, and had been delicately warning the four against making Model A a do-or-die issue, was careful not to gloat. He said that he still wanted to resolve the issue before September. "But we shouldn't simply cross our arms if it slips beyond the summit. I would encourage you to continue your work, to reach out to others." What about compromise measures? The Coffee Club, now far more grandly known as Uniting for Consensus, was willing to consider eight- or ten-year seats, which might serve as trial runs for permanent status. Yes, said the others, but the Africans won't accept a compromise. Ambassador Oshima, always the most cautious of the four, now conceded that nothing could be completed by September. Perhaps the time had come to think along different lines. "We'd like to have positive language in the outcome document," he said. "But what can it be?"

And just like that, the kamikaze option, the train wreck that was going to send reform to kingdom come, vanished. No vote would ever be taken on the issue. The endless months of wrestling toward an utterly foreseeable draw had wasted crucial time that could have been spent resolving other tough questions, had provoked bitter feelings that would not soon subside, and had created four losers who would sulk their way through the subsequent reform process, with India behaving in the most diva-like manner. Still, contrary to the worst fears, the show went on. And Kofi Annan deserved a good deal of credit for this characteristically quiet victory. Annan had spent months holding the hands of the four ambassadors without ever taking their side—talking to their capitals, counseling against unwarranted optimism, stressing the need to focus on the big picture. And in the end it had been not the West or the P5 that had killed expansion but the Africans. Or that's how it would have played out if John Bolton hadn't felt the need to wave the banner of opposition.

CHAPTER TWENTY-TWO

John Bolton's Nuclear Strategy

P RESIDENT PING WAS EXPECTED TO DELIVER THE FINAL draft of the outcome document on September 6, a week before the heads of state arrived for the summit. By late August, however, the whole process was coming unglued. "Everyone is trying to reopen issues," said John Dauth, the Australian ambassador, who was serving as one of Ping's facilitators. "The Russians are the most difficult customers. They're saying no in the most imperious and Soviet way." The Russians hadn't tipped their hand until the last moment, leaving little time to satisfy their concerns. The Chinese, too, suddenly announced deep reservations about management reform, the Peacebuilding Commission, the responsibility to protect, the Human Rights Council. And all too many members of the G77 were taking the view that a summit consecrated to the five-year review of the Millennium Development Goals had, in fact, been hijacked by the West, and its captive Secretariat, in order to dramatize *their* issues. "I think," said Dauth, "we're staring down the barrel of a failed summit."

There was still an optimistic case to be made that both sides would ultimately settle for a balanced package of reforms. And then John Bolton untied the package. On August 29, he began to issue a series of "Dear Colleague" letters, each accompanied by an extensively rewritten version of a section of the draft document. The "amendments" on disarmament and nonproliferation, for example, proposed to eliminate more than half of the existing language and to erase all references to disarmament, to the regulation of small arms, and to treaties the United States opposed. Bolton even suggested drastic revisions in the proposed Peacebuilding Commission, which the United States strongly supported. And on development, the Third World's quid for the quo of security, Bolton delivered the crowning blow. The American text struck out every reference to the Millennium Development Goals, which until that moment the Bush administration had never found exceptionable. An accompanying document offered a hopelessly casuistic-sounding distinction between the goals embraced at Monterrey and other forums and the more highly specified and prescriptive goals contained in the Sachs report. The document also eliminated references to the commitment to reach 0.7 percent of GNP in aid, to the "front-loading" of assistance, to further debt reduction, and to much else that the Bush administration, and in some cases only the Bush administration, opposed.

Though Bolton had often been acting on his own initiative, the bid to rewrite at the eleventh hour a text that had been laboriously assembled over months was taken at the highest levels. "In the run-up to the GA," says Rice, referring to the summit, "we agreed on a course, and that's the course we followed." Rice felt that the Ping document, in whatever draft, had no chance to pass. Issuing an American version, she says, "was a way of getting people focused, and I thought it was terrific." But it also offered other dissatisfied states the perfect pretext to do the same. The American revisions, for all their particular merits, constituted a serious setback for the committed reformers and another unexpected boon for the spoilers. Ambassador Abdallah Baali of Algeria says, "By coming with substantial amendments, Bolton helped to open up the negotiations. We were very grateful to him for that."

And whatever hope the United States had of bringing along moderate states vanished along with the words "Millennium Development Goals." The U.S. Mission was taken by surprise by the ensuing uproar. "I don't think we had any idea about the sort of reaction it might provoke," an American diplomat concedes. But the MDGs represented the core of the developed world's commitment to poor nations; to eliminate the language was to call the commitment itself into question—a commitment that the Bush administration had only grudgingly and partially made.

Washington's last-minute interventions involved both substance and process, and the latter proved every bit as consequential as the former. At a meeting on August 30, the American ambassador announced that the role of Jean Ping and the facilitators had come to an end; the members themselves would take over. Bolton considered this the only way to ensure that language obnoxious to the United States did not remain in the text. What's more, he viewed Ping as a tool of the G77, and he was almost equally suspicious of the Secretariat staff. And for Bolton, though perhaps not for his political masters, a lowest-common-denominator text that did little to reform the UN was much to be preferred to an ambitious text that committed the United States to policies on disarmament or development that in his view violated its national interests.

Bolton's announcement had an almost instantaneous effect. "The first people to seize on it were the Pakistanis, the Egyptians, and the Algerians," says Bob Orr. "These were the countries which also felt quite confident about their ability to tie things in knots when they needed to. His bombshell was a recipe for inaction, shifting the balance to those who were most interested in stopping things from happening." Now, instead of a neutral party sifting the debate for points of consensus, the diplomats kept their own text, placing in brackets any issue that remained unresolved—which was to say, virtually everything. Before long, the number of brackets had climbed well into the hundreds, with only a few days remaining for deliberation. Whatever Bolton's calculations, his behavior struck professional diplomats as stunningly maladroit. "John is hardworking," Kofi Annan would later say. "He's smart. I think he forgot maybe how things work in this house. When you have these kinds of spoilers and you say, 'Let's do this line by line,' you're giving them a shot. And in fact, for these guys, he opened up the floodgates. Until then, we kept saying, 'Do you want to take the blame for the failure of the summit?' And they were sensitive to that. But when they thought somebody else would take the flak, it was much more difficult to rein them in."

In fact, many African members strongly supported the Peacebuilding Commission, as well as the doctrine of the responsibility to protect; many Latin American countries wanted a strong Human Rights Council. But they would not take on the spoilers. One Western ambassador told me that he regularly had members of "the silent majority" over for lunch. "I would say to them, 'Would you please stand up to these clowns?' " Annan called heads of state and implored them to instruct their representatives to show some spine. He later said to me, "My sense is that things get a bit tense when you have these sorts of negotiations; a sort of groupthink develops. And it becomes very difficult and threatening to go outside what is perceived to be the group view and speak for themselves." Or perhaps reforming the UN mattered less to these states than did scoring political points by showing the folks at home that they were standing up to the American hegemon, to whom they otherwise had to submit on really paramount issues like the war on terror.

Back in the middle of August, Mark Malloch Brown had begun speculating about a worst-case scenario he called "the perfect storm." Iran had just begun to convert nuclear precursor material into fissionable material in direct violation of an agreement it had made with France, Germany, and England; there was talk that in early September the issue could be referred to the Security Council, where it was bound to be deeply neuralgic. And as if it weren't bad enough that the council could be fighting over nonproliferation issues while 175 heads of state arrived in New York to solemnize the reform package, which looked increasingly like it might be written on the front of an index card, the Volcker committee had announced that immediately after Labor Day, it would release its third report, which would lay out precisely how the Secretariat and the Security Council had managed the Oil-for-Food Programme. It was conceivable that the UN would celebrate its sixtieth anniversary by going down the drain.

Volcker and reform had been the two great obsessions of the upper reaches of the Secretariat for the last year, and so it was fitting, in a horrible kind of way, that they had reached their climactic moments simultaneously. It had been the nightmare of the Iraq debate, of course, that had launched the reform effort, but as the fear of "another Iraq" ebbed, the Oil-for-Food scandal had taken its place as the existential threat that compelled drastic change. The protracted unfolding of this dismal episode, the growing revelations of ineptitude (rather than corruption), had the effect of shifting the center of the reform debate, at least in some quarters, from the ineluctable fact of American preeminence in the international order to the more addressable, if also more elusive, question of the UN's own culture. This was, at least in theory, the silver lining of the Volcker inquiry. Of course, it wouldn't be much of a silver lining if the findings were so grave that Annan, and perhaps others, were forced to step down.

The committee published its third interim report, spread over five volumes and slightly more than a thousand pages, on September 7. At the core of the report, beneath the lush profusion of detail, was the section labeled "Findings," in annex 3 of volume 1. The language of this passage had been subjected to minute scrutiny for months. One close friend of Annan, who spoke regularly with the report's author, says, "It was very harsh in summary. I said, 'Who's going to read eight hundred pages? It's the conclusions that will get into the press.' " The crucial passage read, "In sum, in light of these circumstances, the cumulative management performance of the Secretary-General fell short of the standards that the United Nations Organization should strive to maintain." Though "fell short of" was scarcely grounds for resignation, the report connected Annan's failure to manage the program adequately with his failure to rigorously investigate Kojo's entanglement with Cotecna, strongly suggesting an overall lack of accountability. And Annan stood alone, for the findings had little to say about the culpability of member states.

A number of Annan's friends worked to get the language changed. And several weeks before the report was to be published, Volcker and several staff members came to Annan's office to discuss their conclusions with the secretary-general and his attorney, Gregory Craig. Officials with the Volcker panel recall that Annan declared that their judgment was so damning that he would be forced to step down. Annan denies this and says he never contemplated quitting. In fact, he said, Craig challenged the one-sided conclusion, asking, "Do you have an agenda? Are you trying to get him to resign?" Annan felt that the Volcker panel had "pulled their punches on the member states and on the council," just as he felt the authors of the Rwanda report had done. In the end, Volcker agreed to move the Cotecna findings to a separate passage, though not to change the language. Most important, a paragraph was added at the beginning of the section noting that the Security Council "failed to clearly define the broad parameters, policies and administrative responsibilities of the Programme . . . Neither the Security Council nor the Secretariat leadership was in overall control."

Indeed, the report called to mind the famous Thomas Nast cartoon of the Tweed Ring, each scalawag pointing an accusing finger at the next one in the circle. Volcker's investigators discovered that as word of Iraqi manipulation of Oil-for-Food filtered in, first to officials with the Office of the Iraq Programme, then to their superiors in the Secretariat and to members of the council's 661 Committee, almost everyone in a position of authority tried to blunt or hide the news. In the summer of 2000, for example, an OIP official reported to Benon Sevan that a Swedish company had complained that the Iraqis were demanding a 15 percent kickback on a contract. In this and subsequent instances, this official later testified, "Mr. Sevan's line was always that his mandate was to get food and medication to the Iraqi people and it was not his job to report about the kickbacks, which he saw as part of Iraqi culture." Sevan suggested that the aggrieved supplier raise the matter with his own diplomats.

Sevan did his best to keep the bad news under wraps. In the course of a meeting of the 661 Committee in December 2000, a British diplomat asked an OIP official about reports of kickbacks and was told that officials had "no knowledge" of such allegations. When the diplomat subsequently asked program officers to prepare a paper on the issue, another official came back with the answer that since OIP had received no "formal, official reports of kickbacks," there was nothing to write—an evasive response that the official later conceded was the "company line." But the member states on the committee were scarcely more eager to pursue allegations of wrongdoing.

In March 2001, the United States, with British backing, submitted a proposal to curtail the illegal Iraqi "commissions" on each contract. The idea received only cursory discussion. An American diplomat raised the topic once again the following month. "The United States underscored the importance of eliminating kickbacks," the Volcker report stated, "in order to ensure that Iraq lacked the funds necessary to develop weapons of mass destruction. Both France and Russia indicated they were awaiting instructions from their capitals regarding the

United States proposals. However, it does not appear that France or Russia ever responded with any definitive positions on these proposals." Russia and France were Iraq's most important supporters on the Security Council, and the Iraqis, in turn, awarded the largest volume of contracts for humanitarian goods to French and Russian companies—who paid, in turn, the largest share of kickbacks. But even the Americans and the British were only intermittently vigilant. The 661 Committee operated according to an unspoken pact in which the United States, and to a lesser extent the U.K., scrutinized contracts for evidence of "dual use" products but waved through almost everything else in order to ensure a steady flow of goods, and thus placate the other members of the P5.

Sevan, who had the rank of under-secretary-general, spoke regularly to Louise Fréchette, the deputy secretary-general, as well as to Iqbal Riza and Kofi Annan. He was loath to report to them, as to the 661 Committee, the growing body of information about systematic bribery and surcharges. But by 2001, these had become matters of common knowledge. Volcker found that Annan's briefing notes for a meeting with the Iraqi foreign minister in February 2001 suggested that he raise the issue of both kickbacks and oil surcharges. The secretary-general appears not to have mentioned either issue. Annan explained to investigators that he believed such subjects belonged in the "technical" talks led by Sevan rather than in the "political" discussions he held. The report notes that Annan also made no reference to these allegations in any of the 90- or 180-day reports on Iraq that he submitted to the Security Council.

For Annan, Fréchette, and Riza, the most damning part of the third interim report was the description of how Oil-for-Food was, or rather wasn't, managed by the thirty-eighth floor. When Annan created the Office of the Iraq Programme, with Sevan at its head, in March 1998, Riza sent a memo to Fréchette delegating to her authority for the "overall supervision" of the program. Fréchette, incredibly, denied to investigators that she had such a role; when shown the memo, she said she had never seen it before. And yet it's easy to see why she never felt that she was in charge. In the upper reaches of the Secretariat, personal relationships easily trumped job titles and official memos; Sevan had known Riza and Annan for years as they climbed together up the UN's career ladder, and he felt perfectly free to sit down with either man for a chat. But Riza, too, disclaimed responsibility, telling investigators that he had "no substantive involvement" in Oil-for-Food, even though he discussed these issues regularly with Sevan and the secretary-general and, as the report notes, met far more frequently with Iraqi officials than Fréchette did.

As for Annan, he had long since accustomed himself to the idea that real power lay with the Security Council, not the Secretariat. The council had imposed sanctions on Iraq and then established Oil-for-Food to mitigate the effect of the sanctions. It had established a committee, as the rules required, to monitor that sanctions regime, and he had established the Office of the Iraq Programme to serve as the bureaucratic arm of that committee. Benon Sevan worked for the council, not for him. He had assumed, wrongly, that Sevan was telling the 661 Committee everything it needed to know. He said that he had often told Sevan to report the kickback allegations in the 90- or 180-day reports and imagined that that must have happened. "Clearly," the report concludes, "Mr. Sevan bears responsibility for withholding information concerning the kickback scheme. Yet, the 38th floor, too, had an obligation to ensure that the Security Council and the 661 Committee were adequately informed."

In fact, Annan did not feel that he had fallen short of the UN's standards or anyone else's. The council, he said, had created a "messy structure" by dividing authority over Iraq among various committees and bodies. The lines of responsibility had been blurred. He had found the passages on the UN's managerial culture "painful to see" but also unfair. "There is a tendency to generalize from the particular," he said. Oil-for-Food was "sui generis": the UN had done nothing like it before, and never would again. He felt that he had been mistreated, but he had held his tongue. "I could have resisted and fought and argued," he said, "but then I would still be feeding the beast."

Volcker came down harder on Fréchette than on her boss. After quoting her to the effect that she was "not aware of any problems involving the Oil-For-Food Programme," the report observes that the DSG in fact knew of the kickback scheme, rampant oil smuggling, and deep dissension inside OIP. After noting that Fréchette "eventually conceded that there 'were a few signals' indicating the Programme was amiss," the passage sardonically concludes, "The documents and witness accounts chronicled herein reveal more than just a 'few signals.' The Deputy Secretary-General knew about—but did not act upon—many reports of serious Programme violations." When I asked Reid Morden, the chief investigator and a former Canadian diplomat who had known and worked with Fréchette for thirty years, if he expected her to resign in the face of such harsh reproach, he said, "I thought she would be giving that serious consideration." But he also recalled that when Fréchette had offered her resignation in the aftermath of the August 19 bombing, Annan had not accepted it. This time around she didn't offer, and Annan didn't ask.

Volcker, who had always maintained that he had accepted the assignment in order to help repair an institution he highly cherished, presented his massive inquiry less as an indictment than as irrefutable proof of the need for drastic managerial reform. The report included a program for change, proposing the creation of a chief operating officer who would report to the secretary-general but have "authority over all aspects of administration." Of course, Louise Fréchette's job had been imagined very much in this light when it had been created in 1997. Volcker also suggested, among other things, the establishment of an independent oversight board to oversee the UN's myriad audit and investigative functions. Annan himself picked up this theme in a speech to the Security Council. In language that for him sounded almost brazen, he said, "The Inquiry Committee has ripped away the curtain and shone a harsh light into the most unsightly corners of the Organization. None of us—Member States, Secretariat, Agencies, Funds or Programmes—can be proud of what it has found. Who among us can now claim that UN management is not a problem or is not in need of reform?"

The Volcker report exploded in the middle of the reform deliberations like a hand grenade—or so it felt to those who already believed that the UN had to be saved from its own managerial culture. "The stakes are so much higher because of Volcker," Bob Orr said the day after the report was released. Orr felt that a combination of Volcker and relentless persuasion might get the debate out of neutral. But I wondered if Orr's optimism wasn't getting the better of him. Every few days I spoke to both Orr and John Dauth, whom I could always count on for a vinegar-coated rather than a sugar-coated account. Dauth was an echt Australian, bluff and gregarious and irreverent—save that he was also one of the very few openly gay members of the diplomatic community. He somehow managed to be bluff and irreverent even about being gay. Dauth was a realist of the most gimlet-eyed variety. He didn't see anyone budging on management reform, or on much else for that matter. The current text, he said, still had 150 brackets. He had tried to skin the cat on nonproliferation by sitting down with "the criminals"— Egypt, Iran, Pakistan, and the United States. But the United States wouldn't give an inch on disarmament, and the others wouldn't budge on proliferation; the whole thing looked doomed. Bolton had joined the spoilers in refusing to allow any issue to come to a vote. Everything would have to be decided by consensus, which was tantamount to saying that nothing would be decided. It was ironic, to say the least, that so pitiless a foe of the institution had seized on one of its most paralyzing rules in order to drive his vision of "reform."

Annan's policy committee met on the morning of September 9, two days after Volcker, and a very solemn meeting it was. Louise Fréchette kicked things off by saying, "What do we do if the summit fails? How do we deal with the morning after?" Shashi Tharoor immediately jumped in; the question had obviously touched a nerve in this institutional loyalist. "It's very important that people understand that the reform continues after the sixteenth of September," he said. "Also, SG, let me say that I joined this organization twenty-seven and a half years ago, and if I had said that the organization I was joining would someday be conducting intrusive inspections for weapons of mass destruction, administering whole territories, monitoring elections all over the world, putting former government leaders in the dock in war-crimes tribunals, they would have told me that you have no idea what kind of organization you've joined. And I could name half a dozen other examples. My point is that the UN has changed profoundly, but we've done so quietly, in a case-by-case manner. I don't think we should allow anyone to tell us that we've failed." It was a splendid speech from a splendid, sometimes splendiferous speaker; Tharoor was defending at once the institution, his own career, and, of course, the secretary-general.

As they spoke, the nine or ten people around the table, Annan's closest advisers, sorted themselves into John Ruggie's two categories: the traditionalists, who, at this moment of duress, wished above all to reaffirm the nobility of the institution; and the modernizers, who saw in the crisis a final opportunity to save the UN from itself. The traditionalists may have believed in reform, but they recoiled from the notion that the UN needed to be "saved." Ibrahim Gambari shared Tharoor's view. The problem, for him, was perception management. "We have to blow our own trumpet," he said. Jean-Marie Guéhenno, Jan Egeland, and Mark Malloch Brown were in the second camp. The UN, said the humanitarian coordinator, had to embrace a "deeper political engagement" in the Middle East, Nepal, northern Uganda.

Tharoor bridled. "Jan, are these problems matters of resources, or are they political problems? Would Museveni *like* us to be engaged in northern Uganda?"

"Museveni might not like it," Egeland retorted, "but there are a hundred ways we could do something." Now Malloch Brown returned to the matter at hand. He was sitting to Annan's right, as always; Iqbal Riza had always positioned himself with due deference at the end of the table. But Riza rarely spoke, and Malloch Brown often did. "Maybe we can break with every secretary-general until now," he said. "Maybe we don't have to go along with the comfortable lie that this was a success. You could say that the summit was a failure."

Now Tharoor was well and truly scandalized. "If you say that the summit was a failure," he asked, "what happens then? Are we saying that the member states are incapable of making a decision?" Malloch Brown emitted an uncharacteristic squeak, and Tharoor plowed passionately onward. "No, I'm serious. I think that's a dangerous path."

And where in all this was Kofi Annan? Was he a traditionalist or a modernizer, a defender at the ramparts or an engineer of the new? After Tharoor's flashing oratory, he said, in his unadorned way, "We have to be coldly realistic in analyzing the results." But then, a moment later: "We've gotten the world to accept that security, development, and human rights are linked. It's a great achievement, intellectually." That scarcely sounded like cold realism. Annan understood, at least abstractly, the need for pitiless self-scrutiny, but his profound love for and identification with the institution made him flinch when he looked too close.

By now the unwieldy mass of negotiators had been cut down, at Ping's urging, first to a "core group" of thirty, and then, when that body had made no headway, to a yet more select group of twelve. On Saturday morning, the tenth—four days after the supposed deadline—the twelve diplomats gathered in conference room 4 in the UN basement, which one ambassador came to call "the dungeon." Bolton had by now been overruled, apparently by Rice, on the MDGs; the United States had also agreed to stipulate that other countries, though not themselves, felt it important to commit to a timetable to reach 0.7 percent, and to carry out the terms of the Kyoto Protocol on global warming. According to several participants, Bolton announced these compromises to the group; but it was too little and far too late. Conference room 4 was a vast space, but soon the members were huddling together by ideology—the G77, with sometimes a subgroup of spoilers like Jamaica and Egypt; the EU and Canada, which chaired the sessions; and the United States, whom nobody wanted to be seen with.

Bolton also staged the kind of confrontation for which he had already become notorious. He said, "I want to be sure that there's no alternate text being prepared somewhere in this building." This was Bolton's consuming fear—that "the bureaucracy" was secretly hatching an October surprise, an anti-American, pro–Third World document to be unveiled at the eleventh hour. He turned to Jean Ping and said, "Please give me assurances that neither you nor the secretary-general are preparing a parallel text." Ping then made an elaborate and opaque speech, during which Bolton became visibly agitated. Bolton then turned to Bob Orr and said, "I want Bob Orr to answer that question." In fact, Orr had been updating the outcome document almost hourly, deleting contentious passages, provisionally adding others that had briefly struggled into the sunlight of consensus before lapsing back into dispute—all to be held in readiness for the moment when the diplomats despaired of reaching agreement among themselves. But Orr looked at Bolton and said, "Our drafting exercise ended on the twenty-first of March when the SG handed his draft to the member states"—a transparent sophistry. "He didn't ask in an artful way," says Orr, by way of mitigation.

Condoleezza Rice insists that this precinct-house interrogation was mere diplomatic stagecraft. "Everybody suspected that there was another document being worked on," she says. "In diplomacy, you very often double-track or even triple-track." It must be said, though, that if Bolton was not simply working one track, he was a far more gifted prevaricator than all prior evidence indicated.

The Group of 12 took up one issue after another, made headway, and then slipped back. The group agreed to a forceful and unambiguous definition of terrorism, but the G77 countries insisted that the ensuing paragraph contain the usual exemption for wars of national resistance—"the right to throw a bomb on a bus," as one Western ambassador put it. So both paragraphs went in the trash bin. The United States wanted language stating that there could be no "impunity" for war criminals, but the EU insisted that such a declaration also acknowledge the role of the International Criminal Court, which the United States opposed; so that went, too. Whatever chance remained of including even vague and hortatory language on nonproliferation vanished when the United States insisted that a standard paragraph acknowledging the goal of a nuclear-free world follow a passage on the urgency of confronting the threat of nuclear terrorism, even though in all previous documents the sequence had been the reverse.

Everything that wasn't nailed down began to delaminate. Even the responsibility to protect, which had the strong support not only of the West but of many African countries and had long ceased to be an article of contention, came under a blistering attack from India, which saw itself as a pillar of the nonaligned movement, and in any case was now sulking about the failure of Security Council expansion. Ambassador Sen delivered a characteristically formalistic and windy attack on the legal and moral foundations of the doctrine. The very name, he said, was offensive. Would the ambassador accept the doctrine under a less provocative moniker? Yes, he would. Junior diplomats were sent to work and came back with five new names: Protecting People from the Crime of Genocide and such. Ambassador Sen began to stall, saying he hadn't yet received instructions from New Delhi. Kofi Annan and

Prime Minister Paul Martin of Canada called Prime Minister Manmohan Singh to urge him to resolve the issue. British ambassador Emyr Jones Parry pressed Sen to make up his mind, and Sen lashed out angrily. Finally, at midnight on Monday, according to one participant, "We said, 'Okay, jerk-off, what's your position on the title?' "

"I don't know yet," said Sen. And the issue remained in brackets.

It quickly became clear that the rules that Bolton had insisted on tipped the advantage to far more experienced and cohesive opponents. Bolton's unwillingness to coordinate strategy with his own allies meant, as one of them says, that "we were disorganized in front of people who were extremely well organized." By early Saturday evening, the group had spent two hours arguing fruitlessly over the Peacebuilding Commission, widely considered the least controversial of the major issues. Bolton would not budge from the American position that the body report solely to the Security Council, rather than first to the council and then to other bodies, though a modest concession almost certainly would have ended the stalemate. One of the spoilers suggested they approve the commission in principle and leave the details to be worked out later by the General Assembly, which could be counted on to make the commission subordinate to itself rather than to the Security Council. Worse still, the spoilers had planned to trade concessions on the peace-building body in order to make a defiant stand on the Human Rights Council. Nevertheless, at about 9:30 p.m., Bolton, frustrated and outmaneuvered, agreed.

With peace-building now safely disposed of, Munir Akram, the Pakistani delegate and a wily negotiator, flourished before the group a "compromise text" on the Human Rights Council that he had been so good as to draw up. The text represented a step backward from language that had been agreed to earlier; countries could be singled out for criticism only in the case of "gross and continuous abuse," a very high standard. The Pakistanis themselves opposed any form of "naming and shaming"; Akram told me later that the failure of the current Human Rights Commission to censure India for its caste system and "its treatment of women" proved that the system was "completely arbitrary" and had more to do with power than with moral status.

But Akram knew that the Chinese, who would not accept any organ that could single them out for criticism, would oppose even this watered-down plan. And the Chinese did so, along with Russia and Egypt. Perhaps, Akram then smoothly suggested, we could approve the council on principle, as we had the Peacebuilding Commission? This would be a genuine catastrophe, for the council was an indispensable symbol of UN renewal as well as a major step forward on human rights. But it was now eleven o'clock, and everyone was getting numb. A European diplomat who had returned from dinner not long before, and still had his wits about him, realized that Bolton and Allan Rock, the Canadian ambassador and a first-time diplomat, were prepared to accept Akram's suggestion. They were outnumbered and outmaneuvered. This official then stepped in to say, "I suggest we reflect on Munir's proposal, and we will be back tomorrow with a counterproposal."

The longer the diplomats talked, the more polarized the conversations became. Who really cared about the UN enough—or, for that matter, cared about any of the reforms enough—to put aside some small measure of national interest in order to ensure a meaningful outcome? Europe, the Anglophone countries (minus the United States), a few Third World outliers. The others were happy to play a game of chicken, threatening to wreck the process in order to block whatever they deemed unacceptable.

The Group of 12 reconvened at 8:00 a.m. on Sunday, only to resume its downward spiral. "We watched the death over a period of four hours of the Human Rights Council, terrorism, and the Peacebuilding Commission," says one ambassador. And now they were running out of time. The heads of state would arrive Wednesday; the outcome document, whatever it would be, had to be completed by Tuesday. Finally, at around midnight, the British, who occupied the EU seat by virtue of their presidency of the organization, volunteered to produce what diplomats call a "harvest document," in which one gathers together the fruits of discussion—which is to say, the points of agreement. This normally represents the terminal stage of negotiation.

The harvest text covered only management reform, the Human Rights Council, and terrorism. The British said they would not include development until some progress had been made on the rest of the agenda; and on the other main issues, like nonproliferation, the group had made so little headway that there was nothing to harvest. And even on the three issues it covered, the text was sketchy to the point of being skeletal. Bob Orr had been speaking regularly to Bolton and his staff. Now, he said, "when I pointed out to him that he was going to lose all of management, all of human rights, and a good chunk of terrorism, and that would be two and a half out of his top three priorities, he said, 'Well, I've always said that reform is not a one-night stand' "—a phrase he had begun to wield repeatedly in the face of criticism. Absolutist that he was, Bolton would not avail himself of the tools of diplomacy, even to his own advantage. "He would not give anything away to get his priorities—even rhetoric," said Orr. "I said, 'If you include "the right to development," we can get concessions on management.' He didn't want to do it. He never traded the MDGs for anything." Bolton struck Orr as oddly nonchalant about the prospect of losing the Human Rights Council and the Peacebuilding Commission.

Orr concluded that Bolton had been pursuing what he called "the ultimate nuclear strategy": "It's either my outcome and we walk out of here alive, or leave the place a smoldering ruin." This appears to be close to the truth. According to an American official deeply involved with the negotiations, "I think we on the U.S. side, and the radicals on their side, thought a lot of this would just disappear. We thought huge portions would fall out because of disagreement, and we would salvage the heart of it. Our guess was we'd end up with somewhere between twelve and fifteen pages." What they ended up with instead, when the utterly exhausted negotiators finally knocked off at 1:00 on Tuesday morning, was a minimal harvest document and a version of the original—Ping 6—with 150 brackets. It was widely agreed that the United States and Cuba ranked first and second, or perhaps second and first, in bracket authorship.

For the previous week, Kofi Annan had been meeting at 8:00 every morning with Jean Ping and Jan Eliasson, the ambassador from Sweden and the incoming president of the General Assembly. They all knew that they might have to call a halt to the marathon wrestling match in conference room 4, but every day Ping and Eliasson said, "Give us another day." The ambassadors were sleepwalking, but they still entertained the collective delusion that they were close to an agreement. Annan was getting more and more agitated. The prospect of declaring the summit a failure, as Malloch Brown had rashly proposed, went against the grain of his entire being. And of course it wouldn't just be *their* failure; it would be his. What was meant to have served as the supreme achievement of his career would instead serve as its epitaph. Still, Annan waited. He knew that he could not intervene until every last possibility had been exhausted.

On Monday afternoon, Annan met once again with his special envoys. "There is the option of 'Do what you can, leave the rest for later,'" Annan said, thinking of the harvest document. "I'm not very pleased with that thought." He urged the envoys to speak to key figures in their regions. "One message we should give is we should think of ending up with nothing when the heads of state come, and that would be a disaster." Joaquim Chissano said he had in fact arranged a meeting with African ambassadors but most had been too busy preparing for their presidents' arrival to come. Annan said the Americans had assured him that they wanted "a real document" and they weren't preparing to pull a three-page statement of principles out of their pocket. Yes, said Ali Alatas of Indonesia, but the Asians fear that if they go with Ping 6 minus the brackets, "this will eliminate 80 percent of their views, and would just give the Americans what they want."

That night the Group of 12 ran into the same brick wall. At his meeting the next morning with Ping and Eliasson, Annan said, "The heads of state are coming in twenty-four hours. What are we going to tell them?" Both men agreed that the time had come to materialize the parallel text that was not supposed to exist and place it before the members.

And now, according to a number of the players, everyone went to battle stations. The two GA presidents began talking to key ambassadors, and Annan's top officials fanned out to speak to their own constituencies. Bob Orr called Condi Rice's aide Shirin Tahir-Kheli to walk her through the outcome document that he and his staff, as well as Ping's staff, were assembling at that very moment. Mark Malloch Brown called Nicholas Burns. And Annan, like the man drawing the short straw, called John Bolton. "Look, John," he said, "I have a hundred, a hundred and forty brackets in the document. If we release that, it's not a document. If we drop the brackets, it's incomplete and incoherent. The president"—that is, Ping—"is going to use his good judgment, having listened to the members."

Bolton bridled. "I'm not sure we're ready for that." He did not sound like a man who had been "double-tracking."

Annan gently persisted. "John, if we give you more time, are you sure you can clean up all the brackets?"

"How much time?"

"I don't think we have more than two to three hours."

"No, we can't do it that fast."

"Then what choice do we have?"

Annan asked Bolton to come to his office to review the document. Bolton arrived at about 9:00; he was a very unhappy man. He said, "When I was asking Ping and Orr whether there was a parallel document, this was what I had in mind." Bolton left without committing himself, though Annan felt that he now saw that the game was up. As Bolton returned to the U.S. Mission, Ping and his facilitators were speaking to other key figures and imploring them to accept half a loaf rather than none. The EU countries had to concede that no further progress would be made on the Human Rights Council; the G77 countries had to accept the language on management reform in order to hold on to the gains they had made on development; the Russians and the Chinese had to agree to the elimination of the language in the Charter branding Germany and Japan "enemy states." There was still last-minute horse-trading to be done. The G77 won the deletion of a strong statement about the need to give the secretary-general more management flexibility. The U.S. Mission asked for eight changes; three, deemed minor, were granted, and five were not. The Americans finally accepted "the right to development," which in fact they had endorsed in various pacts in the previous few years.

I had spoken that morning with John Dauth, who, having no idea of the secret confabulations on the thirty-eighth floor, said he was prepared to tell his prime minister that no outcome at all might be preferable to the "derisory outcome" apparently in the offing. The scheduled meeting of the Group of 12 had been postponed, for reasons not stated, from ten to noon. By 11:45, conference room 4 was surrounded by reporters and cameramen with cables snaking every which way. The ambassadors trooped in; many still had no idea what was happening upstairs. At 12:10, the meeting broke up, to reconvene at 1:00. It was all very confusing; the long-predicted collapse seemed close at hand.

Munir Akram, elegant in houndstooth, glided into the scrum of reporters. "Big picture, Ambassador!" shouted one. "Who's winning?"

"North," Akram said, and then went on his way.

The diplomats did, in fact, return soon after 1:00. But now they had a new document in their hands—Ping 7. By then it was already clear that all but the most recalcitrant of the 191 members had agreed to accept the text as the outcome document. Now the members clamored for an early slot in the schedule of speeches, so that they could put their special stamp of approval on this historic occasion, this extraordinary commitment to renewal, and so on. Annan had been wrong about many things, but he had been right about one big thing: the permanent reps would swallow what they didn't like rather than greet their heads of state empty-handed.

There was a peculiar interval, lasting about twenty-four hours, when the Secretariat was practically euphoric, not to mention profoundly relieved, at having saved the reform package from the trash compactor, while the press took it for granted that they had saved nothing but face, if that. At a press conference that evening after the General Assembly had officially endorsed the outcome document, Annan repeatedly said, in various forms, that "we didn't get everything we wanted" but "we can work with what we have been given." The press, on the other hand, asked the secretary-general how he planned to deal with the "fiasco" of his "watered-down document." Bob Orr, alarmed that the summit was being spun as a failure, held an off-the-record press conference—a poorly attended one—at which he asked the reporters to distinguish between the farcical process and the actual outcome, which, he insisted, contained solid progress in every area save nonproliferation.

It was, in fact, impossible to answer the question "Was the summit a success?" without first asking, "Compared to what?" If one compared the outcome to the expectations that Kofi Annan had raised in his "fork in the road" speech, the summit was a failure. Guidelines for the legitimate use of force, the one reform that could preclude another debacle like Iraq, had barely glimmered into life before falling victim to U.S. opposition. More broadly, the overall package was supposed to hang not on adroit horse-trading but on an acceptance of mutual interdependence—your threat is my threat. Even Annan conceded that al-

though "they walked away verbalizing it, they never really accepted it."
The debate had done far more to limn the differences among blocs of
nations than to diminish them. Now it was obvious that there were two
UNs, one for the North and one for the South—and a third, perhaps,
for the United States.

Compared to the high-level panel report or to "In Larger Freedom,"
or to Ping 3 or to the moment before John Bolton arrived in New York,
the outcome document was a failure. On the other hand, compared to
what virtually everyone expected that very morning, it was quite a success. As one ambassador put it, "The best thing you can say is, 'We
avoided abject humiliation.' " But that wasn't actually the best thing
you could say, for the reform project was plainly a success by the standards of UN history. "These are the most far-reaching reforms in sixty
years," said Steve Stedman, though he was honest enough to add, "God
knows there's not much competition."

On development, the members confirmed the core of the new partnership drawn up at earlier conferences, including the G8 conference
the previous July: The industrialized nations agreed to provide $50 bil-
lion in additional foreign aid by 2010 and to add additional billions by
reaching 0.7 percent by 2015 (a vow made on behalf only of "many developed countries" to satisfy American objections), to forgive the debts
of the most impoverished countries, and to move toward grant-based
rather than loan-based aid. Recipient countries vowed to devise and
implement "national development strategies," to improve governance
and reduce corruption, and to improve the climate for the private sector and private investment. Lengthy passages about "South-South
cooperation," "sustainable development," "gender equality," and other
worthy topics stretched this portion to exactly one-half of the thirty-
five-page document.

On peace and security issues, the members condemned terrorism
"by whomever, wherever and for whatever purposes," though they did
not actually define a terrorist act, as "In Larger Freedom" had; adopted
in unequivocal language the doctrine of the responsibility to protect
(India having finally given way on the subject); and agreed—but only in
principle—to create a Peacebuilding Commission and a Human Rights
Council. On management reform, they agreed to review all mandates
older than five years and invited the secretary-general to submit pro-

posals to the General Assembly "on the conditions and measures necessary for him to carry out his managerial responsibilities effectively."
On the central issues of Security Council expansion, nonproliferation
and disarmament, and rules governing the use of force, the outcome
document was essentially silent.

The final text managed to disappoint almost every one of the UN's
191 members. The extremists in the G77 felt they had made vast concessions in order to essentially codify existing agreements on development. Even the moderates were not especially pleased. Ambassador
Dumisani Kumalo of South Africa, one of Annan's key interlocutors
with developing countries, said that his country, too, had favored including an exemption for wars of national resistance on the definition
of terrorism—"How can *we* say that people living under colonial domination shouldn't fight for their rights?"—and opposed a more muscular
Human Rights Council. South Africa had, he said, favored management reform, but understood very well why others didn't: "Just a small
part of this institution is about development; the rest is about security.
The fear is that if you give the secretary-general authority to move people around, they will just move everything to the Security Council
and give them all these posts." And Kumalo said that while he had
been pleased to see an emerging consensus on development, he recognized that the development agenda was essentially voluntary—we
pledge to do this and that—while the security agenda involved binding
commitments.

But the members hadn't made binding commitments on the security agenda, either. Unable to agree on crucial details, they had left the
real work on terrorism and human rights and peace-building and management reform to the General Assembly, the last institution one would
count on to take a fork in the road. Kofi Annan had warned that the
pressure to act would be off the moment the heads of state went home;
no one, including Annan, was foolhardy enough to forecast success
now that reform was being run through the UN's own paralytic
machinery.

Could it have been otherwise? Most Western diplomats and Secretariat officials believed that something very like Ping 3, minus the various bits of rhetoric intolerable to the United States, could have gained
consensus had John Bolton not lowered his horns and reduced the

whole thing to splinters. Others are less convinced that developing countries would, in fact, have accepted the package. Condoleezza Rice argues that "the real problem was not John but the G4"—that the pointless wrangle over expanding the Security Council diverted crucial, and finite, energies. We'll never know. But there can be little question that UN reform was far more substantive before Bolton arrived than after. And the earlier document would almost certainly have been closer to the Bush administration's professed wishes.

What, then, did Bolton think he was doing? One European diplomat deeply involved in the discussions said, "What they thought they were going to deliver to President Bush on his arrival in New York is still pretty opaque to me. The charitable interpretation is that Bolton may have thought that a process of negotiation will eventually yield a result that's more on U.S. terms. Less charitably, you might suppose that he thought there was still room for a short text. And less charitably still, you might suppose that a UN collapse is no disaster for Bolton's base." Bob Orr put the matter more bluntly: "Either he's not the negotiator he thinks he is, or he has a different agenda from the American position." Perhaps the most positive construction one can put on Bolton's *High Noon*–style of diplomacy is that his deep suspicion of the UN caused him to act in such a way as to perfectly satisfy his own expectations.

But Bolton's failure, and the irony of his rescue by the very institution he held in such low regard, carried a large political meaning as well. The administration he represented was itself divided between those who believed that America faced a hostile and largely uncomprehending world, and thus must be prepared to go its own way, and those who believed that persuasion and diplomacy could, at the very least, diminish differences and reduce tensions. The terrorist attacks of 9/11 had decisively tipped the balance between the two, leaving the professionals in the State Department and the CIA virtually powerless. The failure to win Security Council approval for a resolution authorizing war only vindicated the hard-liners, and the war itself was the highwater mark of the administration's triumphal unilateralism. From then on, though, the White House began to discover the very high price it had paid by going it alone. Professed policy never changed, but from the outset of President Bush's second term the tone of voice became notably chastened, even conciliatory. What catastrophe had done, failed ambitions undid, and the balance tipped back toward diplomacy.

John Bolton was, of course, a charter member of the first camp; 9/11 had only vindicated his views. It was precisely his air of bristling alert, his deep suspicion of diplomacy and of the search for common ground, that endeared him to such as Vice President Cheney. Bolton's very rigidity offered reassurance that he would not be co-opted by the compromising spirit of Turtle Bay. And he was not. He kept his hand firm on the tiller even as the roar of the waterfall ahead grew louder and louder. Perhaps he *wanted* to plunge off the precipice. But that wasn't what his superiors wanted. It may be that Condoleezza Rice always planned to ensure a safe landing, as she herself claims; but it's just as likely that this madcap pilot, and thus the administration he represented, was saved by just the thing he most despised—the finesse, patience, and circumspection of the professional diplomats on the thirty-eighth floor.

On the morning of September 14, President Bush, as head of state of the UN's home country, led off the endless parade of speakers marking the UN's sixtieth anniversary. And it was obvious from the very first, when he recognized "the vital work and great ideals" of the place he called "the You-nahted Nations," that he had come to praise the institution, not to bury it. Yes, he did begin with a weirdly parochial reminder of the various states—Alabama, Mississippi, Louisiana—that had been devastated by Hurricane Katrina a few weeks earlier, but he then went on to thank the world's nations for their response to America's misfortune and to list the reforms, above all in regard to terrorism, that his administration was seeking. And he said, in plain language no one could miss, "We are committed to the Millennium Development Goals." It was widely noted that the president could have saved himself and many others a great deal of suffering by making this ringing declaration a month earlier.

The reform drama had not quite come to an end. On the sixteenth, the General Assembly was to formally adopt the outcome document in a show of consensus. In UN terms, "consensus" means not "everyone agrees" but "everyone who doesn't agree will keep it to himself." Any member can upset the applecart by demanding a vote. And at an early-afternoon meeting with his special envoys, Annan revealed that twenty minutes before, the Venezuelan ambassador had informed him that his country would demand a vote. Venezuela was the spoiler nonpareil—a country with no discernible interest in improving the UN but, under its populist president, Hugo Chávez, an insatiable appetite for theatrical gestures of protest. Annan then spent an hour and a half closeted with Chávez—a tireless monologuist in the mold of Fidel Castro—in the hopes that he could be persuaded not to rain on everyone else's parade.

The ceremony of approval got pushed later and later in the day as the secretary-general tried to reason with this blustering autocrat. Finally, close to 7:00 p.m., Jan Eliasson, the new president of the General Assembly, opened the session and said, "We will move to the draft resolution." First a procedural issue had to be settled. "All agreed?" the president asked. He brought down the gavel. "It is decided." Then he noticed some sort of commotion to one side. "Pardon?" Eliasson recognized the ambassador from Venezuela, Fermín Toro Jiménez. The ambassador thereupon delivered a lengthy harangue against everything in the document save the punctuation. Chávez had apparently agreed not to call for a vote so long as Venezuela could register its own objection and deliver its rant. When at last the ambassador looked up from his text, President Eliasson blandly read off the number of the resolution, waited a split second, and said, "It is so decided." And that was that.

Or not quite. Two countries wished to footnote their position. The first was the United States. Ambassador Bolton graciously thanked one and all, and then got to the point. "The United States understands," he said, that reference in the text to two international conferences and "the use of the phrase 'reproductive health' . . . cannot be interpreted to constitute support, endorsement, or promotion of abortion." It was a tart reminder of American exceptionalism: just as the 0.7 percent target might apply to all developed countries save the United States, so the United States reserved the right to interpret international agreements so as not to conflict with its own preferences or its domestic political imperatives. And then the Cuban ambassador spoke, lambasting the document much as his Venezuelan epigone had.

It was fitting that the two dissenters were the United States and Cuba, the two most effective and relentless forces of obstruction throughout the negotiating process. It was also shocking, at least from the point of view of the confident internationalism that had constituted the mainstream in American foreign policy from the time of FDR. Despite the new tone of accommodation, typified by Condoleezza Rice, the United States, at bottom, defined its interests in such a way as to isolate it from the community even of like-minded nations. Of course there was a tradition, stretching back to the dawn of the Republic, of American exceptionalism. But now the old faith that here was a nation set apart by Providence had mated with a very new sense of vulnerability, and perhaps also with a rogue strain of provincialism, of contempt for the foreign, to produce this unfamiliar, unattractive, and oddly brittle phenomenon of preemptive belligerence.

And the preemptively belligerent America, typified by Vice President Dick Cheney and by John Bolton, his emissary to Turtle Bay, feared, above all, containment. For leading figures in the Bush administration, and for the conservatives who had effectively ruled Congress since 1994, the very act of mingling in the commons of nations, of negotiation and compromise, which required that one accept the validity of competing interests and the plausibility of alternative points of view—the act, in short, of diplomacy—seemed fatally tainted. No fraternizing with the enemy! Jesse Helms might don the UN cap and sup at the UN table, but of American sovereignty one would surrender not an inch.

How could the UN, and Kofi Annan, its consensus-seeking leader, survive the rise of the anti-consensus superpower? The answer was "just barely." Annan had done everything in his power to accommodate the Bush administration's demands, had risked his dignity and his standing within the institution by pulling out a handkerchief every time Washington sneezed. He had done so because in any contest between his dignity and the UN's effectiveness, he would sacrifice the former to the latter. But what had that gotten him, or his institution? Not much. The UN had returned to Iraq, but at a terrible sacrifice. Annan had survived the Oil-for-Food onslaught, but just barely.

What's more, the recalcitrance of the White House had given license to others to misbehave. Cuba was not a problem for the UN—except when Cuba's reflexive defiance of Washington came to represent a posture of self-respect for dozens of other nations who would never think of adopting Cuba's ruinous economic policies. During the Cold War the UN had been divided in half—East versus West, North versus South. Now it was divided in three: the developing world on one side, the United States on the other, and "the West" in the middle. But it all seemed so *unnecessary*: globalization may not have given countries a sense of shared purpose in the face of threats to the international order, as Kofi Annan maintained, but it had certainly compelled a genuine ideological convergence. Virtually all the UN's members practiced some variant of free-market capitalism and at least professed democracy, but the organization felt as polarized as it had been thirty years before, when both capitalism and democracy were under assault.

The UN felt untenable; but at such moments one had to remind oneself that the UN had also felt untenable in the late 1940s, and the early '80s, and the mid-'90s. And a giddy sense of renewal had dawned with the end of the Cold War, and then again with the advent of Kofi Annan. The UN was, by its very nature, too sensitive to the tumult of global politics to enjoy calm seas. Any blow to the international system would leave the UN wobbling. The shock of 9/11, combined with the ideological predispositions of the Bush administration, had launched the United States on an orbit of its own. But the shock of Iraq, and the departure or chastening of some of the ideologues, had drawn the United States steadily, if slowly, back into the solar system. America would always be the UN's outlier, all the more so since Islamic terrorists were obsessed with this gaudy incarnation of Western wealth and power. But President Bush's immediate predecessors had understood that they could get something quite precious from the UN for a very modest price. And in the fall of 2005, John Bolton notwithstanding, there were grounds for hope that that recognition had finally dawned on the White House.

CHAPTER TWENTY-THREE

Model UN

T HE UN FACED A FORK IN THE ROAD, AND IT TOOK THE
path more traveled. We will never know whether something much
closer to "In Larger Freedom" would have been adopted had Washington taken a more pliable approach or had Kofi Annan been operating at
the top of his game, but the fact remains that in the foreseeable future
the UN will muddle along more or less as it has in the past. Even the
one resounding success in the outcome document—the acceptance of
"the responsibility to protect"—had no discernible effect on the debate
over Darfur. And so even a more thoroughgoing reform might not have
altered the UN's essential nature. The United States would resist constraints on its freedom of action even had it agreed to use-of-force
guidelines. The developing world would still bridle at inroads on sovereignty, including those made by a more powerful human rights mechanism. Management reform would not change the view of most members
that the problem with the Secretariat is not that it's ineffective but that
it's a tool of the West.

If we can't change the UN, then perhaps the time has come to
abandon it in favor of something that works better, as we did with the
League of Nations after World War II, or at least transfer its critical
functions to some other body. Of course "works better" begs a question:
Works better at what? Most members of the UN would like it to be a
more effective forum for mobilizing resources and world opinion on behalf of developing nations. But the sense of urgency over reform was

driven by the UN's failures to perform its founding role as policeman of global security, and it is there that the crisis of "irrelevance" lies. The two roles are arguably incompatible and may thus need to be separated. The UN might retain its humanitarian, developmental, and norm-setting roles while ceding much of its political and collective-security function to some new organ. Over the last few years, scholars, pundits, and critics of the organization have put forward several alternative models: an organization of the major Western states plus India and China; an "Anglosphere" consisting of the United States, the U.K., and the Commonwealth; NATO, with a global mandate; a community of liberal democracies.

The exercise is almost certainly a hypothetical one. It took World War I to create the League of Nations, and World War II to necessitate its replacement by the United Nations. The immense political will required to establish a new instrument of collective security clearly does not exist at the moment; a fork in the road is not, thank God, World War III. Only the United States could organize so vast an enterprise, as it did both with the League and with the UN, and these days the United States is far more attracted by the idea of shifting, ad hoc, issue-specific coalitions than by fixed institutions.

But let us imagine for a moment a terrible event that forces us to confront the discrepancy between the stable world of states that the UN was established to manage and the globalized, fragmented, space- and time-annihilating world in which we now live: terrorists simultaneously explode "dirty bombs" in New York and London, or the Marburg virus escapes from Central Africa to become a global pandemic. The Western powers seek to act through the Security Council, but developing countries, backed by China and Russia, prove deeply reluctant to authorize a multinational force to go into the Pakistani province of South Waziristan to hunt down the terrorists, or, in the second case, to intervene in Zimbabwe in order to take over the public health system. Precious days are wasted while a barely acceptable compromise is hammered out. It becomes all too plain that we can no longer put up with the obstacles imposed by a universal body three-quarters of whose members are profoundly reluctant to breach state sovereignty and would rather quarrel about the definition of terrorism than act forcefully against it.

Let us further imagine, then, that the United States and the U.K. issue a call for all democratic nations to band together to form a new instrument of collective security. A number of conservatives, including Newt Gingrich and *New York Times* columnist David Brooks, have called for such a body. But neither of these is a UN hater, and in fact the most fully fleshed-out proposal comes from Ivo Daalder and James Lindsay, foreign-policy scholars and former Clinton administration officials. The Alliance of Democracies, as they call their UN-in-a-bottle, would function as a global version of NATO, with its own military planning and training capacity and a mandate that would include both peacekeeping missions and "high-intensity warfare." The sixty or so members would include not only the Western and industrial states but also India, Brazil, South Africa, and many smaller Third World democracies—but not putatively democratic but effectively authoritarian states like Egypt.

Now let us imagine that the Marburg virus escapes *after* the Alliance is up and running. The United States and several of its allies are prepared to go in. But South Africa's president, Thabo Mbeki, declares that he is deeply troubled by the proposal. South Africa is Zimbabwe's strongest ally, its former partner in revolutionary struggle against white rule. South Africa may be a democracy, but its view of intervention is shaped by its history as a colonized state. And South Africa is not alone in its concerns, for most of the other non-Western members of the Alliance view sovereignty as the ultimate guarantee of "national self-determination." India, after all, had put up ferocious resistance against even including "the responsibility to protect" in the outcome document. The Alliance would probably still be able to act, and far more quickly than the UN, for the weaker members would have little incentive to block the demands of the more powerful. But the debate itself would expose the fallacy of supposing that a state's internal political order determines its relationship to other states.

One of the chief virtues of the Alliance is that it would exclude Russia and China, the twin spoilers of the Security Council, since no meaningful definition of democracy could embrace either. Their absence would remove a major impediment to decisive action. But it would also pose a huge problem. Why would South Korea—or, for that matter, Australia—join an organization that refused to admit China?

Put otherwise: What could the Alliance possibly offer to offset the entirely justified fear of offending the Chinese? And even if the Alliance could, for example, compensate states for whatever financial harms they suffered as a result of joining, the cost of excluding China may be greater than the benefit, for "containing" this emerging superpower—incorporating it, that is, into the confining web of global institutions—is arguably far more important even than containing the United States. The exclusion of Russia would have similar, if perhaps lesser, consequences.

Finally, if the UN's legitimacy springs from its universal character, because through the Security Council "the world," or "the international community," is expressing its will, how will the Alliance of Democracies make its actions stick? Its enforcement measures will be carried out only in nonmembers' territory. Even supposing that the acquiescence of India would grant an element of legitimacy to an enforcement action in Myanmar—an extremely shaky premise—how would the Alliance play a role in the Middle East, a region where no state save Israel would be eligible for membership? Of course intervention in the face of atrocities carries its own legitimacy, as Kofi Annan argued. But this would be a very small part of the Alliance's portfolio, and anything that smacked of *raison d'état* would be that much harder to justify.

What might well doom the Alliance, in any case, is that it simply would not constitute a good enough deal for the United States. The overwhelming majority of those who would be members, Western or otherwise, would have opposed the war in Iraq and generally have taken a dim view of Washington's post-9/11 preoccupation with terrorism. What inducement would they have to grant the United States the latitude that they did not wish to grant it before? What inducement would the United States have to constrain itself in the Alliance's decision-making process? We would get a more sympathetic hearing than we do in the Security Council, but the outcome might be alarmingly similar.

Must we, then, resign ourselves to the rattletrap UN? This is, in fact, the wrong question. The UN once occupied a solitary and majestic position in the firmament of multinational bodies, but that hasn't been so for a decade or more. NATO quietly minded its own business until it became embroiled in the Balkans, where it now fields tens of thousands of peacekeeping troops and where, in Kosovo, it fought a war. No longer constrained by geography, NATO now deploys peacekeeping troops in Afghanistan. The European Union organized the French-led force that briefly occupied Ituri, in eastern Congo, in 2003, and will continue to authorize missions where NATO involvement is problematic. The Organization for Security and Co-operation in Europe has become increasingly engaged in nation-building activities. The G8 is moving into the sphere of social and economic development, as it did in 2005 when heads of state (minus the United States) ratified the goal of giving 0.7 percent of GNP in aid to poor nations.

Africa has developed its own network of institutions as a response to the continent's nonstop military and political crises. The Economic Community of West African States defended the government of Sierra Leone in the late 1990s and took casualties that Western public opinion would never have accepted. The strictly rhetorical Organization of African Unity gave way, in 2002, to the African Union, which now aspires to play a central role in mediation, peacekeeping, and nation-building, though at the moment its reach greatly exceeds its grasp. The New Partnership for Africa's Development seeks to create continent-wide standards for economic and political reform. The Organization of American States, in Latin America, mediates regional disputes, offers technical assistance on elections, and seeks to promote democracy and human rights, though it does not authorize the dispatch of peacekeeping troops.

Perhaps in the future we will stop speaking of multilateralism as if it were synonymous with commitment to the UN; nations that try to resolve disputes through other forums will still be counted as multilateralist. If so, though, we will still value a commitment to fixed institutions. An international system in which different kinds of problems are adjudicated by different kinds of bodies is very different from one in which states pick their own partners as they wish and refuse to acknowledge the binding authority of multilateral institutions when it gets in their way. This, of course, is a description of the United States, with its "core group" on tsunami relief and its Proliferation Security Initiative and its coalitions of the willing and its steadfast refusal to sign treaties accepted by virtually all other nations. If everybody else accepts the constraints of multinational bodies but the United States insists on playing by its own ever-shifting set of rules, then "the international order" is a will-o'-the-wisp. Multilateralism cannot simply mean "acting with others"; it must also mean "acting through rule-based institutions."

The UN already cooperates extensively with these various groups; the Charter, in fact, specifically obliges the UN to work with regional bodies. As this engagement increases, and as these regional bodies come to see themselves less and less as subcontractors and more as equals, the categorical distinction between the one universal body and the many limited or localized ones will begin to blur. The G77 may look to the G8 for meaningful commitments on development issues. The United States and Europe may try to build up the AU's peacekeeping capacity so that "an African solution to an African problem" does not seem like the cynical mockery it does today. Asian nations may downgrade the importance of the UN in favor of regional trade systems and of a perpetual recalibration of relations with China and India.

There is, of course, something melancholy about the prospect of the UN finding its level amid an array of institutions. We cannot help investing the UN with a semireligious awe, and thus with the faith that it might somehow "deliver us from evil," in William Shawcross's phrase. But the UN cannot deliver us from the evils we most fear. And this is so not because of design flaws but because of the structure of the world order itself: one superpower towers above the rest; myriad non-state actors and global forces undermine a state-based system fashioned in the seventeenth century; the West and the global South make demands of each other that neither is willing or fully able to satisfy. A world so fragmented cannot be knit together by a single institution. Difficult though it may be for UN acolytes to acknowledge this fact, it cannot be otherwise.

Of course, even as we pluck the UN off its pedestal, we need to recognize that it will remain indispensable across a wide range of fields. The UN will continue to set norms of behavior with regard to human rights, the obligation of the state to its citizens, and so on, at least so long as we continue to believe in the universality of such standards. It will, or should, remain the central coordinating body in the response to natural disasters. It will continue to provide the overwhelming bulk of peacekeeping troops, at least until regional bodies can take up the slack, which also means that the Security Council will continue to debate and authorize such missions. And the UN's funds and programs will continue to do their work in public health, emergency food aid, and the like. But we will no longer expect it to be both arbiter and executor on all the great questions that vex the world.

If the institution changes, so will the job that, in effect, incarnates the institution. Kofi Annan may turn out to be the last secretary-general to trail such clouds of glory, or for that matter to excite such fierce denunciation. Like Dag Hammarskjöld, Annan expanded the secretary-generalship to its greatest possible dimensions. Hammarskjöld died before the job could collapse back on him, as it probably would have. Annan, of course, experienced his own diminution day by day. The political space available to a secretary-general is a consequence both of his own ambition and skill and of the willingness of the members to have him play such a role. If that willingness disappears, diplomatic gifts avail nothing. And in the current situation, where the UN's leader cannot afford to drift too far from Washington but cannot grow so close that he is seen as a puppet, the secretary-general sometimes seems to be dancing on the head of a pin. It's almost enough to make one nostalgic for the Cold War.

As the members turn to the task of replacing Annan, with the understanding that it is now Asia's "turn" for the job, the candidates whose names have been put forward are mostly uninspiring technocrats. It's true that Annan himself was once an uninspiring technocrat before he blossomed into something else altogether. But his successor, even if he or she possessed such latent gifts, might not be allowed to exercise them. The major powers never want a big secretary-general, but now they may want an even smaller one than usual. That may not be such a bad thing: a technocrat might be best positioned to fix the UN's broken culture, soothe battered feelings, and avoid intractable debates. A lesser SG would help the UN find its level. But he would also leave a hole that no one else would be able to fill. And that would, indeed, be a melancholy note.

Epilogue

T HE ISSUES THAT MOST DEEPLY PREOCCUPIED THE UN IN the middle of 2004 preoccupied it still in the spring of 2006. Iraq had not proved to be the poisoned chalice so many had feared; the UN's successful organization of the election in January 2005 had given it precious credit with the Bush administration. But the harrowing security situation had made it impossible to increase the size or the reach of the tiny UN office there, and the mission had been virtually frozen. The Bush administration was agitating for a bigger presence, but by early 2006 Kofi Annan was worrying that once the United States handed essential security tasks over to the Iraqis, the UN would become so vulnerable that he would have to pull his colleagues out altogether, risking the ire of the White House rather than suffering another August 19.

In Darfur, the Security Council's unwillingness to take decisive action had produced precisely the effects Annan and others had forecast. With the African Union force hopelessly overstretched and overmatched, the rebels continued to attack government forces, Khartoum continued to employ the Janjaweed as its cat's-paw, and bandits exploited the resulting chaos to plunder with impunity. By November 2005, the refugee population had topped two million, but with many of the roads too dangerous for truck caravans, aid groups were forced to deliver supplies by air, and the Sudanese government had responded by cutting off the supply of jet fuel. Desperate refugees were even kidnapping aid workers to dramatize their plight. And the nightmarish situation took yet another downward spiral when the Janjaweed, apparently with Khartoum's active complicity, began crossing the border into Chad to attack and destroy villages populated by the same "African" tribes they had been massacring in Darfur.

Nothing happened until January 12, when the AU, having just about run through the foreign funds that financed the Darfur mission, agreed in principle to permit the UN to take over the peacekeeping mission—just as Annan and others had predicted the organization would once its inadequacy became manifest. On February 2, the Security Council approved a statement submitted by John Bolton, who had just become council president, to "initiate contingency planning without delay" for such a mission. President Bush spoke of doubling the existing strength of seven thousand. The new force would operate under a Chapter 7 mandate permitting much tougher rules of engagement than those under which the AU had operated. It would be tough, and it would be mobile—in theory, at least.

In fact this bold-sounding initiative might have been as empty and cynical an exercise as the May 1994 resolution authorizing a nonexistent force to stop the Rwandan genocide. Peacekeeping officials guessed that organizing the new mission and finding, equipping, and fielding the troops would take as much as a year. And where would the troops come from? Some would consist of the doughty but hopelessly overwhelmed AU force, which would be "re-hatted" as UN peacekeepers; others would be borrowed from UNMIS, the new mission charged with overseeing the cease-fire between the government and the south; and still others would have to be drummed up from among the usual suspects, who were already overstretched. None of them, President Bush made clear, would be American. What's more, Khartoum had consistently said that it would not accept an international, as opposed to an African, force. "Are we going to seek the agreement of the government of Sudan," asked an exasperated Hedi Annabi, deputy head of the peacekeeping department, "or are we planning to shoot our way in with the troops we won't be given?"

Elsewhere in Africa, Robert Mugabe, Zimbabwe's liberator turned tyrant, seemed intent on obliterating his own country. In 2000, he had unleashed soldiers and party loyalists to occupy and expropriate the land of white farmers, satisfying his own restive followers while provoking a reign of terror that led much of Zimbabwe's white population to flee. In the ensuing chaos, agricultural production had plummeted and hunger had become widespread in a country that had not long before been Africa's breadbasket. Almost inconceivably, average life expectancy fell from sixty-three years in the late 1980s to thirty-four years by 2004. Mugabe resisted all attempts to mediate the situation. And then, in the spring of 2005, the increasingly paranoid and isolated leader organized a "slum clearance" program in which policemen and army troops systematically destroyed the shantytowns that dotted every major city, and that Mugabe considered the base of support for the country's chief opposition party. Within two months, 700,000 people had lost their homes, their source of work, or both; an additional 2.4 million—this in a country of 11 million—had suffered less direct harm.

When Annan had tried to intervene, Mugabe had insisted that horrific news reports were "a pack of lies," but he had agreed to let the secretary-general send a special envoy. The envoy's report, issued in July, described the slum-clearance campaign as a humanitarian disaster and possibly a "crime against humanity." Mugabe responded by condemning the report; two weeks later, a squad of riot police leveled a vast settlement outside of Harare, sending twenty thousand people into the bush. The Security Council declined to act; China had openly embraced Mugabe and was prepared to veto any harsh resolution. Annan knew that he would have to depend on Zimbabwe's neighbors, and above all on South Africa, the great regional power and brother in revolution against white rule. Annan regularly urged Thabo Mbeki, South Africa's president and Annan's good friend, to bluntly tell Mugabe that he had gone too far. Mbeki promised to engage in African-style "quiet diplomacy," but in fact, Annan conceded, Mbeki did nothing. And it wasn't hard to understand why. Some of Mbeki's top officials had openly applauded Mugabe's program of vigilante land reform; anything that reduced the role of whites was good. And Mbeki was not about to take on his own left wing in order to intercede on behalf of the Zimbabwean people.

In the fall, Mugabe pushed through legislation amending the constitution to give the state the power to confiscate passports from critics and to expropriate land with no right of appeal. His policemen continued to tear down whatever new shelters desperate dispossessed people erected in the old shantytowns. Mugabe continued to deny the humanitarian crisis he had created, and refused a UN offer to build temporary shelter in advance of the rainy season for the thousands of slum dwellers he had rendered homeless. And no one was willing, or able, to stop him.

Ironically enough, the UN demonstrated its extraordinary value as an instrument of diplomacy not in Africa but in the Middle East, a region whose very geopolitical importance had largely forced the UN to the sidelines. In late August 2004, Lebanon was thrown into violent turmoil when the country's president, widely viewed as a Syrian vassal, announced that rather than step down at the end of his term as required by Lebanon's constitution, he would run once again in an upcoming election. Both Paris and Washington had long-standing ties to the country, and these two capitals, their scars from Iraq still fresh, agreed to deal with the issue through the Security Council. One week later the council passed resolution 1559, calling for fair elections "according to Lebanese constitutional rules" and demanding the withdrawal of "all remaining foreign forces in Lebanon"—that is, Syria's—and the disbanding and disarming of militias, meaning, above all, the gunmen of Hezbollah, supported by Syria and financed by Iran.

The resolution had an electrifying effect on Lebanon's political culture. Rafik Hariri, the country's prime minister and one of its wealthiest and most celebrated figures, resigned rather than accept continued Syrian manipulation of Lebanese politics. On February 14, an immense explosion destroyed Hariri's car as it drove through central Beirut, killing him and twenty others. Syrian involvement was not so much suspected as assumed; Lebanon was convulsed with demonstrations and fresh demands for the Syrian overlords to leave the country. The subsequent Lebanese "investigation" of the murder was widely dismissed as a whitewash whose principal concern was hiding or destroying crucial evidence. In April, the Security Council called for the impaneling of an independent investigative commission.

In its interim report, issued October 19, the commission concluded that the evidence pointed "directly towards Syrian security officials as being involved with the assassination." Though no figures were singled out by name, it was understood that the primary suspect was Syria's intelligence chief, Asef Shawkat, the brother-in-law of President Bashar Assad and, by many accounts, the second most powerful official in the country. The president's brother was also said to have been involved. The report accused the Syrian government of trying to prevent investigators from learning the truth, which might well have led to President Assad himself.

At the end of October, the foreign ministers of the P5 countries gathered in New York to give weight to the collective demand that Syria end its cover-up. Since Russia and China inevitably refused to explicitly threaten sanctions, resolution 1636 stated that Syria would face "further action"—understood to mean sanctions—should it fail to comply. Ten days later Assad himself promised to cooperate with the investigation, but in the same speech he lashed out at his Lebanese critics, the UN, and the West, and hotly vowed not to "bow to anyone in this world." His fury may have been prompted by the dawning realization that, thanks to the UN, Syria was isolated as never before. There was talk of the regime itself toppling.

Though another UN envoy confirmed that Syria had, in fact, withdrawn its forces from Lebanon in conformity with resolution 1559, the security apparatus still had its shadowy network in place. And over the next few months, several prominent Lebanese politicians and journalists were murdered in the same spectacular fashion as Hariri had been. The Syrian regime, evidently torn by indecision, could neither surrender this rich plum of a colony nor defy the whole world by simply devouring it. It remained to be seen whether the UN had the power to deliver to the Lebanese people the liberty that those Security Council resolutions had nobly promised.

Kofi Annan had always maintained that the optimum period for reform would be the days leading up to the arrival of heads of state for the General Assembly session; thereafter, the pressure to reach agreement would dissipate. And so it did. All the reforms that had been left half finished because it had proved impossible to agree on the crucial details continued to languish. When I went to see Bob Orr at the end of

November 2005, I found him the very picture of defeated optimism. Even the Peacebuilding Commission, the least controversial of all major reforms, was endangered. John Bolton was demanding that its activities fall wholly within the purview of the Security Council, and that the P5 enjoy a permanent right of membership—the kind of prerogative that Russia and China used to insist on, but never the United States. The G77 countries had retaliated with impossible demands of their own. Orr had given up hope on a quick resolution of the issue of the Human Rights Council or management reform. Above all, he had given up all hope on Bolton himself. "He is most certainly trying to lead things to a confrontation here," Orr said. "And I have zero confidence that it's in order to make a deal. He's trying to inflame the debate and infuriate the G77." A few days earlier America's trigger-happy ambassador had described the UN as "a target-rich environment" and had warned that if the institution didn't shape up, "we'll turn to some other mechanism to solve international problems."

When I talked to Annan, I found his mood equally dour. He had had a good conversation on reform with Condi Rice, but he wasn't sure it mattered anymore. "Official Washington tells you one thing, but he as the ambassador representing Washington gets to implement the policy. He takes initiatives which do not enhance or enforce the policy in that direction." Annan knew that Rice was hearing just such complaints from diplomats and foreign ministers, but whenever he raised it with her, she would say vaguely, "We'll get on it. We'll send instructions." Rice herself says that she had no problem with Bolton's tactics, and either initiated or signed off on all significant strategic decisions.

By this time, in fact, the administration had concluded that the only way to get reform was to tighten the screws. Bolton announced that absent management reform, the United States would prevent the UN's biennial budget from being passed at the end of the year. This prompted new cries of outrage. Only Japan publicly sided with Washington, but the EU countries, running out of patience, offered quiet support. And Annan, hoping to avert another disaster, signaled to G77 countries that the Secretariat could survive on an interim budget. In the last days of 2005, the General Assembly accepted a six-month budget and adopted a version of the Peacebuilding Commission with an unwieldy membership of thirty-one, including the permanent five.

Washington had been forced to make some concessions on the issue of control: the commission would report at times to the Security Council, but at other, as yet unspecified, phases of the conflict with which it was engaged, it would report to the GA and to the Economic and Social Council.

No real progress was made on either management reform or the Human Rights Council before the end of the year. Bolton himself seemed far more interested in blasting the UN in front of conservative audiences than in hammering out the details of reform. He left Annan to push for most of the important provisions of the Human Rights Council; Bolton said that his top priority was ensuring that bad apples could be ejected from the organization. By mid-February, debate had ground to a halt, as it had in mid-September, and once again the General Assembly president, now Jan Eliasson, submitted a compromise draft. It was an eviscerated version of the body Annan had proposed a year before. Candidates would be chosen not by two thirds of members but by a majority (though they would need a majority of all members rather than merely all those present and voting, as before). Bob Orr believed it was Bolton's own confrontational diplomacy that had put the two-thirds standard out of reach. Still, the council would review the human rights profile of all states, starting with its own members, would meet more often than the commission had, and would have the power to remove the noncompliant.

Most major human rights organizations viewed the proposed council as an acceptable, if highly disappointing, start toward real reform. *The Wall Street Journal* and other conservative media organs derided the proposal as the flimsiest of disguises for the typical UN surrender to despotism, but some liberal outlets, including *The New York Times*, also called for Washington to reject the compromise plan. The White House promptly announced that it could not accept the loss of the two-thirds principle. Bolton asked to have the whole plan reopened for debate. Eliasson, a figure of almost bottomless patience, responded that doing so would open a "Pandora's box" of mischievous demands and suggestions. Virtually every other member, including the most recalcitrant, had signaled that it would vote for the council. The planned vote was delayed again and again in hopes of finding some elusive middle ground. Finally, in mid-March, the proposal was put to a vote in the

General Assembly, where it passed 188 to 4, with the United States joined in opposition by Israel, the Marshall Islands, and Belarus.

Washington may well prove to have been right on the merits. After all, any human rights body that can gain the support of Cuba, Venezuela, China, Iran, Myanmar, and Sudan is fairly likely to be toothless. Of course, what was lost in the righteous calls for repudiation was the White House's own responsibility for the misbegotten creature that Jan Eliasson had been forced to deliver. Here was yet another self-fulfilling prophecy from the administration that had threatened the UN with irrelevance in September 2002 and had then systematically rendered it irrelevant.

But scarcely anyone, oddly enough, asked the question that lay beneath all this political turbulence: Would even a properly fitted-out human rights body have been able to single out abusers and uphold the banner of inalienable human rights? If, after all, the Security Council had not been able to find a means of condemning Robert Mugabe's annihilation of his own country, why should we expect the UN Human Rights Council to do better? Well over half of the members would be drawn from Africa and Asia, where very few nations conformed to the principles of the Universal Declaration of Human Rights. And even the democracies among them were loath to meddle in the affairs of others and were inclined to view human rights as a club wielded by the West. Perhaps the UN was simply not suited to this line of work.

When I had spoken to Rice in late January, she had waved off all criticisms of her ambassador by saying that it was "just a matter of time" before the reforms the United States cared about were passed. But in fact the Human Rights Council had passed in unacceptable form; and by the middle of 2006 the G77, in a spasm of self-righteous opposition to the West, had effectively killed management reform. John Bolton now had all the proof he needed of the UN's incorrigibility. But Condoleezza Rice *wanted* the UN to be effective. Did she wonder, now, if Bolton had gotten the better of her?

Kofi Annan's own immediate world—the world bounded by the upper floors of the Secretariat Building—had changed drastically in the course of 2005. Normally a man in his position would make such wrenching changes after his first term, as President Bush had done, and President Clinton before him. But Annan, of course, hated wrenching change, and had seen no need to alter anything after his supremely successful first term. But disaster—chiefly the nosedive in the UN's relationship with the United States—had forced change upon him. Mark Malloch Brown had replaced Iqbal Riza, Elisabeth Lindenmayer had unceremoniously departed, and Kieran Prendergast had gone off to sip sherry and nurse his grievances for a semester at Harvard, his position taken by the far less forceful and incisive Ibrahim Gambari. Michael Moller, the melancholy Dane, had quite happily left to become SRSG in Cyprus. The deputy secretary-general, Louise Fréchette, having dodged the bullets of August 19 and Oil-for-Food, left under her own steam in April 2006—and was replaced by Mark Malloch Brown, who had in any case been functioning as the UN's de facto number two for the previous year. And Bob Orr had moved up from the thirty-second to the thirty-eighth floor. Between Malloch Brown and Orr, Annan now moved in a world far more attuned to the concerns of Washington, and to Anglo-American opinion generally. The UN loyalists—Riza, Prendergast, Tharoor—had been banished, or removed to a distant orbit. None remained of the old team but Lamin Sise, the genial and ironic keeper of secrets.

Annan's relations with Washington had measurably improved, thanks not only to Malloch Brown and Orr but to Condoleezza Rice and her team. At the same time, Annan's tolerance for John Bolton seemed to diminish as the end of his tenure drew nigh. On December 8, 2005, Louise Arbour, the high commissioner for human rights, had criticized "governments in a number of countries" who claimed that the rise of terrorism required a relaxation of such fundamental human rights as the prohibition on torture. Since the Bush administration was then promoting legislation that would permit torture, if only in some highly circumscribed instances, no one could mistake the identity of the principal country in question. Bolton, never one to turn the other cheek, lashed out at Arbour for discussing "press commentary about alleged American conduct" rather than "serious human rights problems." Annan, in an utterly uncharacteristic jab, instructed his spokesman to say that "the Secretary General has absolutely no disagreement with the statements made by the High Commissioner."

Bolton later apologized to Annan for taking his complaints to the press rather than to him.

A new UN scandal over the procurement of supplies and equipment for peacekeeping missions added fuel to what otherwise seemed to be a dying fire. An internal audit, whose results were published in late January 2006, disclosed that a combination of mismanagement, over-budgeting, and possibly fraud had resulted in serious losses, possibly as high as $300 million. Bolton leaped on the news to vindicate the American drive for "massive management reform." Asked by a reporter whether he agreed with Christopher Burnham, the former State Department official who was now serving as the UN's head of management, that Annan deserved credit for "pushing ahead with reforms," Bolton replied, "I'm glad Chris Burnham is Undersecretary General for management."

In mid-February relations between the two men turned yet more poisonous. That month the United States occupied the presidency of the Security Council, and Bolton had been seeking to hold hearings on the procurement problem. This raised the hackles of the G77 countries yet again, for the General Assembly has jurisdiction over all budgetary matters. The GA, as usual, seemed far more interested in preserving its prerogatives than in getting to the bottom of the issue. At Annan's monthly luncheon with the council, Bolton asked the secretary-general to send an official to brief council members on the progress of the investigation. Annan bridled, saying, as he later told me, "You guys have to decide whether it's the Security Council or the General Assembly" that should hold hearings. "Don't put the Secretariat in the middle." Bolton repeated the request, and Annan added that since outside auditors were currently combing over the books, any official he sent would be severely constrained in what he could disclose. In the course of the exchange, according to one account, Bolton's face grew redder and redder, until finally he exploded: "Do you want me to tell Congress"—several members of which were treating the issue as yet another casus belli with the UN—"that the secretary-general *doesn't* want a debate on this issue?"

"John," said Annan, his voice dropping into a lower register that signaled intense displeasure, at least to those who recognized his signals, "this is intimidation. You really need to stop doing this." Annan added that of course he would send someone to brief the council and admonished everyone—meaning Bolton—not to go out and tell the press otherwise. After lunch, however, Bolton did just that. His insistence on raising the issue in the Security Council precipitated an ugly fight with the defenders of GA privilege, led by South Africa, a country whose good graces the United States needed to cultivate in order to reach a decent outcome on human rights or management reform.

Several days later I asked Annan if he had ever spoken to any ambassador the way he had to Bolton at lunch. "No, I haven't," he said. "I've gotten on with all the previous U.S. ambassadors, who were all really first-rate." None of them, for all their harsh differences, had ever spoken to Annan as Bolton routinely did. "I thought," Annan added, "it was about time to tell him that that sort of language is not appropriate in this building." Even then, for all his cold fury, Annan would not accept that the U.S. ambassador was beyond the reach of persuasion. "I'm not sure whether he doesn't quite understand how this building works," he said. When I accused him of falling back on his usual diplomatic circumlocutions, Annan said, "No, I think there's also a bit of awkwardness, and I think that also plays."

Annan still had to watch himself very carefully in front of Bolton, no matter how he felt. But this was not true of all his tormentors. He had begun firing back at the more bristlingly adversarial members of the press corps. This had begun in September, at the climax of Oil-for-Food, but the confrontation reached operatic, or soap-operatic, heights when several reporters broke the respectful solemnity of the year-end press conference to confront Annan with lingering allegations against him, his staff, and his family. Annan had just finished accusing one reporter of trafficking in "libelous" and "patently false" accusations when James Bone of the *London Times* asked if he had known about, and approved of, Kojo's use of his name to improperly obtain a UN discount on a Mercedes. The question was legitimate, but Bone provocatively added that the Secretary General's "own version of events don't really make sense." At that, Annan exploded, denouncing Bone as "an overgrown schoolboy"— apparently the most withering barb he would let fly in this public setting.

When I saw Annan a few weeks later, he conceded that it had felt good to "slap him down." He felt that he had stood up for his staff, which Bone had been abusing with his perpetual insinuations of malfeasance. It was true that Bone had become something of a journalistic harpy, but Annan, who felt at bottom that the blame for Oil-for-Food, and most everything else, lay with the members rather than with himself or his staff, was also lashing out on his own behalf. What's more, he was taking out years of accumulated frustration on a foe who could wield no weapon more dangerous than a laptop, because he could not permit himself such liberties with the real sources of his pain.

Annan had, in fact, taken a fearful battering over the last few years, and this following a long stretch of adulation that had scarcely prepared him for adversity. At the same press conference he had been asked, in a more sympathetic vein, what advice he had for his successor. Whoever followed him, he said, would need "a thick skin" and the ability to "laugh a lot inside and outside, and at themselves." Like most kindly people, Annan did not have a thick skin, though he thought otherwise, and he had nothing like the kind of self-irony that would let him laugh at his persecutors. He was not suited to the fighting of lonely battles. He was a man who offered bottomless reassurance to others, and needed almost as much himself, but the others had not been there when he had most needed them.

Annan was not a bitter man, not one to dwell on his scars. But he felt ill-used—not so much because he had not been credited sufficiently for his achievements (he had, after all, won the Nobel Peace Prize) as because he believed that he had been unfairly blamed for failures not of his own doing. And this sense of victimization clouded what had once been a serene inner landscape. In our last conversation, I asked if he was a less hopeful man than he had been before, and he unspooled a length of ready-made rhetorical fabric contrasting his "faith in human nature" with his recognition of "man's inhumanity to man." Then I reminded him of his sense of abandonment amid the accusations over Oil-for-Food, when none of the diplomats or foreign secretaries or heads of state usually so eager to launch panegyrics on the secretary-general's behalf had rallied to his side. Now, instead of reaching for another spool, he spoke straight from the heart.

"This is where the secretary-general's position is very lonely," Annan said. "In fact the scandal was in the capitals and in the companies they promoted. One or two said we shouldn't pass the buck to the secretary-general. But you never heard from them. And these were the same guys who were hounding Benon's office and such to get contracts. For them now to say we didn't know, and that it's the incompetent, crooked, fraudulent UN organization, the Secretariat, the secretary-general, when all the action was on their side . . ." Annan didn't finish the sentence or the thought. Perhaps he didn't even finish such thoughts inside himself. He was, as he said, "an optimist by nature." And there were certain painful truths that you could not contemplate, and at the end of the day could not acknowledge, if you wanted to hang on to your optimism in a world that gave so few grounds for it.

A Note on Sources

The chief sources for this book were the several hundred interviews I conducted between the summer of 2004 and the fall of 2005 with current and former UN officials, diplomats, academics, investigators, and American policy makers, as well as refugees in Darfur, peacekeepers and government officials in Congo, and survivors in the tsunami zone. A good deal of the material comes from the meetings of top UN officials—often with outsiders—that Kofi Annan permitted me to attend. I also drew on dozens of conversations I had had in the course of researching articles on the UN since 1998. I read all too many studies and reports produced by the UN and was privy to quite a few secret, or at least nonpublic, communications among UN officials. I monitored the daily activities of the organization through the UN's various news services, through such Web sites as ReliefWeb.int, and through daily newspapers, principally *The New York Times*. I also benefited, to a greater or lesser degree, from the following books:

Albright, Madeleine. *Madam Secretary: A Memoir*. New York: Miramax Books, 2003.

Biermann, Wolfgang, ed. *UN Peacekeeping in Trouble: Lessons Learned from the Former Yugoslavia*. Aldershot, U.K.: Ashgate, 1998.

Blix, Hans. *Disarming Iraq*. New York: Pantheon Books, 2004.

Boutros-Ghali, Boutros. *Unvanquished: A U.N.-U.S. Saga*. New York: Random House, 1999.

Burg, Steven L. *The War in Bosnia-Herzegovina: Ethnic Conflict and International Intervention*. Armonk, N.Y.: M. E. Sharpe, 1999.

Butler, Richard. *The Greatest Threat: Iraq, Weapons of Mass Destruction, and the Crisis of Global Security*. New York: Public Affairs, 2000.

Chesterman, Simon. *You, the People: The United Nations, Transitional Administration, and State-Building*. Oxford: Oxford University Press, 2004.

Cortright, David, and George Lopez. *Sanctions and the Search for Security: Challenges to UN Action*. Boulder, Colo.: Lynne Rienner Publishers, 2002.

Daalder, Ivo H., and James M. Lindsay. *America Unbound: The Bush Revolution in Foreign Policy*. Washington, D.C.: Brookings Institution Press, 2003.

Dallaire, Roméo. *Shake Hands with the Devil: The Failure of Humanity in Rwanda*. New York: Carroll & Graf, 2003.

Dobbins, James, et al., eds. *America's Role in Nation-Building: From Germany to Iraq*. Santa Monica, Calif.: RAND, 2003.

Goulding, Marrack. *Peacemonger*. London: John Murray, 2002.

Hazzard, Shirley. *Defeat of an Ideal: A Study of the Self-Destruction of the United Nations*. Boston: Little, Brown, 1973.

Holbrooke, Richard C. *To End a War*. New York: Random House, 1998.

Kagan, Robert. *Of Paradise and Power: America and Europe in the New World Order*. New York: Alfred A. Knopf, 2003.

Luck, Edward C. *Mixed Messages: American Politics and International Organization, 1919–1999*. Washington, D.C.: Brookings Institution Press, 1999.

Malone, David M. *Decision-Making in the UN Security Council: The Case of Haiti*. Oxford: Clarendon Press, 1998.

———, ed. *The UN Security Council: From the Cold War to the 21st Century*. Boulder, Colo.: Lynne Rienner Publishers, 2004.

Mead, Walter Russell. *Power, Terror, Peace, and War: America's Grand Strategy in a World at Risk*. New York: Alfred A. Knopf, 2004.

Meisler, Stanley. *United Nations: The First Fifty Years*. New York: Atlantic Monthly Press, 1995.

Moynihan, Daniel Patrick. *A Dangerous Place*. Boston: Little, Brown, 1978.

O'Neill, William G. *Kosovo: An Unfinished Peace*. Boulder, Colo.: Lynne Rienner Publishers, 2002.

Packer, George. *The Assassins' Gate: America in Iraq*. New York: Farrar, Straus and Giroux, 2005.

Power, Samantha. *A Problem from Hell: America and the Age of Genocide*. New York: Basic Books, 2002.

Rieff, David. *Slaughterhouse: Bosnia and the Failure of the West*. New York: Random House, 1995.

Rohde, David. *Endgame: The Betrayal and Fall of Srebrenica, Europe's Worst Massacre Since World War II*. New York: Farrar, Straus and Giroux, 1997.

Sachs, Jeffrey D. *The End of Poverty: Economic Possibilities for Our Time*. New York: Penguin Press, 2005.

Schlesinger, Stephen C. *Act of Creation: The Founding of the United Nations*. New York: Westview Press, 2003.

Shawcross, William. *Deliver Us from Evil: Peacekeeping, Warlords, and a World of Endless Conflict*. New York: Simon & Schuster, 2000.

Smith, Michael G. *Peacekeeping in East Timor: The Path to Independence*. Boulder, Colo.: Lynne Rienner Publishers, 2003.

Soderberg, Nancy. *The Superpower Myth: The Use and Misuse of American Might*. Hoboken, N.J.: Wiley, 2005.

Urquhart, Brian. *A Life in Peace and War*. New York: Harper & Row, 1987.

———. *Ralph Bunche: An American Odyssey*. New York: W. W. Norton and Co., 1998.

Weiss, Thomas G., et al., eds. *UN Voices: The Struggle for Development and Social Justice*. Bloomington: Indiana University Press, 2005.

Woodward, Bob. *Bush at War*. New York: Simon & Schuster, 2002.

Acknowledgments

This is the kind of book that cannot be written without the cooperation of its subject, though the subject can exercise no control whatever over the outcome. I am deeply grateful to Kofi Annan for accepting that bargain, which required him not only to speak with me at great length but also to permit me to sit in on meetings, often very sensitive ones, and to quote his remarks as I saw fit. I am similarly grateful to the UN officials who spoke with me regularly and candidly, above all Kieran Prendergast, Bob Orr, Mark Malloch Brown, Shashi Tharoor, and Michael Moller. There are others whose names do not appear in the text, but from whom I gained invaluable insight into the institution: Annika Savill, Stephane Dujarric, Nick Birnback.

Several portions of this book began their life as articles in *The New York Times Magazine*, which largely underwrote my burgeoning interest in the UN and in peace-keeping. For this I owe great thanks to my friend and editor, Gerald Marzorati. Most of the chapters of *The Best Intentions* were read by someone who knew a good deal more about the subject than I did; I am grateful for the sage and tactful counsel of Ed Luck, Simon Chesterman, Ivo Daalder, David Harland, Isabelle Balot, and especially David Malone, who taught me, and teaches me still, how to think about the UN and the international system of which it is a part.

My agent, Andrew Wylie, encouraged me at the outset of this project and congratulated me lavishly at the end (and of course negotiated my contract in between). My editor, Eric Chinski, asked questions and suggested changes with the sole object of making the book I wanted to write as good as it could be—an act of fidelity that every writer craves, but few are lucky enough to receive. Wah-Ming Chang efficiently kept the production schedule on track, while Ingrid Sterner, my all-seeing copy editor and fact-checker, saved me from many a mortifying error. Those that remain are, of course, no one's fault but mine.

Index